LUCRETIU

DE RERUM NATUR

LUCRETIUS
DE RERUM NATURA I

Edited with Introduction, Commentary
and Vocabulary by

P. Michael Brown

Bristol Classical Press

Cover illustration: Epicurus, Roman copy from a Greek portrait statue
of the late 2nd century BC. Metropolitan Museum of Art, New York (no. 11.90).
[Drawing by Patrick Harrison]

First published in 1984 by
Bristol Classical Press
an imprint of
Gerald Duckworth & Co. Ltd
61 Frith Street
London W1D 3JL
E-mail: inquiries@duckworth-publishers.co.uk
Website: www.ducknet.co.uk

Reprinted with minor amendments 1988, 1996, 2000, 2001

A catalogue record for this book is available
from the British Library

ISBN 0-86292-076-0

Printed in Great Britain by
Antony Rowe Ltd., Eastbourne

MATRI CARISSIMAE

PATRISQUE OPTIMI MEMORIAE

CONTENTS

STRUCTURE OF BOOK 1

Though the third and fifth books of Lucretius are
currently the most often read, the first claims attention
not only on the strength of the famous introduction to
the whole poem with which it opens but because its treatment of atoms and void provides the fundamental basis on
which the remaining books depend. A proper understanding
of the philosophical subject-matter is naturally indispensable to a full appreciation of the poetry, and I have
sought to do such justice as I could to both aspects of
the book. The edition, which has long been planned, is
designed to provide all the help required by the comparative beginner in Latin, while at the same time incorporating material which I hope may interest the Lucretian
scholar and specialist. My debt to earlier work, in
particular that of Munro, Duff and Bailey, will be obvious;
I have not normally recorded where I have followed or
disagreed with them on a given point, since my aim was to
write a commentary on Lucretius rather than on Lucretian
scholarship.

I welcomed the opportunity, which the Bristol Classical
Press offered me, of producing my own version of the text;
this shows some sixty or seventy divergences from Bailey's
Oxford Classical Text of 1922, a large proportion of them
involving differences of punctuation or of supplementation
where the manuscripts are defective. My aim has been to
produce a complete, continuously readable version: where
there are lacunae in the manuscripts, I have sacrificed
complete authenticity to continuity and introduced minimum
stopgaps, incorporating a few lines devised by Munro and
three of my own invention. All such supplements, and
restorations of words or parts of words missing in the
manuscripts, are printed in italics. In other directions
I have been more cautious, and have introduced only two

independent conjectures of my own. Textual notes throughout are either excluded or confined to a minimum.

I owe much to the encouragement of Professor D.A. West,
and also of my now retired colleague, Mr. D.A. Malcolm,
who were both kind enough to read an early version of the
Introduction and of the first part of the Notes, and to
make many helpful and detailed suggestions. I am indebted
to the Bristol Classical Press, and to the General Editor,
for agreeing to publish this edition, and for their valuable suggestions and cooperation throughout its preparation.
I am most grateful to Mrs. Jennifer Peat, former secretary
to the Department, for typing the Introduction and Notes
with her usual efficiency and despatch. But possibly my
greatest debt is to Professor P.G. Walsh, without whose
tireless support, prompting and encouragement this work
might never have emerged *dias in luminis oras*.

Department of Humanity
Glasgow University   January 1984

INTRODUCTION

I

THE POEM

Few poems have as clearly defined a purpose as the
De Rerum Natura, in which Lucretius seeks to further the
gospel of Epicurean philosophy and in particular to establish, on the basis of an exposition of Epicurean physics,
that the universe is not subject to divine control or
interference, and that man has no after-life: he thus
hopes to dispel the unhappiness which, as he sees it, mistaken belief and uncertainty about such matters engender.
According to Epicurus, the universe could be wholly explained in terms of an infinite number of indestructible
atoms of matter moving in infinite void in accordance with
unchanging scientific laws: theories of divine control or
intervention, which were seen as rival, inadequate attempts
to explain phenomena, were thus rendered redundant: and
since the souls of men were atomic compounds, which were
dissolved even more quickly than the body at death, death
must mean the end of all consciousness.

The poem's six books fall into three pairs: the first
and second introduce the fundamentals of the system, atoms,
void, and the infinite universe, in which an infinite
number of worlds like our own are included: they describe
atomic motions and varieties, and the effect of these upon
atomic compounds. The third and fourth books are concerned
to establish the material nature of the soul, and to show
how all psychological activities, including perception,
thought, dreaming, willing and emotion can be explained in
atomic terms: they are thus directed principally against
beliefs in an after-life. The fifth and sixth books deal
with our world (to which the others are at least similar),
with its original formation and ultimate destructibility,

its astronomy, the evolution of life and the history of civilisation upon it, and a miscellany of its phenomena from thunderbolts to plague: here, beliefs in divine guidance and intervention are the chief target.

True to the tradition of personal appeal in Epicurean evangelism, the poem takes the form of an attempt to convert one Memmius (see Introduction II below) to Epicurean views: it is only through Memmius that the general reader is addressed.

The work, like Virgil's *Aeneid*, was never fully revised by its author. Though the text is generally more logically ordered than to justify the wholesale transposition of arguments which was once fashionable amongst Lucretian editors, some of the transitions are unsatisfactory as they stand[1] and some arguments might well have been clarified in revision[2]; both types of difficulty seem sometimes to arise from the addition of imperfectly adjusted after-thoughts. And while Lucretius has clearly carried out the bulk of his design[3], the poem may never fully have been completed: the promise of an extended demonstration of the refined atomic structure of the gods, or their abodes, or of both[4] is apparently nowhere fulfilled: and the ending of the poem as we have it, though it has not lacked its defenders, is surely unsatisfactory: can Lucretius really have intended the work to peter out with a grim detail of the account of the Great Plague of Athens? While both deficiencies could be attributed to the loss of some of the text, whose transmission is from a single, occasionally defective archetype, the signs of incomplete revision make it more probable that the passages in question were never in fact composed.

---

[1] See notes e.g. on 1.146-58 and 205-7 below.
[2] See notes e.g. on 1.196ff., 391ff. and 915ff. below.
[3] At 6.92-3 Lucretius announces Book 6 as his last.
[4] 5.155.

THE POET

Lucretius wrote in the first half of the first century
B.C.: beyond that, little can be asserted with confidence
about his life. According to the biographical note of
St. Jerome, the poet was driven insane by a love-potion,
composed his poem in the lucid intervals of insanity
(after which it was 'corrected' by Cicero[5]), and committed
suicide at the age of fourty-four. The validity of this
account is highly dubious: its derivation from Suetonius
(which would increase its reliability) is at least ques-
tionable and it is remarkable that no earlier allusion to
such sensational material has survived, even in writers
hostile to the poet, in the course of some four and a half
centuries after his death. The story may have originated
as a 'pious fiction', designed by religious or philosophical opponents to discredit the poet's views: it may be
based on fanciful inference from parts of the poem - a
procedure for which the ancient biographers of Juvenal
afford parallels. Thus the denunciation of the passion
of love in the fourth book might have suggested that the
poet was a suitable candidate for a love-potion; the
abrupt end of the poem, apparently in the middle of the
grim description of the Athenian plague, might have suggested suicide brought on by morbid depression; in turn
the idea that Cicero 'corrected' the work might have been
inspired by his allusion to it quoted below. Nor can too
much reliance be placed on the accuracy of Jerome's dates
for the poet (94-50 B.C., though there are manuscript

---

[5] Since no *praenomen* is specified, the 'correction' of the poem is
attributed to the orator and not to his less famous brother
Quintus. *emendavit* has been taken to refer to a variety of
activities from criticism before publication to editing and publication itself.

variants), or on the confused account in Donatus' *Life of Virgil*, according to which Lucretius must have died in either 55 or 53 B.C.

Cicero in a well-known passage expresses agreement with his brother's estimate of Lucretius' poetry: *Lucreti poemata, ut scribis, ita sunt, multis luminibus ingeni, multae tamen artis: sed cum veneris*[6]. *ars*, like *ingenium*, is probably complimentary, and the contrast is between natural inspiration and conscious technique: it has, however, sometimes been taken of contrivance and artificiality, an anticipation of some modern criticisms of Lucretius' more technical passages. Apart from this fleeting allusion, Cicero nowhere else mentions the poet. The letter shows that the poem, either in whole or part, was in the brothers' hands by February of 54 B.C. but, since *poemata* may denote either the complete poem or extracts from it[7], we cannot tell whether Lucretius had finished his work on the poem, and may be presumed dead, by this date, or whether the allusion is to passages made available to the Cicero brothers at an earlier stage of composition, possibly for criticism. Whether they had been asked to secure Atticus' aid in publishing the poem is, in turn, a matter of speculation.

Lucretius is generally thought to have been a Roman noble: his name, his familiarity with Roman scenes, and the tone in which he addresses the aristocratic Memmius, though not amounting to conclusive evidence, are all consistent with this view. The Memmius of the poem is traditionally and plausibly identified with C. Memmius, an active politician[8], who was tribune in 66 B.C., and, as praetor in 58, attacked Caesar's legislation of the previous year: in 54, however, he stood for the consulship as a supporter of Caesar,

---

[6] Cicero, *Ad Quintum Fratrem* 2.9.3.
[7] F.H. Sandbach, *Classical Review* 54 (1940) 72ff., favours the view that *poemata* means extracts.
[8] Cf. 1.42-3.

only to suffer exile after conducting a corrupt campaign:
he was dead by 46 B.C. His literary interests included
the composition of amatory verse: as propraetor in
Bithynia in 57 B.C., he included on his staff the poets
Cinna and Catullus, even though the latter came to write of
him with contempt[9]. His predilection for Greek literature,
attested by Cicero[10], helps to explain his patronage of
these Alexandrian-influenced writers, and also fits the
dedication to him of a poem on Epicureanism. The standards
of his private life appear to have fallen short of the
strictness of the Epicurean ethic and might have commended
him to Lucretius as a suitable subject for conversion:
but his quarrel with the Athenian Epicureans, during his
exile in 52 B.C., over the remains of Epicurus' house[11]
suggests that the message was not absorbed. The absence
of Memmius' name from the third, fourth and sixth books,
which may well have been the last composed, may be due
purely to chance; not only is the whole poem conceived
as a personal appeal (which the general reader is allowed
to overhear), but the language associated with Memmius in
the first, second and fifth books is sometimes echoed in
the second person addresses in the three other books: if
Lucretius' failure to name Memmius there is a sign of
estrangement, he must have hoped to find a new dedicatee
and to substitute his name in the first, second and fifth
books in revision[12].

---

[9] Catullus 10 and 28.
[10] Cicero, *Brutus* 247.
[11] Cicero, *Ad Familiares* 13.1.
[12] A novel, speculative view of the dedication and of Lucretius' origins is proposed by L.A. Holland, *Lucretius and the Transpadanes* (1979).

III

EPICUREAN PHILOSOPHY AND LUCRETIUS

The philosophy originally propounded in Athens by Lucretius' master Epicurus (341-270 B.C.) comprised three branches, Logic, Physics and Ethics: of these the Logic, also known as the Canonic, constituted the rules of procedure by which the conclusions of the rest of the system were reached, and the Physics served as the indispensable basis for the Ethics, which was not only the most original but also to Epicurus the most important part of the system.

Logic

In Logic, Epicurus was a thoroughgoing empiricist, insisting on sensation as the first criterion of scientific truth: where it could not provide direct evidence itself, reasoning (on the basis of sense-experience) took over. Unexceptionable as these broad principles appear by modern standards, their application was hampered by lack of the detailed experimental evidence available to the modern scientist and Epicurus sometimes pushed his reliance upon sensation too far: thus he maintained that the sun, moon and stars are not much bigger that they appear to the eye; he also accepted plurality of causes, arguing that where different feasible explanations of a given phenomenon were not contradicted by sensation, each must be valid, at least for the occurrence of that phenomenon in some part of the universe.

Physics

The Epicurean physical system was not formulated in a vacuum, and some account of its background has especial relevance to Lucretius' first book, which includes attacks upon some of Epicurus' predecessors. The story begins in the sixth century B.C., with the Greek physicists of Ionia, the school known as the Monists, who conceived of the whole of the visible world as derived from a single substance:

Thales took this substance to be water (doubtless on the
basis of its observable changes in freezing and evaporation);
Anaximander a substance unknown to perception, which he
called 'the boundless' (τὸ ἄπειρον); Anaximenes air; and
Heraclitus, whose view was important for Stoic physics[13],
fire. The importance of the school lay in the fact that
they were the first to break away from the traditions of
mythology and from the supernatural, the first to search
for some unity lying behind the changing world of appearance and so to assume that the visible world could be explained in terms of scientific law.

Monism did not contain a convincing explanation of the
precise manner in which a single substance could change to
produce the manifold substances of perception. Accordingly,
two developments from it emerge in the fifth century, of
which the first, Pluralism, simply increased the number of
basic substances. The theory was held in different forms:
its foremost exponent, the Sicilian Empedocles, postulated
the four 'elements', earth, air, fire and water, and argued
that they were themselves unchanging but could produce all
other substances as a result of combination in different
proportions. A more radical type of pluralistic theory,
according to which there appear to have been as many basic
substances as are known to experience, seems to have been
part of the system of Anaxagoras, though the full reconstruction of his system is problematical[14].

The other development from Monism was Atomism, of which the
pioneers were the philosophers Leucippus and Democritus.
Arguing that without some limit to the divisibility of objects the world would disintegrate, they arrived at the atom
('the uncuttable'), a solid, indivisible, indestructible

---

[13] See introductory note to 1.635-704 below.
[14] See introductory note to 1.830-920 below.

unit of matter, as the first component of their universe.
Void, the only other component, was postulated in order to
allow motion to the atoms. It was this theory which, after
a century's neglect, was taken over by Epicurus to serve,
with certain modifications, as the foundation of his philosophy.

According to Epicurean atomism, space was infinite, largely
because the alternative was inconceivable: the infinity of
space was thought to entail in turn an infinite number of
atoms. The atoms were homogeneous in substance: they had
three properties only, size, shape and weight, and were
quite devoid of secondary qualities, such as colour, sound
or taste, which could only be acquired by atomic compounds.
Void, on the other hand, had no properties at all: it
could not act or be acted upon. The natural movement of
the atoms was vertically downwards, due to weight, but variation of trajectory was produced by mutual collision, from
which they rebounded: they were also liable to a slight and
unpredictable swerve, postulated as an innovation by Epicurus
in order to escape from the complete mechanical determinism
of Democritus and to leave a loophole for human free will in
the universe[15].

Even in compounds, the atoms remained in constant motion:
the formation of a compound took place when a group of atoms
was driven together and could repeat a pattern of internal
collision without being separated. Once formed, all compounds underwent a continuous give and take of atoms, which
was the basis of Epicurus' account of growth and decay:
they were all, with the sole exception of the gods, ultimately destroyed by resolution into their components.

---

[15] Unpredictability at the atomic level, as set out in modern
quantum physics, has sometimes been similarly invoked to defend
free will; in both cases the argument would appear to prove
too much, making free will purely random and arbitary.

Varieties in compounds were produced by varieties in the
nature, the motions and the arrangement of the constituent
atoms: the more rarefied the compound, the greater the
length of the atoms' trajectories between collisions:
volatile substances contained many tiny, smooth and round
atoms, while those of viscous or solid substances tended
to be larger, rougher and more jagged: pleasant sensations
were generally caused by smooth, round atoms, unpleasant
by a spikier variety. All compounds comprised atoms of
more than one type: there was a limit to the number of
atomic varieties (though the supply of atoms of any given
type was infinite) and a limit also to the possibilities of
combination, in order to account for the limit to the varieties observable in nature.

Each of the infinite number of Epicurean worlds was nothing
more than a complicated, large-scale atomic compound, spherical in shape, and formed initially by the chance concaten-
ation of appropriate matter, within which, by a natural
process of atomic motion, the four elements of the
Pluralists, earth, air, fire and water, next separated out.
The earth, together with its ocean, occupied the centre of
the sphere, and was pictured as a flat dish, surrounded
both above and (less convincingly) below by air, which comprised the inner atmosphere: beyond this, an envelope of
fiery ether, in which the heavenly bodies were denser concentrations of fire, formed the outermost limits of the
sphere. The earth contained a stock of every type of atom:
as a consequence of chance atomic motions within the earth,
the familiar objects of our world arose from it, including
vegetable and animal life, the latter from wombs put forth
from the earth. Some species were better equipped than
others to survive[16].

---

[16] Though Epicurus believed in fixity of species, he anticipated,
in principle, the Darwinian theory of natural selection.

All consciousness and mental processes depended on the soul, which was formed of a combination of especially refined atoms and comprised two parts, one distributed throughout the body and responsible for sensation, the other concentrated in the breast and responsible for thought, dreams, will and emotion. Sensation was the by-product of certain motions of soul and body atoms, and was always initiated by some physical impulse: the mechanism of vision, hearing, taste and smell was similar to that of touch, and involved subtle emanations of atoms from the object perceived making contact with the sense-organs, and affecting the pattern of atomic motions therein. The more complicated activities of the soul in the breast were attributed equally to atomic motions.

Ethics

On this physical system Epicurus based his Ethics, which embraced firstly the two conclusions so important to Lucretius, the non-participation of the gods in the workings of the universe, and the mortality of the soul: fear of the gods and of death was thus no more than groundless superstition. But though denying the gods control of the universe, Epicurus did allow their existence, on the strength of their constant appearance to men, especially in dreams: this must be due to atomic emanations from their bodies entering men's souls. The Epicurean gods were anthropomorphic and immortal beings, of a very refined atomic texture: though there is no evidence that they differed in identity from the traditional Olympians, they certainly differed in moral status, since they exemplified the Epicurean moral ideal of peace and tranquillity, and in location, for they dwelt in the spaces between worlds. The physical status of these gods is extremely puzzling: by accepting the existence of a form of eternal atomic compound (whatever the precise mechanical details involved in such a phenomenon may have been), Epicurus would appear to have sacrificed the unity of his system: again, other explanations of the pre-

sence of the gods in mental processes would appear, in view
of his account of other psychological phenomena, to have
been readily available to him: one is accordingly tempted
to wonder quite how literal his account is intended to be.
But there is no question of the importance to Epicurus of
the religious role of his gods: contemplation and imitation
of their ideally peaceful life amounted to acts of worship
and piety respectively[17]: indeed, Epicurus seems to have
recommended his disciples to participate in traditional
religious observance as constituting at least a step towards
proper Epicurean worship.

The main body of Epicurean Ethics aimed to provide a complete code of conduct to which men could cling in the moral
confusion of the Hellenistic age. The starting-point lay
once more in the physical theory, and in the contention
that every human action or experience was accompanied by
a feeling of pleasure or pain. This feeling was the first
criterion of practical, ethical knowledge, just as sensation
was the first criterion in the theoretical sphere: pleasure
dictated that the course of action involving it was to be
pursued, pain that it was to be avoided. Such a view lends
itself to misinterpretation; Epicurus was not recommending
the 'let us eat, drink and be merry' philosophy which subsequently became associated with his name; arguing that the
true end of pleasure was the removal of pain and that, once
this had been achieved, pleasure could not be increased but
only varied, he defined the true end of life not as incessant sensual delectation, but as a more negative, passive
state of ἀπονία and ἀταραξία (freedom from bodily pain and
from mental disturbance). Man's basic needs were few:
accordingly, as was appropriate in what was intended as a
popular philosophy, the achievement of self-sufficiency,
ensuring at least a preponderance of pleasure over pain,

---

[17] Cf. Lucretius 6.68-78.

lay within the reach of practically everyone. The body's
only requirements were sufficient food, clothing and shelter
to ward off the pains of hunger, cold, and the like: a
rather greater number of potential sources of distress con-
fronted the mind. Not only must it be free from the two
great religious fears, of the gods and an after-life, against which the only sure protection was the study of
Epicurean philosophy: it had also to avoid all unnecessary
desires whose pursuit was liable to involve disproportionate
pain. The quest for riches and office, which, apart from
making enemies, was usually disappointed, was accordingly
ruled out: 'live your life unnoticed' (λάθε βιώσας), was
here the Epicurean motto. Love, too, could occasion the
most disastrous emotional disturbances: sexual desire could
be gratified only if emotional independence remained unim-
paired: and even family life was frowned upon, because of
the 'distractions and unpleasantnesses' thought to be involved. Further essential requirements for the mind were
a feeling of security from other men, and freedom from the
pangs of guilty conscience, which were attributed entirely
to fear of retribution: to achieve these goals, conformity
with justice was essential: in Epicurus' egoistic system
justice was a sort of Hobbesian social contract not to harm
and not to be harmed: it was not altruistic, but an essential means to an end. The Epicurean concept of pleasure
thus appears a very restricted, largely negative one: the
two highest, most positive pleasures open to the Epicurean
seem to have been friendship (though even this was justified
in the first instance on utilitarian grounds) and the contemplation of the true nature of the universe as revealed in
Epicurean philosophy.

Lucretian Epicureanism
Lucretius, despite his concentration on the Physics and its
two vital implications about the gods and an after-life,
shows himself an equally faithful disciple of his master in
Logic and in Ethics: though these subjects are not treated

systematically, all their most fundamental points are
stressed in the course of the poem. Of Epicurus' voluminous
writings, only a collection of *Principal Sayings* and three
letters to disciples (one of which is of dubious authenticity) survive in their entirety: the rest of our knowledge
depends upon fragments and secondary sources. Nothing suggests that Lucretius, who makes no claim to philosophical
originality, introduced any innovations or amendments of
his own into his exposition, even if many of his copious
illustrations are of his own invention. He is often to be
observed closely following Epicurus' *Letter to Herodotus*[18],
which provides a summary of the physical system, and may be
presumed to have drawn on other of his master's works with
similar fidelity.

Lucretius' emphasis on the two 'religious' conclusions of
Epicureanism has sometimes been thought anachronistic and
more appropriate to the climate of opinion in the Greece
of Epicurus than in first century Rome, where the educated
classes (the only audience Lucretius could hope to reach
directly with the poem) are sometimes sceptical of the state
religion and disavow belief in an after-life: the poem also
gives considerable prominence to the cruder forms of popular belief. While Lucretius may have somewhat overesti-
mated the religious fears of his contemporaries, or indulged
in what Kenney has called 'satirical overkill'[19], it is a
mistake to suppose that primitive superstition is his only
target: his object is to establish correct belief about
the gods and the mortality of the soul, for which in his
view Epicurean philosophy provided the only sound basis:
he is thus opposing any opinion on these subjects which is
non-Epicurean, and aiming not only at superstition and traditional religion, but also at rival philosophical views

---

[18] E.g. 1.149ff., 418ff., 599ff. and 951ff.
[19] E.J. Kenney, *Lucretius, Greece and Rome*, New Surveys in the
Classics, no. 11 (1977).

(to whose refutation much space is devoted). To Lucretius even the professed but non-Epicurean sceptic needed conversion, since scepticism without the sound scientific basis of Epicureanism was liable to break down in time of stress[20].

The passionate fervour with which Lucretius conveys his message is certainly an un-Epicurean trait: it may be that of the convert, reacting against his own former beliefs, though psychological plausibility does not amount to proof. His fervour certainly affords no clue that he was still trying to convince himself of the validity of his own conclusions: the persistent theory, according to which there are signs in Lucretius of an Anti-Lucretius unable to accept the Epicurean message, is probably more informative about the religious persuasions of its champions than about Lucretius' own. A similar fervour animates the poet's moral disquisitions, his attacks on money-making and political ambition (his most frequent moral targets) and on the passion of love: in these fields it is certainly not surprising that he saw the Epicurean message as vitally relevant to the Roman contemporary scene.

IV

LUCRETIUS' POETIC MEDIUM AND ACHIEVEMENT

Epicureanism had been propounded at Rome since the second century B.C.: Lucretius' originality lies in his use of poetry as a medium for its exposition. The tradition of didactic poetry (regarded by the Greeks as a branch of epic) went back to Hesiod, whose *Works and Days* displays a similar moral earnestness to that which animates Lucretius. This feature seems to have been largely conspicuous by its

---

[20] 3.41-54.

absence in the great proliferation of the genre with the
Alexandrian poets, whose generally abstruse and technical
subject-matter reflects their preoccupation with learning
and with literary form as an end in itself: their works
were popular with the Romans and were to exercise a widespread influence on Roman didactic. Cicero's *Aratea* , a
youthful version of the astronomical and meteorological
poetry of Aratus, had appeared fairly recently when Lucretius
started to write: but, while occasionally echoing Cicero's
language, Lucretius differs radically in spirit. A much
older and far more influential precedent lay in the philosophical poetry of three early Greek thinkers: in the sixth
century Xenophanes, in addition to attacking the crudities
of Olympian theology in satirical verses, had probably also
composed a hexameter poem *On Nature*: certainly in the fifth
Parmenides and Empedocles had expounded their philosophical
ideas in didactic hexameters, continuing the Hesiodic tradition in a novel field and to some extent rivalling, or
seeking to replace, the subject-matter of Hesiod's *Theogony*.
The surviving fragments suggest that of this trio Empedocles
alone rose to any great poetic heights: the example of his
poem *On Nature* clearly exerted a profound literary influence
upon Lucretius, in whom various reminiscences are detectable,
and whose rapturous eulogy[21] is not inspired solely by philosophical sympathy. In Latin, although Ennius had composed
two philosophical works based on Greek sources, the *Epicharmus*
(on nature and the four elements) and the *Euhemerus* (a
rationalistic account of the gods of mythology), the former
employed a trochaic metre rather than the hexameter and the
latter was a prose work.

Whatever the precedents, Epicurus' unsympathetic attitude to
the arts in general might have seemed to weigh against the
medium of poetry: regarding Epicurean philosophy as the only
essential study, he treated other forms of culture, which he

---

[21] **1.716-33.**

doubtless saw as a rival moral influence, with some hostility. That he would seriously have objected to a poem
preaching Epicureanism is unlikely, and Lucretius is careful to point out that the ultimate purpose of his poetry
is the more effective achievement of his philosophical
end[22]: a poem on Epicureanism was also likely to arouse a
wider interest in the literary circles of his day than a
scientific prose tract on the same subject[23]. In embarking
upon poetry and the figurative language essential to it,
he was certainly liable to technical violation of one of the
rules of Epicurean Canonic, according to which words must be
used in their basic, most obvious senses: he nevertheless
shows himself aware of this rule in connection with technical
terminology[24], and of the need for lucidity in philosophical
exegesis[25], while he also points out the dangers involved
in one type of poetic licence[26].

These considerations are, in fact, peripheral: the ultimate
reason for Lucretius' 'choice' of poetry lies in the poetic
nature of the inspiration afforded him by Epicurean philosophy and in the consciousness that it was only in poetry
that he could most adequately and effectively express the
Epicurean message. Certainly formidable difficulties con-
fronted him if a poem worthy of the name was to be achieved.
Even the metrical problems were considerable[27]: words awkward or inadmissible in the Latin hexameter might include
crucial technical or semi-technical terms: thus *primordia*,
one of his words for the primary particles, had to be replaced in the genitive, dative and ablative by *principia*, and
magnitudo by such words as *figura*, *filum*, or the coined

---

[22] 1.935-50.
[23] See note on 1.945 below.
[24] E.g. 1.458.
[25] 1.639-44 and 933-4.
[26] 2.655-60.
[27] This was an aspect of the *patrii sermonis egestas* of which
Lucretius complains; see note on 1.136-45 below.

maximitas. Further, Epicurean physics, which was to occupy
the bulk of the work, was not only a factual but also a
vastly complicated subject, some of whose aspects, like the
doctrine of the 'least parts' of the atom[28], were highly
technical and difficult enough to manage metrically, let
alone invest with poetic power. But the poetic potential of
the subject is equally obvious. However involved its details
may sometimes be, its essential concept, of an infinite universe comprising atoms and void, is of a simplicity and at
the same time of a breadth to commend it to the poet's imagination. Again, Epicurean argument for imperceptible processes (the most crucial of which were at the atomic level)
generally proceeded, as has been seen, from observed phenomena, so that even unpromising technical topics afforded
abundant opportunities for precise natural description, which
was not gratuitous poetic adornment, but an integral part of
the scientific argument: a comparison between Lucretius and
the surviving works of Epicurus (even allowing for the fact
that these are no more than summaries) suggests that the
Roman poet, with his vivid and precise pictorial imagination,
has exploited the possibility of such illustration to a remarkable degree[29]. At the same time, the subject-matter
also allows ample scope for Lucretius' notable bent for satirical poetry, when he mocks human folly or ridicules rival
theories[30]. Above all, if Epicurean physics was a factual
subject, it evoked an emotional response in its true adher-
ents: contemplation of the realities of the universe was
not only the source of the highest form of pleasure, but did
not exclude a feeling of wonder and awe that these realities

---

[28] 1.599-634.

[29] E.g. 1.250-64, 271-328, 348-55 and 489-96.

[30] Conspicuous examples are to be found in the denunciation of
religio (1.80-101) and in the course of the philosophical
attacks on Ennius (1.120-6), Heraclitus (1.635-704),
Anaxagoras (1.830-920), and the centripetalists (1.1052ff.).

should obtain: so Lucretius talks of the *divina voluptas*
and the *horror* inspired by Epicurus' revelation of nature's
secrets[31]. Moreover, the whole purpose of the factual exposition was ultimately practical and moral: what was more
worthy to be enshrined in poetry that what Lucretius saw as
the ultimate physical and moral truths of the universe?

There is no greater indirect testimony to Lucretius' poetic
success than the pervasive influence which he exerted upon
Virgil, not only in the *Georgics* but in his whole output.
Merrill finds that one Virgilian line in twelve echoes
Lucretius, whether consciously or unconsciously[32]. Modern
critics freely acknowledge the poetic stature of Lucretian
'purple patches', which include not only the introductions
and the so-called 'digressions' where he dilates upon his
central philosophical aims and conclusions, but also a
number of passages which occur in the course of scientific
exposition: but they often complain that at least large
expanses of the argumentation are arid, pedestrian and prosaic. It is certainly true that the poem, like the *Georgics*,
is not always on the same poetic plane: indeed, given his
subject-matter, Lucretius obviously did not hope or aim to
rise consistently to the same level of inspiration. Broadly
speaking, the expository passages are written in a plainer
style, appropriate to their purpose of instruction, while
the non-expository passages are pitched in a grander style
and make a stronger and more consistent appeal to the emotions.
Certainly Lucretian exposition involves features of style
which are not typical of Roman poetry: his sentences are
sometimes unusually long and involve unusual degrees of sub-
ordination, but the dexterity with which they are handled
and the *ars* which lies behind them is often seriously under-

---

[31] 3.28-30.
[32] W.A. **Merrill**, *Parallels and Coincidences in Lucretius and
Virgil* (**1918**).

estimated[33]. Again, he is not afraid to use words like *res*,
constare and *videtur* in different senses at close range,
trusting the context to make the meaning clear, or conversely
to repeat words at close range in the same sense, as lucidity
or emphasis requires, though this should not obscure the resource with which he constantly varies his vocabulary for
concepts central to the argument[34]. His word-order, though
often illustrative (see Introduction V c below) and generally
lucid, occasionally strains the greater flexibility natural
in poetry to its limits: his exploitation of the postponed
conjunction, in particular, can sometimes baffle the beginner. Unlike the Augustans, he has no inhibitions about the
use of demonstrative pronouns in prominent positions or
about placing the verb 'to be', even when unemphatic, at the
beginning or end of a line. His signposting of arguments
with recurrent introductory formulae like *primum, praeterea,
quin etiam, huc accedit uti, denique* and *postremo* is uncompromis-
ingly functional, even if it may, together with the repetition of key lines and phrases[35] and the use of periphrases
with a genitive like *vis* and *natura*[36], be a conscious replacement for the repeated formulae of epic, so suggesting a
rivalry between the epic of action and Lucretius' more
serious, more important epic of thought.

Despite such 'prosaic' elements, the unevenness of the poem
is often much exaggerated: the poetic 'honey' is more gen-
erously spread than is always appreciated. The contribution
of archaism, of alliteration and assonance, and of imitative
effects will be considered in the next section: they are as
pervasive in the expository as in the non-expository passages.
The general richness of the poem's language (to which archaism

---

[33] E.g. 1.584-98, where the two long sentences which express a
new and complete argument not only form a carefully balanced
antithesis, but are chiasmically arranged.
[34] Cf. e.g. 1.299-301 and 348-55.
[35] E.g. 1.75-7, 146-8, 505 and 670-1.
[36] See note on 1.131 below.

itself contributes) is all the more striking when compared
with the flat, technical-sounding Greek of Epicurus: arrange
Lucretius' words in prose order, and what Horace calls the
disiecti membra poetae[37] emerge with considerable regularity.
A significant illustration of the avoidance of the prosaic
is provided by the poet's approach to the problem of technical terminology: here, the absence in Latin of any ready-
made scientific or philosophical vocabulary was, despite his
complaints (see fn. 27 above), something of a blessing in
disguise, for it generally enabled him to avoid terms with
the inherent prosaic associations of words like, for example,
the English 'atoms' or 'elements': thus, to refer to his
primary particles he never transliterates the Greek ἄτομοι,
but prefers more general terms, often involving a degree of
metaphor, like *primordia* and *semina*[38], which correspond respectively to the Greek ἀρχαί and σπέρματα: again, his
terms for atomic combination and dissolution, *concilium* and
discidium[39], suggest personification of the atoms, and carry
political and legal overtones. Such personification of the
inanimate, which can scarcely be labelled 'prosaic', is widespread in the poem, and is especially common in the case of
the atoms, which much of the time take on the role of
'heroes' in the Lucretian epic. Nor is this approach scientifically indefensible: certainly the atoms were not conscious agents[40] but, since Epicureanism presupposed a degree
of uniformity in the processes of nature at different levels
on the scale of size, observable phenomena involving persons
might serve as a perfectly legitimate analogue for unobserv-
able processes at the atomic level: thus an atom, like a
phalanx of men, owed its strength to the solidity of its
formation[41]. This personification, as in the examples cited,

---

[37] Horace, *Satires* 1.4.62.
[38] See notes on 1.55 and 59 below.
[39] See notes on 1.183 and 220 below.
[40] This idea is ridiculed at 1.1021ff.
[41] 1.605-6, where it is the 'least parts' of the atom which are
personified.

often involves a specific metaphor: the richness of Lucretian imagery, to which commentators are not always
sufficiently sensitive[42], is not confined to the 'purple
patches', any more than is the subtle linking of sound with
sense by the use of alliteration and assonance and expressive
words, word-order and rhythm. All these factors assist in
giving a measure of stylistic unity to the poem: it has,
further, an emotional unity, which depends not only on
Lucretius' deep spiritual satisfaction, combined with a sense
of wonder, inspired by contemplation of the manifold facets
of nature, but also on his passionate conviction of the
validity of every aspect of the philosophy which he is ex-
pounding and on his fervent desire to communicate it and to
achieve thereby his readers' salvation.

V

STYLE

In addition to the considerations touched on in the preceding section, the following aspects of Lucretian style
may be singled out for especial mention.

(a) *Archaism*
A strong archaic flavour is imparted to the poem by the
generous, but intermittent, incorporation of archaic gram-
matical forms and vocabulary, and by the more sparing adoption
of archaic syntax. That archaism could invest poetry with
dignity and solemnity is attested by Cicero[43]: the extremely
rare and isolated instances of archaism in Virgil seem designed to produce a similar effect much more occasionally and
to pay tribute to a tradition. In Lucretius, the tendency
was clearly influenced in no small degree by his admiration

---

[42] For a salutary corrective, see D. West, *The Imagery and Poetry
of Lucretius* (1969).

[43] Cicero, *de Oratore* 3.153.

for Ennius, the father of Roman poetry, who had first introduced the hexameter from Greek into Latin, in his historical
epic, the *Annales*: the numerous Lucretian echoes of Ennian
phraseology and the direct tribute to Ennius' literary achievement[44] confirm that he saw Ennius as his main literary model
in Latin.

Two conspicuous examples of archaism in grammar are the disyllabic first declension genitive singular in $-\bar{a}\bar{\imath}$ for the
normal $-ae$[45] and the passive or deponent infinitive in
$-ier$ for the usual $-i$[46]. In vocabulary, apart from
the frequent use of old words like *dius*, *cluere*, *pauxillus* or
suppus (22, 119. 835, 1061), and of words in archaic, often
root senses[47], Lucretius shows a great fondness for archaic
compound adjectives[48], for rare compound verbs (e.g. *praepandere*
and *convisere* 144-5). for adverbs in *-im* (e.g. *moderatim*
323) and for abstract nouns of the fourth declension (e.g.
comptus 87, *mactatus* 99 and *conciliatus* 575): many words
in all four categories occur for the first or only time in
Lucretius, and he has clearly often exploited the archaic
tendency to coin words freely, so that his archaism has its
creative side. In his syntax, which naturally exhibits many
constructions common to the Roman poets in general, the archaising tendency is less marked, but is exemplified in the
final dative with a gerundive construction[49], the indicative
with concessive *cum* (e.g. 726-7), and the genitive of
separation[50]. A number of indiosyncrasies, including some
of his fluctuations of declension (e.g. *materia* / *materies,*
exanimus for *exanimis*[51]), of conjugation (e.g. *condensēre*
foi *condensare* 392) or between transitive and intransitive usages[52]. should not be regarded as genuinely

---

[44] 1.117-9.
[45] See note on 1.29 below.
[46] See note on 1.207 below.
[47] See notes e.g on *templa* 1.120 and *cogi* 1.1020 below.
[48] See note on *navigerum* and *frugiferentis* 1.3 below.
[49] See note on 1.24 below.
[50] See note on *aversa viai* 1.1041 below.
[51] See notes on 1.58 and 774 below.
[52] See notes on *movendi* 1.383 and *trahere* 1.397 below.

archaic, but rather as reflecting a genuine fluidity
in the language of his day: nevertheless a considerable
proportion of his 'archaism' remains irreducible, and
is obviously studied.

The alternation between archaic and contemporary forms and
usages adds variety to the poem and is of enormous metrical
advantage: when the archaic form is not the only one
readily admissible in the hexameter (as it is, e.g., with
indugredi 82), it is often at least far more metrically convenient. But an older form is often preferred where the
standard usage is metrically identical, as with *rursum* and
prorsum for *rursus* and *prorsus* (57 and 1005), *reddunda* for *reddenda*
(59) or *ollis* for *illis* (672): and whether metrically advantageous or not, the archaising tendency has the artistic
justification of lending the poem added solemnity, dignity
and grandeur; this effect is perhaps nowhere more notice-
able than in the sonorous -*ai* genitive, to which Lucretius
often gives emphasis by placing it at the end of the line.

(b) *Alliteration and assonance*
Alliteration, involving the repetition of a consonant (not
necessarily initial), and assonance, involving the repetition of a vowel sound or of a syllable, are exploited by
Lucretius to a far greater extent than by any other fully
extant Roman poet, and make a fundamental contribution to
the music of his verse. The older Roman poets had been
fond of these effects, which are frequent in the fragments
of Ennius, and to this extent their prevalence in Lucretius
reflects his archaising tendency: but, not unnaturally, he
shows far greater subtlety in their employment. Ennius had
sometimes given single letters an exaggerated or even grotesque predominance[53]: Lucretius more often prefers to
interweave a variety of repeated sounds (while often giving

---

[53] See note on 1.200-2, where Lucretius may be deliberately
parodying Ennius.

them greater prominence than was later to prove to Virgil's taste). The literary contribution of these practices is manifold (in some contexts an assonance can seem to take on an air of mockery[54]) and naturally cannot be too precisely categorised, but sometimes (as with *fera moenera militiai* 29 or *flammantia moenia mundi* 73) they help to add unity and impressiveness to a phrase: in many cases they acquire, in their context, an expressive effect (see also (c) below, as also for 'meaningful' assonance), most obviously as when a repeated *m* echoes the rumble of thunder (e.g. 68-9) or when v, especially in combination with $\bar{i}$, is repeated in a context of vigour (e.g. 72) or violence (e.g. 271): in addition, they contribute not only to the music, but to the continuity of the verse, serving, like the relentless hexameter itself, to carry the reader more speedily through the argument to the philosophical conclusion.

(c) *Meaningful word-play and expressive use of language*
According to Epicurean theory, language was in origin natural, rather than conventional, and began because men of the same race tended spontaneously to produce the same sort of sound in the same sort of situation: it was only at a later stage, when the advantages of language became apparent, that names came also to be deliberately allocated, by convention. Lucretius faithfully summarises this doctrine (5.1028-90), appealing to the analogy of animals, which spontaneously utter different sounds in different situations according to their kind: in describing these sounds, he makes conspicuous use of expressive, onomatopoeic language, as if to suggest the further argument that man's vocabulary for animal noises stems from a spontaneous, natural imitation of them.

As was first pointed out by Friedländer, recently followed up by Snyder[55], the Epicurean view that language was in

---

[54] See notes on 1.667 and 787 below.
[55] P. Friedländer, 'Pattern of Sound and Atomistic Theory in Lucretius', *American Journal of Philology* 62 (1941) 16-34; J.M. Snyder *Puns and Poetry in Lucretius' De Rerum Natura* (1980).

origin natural helps to explain the prevalence of certain
features of Lucretius' style. He is especially fond of
employing similarities between words in order to draw attention to similarities in the world; this literary effect is
not confined to Lucretius[56], but in his case appears
often to have a scientific basis in Epicurean theory. If
language is basically natural, similarities between words
would tend often not to be merely fortuitous, but to arise
because two distinct, but related types of object or event
spontaneously evoked two distinct, but related sounds.
Lucretius seems often clearly to be suggesting that verbal
correspondences are not accidental, especially where he
juxtaposes words of the same root, as if to remind us of
their derivation and so to enrich their meaning[57], or where
(more important) he suggests an etymology of certain key concepts, such as *natura* (*nasci*) 21-5, *superstitio* (*superstare*) 65,
materies (*mater*) 167-71, and *religio* (*religare*) 932[58]. A clear
indication that he is fully aware of the scientific basis of
his practice lies in his fondness for the analogy which he
draws between the atoms in compounds and the letters in
words, which is invoked on three occasions in the first book
(196-7, 823-9 and 907-14): just as different combinations
of different letters make up different words, so different
combinations of different types of atom make up different
types of compound object: significantly, he suggests that
words for closely related types of object sometimes contain
many letters in common, just as closely related types of com-

---

[56] Cf. e.g. Shakespeare, *Macbeth*, Act I, Scene vii - 'If the
assassination / Could trammel up the consequence, and catch /
With his *surcease*, *success*.' - where, in Macbeth's wishful
thinking, Duncan's death seems almost literally to spell triumph;
or *Othello*, Act III, Scene iii - 'But, O, what damned minutes
tells he o'er, / Who *dotes*, yet *doubts*.' - where the verbal
correspondence suggests how closely associated love and jealousy
can be.

[57] See notes, e.g., on *corripiunt rapidi* 1.294 and *annis anulus*
1.311-2 below.

[58] See notes *ad locc.* below.

pound (like wood and fire, into which wood can pass) will
tend to contain many types of atom in common: the specific
example of *lignum* and *ignis* is adduced at 912-4.

But if Lucretius saw a scientific justification for his
habit of word-play and meaningful assonance, it is equally
clear that he extends it to cases where, even allowing for
the crudities of ancient etymology, he must have realised
that the verbal similarity was purely fortuitous: indeed,
he sometimes uses a verbal echo to obtain a paradox, and to
focus not on a correspondence, but on an opposition in the
world, as if the similarity of the words was potentially
misleading (e.g. *deceptaque non capiatur* 941 or *effugiumque fugae
prolatet copia* 983).   Epicurean theory, moreover, left room
for such fortuitous verbal correspondences, which might be
expected to arise from the arbitrary allocation of names
which was an important secondary stage in the development of
language.   Thus the echo of *Ennius* in *perenni* (117-8), while
calculated to bring out the appropriateness of Ennius' name,
is certainly not intended to suggest that the name predes-
tined him to literary immortality: and the correspondence
between *officium corporis* and *officere* (336-7), which underlines the point that matter and its property of 'getting in
the way' are inseparable, is obviously, on inspection,
purely accidental, since the combination of *officium* with any
genitive (even the antonym *inanis*, 'the function of void')
would produce an identical, but less scientifically appropriate, verbal echo.   But though not all Lucretian word-
plays have any serious claim to etymological or scientific
justification, he constantly exploits them meaningfully,
as though they had: their most frequent function, whether
their scientific basis is plausible or entirely specious,
is to reinforce the logic of an assertion or argument, by
suggesting that the verbal similarity reflects an actual
similarity existing in nature[59].

---

[59]   E.g. 1.336-7 cited above; cf. note on *flamina / flumen* 1.290-
1 below.

But the Epicurean theory of language has far wider implications for Lucretian style, apart from the more specific
question of word-play. If language is in origin imitative,
its word-patterns would often automatically tend to reflect
the patterns in the world which it is describing. Lucretius
frequently exploits the flexibility possible in poetry to
arrange his words to match the pattern in nature which he is
presenting, a habit which West has called 'syntactical ono-
matopoea'[60]. Examples are not only too numerous but too
felicitous to be ascribed to mere coincidence, and are often
didactically and argumentatively illustrative[61]. Again, if
language is to a large extent 'natural', many of its sounds
would tend to have at least a general appropriateness to the
sense, and sometimes to be more positively expressive or
onomatopoeic. This applies not only to complete words, but
also to individual letters or groups of letters, which might
tend to have their own special associations and appropriateness to certain categories of description, e.g. liquids to
pleasant, restful contexts, plosives to contexts of greater
vigour and astringency (e.g. 372-4): in terms of the favourite Lucretian analogy, the former letters would correspond to
the smooth atoms responsible for fluidity and for generally
pleasant sensations, the latter to atoms of a rougher, more
jagged type. Lucretian alliteration and assonance are indeed
remarkably expressive: while the interplay of sound and
sense can only properly be appreciated by reading the poem
aloud, attempts will be made in the notes to draw attention
to some of the more obvious examples. There can be no doubt
that the poet consciously realised that such imitative and
expressive use of language was entirely consistent with the
Epicurean theory of its origin.

---

[60] *Op. cit.* (fn. 42 above) 119.
[61] See notes, e.g., on 1.33, 37, 38-9, 367, 375-6, 385-6, 114-5,
998-1000 and 1106-8 below.

(d) *Metre*

Despite the various reminiscences of Ennius in the poem, to
which a characteristically Ennian cadence may at times contribute, the Lucretian hexameter naturally exhibits significant differences from that of his pioneering predecessor:
equally naturally, it possesses features which the refined
taste of Virgil, the acknowledged master of the medium, was
later to avoid: indeed, the canons for the epic, didactic
and elegiac hexameter tended to become more numerous and re-
strictive throughout its history from Ennius to the
Augustans[62]. The following comparative summary should not be
taken to imply that the Virgilian hexameter would in any
fundamental respect have been a better instrument for
Lucretius, or one as well suited to his subject-matter.

Two types of accent or emphasis fall upon syllables in Latin
verse: *ictus*, or metrical emphasis, which in the hexameter
falls upon the first syllable of each foot, and *stress*, the
accentuation of normal prose pronunciation. Disyllabic words
were stressed on the first syllable (*álma*, *máre*) : words of
three or more syllables on the penultimate, if long (*volúptas*),
and on the antepenultimate, if the penultimate was short
 (*hóminum*): words of four or more syllables probably bore a
secondary stress earlier in the word (*ànimántum*, *frùgiferéntis*).
As Greek had no stress accent, one of the main problems confronting the Romans in their adaptation of the Greek hexameter
was to decide how far ictus and stress should be made to co-
incide or to clash. The general preference which emerged was
for some measure of clash within the first four feet, and for
coincidence in the last two, so that the normal prose pronunciation brought out the metre at the end of the line. Ennius,
whether consciously or not, made an important contribution to
this pattern: his preference for the strong (or 'masculine')
caesura (- ‖ ‿‿) in the third or fourth foot over the weak

---

[62] The hexameter of satire had canons of its own, notwithstanding
the epic or mock-epic style sometimes cultivated in this genre,
most conspicuously by Juvenal.

(or 'feminine') caesura (–⏑ || ⏑), which is far more common in the Greek hexameter, automatically secured more conflict in the middle of the line than would otherwise have resulted. But, while it is unfair to dismiss the Ennian hexameter as 'haphazard', he certainly exhibits a greater proportion of departures from final coincidence than his successors: in Virgil, such exceptions seem only to be allowed in special circumstances, usually where a Greek word or context justifies a Greek type of line-ending, or where some expressive effect, which may vary considerably according to context, is intended. Lucretius generally has a high proportion of final coincidence, and though some of his deviations from it seem to be concessions to the difficulties of the metre and the subject-matter, many of them appear as appropriate and effective as Virgil's (e.g. 13, 33 and 69). At the same time Lucretius is by no means as fastidious as Virgil as to the precise type of final coincidence employed; Virgil, partly at least out of a desire to secure emphatic coincidence, normally restricts himself to three types of line-ending, exemplified by *únde Latínum*, *cónderet úrbem* and *prímus ab óris*, allowing word-breaks in the last two feet only after the first two or three syllables, or after both: Lucretius readily admits, as occasional additions, other types which secure at least a high degree of coincidence. Thus a word of five syllables (e.g. *frùgiferéntis*) sometimes closes the line, a favourite type with Lucretius (the technical words *materiai* and *principiorum* account for many of his examples), as earlier with Ennius: again, a high proportion of his lines which end with quadrisyllabic or monosyllabic words, which in most combinations produce a strong conflict within the last two feet, are 'protected' by a preceding monosyllable, or, in the case of quadrisyllabic words, by a preceding elision (*néc minitánti*, *córpore quáe sunt*, *natúra animántum*); these combinations secure greater coincidence, even though they involve an element of clash, arising from the secondary stress on the initial syllable of the quadrisyllabic word and the accentuation accorded to the final monosyllabic word.

Whatever Virgil's gain in refinement from his normal
avoidance of such endings, the Lucretian hexameter is
in this respect at least richer in variety than the Virgilian.
Within the first four feet, Roman poets avoid monotony by regularly varying the incidence of conflict from line to line,
but here too characteristic tendencies emerge. In the first
foot, Lucretius and later writers have more coincidence than
Ennius, thus more often characterising the metre at the beginning of the line, as well as at the end: in the second,
coincidence becomes increasingly exceptional, though Lucretius
has a number of examples, for instance where the first two
feet are self-contained (e.g. 72, 87 and 468). The strong
caesura normal in the third or fourth foot automatically produces clash in one or other: Lucretius has more instances than
Virgil of elision at the main caesura (e.g. 234), and of a main
fourth foot caesura unaccompanied by a strong caesura in the
second foot (e.g. 468): in the fourth foot, Virgil exhibits
more instances of clash than Lucretius, thus more often
avoiding coincidence in the whole of the second half of the
line.

But many characteristics of the Lucretian hexameter are independent of the relation of ictus and stress. He avails
himself only sparingly of the spondaic fifth foot, which is
common in the Greek hexameter, and comparatively popular
with Ennius and with the Alexandrian school of Roman poets:
the seven instances in the first book all seem in different
ways appropriate to their context (most obviously perhaps 64
and 991). His use of *tmesis* (which is sometimes expressive)
stands midway between the extravagance of Ennius and the re-
straint of Virgil[63]. His elision of final -*s*, of which he is
apparently the last writer to make any extended use[64], may be
seen as part of his archaising tendency. His higher proportion of end-stopped lines as compared with Virgil, which has
been criticised as 'monotonous', should not obscure the

---

[63] See note on 1.318 below.
[64] See note on 1.159 below.

pauses which he engineers at other points in the line, and
is to a large extent dictated by the subject-matter: the
end of the line is the natural place to conclude an argument
or illustration, from which subtle Virgilian enjambement
would only be a distraction;   indeed, a reader attending to
the argument is unlikely to sense any rhythmic monotony.   He
shows himself just as aware of the imitative and expressive
possibilities of rhythm as of those of language[65], even though
these effects are usually less subtle than Virgil's, as befits their illustrative didactic purpose, and even though not
every accumulation of elisions or every heavily spondaic line
has an obvious appropriateness to the sense.   Not unnaturally,
given the nature of some of his subject-matter and his date
in history, Lucretius sometimes lacks smoothness and polish:
thus he is readier than the Augustans to admit, for example,
an occasional harsh *synizesis* (*cuius* 149) or consonantalisation
(*suo* 1022), or occasionally to append -*que* to short *e*[66] or to
allow a short final vowel before a double consonant[67].   Such
traces of harshness and ruggedness are however not necessarily a defect in Lucretius, but rather reflect the relentless
zeal with which he presses on, whatever the obstacles, towards his philosophical goal.

---

[65]   See notes e.g. on 1.150, 233-4, 337, 348-9, 662-3, 742-3, 843,
938 and 1003-4 below.
[66]   See note on 1.134 below.
[67]   See note on 1.372 below.

SELECT BIBLIOGRAPHY

AMORY,A.: '*Obscura de re lucida carmina*: Science and poetry in *De Rerum Natura*', *YCS* 21 (1969) 143-168.

BAILEY,C.: *Titi Lucreti Cari De Rerum Natura*, 3 vols. (1947).

BOYANCÉ,P.: *Lucrèce et l'épicurisme* (1963).

COX,A.: 'Didactic Poetry', in *Greek and Latin Literature: a Comparative Study*, ed. J. Higginbotham (1969) 124-161.

DALZELL,A.: 'A Bibliography of Work on Lucretius, 1945-1972', *CW* 66 (1972-3) 385-427 and 67 (1973-4) 65-112.

DUDLEY,D.R. ed.: *Lucretius, Studies in Latin Literature and its Influence* (1965).

DUFF,J.D.: *T. Lucreti Cari Liber Primus* (1923).

FRIEDLÄNDER,P.: 'Pattern of Sound and Atomistic Theory in Lucretius', *AJP* 62 (1941) 16-34.

FURLEY,D.J.: 'Lucretius and the Stoics', *BICS* 13 (1966) 13-33.

GIANCOTTI,F.: *Il preludio di Lucrezio* (1959).

GIUSSANI,C.: *Titi Lucreti Cari De Rerum Natura* (1896-8).

GUTHRIE,W.K.C.: *A History of Greek Philosophy*, vols. I and II (1962-5).

HADZSITS,G.D.: *Lucretius and his Influence* (1935).

HOLLAND,L.A.: *Lucretius and the Transpadanes* (1979).

KENNEY,E.J.: *Lucretius, Greece and Rome*, New Surveys in the Classics no. 11 (1977).

KIRK,G.S. and RAVEN,J.E.: *The Presocratic Philosophers: a Critical History with a Selection of Texts* (1957).

LONG,A.A.: *Hellenistic Philosophy: Stoics, Epicureans and Sceptics* (1974).

MUNRO,H.A.J.: *T. Lucreti Cari De Rerum Natura*, 3 vols. (1893).

OTT,W.: *Metrische Analysen zu Lukrez De Rerum Natura, Buch I* (1974).

RIST,J.M.: *Epicurus: an Introduction* (1972).

SANTAYANA,G.: *Three Philosophical Poets: Lucretius, Dante and Goethe* (1935).

SELLAR,W.Y.: *The Roman Poets of the Republic* (1889).

SNYDER,J.M. *Puns and Poetry in Lucretius' De Rerum Natura* (1980).

SYKES DAVIES,H.: 'Notes on Lucretius', *The Criterion* 11 (1931-2) 25-42.

WASZINK,J.H.: 'Lucretius and Poetry', *Mededelingen der Koninklijke Nederlandse Akademie van Wetenschapen*, Afd. Letterkunde n.s. 17 (1954) 243-257.

WEST,D.: *The Imagery and Poetry of Lucretius* (1969).

Kenney's invaluable survey provides a splendid amplification of much that is outlined in the Introduction to the present volume. Long and Rist should be consulted for further information on Epicurean philosophy; Guthrie and Kirk-Raven on the Presocratics attacked at 1.635-920 and on Epicurus' Atomist predecessors. Fuller bibliographies of work up to 1977 are to be found in Dalzell and Kenney.

Note:

Full references to other works, which are cited only once in the introduction and notes, are given in the course of the text: references to works included in the bibliography are made by the author's surname and, where appropriate, page numbers.

LUCRETIUS

DE RERUM NATURA I

1 - 145 : INTRODUCTION

Prayer to Venus (1-43)

Aeneadum genetrix, hominum divumque voluptas,
alma Venus, caeli subter labentia signa
quae mare navigerum, quae terras frugiferentis
concelebras, per te quoniam genus omne animantum
5   concipitur visitque exortum lumina solis:
te, dea, te fugiunt venti, te nubila caeli
adventumque tuum, tibi suavis daedala tellus
summittit flores, tibi rident aequora ponti
placatumque nitet diffuso lumine caelum.
10 nam simul ac species patefactast verna diei
et reserata viget genitabilis aura favoni,
aeriae primum volucres te, diva, tuumque
significant initum perculsae corda tua vi.
inde ferae pecudes persultant pabula laeta   (15)
15 et rapidos tranant amnis: ita capta lepore   (14)
te sequitur cupide quo quamque inducere pergis.
denique per maria ac montis fluviosque rapaces
frondiferasque domos avium camposque virentis
omnibus incutiens blandum per pectora amorem
20 efficis ut cupide generatim saecla propagent.
quae quoniam rerum naturam sola gubernas
nec sine te quicquam dias in luminis oras
exoritur neque fit laetum neque amabile quicquam,

```
        te sociam studeo scribendis versibus esse
25   quos ego de rerum natura pangere conor
     Memmiadae nostro, quem tu, dea, tempore in omni
     omnibus ornatum voluisti excellere rebus.
     quo magis aeternum da dictis, diva, leporem.
     effice ut interea fera moenera militiai
30   per maria ac terras omnis sopita quiescant.
     nam tu sola potes tranquilla pace iuvare
     mortalis, quoniam belli fera moenera Mavors
     armipotens regit, in gremium qui saepe tuum se
     reicit aeterno devictus vulnere amoris,
35   atque ita suspiciens tereti cervice reposta
     pascit amore avidos inhians in te, dea, visus
     eque tuo pendet resupini spiritus ore.
     hunc tu, diva, tuo recubantem corpore sancto
     circumfusa super, suavis ex ore loquelas
40   funde petens placidam Romanis, incluta, pacem.
     nam neque nos agere hoc patriai tempore iniquo
     possumus aequo animo nec Memmi clara propago
     talibus in rebus communi desse saluti.



     First Syllabus (50-61)


50   quod superest, Memmi, vacuas auris animumque
     semotum a curis aᵈʰibe veram ad rationem,
     ne mea dona tibi studio disposta fideli,
     intellecta prius quam sint, contempta relinquas.
     nam tibi de summa caeli ratione deumque
55   disserere incipiam et rerum primordia pandam,
     unde omnis natura creet res auctet alatque
     quove eadem rursum natura perempta resolvat,
     quae nos materiem et genitalia corpora rebus
     reddunda in ratione vocare et semina rerum
60   appellare suemus et haec eadem usurpare
     corpora prima, quod ex illis sunt omnia primis.
```

humana ante oculos foede cum vita iaceret
in terris oppressa gravi sub religione
quae caput a caeli regionibus ostendebat
65 horribili super aspectu mortalibus instans,
primum Graius homo mortalis tollere contra
est oculos ausus primusque obsistere contra,
quem neque fama deum nec fulmina nec minitanti
murmure compressit caelum, sed eo magis acrem
70 irritat animi virtutem, effringere ut arta
naturae primus portarum claustra cupiret.
ergo vivida vis animi pervicit, et extra
processit longe flammantia moenia mundi
atque omne immensum peragravit mente animoque,
75 unde refert nobis victor quid possit oriri,
quid nequeat, finita potestas denique cuique
quanam sit ratione atque alte terminus haerens.
quare religio pedibus subiecta vicissim
obteritur, nos exaequat victoria caelo.

Religion is more impious than its opponents (80-101)

80 illud in his rebus vereor, ne forte rearis
impia te rationis inire elementa viamque
indugredi sceleris. quod contra saepius illa
religio peperit scelerosa atque impia facta.
Aulide quo pacto Triviai virginis aram
85 Iphianassai turparunt sanguine foede
ductores Danaum delecti, prima virorum.
cui simul infula virgineos circumdata comptus
ex utraque pari malarum parte profusast,
et maestum simul ante aras adstare parentem
90 sensit et hunc propter ferrum celare ministros
aspectuque suo lacrimas effundere civis,
muta metu terram genibus summissa petebat.
nec miserae prodesse in tali tempore quibat

quod patrio princeps donarat nomine regem.
95 nam sublata virum manibus tremibundaque ad aras
deductast, non ut sollemni more sacrorum
perfecto posset claro comitari Hymenaeo,
sed casta inceste nubendi tempore in ipso
hostia concideret mactatu maesta parentis,
100 exitus ut classi felix faustusque daretur.
tantum religio potuit suadere malorum.

Fears about the hereafter must be forestalled : the
syllabus expanded (102-135)

tutemet a nobis iam quovis tempore vatum
terriloquis victus dictis desciscere quaeres.
quippe etenim quam multa tibi iam fingere possunt
105 somnia quae vitae rationes vertere possint
fortunasque tuas omnis turbare timore!
et merito. nam si certam finem esse viderent
aerumnarum homines, aliqua ratione valerent
religionibus atque minis obsistere vatum.
110 nunc ratio nulla est restandi, nulla facultas,
aeternas quoniam poenas in morte timendumst.
ignoratur enim quae sit natura animai,
nata sit an contra nascentibus insinuetur,
et simul intereat nobiscum morte dirempta
115 an tenebras Orci visat vastasque lacunas
an pecudes alias divinitus insinuet se,
Ennius ut noster cecinit, qui primus amoeno
detulit ex Helicone perenni fronde coronam
per gentis Italas hominum quae clara clueret;
120 etsi praeterea tamen esse Acherusia templa
Ennius aeternis exponit versibus edens,
qua neque permaneant animae neque corpora nostra
sed quaedam simulacra modis pallentia miris;
unde sibi exortam semper florentis Homeri
125 commemorat speciem lacrimas effundere salsas
coepisse et rerum naturam expandere dictis.

4.

quapropter bene cum superis de rebus habenda
nobis est ratio, solis lunaeque meatus
qua fiant ratione, et qua vi quaeque gerantur
130 in terris, tunc cum primis ratione sagaci
unde anima atque animi constet natura videndum,
et quae res nobis vigilantibus obvia mentis
terrificet morbo adfectis somnoque sepultis,
cernere uti videamur eos audireque coram,
135 morte obita quorum tellus amplectitur ossa.

Difficulty of the task (136-145)

nec me animi fallit Graiorum obscura reperta
difficile inlustrare Latinis versibus esse,
multa novis verbis praesertim cum sit agendum
propter egestatem linguae et rerum novitatem;
140 sed tua me virtus tamen et sperata voluptas
suavis amicitiae quemvis efferre laborem
suadet et inducit noctes vigilare serenas
quaerentem dictis quibus et quo carmine demum
clara tuae possim praepandere lumina menti,
145 res quibus occultas penitus convisere possis.

146 - 328 : THE EXISTENCE OF PERMANENT, INVISIBLE
CONSTITUENTS OF MATTER

Things are not created out of nothing, but out
of the appropriate matter (146-214)

Introduction (146-158)

hunc igitur terrorem animi tenebrasque necessest
non radii solis neque lucida tela diei
discutiant sed naturae species ratioque.

                principium cuius hinc nobis exordia sumet,
150   nullam rem e nilo gigni divinitus umquam.
                quippe ita formido mortalis continet omnis,
                quod multa in terris fieri caeloque tuentur
                quorum operum causas nulla ratione videre
                possunt ac fieri divino numine rentur.
155   quas ob res ubi viderimus nil posse creari   (156)
                de nilo, tum quod sequimur iam rectius inde
                perspiciemus, et unde queat res quaeque creari
                et quo quaeque modo fiant opera sine divum.   (155)

        Proof i (159-173)

                nam si de nilo fierent, ex omnibu' rebus
160   omne genus nasci posset, nil semine egeret.
                e mare primum homines, e terra posset oriri
                squamigerum genus et volucres erumpere caelo;
                armenta atque aliae pecudes, genus omne ferarum,
                incerto partu culta ac deserta tenerent.
165   nec fructus idem arboribus constare solerent,
                sed mutarentur, ferre omnes omnia possent.
                quippe, ubi non essent genitalia corpora cuique,
                qui posset mater rebus consistere certa?
                at nunc seminibus quia certis quaeque creantur,
170   inde enascitur atque oras in luminis exit,
                materies ubi inest cuiusque et corpora prima;
                atque hac re nequeunt ex omnibus omnia gigni,
                quod certis in rebus inest secreta facultas.

        Proof ii (174-183)

                praeterea cur vere rosam, frumenta calore,
175   vitis autumno fundi suadente videmus,
                si non, certa suo quia tempore semina rerum
                cum confluxerunt, patefit quodcumque creatur,
                dum tempestates adsunt et vivida tellus

                                          6.

tuto res teneras effert in luminis oras?
180 quod si de nilo fierent, subito exorerentur
incerto spatio atque alienis partibus anni,
quippe ubi nulla forent primordia quae genitali
concilio possent arceri tempore iniquo.

Proof iii (184-191)

nec porro augendis rebus spatio foret usus
185 seminis ad coitum, si e nilo crescere possent.
nam fierent iuvenes subito ex infantibu' parvis
e terraque exorta repente arbusta salirent.
quorum nil fieri manifestum est, omnia quando
paulatim crescunt, ut par est, semine certo;
190 crescentesque genus servant, ut noscere possis
quidque sua de materia grandescere alique.

Proof iv (192-198)

huc accedit uti sine certis imbribus anni
laetificos nequeat fetus summittere tellus
nec porro secreta cibo natura animantum
195 propagare genus possit vitamque tueri;
ut potius multis communia corpora rebus
multa putes esse, ut verbis elementa videmus,
quam sine principiis ullam rem exsistere posse.

Proof v (199-207)

denique cur homines tantos natura parare
200 non potuit, pedibus qui pontum per vada possent
transire et magnos manibus divellere montis
multaque vivendo vitalia vincere saecla,
si non, materies quia rebus reddita certast
gignundis e qua constat quid possit oriri?

205 nil igitur fieri de nilo posse fatendumst,
semine quando opus est rebus quo quaeque creatae
aeris in teneras possint proferrier auras.

Proof vi (208-214)

postremo quoniam incultis praestare videmus
culta loca et manibus meliores reddere fetus,
210 esse videlicet in terris primordia rerum
quae nos fecundas vertentes vomere glebas
terraique solum subigentes cimus ad ortus.
quod si nulla forent, nostro sine quaeque labore
sponte sua multo fieri meliora videres.

Things are not destroyed into nothing, but into
their component matter (215-264)

Statement and proof i (215-224)

215 huc accedit uti quidque in sua corpora rursum
dissoluat natura neque ad nilum interimat res.
nam si quid mortale e cunctis partibus esset,
ex oculis res quaeque repente erepta periret.
nulla vi foret usus enim quae partibus eius
220 discidium parere et nexus exsolvere posset.
quod nunc, aeterno quia constant semine quaeque,
donec vis obiit quae res diverberet ictu
aut intus penetret per inania dissoluatque,
nullius exitium patitur natura videri.

Proof ii (225-237)

225 praeterea quaecumque vetustate amovet aetas,
si penitus perimit consumens materiem omnem,
unde animale genus generatim in lumina vitae

```
        redducit Venus, aut redductum daedala tellus
        unde alit atque auget generatim pabula praebens?
230     unde mare ingenui fontes externaque longe
        flumina suppeditant? unde aether sidera pascit?
        omnia enim debet, mortali corpore quae sunt,
        infinita aetas consumpse anteacta diesque.
        quod si in eo spatio atque anteacta aetate fuere
235     e quibus haec rerum consistit summa refecta,
        immortali sunt natura praedita certe;
        haud igitur possunt ad nilum quaeque reverti.
```

Proof iii (238-249)

```
        denique res omnis eadem vis causaque vulgo
        conficeret, nisi materies aeterna teneret,
240     inter se nexu minus aut magis indupedita.
        tactus enim leti satis esset causa profecto,
        quippe ubi nulla forent aeterno corpore, quorum
        contextum vis deberet dissolvere quaeque.
        at nunc, inter se quia nexus principiorum
245     dissimiles constant aeternaque materies est,
        incolumi remanent res corpore, dum satis acris
        vis obeat pro textura cuiusque reperta.
        haud igitur redit ad nilum res ulla, sed omnes
        discidio redeunt in corpora materiai.
```

Proof iv (250-264)

```
250     postremo pereunt imbres, ubi eos pater aether
        in gremium matris terrai praecipitavit;
        at nitidae surgunt fruges ramique virescunt
        arboribus, crescunt ipsae fetuque gravantur;
        hinc alitur porro nostrum genus atque ferarum,
255     hinc laetas urbes pueris florere videmus
        frondiferasque novis avibus canere undique silvas;
        hinc fessae pecudes pingui per pabula laeta
```

corpora deponunt et candens lacteus umor
uberibus manat distentis; hinc nova proles
260   artubus infirmis teneras lasciva per herbas
ludit lacte mero mentis perculsa novellas.
haud igitur penitus pereunt quaecumque videntur,
quando alid ex alio reficit natura nec ullam
rem gigni patitur nisi morte adiuta aliena.

The assumption of invisible 'seeds' of matter
is perfectly feasible (265-328)

265   nunc age, res quoniam docui non posse creari
de nilo neque item genitas ad nil revocari,
ne qua forte tamen coeptes diffidere dictis,
quod nequeunt oculis rerum primordia cerni,
accipe praeterea quae corpora tute necessest
270   confiteare esse in rebus nec posse videri.

Example i (271-297)

principio venti vis verberat incita pontum
ingentisque ruit navis et nubila differt,
interdum rapido percurrens turbine campos
arboribus magnis sternit montisque supremos
275   silvifragis vexat flabris: ita perfurit acri
cum fremitu saevitque minaci murmure ventus.
sunt igitur venti nimirum corpora caeca
quae mare, quae terras, quae denique nubila caeli
verrunt ac subito vexantia turbine raptant,
280   nec ratione fluunt alia stragemque propagant
et cum mollis aquae fertur natura repente
flumine abundanti, quam largis imbribus auget
montibus ex altis magnus decursus aquai
fragmina coniciens silvarum arbustaque tota,
285   nec validi possunt pontes venientis aquai
vim subitam tolerare: ita magno turbidus imbri

```
        molibus incurrit validis cum viribus amnis.
        dat sonitu magno stragem volvitque sub undis
        grandia saxa ruitque et quidquid fluctibus obstat.
290     sic igitur debent venti quoque flamina ferri,
        quae veluti validum cum flumen procubuere
        quamlibet in partem, trudunt res ante ruuntque
        impetibus crebris, interdum vertice torto
        corripiunt rapidique rotanti turbine portant.
295     quare etiam atque etiam sunt venti corpora caeca,
        quandoquidem factis et moribus aemula magnis
        amnibus inveniuntur, aperto corpore qui sunt.
```

Example ii (298-304)

```
        tum porro varios rerum sentimus odores
        nec tamen ad naris venientis cernimus umquam,
300     nec calidos aestus tuimur nec frigora quimus
        usurpare oculis nec voces cernere suemus;
        quae tamen omnia corporea constare necessest
        natura, quoniam sensus impellere possunt.
        tangere enim et tangi, nisi corpus, nulla potest res.
```

Example iii (305-310)

```
305     denique fluctifrago suspensae in litore vestes
        uvescunt, eaedem dispansae in sole serescunt.
        at neque quo pacto persederit umor aquai
        visumst nec rursum quo pacto fugerit aestu.
        in parvas igitur partis dispergitur umor
310     quas oculi nulla possunt ratione videre.
```

Example iv (311-321)

```
        quin etiam multis solis redeuntibus annis
        anulus in digito subter tenuatur habendo,
```

11.

stilicidi casus lapidem cavat, uncus aratri
ferreus occulte decrescit vomer in arvis,
315 strataque iam vulgi pedibus detrita viarum
saxea conspicimus; tum portas propter aena
signa manus dextras ostendunt attenuari
saepe salutantum tactu praeterque meantum.
haec igitur minui, cum sint detrita, videmus;
320 sed quae corpora decedant in tempore quoque,
invida praeclusit speciem natura videndi.

Example v (322-328)

postremo quaecumque dies naturaque rebus
paulatim tribuit, moderatim crescere cogens,
nulla potest oculorum acies contenta tueri;
325 nec porro quaecumque aevo macieque senescunt
nec, mare quae impendent, vesco sale saxa peresa
quid quoque amittant in tempore cernere possis.
corporibus caecis igitur natura gerit res.

329 - 417 : THE EXISTENCE OF VOID

Introduction (329-334)

nec tamen undique corporea stipata tenentur
330 omnia natura; namque est in rebus inane.
quod tibi cognosse in multis erit utile rebus
nec sinet errantem dubitare et quaerere semper
de summa rerum et nostris diffidere dictis.
quapropter locus est intactus inane vacansque.

Proof i (335-345)

335 quod si non esset, nulla ratione moveri

res possent; namque officium quod corporis exstat,
officere atque obstare, id in omni tempore adesset
omnibus; haud igitur quicquam procedere posset,
principium quoniam cedendi nulla daret res.
340 at nunc per maria ac terras sublimaque caeli
multa modis multis varia ratione moveri
cernimus ante oculos, quae, si non esset inane,
non tam sollicito motu privata carerent
quam genita omnino nulla ratione fuissent,
345 undique materies quoniam stipata quiesset.

Proof ii (346-357)

praeterea quamvis solidae res esse putentur,
hinc tamen esse licet raro cum corpore cernas.
in saxis ac speluncis permanat aquarum
liquidus umor et uberibus flent omnia guttis.
350 dissipat in corpus sese cibus omne animantum;
crescunt arbusta et fetus in tempore fundunt
quod cibus in totas usque ab radicibus imis
per truncos ac per ramos diffunditur omnis.
inter saepta meant voces et clausa domorum
355 transvolitant, rigidum permanat frigus ad ossa.
quod nisi inania sint, qua possent corpora quaeque
transire, haud ulla fieri *haec* ratione videres.

Proof iii (358-369)

denique cur alias aliis praestare videmus
pondere res rebus nilo maiore figura?
360 nam si tantundemst in lanae glomere quantum
corporis in plumbo est, tantundem pendere par est,
corporis officiumst quoniam premere omnia deorsum,
contra autem natura manet sine pondere inanis.
ergo quod magnumst aeque leviusque videtur,
365 nimirum plus esse sibi declarat inanis;

at contra gravius plus in se corporis esse
dedicat et multo vacui minus intus habere.
est igitur nimirum id quod ratione sagaci
quaerimus, admixtum rebus, quod inane vocamus.

Refutation of rival views (370-397)

370 illud in his rebus ne te deducere vero
possit, quod quidam fingunt, praecurrere cogor.
cedere squamigeris latices nitentibus aiunt
et liquidas aperire vias, quia post loca pisces
linquant, quo possint cedentes confluere undae.
375 sic alias quoque res inter se posse moveri
et mutare locum, quamvis sint omnia plena.
scilicet id falsa totum ratione receptumst.
nam quo squamigeri poterunt procedere tandem,
ni spatium dederint latices? concedere porro
380 quo poterunt undae, cum pisces ire nequibunt?
aut igitur motu privandumst corpora quaeque
aut esse admixtum dicendumst rebus inane
unde initum primum capiat res quaeque movendi.
postremo duo de concursu corpora lata
385 si cita dissiliant, nempe aer omne necessest,
inter corpora quod fiat, possidat inane.
is porro quamvis circum celerantibus auris
confluat, haud poterit tamen uno tempore totum
compleri spatium; nam primum quemque necessest
390 occupet ille locum, deinde omnia possideantur.
quod si forte aliquis, cum corpora dissiluere,
tum putat id fieri quia se condenseat aer,
errat; nam vacuum tum fit quod non fuit ante
et repletur item vacuum quod constitit ante,
395 nec tali ratione potest denserier aer,
nec, si iam posset, sine inani posset, opinor,
ipse in se trahere et partis conducere in unum.

14.

         quapropter, quamvis causando multa moreris,
         esse in rebus inane tamen fateare necessest.
400 multaque praeterea tibi possum commemorando
         argumenta fidem dictis corradere nostris.
         verum animo satis haec vestigia parva sagaci
         sunt per quae possis cognoscere cetera tute.
         namque canes ut montivagae persaepe ferai
405 naribus inveniunt intectas fronde quietes,
         cum semel institerunt vestigia certa viai,
         sic alid ex alio per te tute ipse videre
         talibus in rebus poteris caecasque latebras
         insinuare omnis et verum protrahere inde.
410 quod si pigraris paulumve recesseris ab re,
         hoc tibi de plano possum promittere, Memmi:
         usque adeo largos haustus e fontibu' magnis
         lingua meo suavis diti de pectore fundet,
         ut verear ne tarda prius per membra senectus
415 serpat et in nobis vitai claustra resolvat,
         quam tibi de quavis una re versibus omnis
         argumentorum sit copia missa per auris.

         418 - 482 : EVERYTHING CAN BE EXPLAINED IN TERMS OF
                        MATTER AND VOID

         Matter and void exist in their own right: there is no
         third category of independent existence (418-448)

         sed nunc ut repetam coeptum pertexere dictis,
         omnis, ut est igitur per se, natura duabus
420 constitit in rebus; nam corpora sunt et inane,
         haec in quo sita sunt et qua diversa moventur.
         corpus enim per se communis dedicat esse
         sensus, cui nisi prima fides fundata valebit,
         haud erit occultis de rebus quo referentes

                        15.

425 confirmare animi quicquam ratione queamus.
　　 tum porro locus ac spatium, quod inane vocamus,
　　 si nullum foret, haud usquam sita corpora possent
　　 esse neque omnino quoquam diversa meare;
　　 id quod iam supera tibi paulo ostendimus ante.
430 praeterea nil est quod possis dicere ab omni
　　 corpore seiunctum secretumque esse ab inani,
　　 quod quasi tertia sit numero natura reperta.
　　 nam quodcumque erit, esse aliquid debebit id ipsum;
　　 cui si tactus erit quamvis levis exiguusque,　　　 (435)
435 augmine vel grandi vel parvo denique, dum sit,　　(434)
　　 corporis augebit numerum summamque sequetur.
　　 sin intactile erit, nulla de parte quod ullam
　　 rem prohibere queat per se transire meantem,
　　 scilicet hoc id erit, vacuum quod inane vocamus.
440 praeterea per se quodcumque erit, aut faciet quid
　　 aut aliis fungi debebit agentibus ipsum
　　 aut erit ut possint in eo res esse gerique.
　　 at facere et fungi sine corpore nulla potest res
　　 nec praebere locum porro nisi inane vacansque.
445 ergo praeter inane et corpora tertia per se
　　 nulla potest rerum in numero natura relinqui,
　　 nec quae sub sensus cadat ullo tempore nostros
　　 nec ratione animi quam quisquam possit apisci.

Everything else is a 'property' or 'accident' of
matter and void (449-482)

　　 nam quaecumque cluent, aut his coniuncta duabus
450 rebus ea invenies aut horum eventa videbis.
　　 coniunctum est id quod nusquam sine permitiali
　　 discidio potis est seiungi seque gregari,
　　 pondus uti saxis, calor ignist, liquor aquai,
　　 tactus corporibus cunctis, intactus inani.
455 servitium contra paupertas divitiaeque
　　 libertas bellum concordia, cetera quorum
　　 adventu manet incolumis natura abituque,

haec soliti sumus, ut par est, eventa vocare.
tempus item per se non est, sed rebus ab ipsis
460 consequitur sensus, transactum quid sit in aevo,
tum quae res instet, quid porro deinde sequatur.
nec per se quemquam tempus sentire fatendumst
semotum ab rerum motu placidaque quiete.
denique Tyndaridem raptam belloque subactas
465 Troiugenas gentis cum dicunt esse, videndumst
ne forte haec per se cogant nos esse fateri,
quando ea saecla hominum, quorum haec eventa fuerunt,
irrevocabilis abstulerit iam praeterita aetas.
namque aliud terris, aliud regionibus ipsis
470 eventum dici poterit quodcumque erit actum.
denique materies si rerum nulla fuisset
nec locus ac spatium, res in quo quaeque geruntur,
numquam Tyndaridis formae conflatus amore
ignis Alexandri Phrygio sub pectore gliscens
475 clara accendisset saevi certamina belli,
nec clam durateus Troianis Pergama partu
inflammasset equus nocturno Graiugenarum;
perspicere ut possis res gestas funditus omnis
non ita uti corpus per se constare neque esse,
480 nec ratione cluere eadem qua constet inane,
sed magis ut merito possis eventa vocare
corporis atque loci, res in quo quaeque gerantur.

483 - 634 : THE ATOMIC NATURE OF MATTER

Introduction (483-502)

corpora sunt porro partim primordia rerum,
partim concilio quae constant principiorum.
485 sed quae sunt rerum primordia, nulla potest vis
stinguere; nam solido vincunt ea corpore demum.
etsi difficile esse videtur credere quicquam
in rebus solido reperiri corpore posse.

17.

```
        transit enim fulmen caeli per saepta domorum,
490     clamor ut ac voces; ferrum candescit in igni
        dissiliuntque fero ferventi saxa vapore;
        cum labefactatus rigor auri solvitur aestu,
        tum glacies aeris flamma devicta liquescit;
        permanat calor argentum penetraleque frigus,
495     quando utrumque manu retinentes pocula rite
        sensimus infuso lympharum rore superne.
        usque adeo in rebus solidi nil esse videtur.
        sed quia vera tamen ratio naturaque rerum
        cogit, ades, paucis dum versibus expediamus
500     esse ea quae solido atque aeterno corpore constent,
        semina quae rerum primordiaque esse docemus,
        unde omnis rerum nunc constet summa creata.


        Proof i (503-539)


        principio quoniam duplex natura duarum
        dissimilis rerum longe constare repertast,
505     corporis atque loci, res in quo quaeque geruntur,
        esse utramque sibi per se puramque necessest.
        nam quacumque vacat spatium, quod inane vocamus,
        corpus ea non est; qua porro cumque tenet se
        corpus, ea vacuum nequaquam constat inane.
510     sunt igitur solida ac sine inani corpora prima.
        praeterea quoniam genitis in rebus inanest,
        materiem circum solidam constare necessest,
        nec res ulla potest vera ratione probari
        corpore inane suo celare atque intus habere
515     si non, quod cohibet, solidum constare relinquas.
        id porro nil esse potest nisi materiai
        concilium, quod inane queat rerum cohibere.
        materies igitur, solido quae corpore constat,
        esse aeterna potest, cum cetera dissoluantur.
520     tum porro si nil esset quod inane vacaret,
        omne foret solidum; nisi contra corpora certa
        essent quae loca complerent quaecumque tenerent,
```

omne quod est spatium vacuum constaret inane.
alternis igitur nimirum corpus inani
525 distinctumst, quoniam nec plenum naviter exstat
nec porro vacuum. sunt ergo corpora certa
quae spatium pleno possint distinguere inane.
haec neque dissolui plagis extrinsecus icta
possunt nec porro penitus penetrata retexi
530 nec ratione queunt alia temptata labare;
id quod iam supra tibi paulo ostendimus ante.
nam neque collidi sine inani posse videtur
quicquam nec frangi nec findi in bina secando
nec capere umorem neque item manabile frigus
535 nec penetralem ignem, quibus omnia conficiuntur.
et quo quaeque magis cohibet res intus inane,
tam magis his rebus penitus temptata labascit.
ergo si solida ac sine inani corpora prima
sunt ita uti docui, sint haec aeterna necessest.

Proof ii (540-550)

540 praeterea nisi materies aeterna fuisset,
antehac ad nilum penitus res quaeque redissent
de niloque renata forent quaecumque videmus.
at quoniam supra docui nil posse creari
de nilo neque quod genitum est ad nil revocari,
545 esse immortali primordia corpore debent,
dissolui quo quaeque supremo tempore possint,
materies ut suppeditet rebus reparandis.
sunt igitur solida primordia simplicitate
nec ratione queunt alia servata per aevum
550 ex infinito iam tempore res reparare.

Proof iii (551-564)

denique si nullam finem natura parasset
frangendis rebus, iam corpora materiai

19.

```
     usque redacta forent aevo frangente priore,
     ut nil ex illis a certo tempore posset
555  conceptum summum aetatis pervadere ad auctum.
     nam quidvis citius dissolvi posse videmus
     quam rursus refici; quapropter longa diei
     infinita aetas anteacti temporis omnis
     quod fregisset adhuc disturbans dissoluensque,
560  numquam relicuo reparari tempore posset.
     at nunc nimirum frangendi reddita finis
     certa manet, quoniam refici rem quamque videmus
     et finita simul generatim tempora rebus
     stare quibus possint aevi contingere florem.
```

Proof iv (565-576)

```
565  huc accedit uti, solidissima materiai
     corpora cum constant, possint tamen omnia reddi,
     mollia quae fiunt, aer aqua terra vapores,
     quo pacto fiant et qua vi quaeque gerantur,
     admixtum quoniam semel est in rebus inane.
570  at contra si mollia sint primordia rerum,
     unde queant validi silices ferrumque creari
     non poterit ratio reddi; nam funditus omnis
     principio fundamenti natura carebit.
     sunt igitur solida pollentia simplicitate
575  quorum condenso magis omnia conciliatu
     artari possunt validasque ostendere viris.
```

Proof v (577-583)

```
     porro si nullast frangendis reddita finis
     corporibus, tamen ex aeterno tempore quaeque
     nunc etiam superare necessest corpora rebus,
580  quae nondum clueant ullo temptata periclo.
     at quoniam fragili natura praedita constant,
     discrepat aeternum tempus potuisse manere
```

innumerabilibus plagis vexata per aevum.

Proof vi (584-598)

denique iam quoniam generatim reddita finis
585 crescendi rebus constat vitamque tenendi,
et quid quaeque queant per foedera naturai,
quid porro nequeant, sancitum quandoquidem exstat,
nec commutatur quicquam, quin omnia constant
usque adeo, variae volucres ut in ordine cunctae
590 ostendant maculas generalis corpore inesse,
immutabili' materiae quoque corpus habere
debent nimirum. nam si primordia rerum
commutari aliqua possent ratione revicta,
incertum quoque iam constet quid possit oriri,
595 quid nequeat, finita potestas denique cuique
quanam sit ratione atque alte terminus haerens,
nec totiens possent generatim saecla referre
naturam mores victum motusque parentum.

Proof vii (599-634)

tum porro quoniam est extremum quodque cacumen
600 corporis illius quod nostri cernere sensus
iam nequeunt, id nimirum sine partibus exstat
et minima constat natura nec fuit umquam
per se secretum neque posthac esse valebit,
alterius quoniamst ipsum pars, primaque et una,
605 inde aliae atque aliae similes ex ordine partes
agmine condenso naturam corporis explent,
quae quoniam per se nequeunt constare, necessest
haerere unde queant nulla ratione revelli.
sunt igitur solida primordia simplicitate,
610 quae minimis stipata cohaerent partibus arte,
non ex illarum conventu conciliata,
sed magis aeterna pollentia simplicitate,

21.

unde neque avelli quicquam neque deminui iam
concedit natura reservans semina rebus.
615 praeterea nisi erit minimum, parvissima quaeque
corpora constabunt ex partibus infinitis,
quippe ubi dimidiae partis pars semper habebit
dimidiam partem nec res praefiniet ulla.
ergo rerum inter summam minimamque quid escit?
620 nil erit ut distet; nam quamvis funditus omnis
summa sit infinita, tamen, parvissima quae sunt,
ex infinitis constabunt partibus aeque.
quod quoniam ratio reclamat vera negatque
credere posse animum, victus fateare necessest
625 esse ea quae nullis iam praedita partibus exstent
et minima constent natura. quae quoniam sunt,
illa quoque esse tibi solida atque aeterna fatendum.
denique si minimas in partis cuncta resolvi
cogere consuesset rerum natura creatrix,
630 iam nil ex illis eadem reparare valeret
propterea quia, quae nullis sunt partibus aucta,
non possunt ea quae debet genitalis habere
materies, varios conexus pondera plagas
concursus motus, per quae res quaeque geruntur.

635 - 920 : REFUTATION OF RIVAL ANALYSES OF MATTER

(A) The Monists, represented by Heraclitus and the
     fire theorists (635-704)

*Introduction : Heraclitus' obscurity recommends him
to his disciples (635-644)*

635 quapropter qui materiem rerum esse putarunt
ignem atque ex igni summam consistere solo,
magno opere a vera lapsi ratione videntur.
Heraclitus init quorum dux proelia primus,
clarus *ob* obscuram linguam magis inter inanis

640 quamde gravis inter Graios qui vera requirunt.
    omnia enim stolidi magis admirantur amantque,
    inversis quae sub verbis latitantia cernunt,
    veraque constituunt quae belle tangere possunt
    auris et lepido quae sunt fucata sonore.

Fire cannot produce the variety observable in nature (645-689)

645 nam cur tam variae res possent esse requiro,
    ex uno si sunt igni puroque creatae.
    nil prodesset enim calidum denserier ignem
    nec rarefieri, si partes ignis eandem
    naturam quam totus habet super ignis haberent.
650 acrior ardor enim conductis partibus esset,
    languidior porro disiectis *dis*que sipatis.
    amplius hoc fieri nil est quod posse rearis
    talibus in causis, nedum variantia rerum
    tanta queat densis rarisque ex ignibus esse.
655 id quoque, si faciant admixtum rebus inane,
    denseri poterunt ignes rarique relinqui.
    sed, quia multa sibi cernunt contraria, mus*sant*
    et fugitant in rebus inane relinquere purum;
    ardua dum metuunt, amittunt vera viai;
660 nec rursum cernunt exempto rebus inani
    omnia denseri fierique ex omnibus unum
    corpus, nil ab se quod possit mittere raptim;
    aestifer ignis uti lumen iacit atque vaporem,
    ut videas non e stipatis partibus esse.
665 quod si forte alia credunt ratione potesse
    ignis in coetu stingui mutareque corpus,
    scilicet ex nulla facere id si parte reparcent,
    occidet ad nilum nimirum funditus ardor
    omnis et e nilo fient quaecumque creantur.
670 nam quodcumque suis mutatum finibus exit,
    continuo hoc mors est illius quod fuit ante.
    proinde aliquid superare necessest incolume ollis,

ne tibi res redeant ad nilum funditus omnes
de niloque renata vigescat copia rerum.
675 nunc igitur quoniam certissima corpora quaedam
sunt quae conservant naturam semper eandem,
quorum abitu aut aditu mutatoque ordine mutant
naturam res et convertunt corpora sese,
scire licet non esse haec ignea corpora rerum.
680 nil referret enim quaedam decedere, abire,
atque alia attribui, mutarique ordine quaedam,
si tamen ardoris naturam cuncta tenerent;
ignis enim foret omnimodis quodcumque crearent.
verum, ut opinor, itast: sunt quaedam corpora, quorum
685 concursus motus ordo positura figurae
efficiunt ignis, mutatoque ordine mutant
naturam neque sunt igni simulata neque ulli
praeterea rei quae corpora mittere possit
sensibus et nostros adiectu tangere tactus.

Concluding objections (690-704)

690 dicere porro ignem res omnis esse neque ullam
rem veram in numero rerum constare nisi ignem,
quod facit hic idem, perdelirum esse videtur.
nam contra sensus ab sensibus ipse repugnat
et labefactat eos, unde omnia credita pendent,
695 unde hic cognitus est ipsi quem nominat ignem.
credit enim sensus ignem cognoscere vere,
cetera non credit, quae nilo clara minus sunt.
quod mihi cum vanum tum delirum esse videtur.
quo referemus enim? quid nobis certius ipsis
700 sensibus esse potest, qui vera ac falsa notemus?
praeterea quare quisquam magis omnia tollat
et velit ardoris naturam linquere solam,
quam neget esse ignis, *quidvis* tamen esse relinquat?
aequa videtur enim dementia dicere utrumque.

24.

Transition to the Pluralists : praise of Empedocles (705-733)

705 quapropter qui materiem rerum esse putarunt
ignem atque ex igni summam consistere posse,
et qui principium gignundis aera rebus
constituere, aut umorem quicumque putarunt
fingere res ipsum per se, terramve creare
710 omnia et in rerum naturas vertier omnis,
magno opere a vero longe derrasse videntur.
adde etiam qui conduplicant primordia rerum
aera iungentes igni terramque liquori,
et qui quattuor ex rebus posse omnia rentur
715 ex igni terra atque anima procrescere et imbri.
quorum Acragantinus cum primis Empedocles est,
insula quem triquetris terrarum gessit in oris,
quam fluitans circum magnis anfractibus aequor
Ionium glaucis aspergit virus ab undis,
720 angustoque fretu rapidum mare dividit undis
Italiae terrarum oras a finibus eius.
hic est vasta Charybdis et hic Aetnaea minantur
murmura flammarum rursum se colligere iras,
faucibus eruptos iterum vis ut vomat ignis
725 ad caelumque ferat flammai fulgura rursum.
quae cum magna modis multis miranda videtur
gentibus humanis regio visendaque fertur,
rebus opima bonis, multa munita virum vi,
nil tamen hoc habuisse viro praeclarius in se
730 nec sanctum magis et mirum carumque videtur.
carmina quin etiam divini pectoris eius
vociferantur et exponunt praeclara reperta,
ut vix humana videatur stirpe creatus.

hic tamen et supra quos diximus inferiores
735   partibus egregie multis multoque minores,
quamquam multa bene ac divinitus invenientes
ex adyto tamquam cordis responsa dedere
sanctius et multo certa ratione magis quam
Pythia quae tripodi a Phoebi lauroque profatur,
740   principiis tamen in rerum fecere ruinas
et graviter magni magno cecidere ibi casu;
primum quod motus exempto rebus inani
constituunt et res mollis rarasque relinquunt,
aera solem imbrem terras animalia fruges,
745   nec tamen admiscent in eorum corpus inane;
deinde quod omnino finem non esse secandis
corporibus faciunt neque pausam stare fragori
nec prorsum in rebus minimum consistere qui*cquam;*
cum videamus id extremum cuiusque cacumen
750   esse quod ad sensus nostros minimum esse videtur,
conicere ut possis ex hoc, quae cernere non quis
extremum quod habent, minimum consistere *rebus.*
huc accedit item, quoniam primordia rerum
mollia constituunt, quae nos nativa videmus
755   esse et mortali cum corpore funditus, utqui
debeat ad nilum iam rerum summa reverti
de niloque renata vigescere copia rerum;
quorum utrumque quid a vero iam distet habebis.
deinde inimica modis multis sunt atque veneno
760   ipsa sibi inter se; quare aut congressa peribunt
aut ita diffugient ut tempestate coacta
fulmina diffugere atque imbris ventosque videmus.

The crucial dilemma of Pluralism (763-781)

denique quattuor ex rebus si cuncta creantur
atque in eas rursus res omnia dissoluuntur,
765   qui magis illa queunt rerum primordia dici

quam contra res illorum retroque putari?
alternis gignuntur enim mutantque colorem
768 et totam inter se naturam tempore ab omni.
770 sin ita forte putas ignis terraeque coire
corpus et aerias auras roremque liquoris,
nil in concilio naturam ut mutet eorum,
nulla tibi ex illis poterit res esse creata,
non animans, non exanimo cum corpore, ut arbor.
775 quippe suam quidque in coetu variantis acervi
naturam ostendet mixtusque videbitur aer
cum terra simul atque ardor cum rore manere.
at primordia gignundis in rebus oportet
naturam clandestinam caecamque adhibere,
780 emineat ne quid quod contra pugnet et obstet
quominus esse queat proprie quodcumque creatur.

*Attack on the theory that the four elements change
into one another (782-802)*

quin etiam repetunt a caelo atque ignibus eius
et primum faciunt ignem se vertere in auras
aeris, hinc imbrem gigni terramque creari
785 ex imbri, retroque a terra cuncta reverti,
umorem primum, post aera, deinde calorem,
nec cessare haec inter se mutare, meare
a caelo ad terram, de terra ad sidera mundi.
quod facere haud ullo debent primordia pacto.
790 immutabile enim quiddam superare necessest,
ne res ad nilum redigantur funditus omnes.
nam quodcumque suis mutatum finibus exit,
continuo hoc mors est illius quod fuit ante.
quapropter quoniam quae paulo diximus ante
795 in commutatum veniunt, constare necessest
ex aliis ea, quae nequeant convertier usquam,
ne tibi res redeant ad nilum funditus omnes.
quin potius tali natura praedita quaedam
corpora constituas, ignem si forte crearint,

800 posse eadem demptis paucis paucisque tributis,
ordine mutato et motu, facere aeris auras,
sic alias aliis rebus mutarier omnis?

The argument from nutrition does not prove
Pluralism (803-829)

'at manifesta palam res indicat' inquis 'in auras
aeris e terra res omnis crescere alique;
805 et nisi tempestas indulget tempore fausto
imbribus, ut tabe nimborum arbusta vacillent,
solque sua pro parte fovet tribuitque calorem,
crescere non possint fruges arbusta animantes.'
scilicet et nisi nos cibus aridus et tener umor
810 adiuvet, amisso iam corpore vita quoque omnis
omnibus e nervis atque ossibus exsoluatur.
adiutamur enim dubio procul atque alimur nos
certis ab rebus, certis aliae atque aliae res.
nimirum quia multa modis communia multis
815 multarum rerum in rebus primordia mixta
sunt, ideo variis variae res rebus aluntur.
atque eadem magni refert primordia saepe
cum quibus et quali positura contineantur
et quos inter se dent motus accipiantque;
820 namque eadem caelum mare terras flumina solem
constituunt, eadem fruges arbusta animantis,
verum aliis alioque modo commixta moventur.
quin etiam passim nostris in versibus ipsis
multa elementa vides multis communia verbis,
825 cum tamen inter se versus ac verba necessest
confiteare et re et sonitu distare sonanti.
tantum elementa queunt permutato ordine solo.
at rerum quae sunt primordia, plura adhibere
possunt unde queant variae res quaeque creari.

(c) Anaxagoras and the theory of 'like parts'
(830-920)

Homoeomeria *explained : initial objections*
(830-858)

830 nunc et Anaxagorae scrutemur homoeomerian
     quam Grai memorant nec nostra dicere lingua
     concedit nobis patrii sermonis egestas;
     sed tamen ipsam rem facilest exponere verbis.
     principio, rerum quam dicit homoeomerian,
835 ossa videlicet e pauxillis atque minutis
     ossibus hic et de pauxillis atque minutis
     visceribus viscus gigni sanguenque creari
     sanguinis inter se multis coeuntibu' guttis
     ex aurique putat micis consistere posse
840 aurum et de terris terram concrescere parvis,
     ignibus ex ignis, umorem umoribus esse,
     cetera consimili fingit ratione putatque.
     nec tamen esse ulla parte idem in rebus inane
     concedit neque corporibus finem esse secandis.
845 quare in utraque mihi pariter ratione videtur
     errare atque illi, supra quos diximus ante.
     adde quod imbecilla nimis primordia fingit,
     si primordia sunt, simili quae praedita constant
     natura atque ipsae res sunt aequeque laborant
850 et pereunt neque ab exitio res ulla refrenat.
     nam quid in oppressu valido durabit eorum,
     ut mortem effugiat, leti sub dentibus ipsis?
     ignis an umor an aura? quid horum? sanguen an ossa?
     nil, ut opinor, ubi ex aequo res funditus omnis
855 tam mortalis erit quam quae manifesta videmus
     ex oculis nostris aliqua vi victa perire.
     at neque reccidere ad nilum res posse neque autem
     crescere de nilo testor res ante probatas.

　　　praeterea quoniam cibus auget corpus alitque,
860　scire licet nobis venas et sanguen et ossa
　　　et nervos alienigenis ex partibus esse.
　　　sive cibos omnis commixto corpore dicent
　　　esse et habere in se nervorum corpora parva
　　　ossaque et omnino venas partisque cruoris,
　　　fiet uti cibus omnis, et aridus et liquor, ipse
865　ex alienigenis rebus constare putetur,
　　　ossibus et nervis sanieque et sanguine mixto.
　　　praeterea quaecumque e terra corpora crescunt
　　　si sunt in terris, terram constare necessest
　　　ex alienigenis, quae terris exoriuntur.
870　transfer item, totidem verbis utare licebit.
　　　in lignis si flamma latet fumusque cinisque,
872　ex alienigenis consistant ligna necessest,
874　ex alienigenis, quae lignis exoriuntur.

The solution cannot be that all things are hidden
in all things (875-896)

　　　linquitur hic quaedam latitandi copia tenvis,
　　　id quod Anaxagoras sibi sumit, ut omnibus omnis
　　　res putet immixtas rebus latitare, sed illud
　　　apparere unum cuius sint plurima mixta
　　　et magis in promptu primaque in fronte locata.
880　quod tamen a vera longe ratione repulsumst.
　　　conveniebat enim fruges quoque saepe, minaci
　　　robore cum saxi franguntur, mittere signum
　　　sanguinis aut aliquid, nostro quae corpore aluntur,
　　　cum lapidi in lapidem terimus, manare cruorem.
885　consimili ratione herbas quoque saepe decebat
　　　et latices dulcis guttas similique sapore
　　　mittere, lanigerae quali sunt ubere lactis,
　　　scilicet et glebis terrarum saepe friatis
　　　herbarum genera et fruges frondisque videri

890 dispertita inter terram latitare minute,
postremo in lignis cinerem fumumque videri,
cum praefracta forent, ignisque latere minutos.
quorum nil fieri quoniam manifesta docet res,
scire licet non esse in rebus res ita mixtas,
895 verum semina multimodis immixta latere
multarum rerum in rebus communia debent.

The argument from forest-fires does not support
Anaxagoras (897-914)

'at saepe in magnis fit montibus' inquis 'ut altis
arboribus vicina cacumina summa terantur
inter se, validis facere id cogentibus austris,
900 donec flammai fulserunt flore coorto.'
scilicet et non est lignis tamen insitus ignis,
verum semina sunt ardoris multa, terendo
quae cum confluxere, creant incendia silvis.
quod si facta foret silvis abscondita flamma,
905 non possent ullum tempus celarier ignes,
conficerent vulgo silvas, arbusta cremarent.
iamne vides igitur, paulo quod diximus ante,
permagni referre eadem primordia saepe
cum quibus et quali positura contineantur
910 et quos inter se dent motus accipiantque,
atque eadem paulo inter se mutata creare
ignis et lignum? quo pacto verba quoque ipsa
inter se paulo mutatis sunt elementis,
cum ligna atque ignis distincta voce notemus.

Reductio ad absurdum (915-920)

915 denique iam quaecumque in rebus cernis apertis
si fieri non posse putas, quin materiai
corpora consimili natura praedita fingas,
hac ratione tibi pereunt primordia rerum:

31.

```
       fiet uti risu tremulo concussa cachinnent
920    et lacrimis salsis umectent ora genasque.




       921 - 1117 : THE INFINITY OF THE UNIVERSE
                    AND ITS TWO CONSTITUENTS


       Introduction : the author's mission (921-950)


       nunc age quod superest cognosce et clarius audi.
       nec me animi fallit quam sint obscura; sed acri
       percussit thyrso laudis spes magna meum cor
       et simul incussit suavem mi in pectus amorem
925    musarum, quo nunc instinctus mente vigenti
       avia Pieridum peragro loca nullius ante
       trita solo. iuvat integros accedere fontis
       atque haurire, iuvatque novos decerpere flores
       insignemque meo capiti petere inde coronam
930    unde prius nulli velarint tempora musae;
       primum quod magnis doceo de rebus et artis
       religionum animum nodis exsolvere pergo,
       deinde quod obscura de re tam lucida pango
       carmina, musaeo contingens cuncta lepore.
935    id quoque enim non ab nulla ratione videtur;
       sed veluti pueris absinthia taetra medentes
       cum dare conantur, prius oras pocula circum
       contingunt mellis dulci flavoque liquore,
       ut puerorum aetas improvida ludificetur
940    labrorum tenus, interea perpotet amarum
       absinthi laticem deceptaque non capiatur,
       sed potius tali pacto recreata valescat,
       sic ego nunc, quoniam haec ratio plerumque videtur
       tristior esse quibus non est tractata, retroque
945    vulgus abhorret ab hac, volui tibi suaviloquenti
       carmine Pierio rationem exponere nostram
       et quasi musaeo dulci contingere melle,
       si tibi forte animum tali ratione tenere
```

versibus in nostris possem, dum perspicis omnem
950 naturam rerum qua constet compta figura.

The new topic (951-957)

sed quoniam docui solidissima materiai
corpora perpetuo volitare invicta per aevum,
nunc age, summai quaedam sit finis eorum
necne sit, evoluamus; item quod inane repertumst
955 seu locus ac spatium, res in quo quaeque gerantur,
pervideamus utrum finitum funditus omne
constet an immensum pateat vasteque profundum.

Infinity of the universe and of space (958-1007)

Proof i (958-967)

omne quod est igitur nulla regione viarum
finitumst; namque extremum debebat habere.
960 extremum porro nullius posse videtur
esse, nisi ultra sit quod finiat; ut videatur
quo non longius haec sensus natura sequatur.
nunc extra summam quoniam nil esse fatendum,
non habet extremum, caret ergo fine modoque.
965 nec refert quibus adsistas regionibus eius;
usque adeo, quem quisque locum possedit, in omnis
tantundem partis infinitum omne relinquit.

Proof ii (968-983)

praeterea si iam finitum constituatur
omne quod est spatium, si quis procurrat ad oras
970 ultimus extremas iaciatque volatile telum,
id validis utrum contortum viribus ire
quo fuerit missum mavis longeque volare,

an prohibere aliquid censes obstareque posse?
alterutrum fatearis enim sumasque necessest.
975 quorum utrumque tibi effugium praecludit et omne
cogit ut exempta concedas fine patere.
nam sive est aliquid quod probeat officiatque
quominu' quo missum est veniat finique locet se,
sive foras fertur, non est a fine profectum.
980 hoc pacto sequar atque, oras ubicumque locaris
extremas, quaeram quid telo denique fiat.
fiet uti nusquam possit consistere finis
effugiumque fugae prolatet copia semper.

Proof iii (984-997)

praeterea spatium summai totius omne
985 undique si inclusum certis consisteret oris
finitumque foret, iam copia materiai
undique ponderibus solidis confluxet ad imum
nec res ulla geri sub caeli tegmine posset
nec foret omnino caelum neque lumina solis,
990 quippe ubi materies omnis cumulata iaceret
ex infinito iam tempore subsidendo.
at nunc nimirum requies data principiorum
corporibus nullast, quia nil est funditus imum
quo quasi confluere et sedis ubi ponere possint.
995 semper in assiduo motu res quaeque geruntur:
partibus *e* cunctis infernaque suppeditantur
ex infinito cita corpora materiai.

Proof iv (998-1001)

postremo ante oculos res rem finire videtur;
aer dissaepit collis atque aera montes,
1000 terra mare et contra mare terras terminat omnis;
omne quidem vero nil est quod finiat extra.

est igitur natura loci spatiumque profundi
quod neque clara suo percurrere fulmina cursu
perpetuo possint aevi labentia tractu
1005   nec prorsum facere ut restet minus ire meando;
usque adeo passim patet ingens copia rebus
finibus exemptis in cunctas undique partis.

The universe must comprise both infinite
space and infinite matter (1008-1051)

ipsa modum porro sibi rerum summa parare
ne possit, natura tenet, quae corpus ·inani
1010   et quod inane autem est finiri corpore cogit,
ut sic alternis infinita omnia reddat,
aut etiam alterutrum, nisi terminet alterum eorum,
simplice natura pateat tamen immoderatum.
sed spatium supra docui sine fine patere.
si finita igitur summa esset materiai,
nec mare nec tellus neque caeli lucida templa
1015   nec mortale genus nec divum corpora sancta
exiguum possent horai sistere tempus.
nam dispulsa suo de coetu materiai
copia ferretur magnum per inane soluta,
sive adeo potius numquam concreta creasset
1020   ullam rem, quoniam cogi disiecta nequisset.
nam certe neque consilio primordia rerum
ordine se suo quaeque sagaci mente locarunt
nec quos quaeque darent motus pepigere profecto,
sed, quia multa modis multis mutata per omne
1025   ex infinito vexantur percita plagis,
omne genus motus et coetus experiundo
tandem deveniunt in talis disposituras,
qualibus haec rerum consistit summa creata,
et multos etiam magnos servata per annos,
1030   ut semel in motus coniectast convenientis,

35.

```
       efficit ut largis avidum mare fluminis undis
       integrent amnes et solis terra vapore
       fota novet fetus summissaque gens animantum
       floreat et vivant labentes aetheris ignes;
1035   quod nullo facerent pacto, nisi materiai
       ex infinito suboriri copia posset,
       unde amissa solent reparare in tempore quaeque.
       nam veluti privata cibo natura animantum
       diffluit amittens corpus, sic omnia debent
1040   dissolui simul ac defecit suppeditare
       materies aliqua ratione aversa viai.
       nec plagae possunt extrinsecus undique summam
       conservare omnem quaecumque est conciliata.
       cudere enim crebro possunt partemque morari,
1045   dum veniant aliae ac suppleri summa queatur;
       interdum resilire tamen coguntur et una
       principiis rerum spatium tempusque fugai
       largiri, ut possint a coetu libera ferri.
       quare etiam atque etiam suboriri multa necessest;
1050   et tamen, ut plagae quoque possint suppetere ipsae,
       infinita opus est vis undique materiai.
```

Refutation of the theory of centripetal
matter (1052-1113)

```
       illud in his rebus longe fuge credere, Memmi,
       in medium summae quod dicunt omnia niti,
       atque ideo mundi naturam stare sine ullis
1055   ictibus externis neque quoquam posse resolvi,
       summa atque ima quod in medium sint omnia nixa
       (ipsum si quicquam posse in se sistere credis);
       et quae pondera sunt sub terris omnia sursum
       nitier in terraque retro requiescere posta,
1060   ut per aquas quae nunc rerum simulacra videmus.
       et simili ratione animalia suppa vagari
       contendunt neque posse e terris in loca caeli
       reccidere inferiora magis quam corpora nostra
```

```
        sponte sua possint in caeli templa volare;
1065    illi cum videant solem, nos sidera noctis
        cernere, et alternis nobiscum tempora caeli
        dividere et noctes parilis agitare diebus.
        sed vanus stolidis haec error falsa probavit,
        amplexi quod habent perversa rem ratione;
1070    nam medium nil esse potest, quando omnia constant
        infinita. neque omnino, si iam medium sit,
        possit ibi quicquam consistere eam magis ob rem,
        quam quavis alia longe ratione repelli:
        omnis enim locus ac spatium, quod inane vocamus,
1075    per medium, per non medium, concedere debet
        aeque ponderibus, motus quacumque feruntur.
        nec quisquam locus est, quo corpora cum venere,
        ponderis amissa vi possint stare in inani;
        nec quod inane autem est ulli subsistere debet,
1080    quin, sua quod natura petit, concedere pergat.
        haud igitur possunt tali ratione teneri
        res in concilium medii cuppedine victae.
        praeterea quoniam non omnia corpora fingunt
        in medium niti, sed terrarum atque liquoris,
1085    umorem ponti magnasque e montibus undas,          (1086)
        et quasi terreno quae corpore contineantur,       (1085)
        at contra tenuis exponunt aeris auras
        et calidos simul a medio differrier ignis,
        atque ideo totum circum tremere aethera signis
1090    et solis flammam per caeli caerula pasci,
        quod calor a medio fugiens se ibi colligat omnis,
        nec prorsum arboribus summos frondescere ramos
        posse, nisi a terris paulatim cuique cibatum
        ignea vis tribuat surgens et ad aethera tendens,
        scilicet incerto diversi errore vagantes
        argumenta sibi prorsum pugnantia fingunt.
        quin etiam si iam vere differrier ignis
        a medio dicant, video tamen esse timendum
1102    ne volucri ritu flammarum moenia mundi
        diffugiant subito magnum per inane soluta
        et ne cetera consimili ratione sequantur,
```

1105 neve ruant caeli tonitralia templa superne
     terraque se pedibus raptim subducat et omnis
     inter permixtas rerum caelique ruinas
     corpora solventis abeat per inane profundum,
     temporis ut puncto nil exstet reliquiarum
1110 desertum praeter spatium et primordia caeca.
     nam quacumque prius de parti corpora desse
     constitues, haec rebus erit pars ianua leti,
     hac se turba foras dabit omnis materiai.

Conclusion : exhortation of Memmius (1114-1117)

     haec si pernosces, parva perductus opella
     cetera percipies quae restant cumque docenda;
1115 namque alid ex alio clarescet nec tibi caeca
     nox iter eripiet quin ultima naturai
     pervideas; ita res accendent lumina rebus.

LIST OF ABBREVIATIONS USED IN THE NOTES

abl.	ablative	perf.	perfect
acc.	accusative	pl.	plural
adj.	adjective	plupf.	pluperfect
conj.	conjugation	rel.	relative
dat.	dative	sing.	singular
decl.	declension	subj.	subjunctive
fem.	feminine	*TAPA*	*Transactions and Proceedings*
fut.	future		*of the American Philological*
gen.	genitive		*Association*
impf.	imperfect	*TGF*	*Tragicorum Graecorum*
indic.	indicative		*Fragmenta,* Nauck (revised
infin.	infinitive		Snell, 1964)
L	Lucretius	*TRF*	*Tragicorum Romanorum*
lit.	literally		*Fragmenta,* Ribbeck
masc.	masculine		(revised 1962)
neut.	neuter	transl.	translate
nom.	nominative		

The numbering of references to Presocratic philosophers corresponds with Diels, *Fragmente der Vorsokratiker* (revised Kranz, 1951), to Ennius with Vahlen, *Ennianae Poesis Reliquiae* (3rd edition, 1963).

Titles of classical works are cited in full, except for Epicurus, *ad Herodotum* (*ad Hdt.*).

Works included in the bibliography are referred to only by author's surname (and, where appropriate, page number). Full references to other works, which are cited only once, are given in the course of the notes.

Cross references to L's own work are given in the form of simple line numbers when the reference is to book 1, of book and line number when the reference is to another book (e.g. 2.920, 6.427); where a number of consecutive references are to the same book they appear in the form 5. 247, 386, 478 and 821. [The same is true of the Introduction, though in the footnotes there references to book 1 are so prefixed (e.g. 1.237).]

NOTES

1-145 INTRODUCTION

The passage comprises an eloquent preface not only to book
1 but to the whole poem. Though the individual sections
are justly admired, the overall structure has been sub-
jected to exaggerated criticism and has been thought to
reflect the unrevised state of the work as a whole. Set-
ting aside the textual problems presented by 44-50 (see
notes below), the only real structural difficulties are
the transition at 62, which is rather abrupt, and that
at 146-8, which is somewhat awkward (see on 146-58 below).
While these could be indications that parts, or indeed
the whole, of 62-148 were later additions of the poet,
the arrangement is otherwise perfectly logical and natural
throughout. How L might have removed such possible de-
fects in revision it is idle to speculate.

1-43 Prayer to Venus

L asks the goddess (a) to aid him in the composition of
the poem (b - 29ff.) to secure the peace of the Roman
world as a prerequisite by interceding with her lover,
the war-god Mars.

Since the Epicurean gods, unlike the Venus and Mars
depicted here, did not control the workings of nature
or intervene in human affairs, the prayer has symbolic,
rather than literal, meaning for the poet and can be
understood as an expression of the pious hope that, as
far as the writing of the poem is concerned, the forces
of creativity and peace (symbolised in Venus) may favour
the poet and prevail over the forces of war and destruction (symbolised in Mars). Venus certainly exhibits
features drawn from traditional religion and mythology
and without literal meaning for L: thus she is mother
of Aeneas (1) and lover of Mars (31-40): but her symbolic
role is carefully derived and developed from her more
traditional associations.

In 1-20, she personifies creative forces in the field
of sexual reproduction. This role as a life-urge (the
Roman *Venus physica*) was a natural extension of her
conventional role as goddess of love and was already
familiar in antiquity; it can be traced in Homeric Hymn
4 (1-5), Euripides' *Hippolytus* (esp. 447-50 and 1272-
81) and in two of L's predecessors in the field of
philosophical poetry, Parmenides (Diels B.12.3-6) and

Empedocles (Diels B.17, 22, 35 and 71), all of which
may have influenced this part of the portrait. (L
presents Venus in an identical role more briefly at 228:
comparison may also be made with her introduction as a
synonym for love at 4.1058ff., where it emerges that
her influence in this field is not as universally bene-
ficent as 1-20 suggest.) But at 21ff. L uniquely extends
Venus' province to embrace every type of creation, including literary and artistic production. Her identification with *voluptas* (1; cf. her association with
lepor in 15 and 28) is a vital aspect of her creative
function, since pleasure in Epicurean theory was the
motive force behind creativity in both the sexual and
the artistic field. (Bignone, *Storia della letteratura
latina* vol. 2 (1945) 437-44, presses the identification
too far in making the Venus of the invocation embody two
highly technical Epicurean concepts in turn, 'kinetic'
pleasure in 1-28 and 'static' pleasure in 29-43.)

At 29-40 Venus, despite her more anthropomorphic, out-
wardly more conventional guise as lover of Mars, fully
retains the creative role of 1-28 and is simultaneously
associated with peace: she is to placate Mars, who as
war-god is destructive not only of life but also of the
conditions conducive to intellectual creativity (41-3).
The association of creativity with peace, like that of
war with destruction, is natural enough and has already
been foreshadowed in the initial portrait. At 6-9 Venus
is responsible for the peaceful environment of spring
which most favours physical generation; so at 29ff. she
is asked to secure the peaceful conditions essential for
the creativity involved both in L's composition of the
poem and his reader's study of it. The mythological
imagery, whereby Venus and Mars appear as lovers, may
have been suggested to L by Empedocles, who had used the
union and separation of Ares and Aphrodite to symbolise
the alternate predominance of his two philosophical
principles of Love and Strife (see on 705-829 below).

The personification of creative forces in Venus may be
compared with L's frequent personification of Nature in
a creative role (e.g. 56 and 629 *rerum natura creatrix*).
From the point of view of Epicurean science, the creative
and destructive principles embodied by Venus and Mars
are no more than abstractions: though there is no need to
suppose too precise an allegory, comparison may be made
with 2.569-72, where L refers in a purely scientific
context to the opposing forces of construction and destruction in nature (*motus genitales auctificique, motus
exitiales*). The symbolism is an extension of the poetic
licence defended at 2.655-60, whereby the names of gods
are used with reference to their traditional spheres of

influence.

Such a symbolic interpretation (along the lines suggested
by Giancotti) gives the passage real and consistent meaning for the poet and accounts for the fundamental and
glaring discrepancies between the Venus and Mars of the
invocation and the gods of Epicurean orthodoxy. While
a reader uninitiated in Epicurean theology might have
been temporarily misled, the boldness of the symbolism
is less surprising at the beginning of the poem than it
would be elsewhere; L may have in mind such precedents
as the allegory with which the poem of Parmenides had
opened. In expressing his hopes for poetic success and
for peace in the form of an appeal to his symbolic
Venus, L is clearly influenced by poetic convention and
the poetic advantages to be derived from it; cf. 6.92-
5, where, like Empedocles before him (Diels B.131), he
expresses the first hope in the more exclusively conventional form of an appeal to the Muse Calliope. At the
same time Venus' association with creative processes
and with peace makes her a genuine object of the poet's
reverence: his awe and wonder at the creative processes
of nature is especially evident in the description and
helps to impart a type of genuine religious feeling to
the invocation.

The interpretation of the passage is complicated by the
appearance after line 43 in the Mss of the following
six lines, which occur also at 2.646-51 and describe the
life of the true Epicurean gods to which Venus and Mars
fail so conspicuously to conform:

> omnis enim per se divum natura necessest
> immortali aevo summa cum pace fruatur   45
> semota ab nostris rebus seiunctaque longe.
> nam privata dolore omni, privata periclis,
> ipsa suis pollens opibus, nil indiga nostri,
> nec bene promeritis capitur neque tangitur ira.

These lines should probably be deleted from book 1, despite
the consensus of most recent scholars in their favour.
Retained, with the theme of peace serving as the connect-
ing link with the preceding lines (Bignone, who posits an
intervening lacuna, *Rivista di Filologia* 47 (1919) 423ff.;
Friedländer, *TAPA* 70 (1939) 368ff.; Bailey), the lines
make L associate his Mars and Venus with the orthodox
Epicurean gods, whilst simultaneously emphasising the
fundamental inconsistencies. The description of the peace
of the gods (45), though entirely appropriate to Venus,
certainly does not fit Mars, and the stress on the gods'
self-sufficiency and their consequent indifference to
human affairs and behaviour, conveyed by *per se* (44) and
by the whole of 46-9, does not fit Mars or Venus. Again

the allusion to the gods' immortality (45), which in book
2 corrects the myth of Jupiter's infant cries, has no
obvious relevance in the present context. Even if L has
deliberately started from conventional religious assumptions and is now proceeding to refine them in Epicurean
terms (cf. Kleve, *Symbolae Osloenses* 41 (1966) 86-94),
he could scarcely have carried out his intention in a
clumsier ,or more misleading way. The hypothesis of a
lacuna after either 43 or 49, where L either planned or
actually completed a missing passage explaining and
rationalising the non-literal theology of 1-43 (Diels,
1923 text; Giancotti) makes 44-9 relevant to their context; but despite parallels for rationalisation in L
and his predecessors, any explicit suggestion at this
point that the divinity of his Mars and Venus was ,suspect
would have destroyed the poetic illusion on which the invocation depends for its artistic effect. An older solution of the problem therefore remains the most convincing,
that a marginal reference to, or quotation of, the lines
from book 2 has led to their early incorporation, together
with the rubric ΤΟ ΜΑΚΑΡΙΟΝ ΚΑΙ ΑΦΘΑΡΤΟΝ, in the text of
book 1: the purpose of such a note might have been to draw
attention to the divergence between the Venus and Mars of
1-43 and the true Epicurean gods; but another possible
source for it is 54 below, where a scientific account
of theology is promised. The repetition of 1.153-4 at
6.56-7 and 90-1 is likely to have arisen from the latter
type of reference.

The invocation contains all the traditional elements of
a Greek prayer: (a) identification and praise of the
deity (the identification of Venus proceeds throughout
the prayer and overlaps with the other contents); (b)
petitions (24-5 and 29-30) and grounds, including re-
minders of competence (21-3, 26-8 and 31-40); (c) necessity for (second) petition (41-3).

1-9 The rhetorical structure of the sentence reflects the
impassioned, hymnic nature of the address. 1-5 comprise
a long apostrophe, opening (1-2) with a tricolon of
vocative phrases which reach a climax with the naming of
the goddess, and continuing (2-5) with a relative clause,
with anaphora of *quae*, which is further developed by a
quoniam clause. The main clauses (6-9) are linked by
hymnic anaphora (*te . . . te . . . te . . . tuum, tibi
. . . tibi* (cf. *per te* 4): the use with the second *tibi*
of two clauses linked by *-que* makes the final member
fittingly climactic.

1 Aeneadum genetrix: at the most obvious level, the description
conveys the tradition that Venus was mother of Aeneas and

so of his descendants, the Roman race, and strikes
a national note, since L is introducing Greek philosophy
to a Roman audience (cf. *Romanis* 40). But as *Venus
physica*, the goddess was responsible for the origin of
the Romans, and of every race, in a sense more real to
the poet. The first decl. gen. pl. in -*um* is found
chiefly, as here, with nouns borrowed from Greek.
hominum divumque voluptas: at the conventional level, Venus
as goddess of love confers general sexual pleasure: but
voluptas, subject to certain safeguards, was the *summum
bonum* of Epicurean moral theory, and L here follows the
hedonistic tradition in which Aphrodite / Venus was identified with Pleasure; cf. *dux vitae, dia voluptas* 2.172,
where Pleasure is both 'guide of life' and 'divine'.
voluptas is a vital aspect of Venus' central, creative,
role (see introductory note above): though the pleasure
with which she is associated is throughout 2-20 primarily sexual, her control of artistic creativity (21-5)
makes her also representative of the higher forms of
pleasure; cf. 6.94, where the Muse Calliope is similarly
described as *requies hominum divumque voluptas*. *divum*
is applicable either to the traditional or to the
Epicurean gods, even though the latter imposed important
restrictions on their pleasures (Introduction III). *hominum divumque* (Kenney 13) is an Ennian phrase (*Annales* 249)
which evokes the Homeric ἀνδρῶν τε θεῶν τε, immediately
signalling the epic nature of the work. *divum* is one of
a number of second decl. words which frequently retain
the original form of the gen. pl. (-*um* for -*orum*) in the
classical period (cf. *deum* 54 and 68; *virum* 95 and 728):
so too with Greek proper names (cf. *Danaum* 86).

2-3 alma: a stock epithet of deities, but the root connection
with *alere*, to nurture, makes it especially applicable
to Venus in her generative role: to the Epicurean, birth
and growth, generation and nurture, were different aspects of a continuous process.
caeli . . . signa: part of the rel. clause which continues
in 3-4; the first *quae* is postponed to an emphatic position. *signa* probably has its widest Lucretian sense,
including sun and moon as well as stars.
caeli . . . mare . . . terras: L often utilises this
traditional triple division of the world, which corresponds to some extent with Epicurean physics: technically
the heavens comprised both air and fire, which, with
earth and water, made up the four Empedoclean 'elements'
(see on 705-829 below); cf. 6-9, where the fourfold division
can perhaps be detected, with air represented in 6 and
fire (as light) in 9.
navigerum . . . frugiferentis: the adjs. are not purely
ornamental but reinforce the idea of a world teeming with
activity and life, for all forms of which, both animal
and vegetable, Venus is responsible. Compound words of

this type, as distinct from those involving a prepositional prefix, are common in Greek and in the early Roman poets. Their free employment and coinage by L adds to the archaic flavour of his style (Introduction V a). With certain exceptions (e.g. L's *armipotens* (33) is used by Virgil), later Latin writers seem to have regarded such words as unsuited to the language; cf. Quintilian 1.5.70. On the final pentasyllable, see Introduction V d.

4 concelebras: Venus makes the world abundantly *celeber* (the prefix is intensive) by peopling it richly; contrast the senses at 2.345 and 5.1381.

quoniam: the clause explains and justifies the claim just made. The position of *per te* is emphatic — 'since it is through thee that . . .'

animantum: in poetry, this form of the gen. pl. of participial words is common, for the metrically awkward *-ium*. The final quadrisyllable is here 'protected' by the preceding elision (cf. e.g. 194 and see Introduction V d).

5 concipitur . . . exortum: the allusions to conception and birth develop and help to explain the image of *genetrix* (1).

lumina: poetic pl.

6 venti . . . nubila: i.e. of winter; Venus here appears as goddess of spring; cf. *verna* 10.

7 suavis: acc. pl.

daedala: the adj. is here active, as in the Greek proper name, and personifies *tellus*.

8 rident: the calm shimmering of the sea, after the storms of winter, is here represented as a smile of welcome at Venus' arrival. In L this metaphor, whether applied to the sea or to the cloudless sky of the gods (3.22, in a passage very reminiscent of the lines on spring), consistently suggests tranquillity; cf. *placatum* of the sky in 9.

aequora ponti: the literal sense, 'level surfaces of the sea', fits the calm sea in spring, though *aequor* and *aequora* alone are often mere synonyms for *mare*, as e.g. at 718.

9 The repetition of liquids and of long *a* and *u* adds to the music of the line and helps to make it an expressively peaceful climax. Like Virgil, L here employs a word of three long syllables before the final dactyl and spondee to close the period.

10 nam: it must be Venus whom the elements welcome in spring, for spring is the time when she manifests her arrival by initiating mating.

species . . . verna diei: 'the face of springtime'; the adj.
is transferred from *diei*, which here denotes 'season',
to *species*. For the hypallage, cf. on 54 below and 81,
474 and 1102.
patefactast: the spelling reflects that, when *est* is preceded by a final vowel (or vowel followed by *m*), pro-
delision rather than elision takes place.

11 reserata: the metaphor would suggest to the Roman reader
the myth of the winds imprisoned in Aeolus' cave.
genitabilis picks up the root in *genetrix* (1). The adj.
(nom. with *aura*, rather than gen. with *favoni*) is here
a variant for *genitalis* which L always uses elsewhere;
for the fairly rare active force of an adj. in *-bilis*,
cf. *manabile frigus* 534.

13 perculsae corda: 'stricken in their hearts', with *corda*
an acc. of respect or 'part affected', a Greek rather
than a native Latin idiom, which is commonly adopted
by Roman poets.
tua vi: the monosyllabic ending disrupts the coincidence
of ictus and stress in the last two feet but the 'violence'
of the rhythm fits the sense; cf. Introduction V d.

14 inde: 'next', answering *primum* (12).
ferae pecudes: 'wild beasts and tame', with the same
archaising asyndeton as at 163; for equally abrupt
examples, cf. *proelia pugnas* (2.118 and 4.1009), *alit
auget* (5.257).
pabula laeta: though usually applied by L to farmland
(where *ferae* do not belong, even in spring), the phrase
covers the pastures of wild animals at 2.596. *laeta* is
used primarily in the 'agricultural' sense of 'rich',
'fruitful', but the non-specialised sense of 'glad',
which would involve the same personification of inanimate
nature as *rident aequora ponti* (8), is probably not excluded from the poet's mind. The description of the
background is not merely ornamental; cf. on 3 above.
The strongly marked alliteration with *p*, *t* and *l* adds
to the vigour of the line.

15 rapidos: derived, like *rapax* (17), from *rapere*; L often
-6 seems to have in mind the root sense, as much as the idea
of speed (see on 273 and 294 below). Here the beasts
defy the rushing waters which threaten to carry them off.
capta . . . sequitur: the military metaphor (cf. *fugiunt*
6) is taken up in 34, where Mars is the victim. The
subject is *quaeque* ('each beast'); the pronoun is idiomatically attracted inside the local rel. clause of 16.
lepore: a quality possessed by Venus, as befits her identification with *voluptas* (1), to an irresistible degree,
which L accordingly asks her to bestow on his poem in
28; cf. also 934.

17 **denique**: 'in short', 'yes', summing up and generalising
from the two previous examples, which are hinted at
again in 18; cf. 3.50 and contrast the enumerative and
climactic uses (see on 199 and 76 below).

18 **frondiferas . . . virentis**: the adjs. are again not merely
picturesque; see on 3 and 14 above, and on 3 above for
the archaic type of compound.

19 **omnibus**: dat. with *incutiens* but doing the work of a possessive with *pectora*, according to the normal idiom with
parts of the body; cf. 87, 416f., 924, 930 and 948.
blandum: the adj. again stresses Venus' *lepor* (15); its
juxtaposition with the violent *incutiens*, which is more
often used of inspiring fear than *amor*, brings out the
element of oxymoron in the whole phrase; cf. 924.

20 **saecla**: L frequently uses this syncopated form of *saecula*
in an extended sense, as equivalent to *genera* (a plural
awkward or inadmissible in the hexameter), as here and
at 597. But at 202 and 467 the word has its normal
sense, 'generations'.

21 **quae quoniam**: 'since thou'; the rel. is connective.
rerum naturam: answered by *de rerum natura*, the title of
the poem, in 25: L's subject-matter makes Venus an appropriate deity to entreat. Venus 'alone steers the
nature of things' because she is creative, a point
summed up more explicitly in the next clause (*nec . . .
exoritur* 22-3). On its first appearance in the poem
natura is used in a context clearly suggesting its root
meaning, 'birth'; see also on *nata* 113 below and cf.
rerum natura creatrix 629. On L's habit of suggesting
an etymology for key concepts, see Introduction V c.

22 **nec . . . exoritur**: not only helping to explain *rerum
-3 naturam sola gubernas*, but also introducing a second
reason for entreating Venus: the poem cannot come into
being in the first place without her.
dias: the adj. is another form of *divus* (1, 12, 28 and
38); here the primary sense 'bright' (cf. *di-es*; *Di-
espiter*, the sky-god), from which the sense 'divine' is
developed, predominates but does not preclude a responsion with *diva* (28 and 38). Cf. also Homeric δῖος.
in luminis oras: an Ennian phrase, recurrent in L (cf.
170 and 179) and imitated by other Latin poets. *orae*
(lit. 'borders') comes, like *fines*, to denote the regions
included and here emphasises the point of transition
from darkness to light.
neque fit . . . quicquam: Venus is being asked not only to
help the poem to come into existence but to make it
fruitful (*laetum*; cf. 14) and attractive (*amabile*; cf.
lepore 15, *blandum amorem* 19 and *leporem* 28). This will

make it, in its turn, creative - of pleasure, and of
Epicurean conviction and joy, in the reader. The two
clauses of 22-3 are chiasmically arranged.

24 **scribendis versibus**: final dat. ('for the composition of
my verses'; closely with *sociam*), an old construction
which is usually replaced e.g. by *ad* + acc. The conser-
vatism of administrative language provides a close parallel (e.g. *tresviri agris dandis*). L is fond of this
type of construction; cf. 184, 547 and 707, and for less
clear-cut examples see on 203-4 and 746-7 below.

25 **de rerum natura**: L's title is modelled on the Greek Περὶ
Φύσεως, the title of (amongst other philosophical works)
both the scientific poem of Empedocles and the thirty-
seven book treatise which was the most important of
the lost works of Epicurus.
   pangere: a metaphor from building; the word comes commonly
to be applied to literary composition.

26 **Memmiadae**: the coined patronymic provides a metrical
-7 equivalent for the inadmissible Memmiō, but is not without poetic and honorific effectiveness; cf. *Memmi clara
propago* 42. On Memmius, see Introduction II.
   quem tu . . . rebus: the compliment has point, for coins show
that Venus was patron goddess of the Memmii, an incidental factor increasing the appropriateness of L's appeal
to her.
   tempore in omni: 'at all times'; *in* is redundant with a
temporal abl. where the noun itself contains the idea
of time, and the normal meaning would be 'in every crisis':
The otiose use of prepositions has considerable metrical
advantages and is a feature of L's style. The juxtaposition of the emphatically placed *omni omnibus* heightens
the emphasis on them.

28 **quo magis**: Venus has all the more reason to assist L, because
the poem is addressed to her favourite, Memmius, and moreover is designed to confer on him the greatest possible
blessing, conversion to Epicureanism.
   aeternum: regularly applied by L to poetic immortality (cf.
121), naturally enough despite his belief in the ultimate
mortality of this world and all its works. More start-
ling is the poetic, non-scientific application of the
word to objects like the *mundus* itself, as at 5.514.
   leporem: picking up *amabile* 23; cf. also on 15 above.

29 **fera moenera militiai**: with nouns of the first decl., L
has slightly more examples of the archaic *-ai* gen., which
is disyllabic, than of the classical *-ae* (Virgil has four
such instances) and frequently employs it at the end of
the line, where, especially in polysyllabic words, its

sonority is most conspicuous; see Introduction V a.
Coupled with the archaic form of *munera*, which gives a
harsher and so more appropriate sound, it adds to the
impressiveness of the whole phrase, which is linked together by the assonance with *-era* and the *m* alliteration; cf. *belli fera moenera Mavors* 32, where the repeated *m* links Mars with his sphere. The harsh sound
of these two expressions contrasts with the smoother,
more liquid sounds of the two intervening lines.

31 tranquilla pace: cf. *placidam pacem* 40; peace is already
associated in L's mind with the Epicurean moral ideal
of mental calm (ἀταραξία; Introduction III), to which
explicit allusion is made in 42, *aequo animo*.

32 Mavors: this archaic form of *Mars* (not peculiar to L
amongst Roman poets) in the context of *mortalis* (those
subject to *mors*) suggests that L has in mind the equa-
tion *Mavors* = *mors*, and regards the words as etymologically connected (Introduction V c). Mars, through
Romulus, was the conventional father of the Romans, just
as Venus, through Aeneas, was their mother. Venus is
thus to deliver them from the martial aspect of their
heritage.

33 armipotens: see on *navigerum* 3.
tuum se: the verbal matches the physical juxtaposition. On
the monosyllabic ending, which is not inappropriate to
the 'heaviness' of the sense, see Introduction V d. The
graphic beauty of the description from here to 40, whether
or not inspired by some ancient work of art, should not
obscure the fact that L, while welcoming the suppression
of Mars' belligerency and while not disapproving of sexual pleasure in itself, does not sympathise with Mars'
emotion, for it appears to be the passionate type of love
condemned in book 4; cf. Introduction III.

34 aeterno . . . amoris: the image of the god of war utterly
conquered by an eternal wound *of love* is particularly
apposite. Venus' physical position above Mars in 35-
9 symbolises her conquest and the god's subjection to her.

35 reposta: poetic syncopation for *rĕpŏsĭtā*; cf. *disposta* 52
and *posta* 1059.

36 pascit amore avidos . . . visus: a sustained image, 'he
feeds his greedy eyes with love'. *visus* is abstract
for concrete.
inhians in te: 'gaping longingly at thee'; the verb covers
a physical, and also the accompanying mental, state.

37 resupini: (sc. *eius*) 'and his breath, as he lies back,
hangs on thy lips.' The juxtaposition of *spiritus ore*

is again effective; cf. on 33 above.

38 hunc . . . recubantem: the acc. is governed by the *circum*
-9   of the passive *circumfusa* ('embracing him'); the analogy
    of the deponent *amplector* with acc. perhaps facilitates
    the construction. The interweaving of words in *hunc*
    . . . *circumfusa* matches the physical intertwining of
    the lovers.
    tuo . . . corpore sancto: probably instrumental abl. with
    circumfusa. The combination of possessive with another
    adj. is unusual and an archaic feature; cf. 413 and
    Virgil, *Aeneid* 6.185.
    super: 'from above'; see on 34 above.

41 nos: an 'editorial' pl., as e.g. at 429 and 499. In some
    contexts the pl. may be genuine, and denote 'we Epicur-
    eans' (e.g. 102) or 'we Roman Epicureans' (e.g. 58-60
    and 458).
    agere hoc: 'attend to my task': but in addition to the idea
    of concentration (contrast *aliud agere*, 'to be inatten-
    tive'), the discharge of a sacred duty is suggested, *hoc
    age* being a sacrificial formula. The religious sense
    has especial point: L likes to stress that his philo-
    sophy is more truly 'sacred' and 'religious' than ortho-
    dox religion; cf. 736-9.
    patriai tempore iniquo: 'at a time of trouble for our
    country', a phrase applicable to any period at the fall
    of the Republic, which in itself provides no clue to the
    date of the poem's composition.

42 aequo animo: 'with untroubled mind', the Epicurean moral
    ideal; see on 31 above. *aequo* is opposed to *iniquo* (=
    non aequo) 41. The 'word-play' (see Introduction V c)
    reflects the inevitable connection between political
    and mental turmoil.

43 communi desse saluti: 'fail to support the common safety'
    (*desse* is a common poetic contraction of *deesse*). Strict
    Epicurean ethics forebade participation in political life
    (Introduction III), although Roman Epicureans, notably
    the conspirator Cassius, often failed to conform. L here
    offers an incidental justification for Memmius' political
    activities: the situation leaves no alternative. Concern
    for 'the common safety' implies loyalty to the constitut-
    ional, or senatorial, cause: Memmius must accordingly have
    been opposed to Caesar at the time of writing, which,
    assuming the traditional identification, must be prior to
    Memmius' defection in 54 B.C. Though the lines would be
    especially appropriate to his praetorship in 58 B.C.,
    they cannot be assigned to this date with any certainty.

50-61 First Syllabus

A summary of contents is a regular item in a Lucretian
introduction. This one alludes briefly to the subject-
matter of books 1, 2, 5 and 6 - atomic physics and the
non-participation of the gods in the workings of the
universe. The contents of books 3 and 4 (the nature of the
soul and of perception) are summarised in a second syllabus
at 130-5. The double syllabus is not in itself a sign that
the proem of book 1 is incomplete. It is certainly possible that 3 and 4 were not part of L's original scheme
and were composed later than 5, necessitating the later
addition of the second syllabus in 1; but, even if that
were so, L had no reason to contemplate any subsequent
amalgamation of the two passages, since the two categories of subject-matter are quite distinct and are
studied for different reasons: the first, to eliminate
fear of divine intervention; the second, as is explicitly
stated at 102-26, to eliminate the fear of death.

50 Sauppe's restoration of the line, which is incomplete in the
    Mss, is here adopted. The inclusion of the vocative
    obviates the need to suppose a preceding lacuna in which
    L turned from Venus to Memmius. The scholiast on Virgil
    (*Georgics* 3.3), from whom the alternative supplement
    animumque sagacem is derived, may have conflated the line
    with 4.912.
  quod superest: 'to proceed' (lit. 'as to what remains';
    the antecedent of *quod*, if expressed, would be the ad-
    verbial acc. *id*). The frequency in the later books of
    this formula of transition to a new point or topic re-
    flects the urgency with which L constantly presses on
    towards his ultimate goal.
  vacuas: 'unpreoccupied'; the idea is picked up in *semotum
    a curis* 51, a clear reference, like *aequo animo* 42, to
    the ἀταραξία essential for philosophic study.

51 veram ad rationem: 'to the true philosophy' of Epicurus.
    On the line-ending, with 'protected' quadrisyllable,
    see Introduction V d.

52 disposta . . . contempta relinquas: the poem is pictured as
-3   a feast spread before Memmius, at which L does not want
    him to turn up his nose.
  fideli: to Epicurus, as becomes clearer after 62ff.

54 de summa caeli ratione deumque: 'on the lofty lore of the
    heavens and the gods'; *summa* is perhaps transferred from
    caeli to *ratione* (see on 10 above) but is appropriate
    to *ratione* itself in an emotive sense; cf. *superis de*

rebus (= Epicurus' περὶ τῶν μετεώρων) 127. Astronomy
is covered in book 5, atmospheric phenomena in 6: L's
only accounts of the true nature of the gods appear at
2.646-51, 3.18-24 and 5.148-55, where a fuller treatment is promised (Introduction I). *caeli deumque* are
naturally linked, since popular superstition set the
gods in the heavens and attributed celestial phenomena
in particular to this agency; cf. 63-5 and 68-9, for
which 54 prepares. Both subjects must be studied to
eradicate fear of divine intervention.

55 et . . .: L here turns to the atomic theory of books 1
and 2, a prerequisite for the understanding of the
topics just mentioned and of the whole system.
rerum primordia: 'the first-beginnings of things' (according to Epicurean theory, the atoms). *primordia*,
like *principia* which replaces it in the gen., dat.,
and abl. (where *primordiōrum* and *primordiīs* are metrically inadmissible), is less intrinsically technical
than the Greek ἄτομοι which L never transliterates (cf.
Introduction IV): the terms correspond to the Greek
ἀρχή or ἀρχαί, which were applied by other Greek physicists, as well as the Atomists, to their differing
concepts of primary matter. The word 'atom' should
never in fact figure in a translation of L: its repeated use does no justice to the resource and variety
of his vocabulary and to his avoidance of the prosaically
technical, while in book 1 such a rendering is not conducive, but positively prejudicial, to scientific clarity,
for the arguments that the 'first-beginnings' are 'atoms'
are not complete until 920; see on 146-328 below.

56 unde : = *ex quibus*, just as *quo* 57 = *in quae*; L is fond of
picking up an antecedent noun with a local rel.; cf. e.g.
122, 356, 374, 383, 421, 502 and 546.
omnis . . . res: i.e. all compound objects; cf. *rerum* and
rebus in 55, 58 and 59.
natura: L's frequent personification of Nature, especially
in a creative or destructive capacity (cf. e.g. 199, 216,
224, 263f., 328, 551, 614 and 629) would be understandable
enough in prose, let alone poetry, and does not of course
imply that a purposive agency controls the universe.
auctet alatque: synonyms standing in asyndeton with *creet*:
L considers (a) creation (b) growth. *alat* is partly
metaphorical: the description includes inorganic compounds, whose 'nurture' consists of the intake of appropriate *primordia*. The subjs. in 56-7 are of virtual
oratio obliqua after *pandam* 55; contrast the indics.
suemus and *sunt* 60-1, which state the facts (in the first
case of terminology, rather than of central doctrine)
more categorically.

57 'And into which, in turn, nature resolves them again when

they are destroyed'. *-ve* is sometimes used with the force
of *et* (lit. 'or', sc. 'as the case may be'). *perempta* is
neut. pl. as if *omnia*, not *omnis res*, had preceded, a
common enough Lucretian *constructio ad sensum*. *eadem*
(nom. fem. sing.; cf. 306 and 630) idiomatically points
the contrast between nature as a creative and destructive
agent. For the older form of *rursus*, which L sometimes
prefers, cf. e.g. 215, 308 and 660.

58 The list of synonyms is not exhaustive: it does not include
-61   *elementa*, for which see on 197 below.

58 **materiem:** 'matter', more lit. 'source material' (= Greek
      ὕλη), the generic term for the ultimate particles. At
      171 (see note) L brings out the connection with *mater*:
      all three terms in 58-9 involve related metaphors. L
      prefers the fifth to the first decl. form of the word
      in the nom. and acc.
   genitalia corpora rebus: 'bodies which give birth to things';
      the dat., doubtless preferred to the gen. to provide var-
      iety with *semina rerum* at the end of 59, is most easily
      taken closely with *genitalia*.

59 **reddunda:** L is fond of this older form of the gerundive of
      third and fourth conj. verbs; cf. 204, 707, 778 and 1026.
   semina: 'seeds' (= Greek σπέρματα); like ἀρχαί, this meta-
      phorical term was not peculiar to atomist philosophers.

60 **appellare . . . usurpare:** L seems playfully to demonstrate
      his versatility by finding synonyms for *vocare* 59, as well
      as for the primary particles. *usurpare* is basically to
      make use of, often, as here, as a name or term. For the
      spondaic fifth foot, cf. Introduction V d: the heavy
      rhythm is perhaps a playful indication of the difficulty
      of finding yet another synonym (cf. e.g. on 139 below).
      In a spondaic hexameter, a final quadrisyllabic word
      provides the same coincidence of ictus and stress as a
      final pentasyllable in the normal dactylic line.
   suemus: a contraction of *suevimus*, by analogy with the more
      familiar forms *suesti*, *suestis* and *suerunt*. L is not
      only fond of standard contractions of the perf. and al-
      lied tenses (e.g. *turparunt* 85, *donarat* 94, *cognosse* 331,
      quiesset 345, *pigraris* 410 and *inflammasset* 477), but
      sometimes goes beyond them (see e.g. on *irritat* 70 and
      consumpse 233 below). The u of *suemus*, normally conson-
      antal (as at 301), is here a vowel; cf. e.g. *dissoluat*
      216, and for the converse *tenvis* 875 and (more unusually)
      monosyllabic *suo* 1022.
   haec: = *quae*; Latin sometimes replaces a repeated rel. with
      a demonstrative, as here and at 721, or omits it, even in
      a new case, as at 154, 686 and 850.
   eadem: 'also', 'as well', idiomatically pointing a corres-
      pondence, rather than a contrast as at 57 above.

61 corpora prima: 'first bodies' (= σώματα πρῶτα).
primis: predicative: 'it is from them in the first place
that all things exist.'

62-79 Praise of Epicurus

Similar eulogies introduce books 3, 5 and 6, and reveal
L's attitude of quasi-religious awe for his master, whom
he goes so far as to call *deus* at 5.8. Whereas in the
other books the eulogies replace the epic invocation of
a traditional god (and stress Epicurus' greater claim to
real divinity, as in 5), that of 1 accompanies the invocation of Venus. Indeed, Venus and Epicurus have important
aspects in common: Epicurus is creative (and L gives emphasis to his originality in 66-7 and 71) of what is most
vital to human happiness and, by his victory over the
monster *religio*, has given man the opportunity of embracing the most valuable form of peace (ἀταραξία, mental calm).

62 ante oculos . . . iaceret: 'lay prostrate for all to see'.

63 in terris: 'upon the face of the earth'; the pl., frequent
in L with *terra* (e.g. 130, 152 and 210), here perhaps indicates that all nations were in the same plight, so
preparing for *Graius* 66.
gravi sub religione: 'beneath the burden of religion'.
religio denotes (i) a feeling of religious awe, (ii)
the rites performed to settle this emotion, and so (iii)
the organised worship of the gods: in L the sense is usually close to 'religious fear', 'religious scruple',
according to (i), and suggesting in particular the fears
of divine intervention and death which the poem seeks to
banish. The Romans derived the word variously from
relegere (the ritual is regularly repeated) and *religare*
(*religio* binds one). L favours the latter account at 932,
where he talks of 'knots' of *religiones*, so suggesting
an etymology for a key concept by a word-play (Introduction V c; cf. on *super instans* 65 below). As with
relicuo (560), the long e in L is due to the double pronunciation of the *l*, which reveals a formation with the
archaic *red-* (which survives e.g. in classical *reddere*)
for *re-*; cf. the archaic forms *redducit*, *redductum* (228),
reccidere (857 and 1063). The final pentasyllabic word
here weighs down the line, as if mirroring *religio*'s
effect on mankind.

64 Religion is pictured as a monster lowering at mankind. Its
abode is in the heavens because popular belief set the
gods there and because celestial phenomena were a prime

source of religious fear (cf. on 54 above); 68-9 help
to explain the image.
ostendebat: the spondaic fifth foot (Introduction V d) fits
the heavy, sinister, menacing sense.

65 super . . . instans: 'standing ever over'; the words clearly
hint at the noun *superstitio* (lit. 'a standing over') and
its etymology, and suggest that superstition is to be
equated with *religio*: to L, the terms are interchangeable.
Friedländer 19 draws attention also to the echo of *RELIGIONe*
in *caeLI REGIONibus* earlier in the sentence: while the assonance underlines the link between religion and the skies,
L can scarcely be offering a serious etymology, which is
postponed until 932.

66 primum . . . primusque: 'for the first time . . . and to
-7 be the first to . . .'; Epicurus' originality (cf. *primus*
71) is forcibly stressed. Though he went to extraordinary
lengths in denying indebtedness to previous philosophers,
the bulk of his physics derived from the Atomists Leucippus
and Democritus and even in the most original part of his
system, his ethics, certain conclusions seem to have been
anticipated. L in turn has been criticised for consistently depicting Epicurus as a pioneer (cf. 3.2) but, while
he finds time for a handsome tribute to earlier thinkers
at 716-39, a eulogy inspired by quasi-religious fervour
is not the place for a meticulous account of debts to predecessors and he saw Epicurus as first to propound a
completely true system and so to oppose religion success-
fully.
Graius homo: in none of the four eulogies does L name
Epicurus, as if debarred by religious taboo. This, together with the emphasis on his originality, has led to
some strange theories about the identity of the 'man of
Greece', who is indubitably Epicurus.
contra . . . contra: the emphatic repetition at the end of
each line effectively conveys Epicurus' stubborn, un-
flinching resistance.

68 fama deum: 'stories of the gods'; the *m* alliteration down
-9 to *caelum* suggests, in the context, menace in general
and the rumble of thunder in particular.
eo magis acrem: the two final disyllables have much the same
effect on the pattern of ictus and stress as a final quadrisyllable (Introduction V d); the degree of clash is reduced by the 'protection' of a preceding monosyllable
(e.g. 246 and 724) or a preceding elision (e.g. 741).
The unusual 'violence' of the rhythm (as also in the 'protected' instances cited) is not out of place in the context.

70 irritāt: a contraction of *irritavit*, by analogy with more
-1 established first conj. forms like *turparunt* 85 and

donarat 94; cf. 5.396 and 6.587 and see on *suemus* 60.

effringere . . .: the original picture, Epicurus' confront-
ation with the monster *religio*, is now lost sight of until
the climax of the passage at 78-9. As at 31ff., in the port-
rayal of Venus, new imagery appropriate to the central
theme now occurs to the poet's pictorial mind. Epicurus
now appears as a military campaigner, eager to 'burst open
the tight-set bolts on nature's doors' (by discovering her
closely guarded secrets): in 72ff., the conquest of this
key citadel opens up the infinite universe beyond the walls
of our own world and enables him to extend the frontiers of
human knowledge throughout it. Cf. Cicero, *pro Murena* 33,
where the context is purely military - *eam urbem sibi Asiae
ianuam fore, qua effracta et revulsa tota pateret provincia.*
The military and the monster-slaying imagery implies a
challenge to traditional epic values, since L sees Epicurus'
achievements as far greater than those of any literal general or monster-slayer, as is made clear in the climacti-
cally arranged list of great men at 3.1024-44 and the
eulogy at 5.1-54.

primus: closely with *effringere*, rather than *cupiret*, which
is an archaic fourth conj. form of *cuperet*.

72 **vīvida vīs animī pervīcit:** the assonance, like the alliter-
ative pattern with initial *p* and *c* in 71 above, matches
Epicurus' vigour and insistence. L is fond of the sound
vī in a vigorous or violent context: the roots of *vivere,
vis* and *vincere* here each contribute one example, a correspondence which L may have thought meaningful (Introduction V c).

extra governs *moenia* 73; its position links the two lines
together, so helping to emphasise the length of Epicurus'
vast journey.

73 **processit:** Epicurus, not *vis*, is now the subject.

flammantia moenia mundi: i.e. the fiery envelope of ether,
in which our world was enclosed and which formed its outer
visible limits: each of the infinite number of worlds
in the universe had its own heavenly bodies, so that one
could never see out into the universe beyond the 'ramparts'
of one's own world: man's knowledge was thus encircled
and confined until Epicurus transcended them, passing
beyond the *caelum* from which *religio* had lowered. *moenia
mundi* (cf. 1102) is a regular Lucretian image for this
envelope, but here fits the campaigning metaphor. *flammantia*, which is literal, makes the obstacle more formidable, but the flames fail to deter the intrepid general.
The *m* alliteration lends unity and majesty to this impressive phrase.

74 **omne immensum:** 'the boundless universe'; L uses the neut. adj.
omne as a noun in a technical sense (= Epicurus' τὸ πᾶν).

mente animoque: 'by the power of his intellect'; the nouns
are synonymous. Virgil (*Aeneid* 6.11) imitates the phrase,
which involves a 'protected' quadrisyllabic ending, like 4.

75 refert: not simply 'reports'; the combination with *victor*
suggests a triumphing general, who 'brings back as the
prize of victory (knowledge of)'; cf. Virgil, *Aeneid* 4.
93. *refert* governs the three indirect questions *quid
possit . . . haerens* 77: these presuppose the operation
of natural, scientific law, which rules out the fear
of divine caprice inspired by *religio*; they thus constitute a key passage which L thrice repeats elsewhere,
in 1 at 594-6. L's habit of often almost catechistic
repetition is a useful didactic instrument, and may
in part be a conscious adaptation of the rather different
repetitions of Homeric epic; cf. e.g. on 505, 670-1, 673-
4, 738-9 and 908-10 below and see also W.B. Ingalls, *Phoenix*
25 (1971) 227-36.

76 finita . . . ratione: 'on what principle indeed each
-7 class of thing has its powers restricted . . .'. *denique*
marks the third question as the climax; cf. 278, and
contrast the senses at 17 and 199. The postponement of
quanam ratione throws emphasis on to the key idea of
limitation (*finita*), with which the clause also ends
(*terminus*). *cuique* ('each thing') embraces 'each type
of thing': as often where L is referring to scientific
law, the second idea is in mind, for objects of a given
category behave uniformly.
　alte terminus haerens: 'a deep-set boundary stone'; like
the matching *finita potestas* (which has a legal ring)
and the triumph image, the metaphor, from the stone pillar
marking the boundary between properties, is characteristically Roman.

78 L here returns to the opening image, with the position of 62-
-9 5 now dramatically reversed, as *vicissim* underlines: mankind, previously prostrate and *oppressa in terris*, is now
exalted to the skies, and has changed places with the
monster, previously *super instans* but now *pedibus subiecta* and trampled underfoot (*obteritur*). *victoria*,
echoing *victor* 75, helps to link the two different but
harmonising images of Epicurus as all-conquering general
and monster-slaying hero. *pedibus subiecta* is imitated
by Virgil in his tribute to L at *Georgics* 2.492.
　caelo: opposed to *in terris* 63, and answering *caeli* 64 -
not simply a metaphor for triumph, but also a poetic
allusion to the Epicurean gods, whose literal home was
beyond the *caelum* in the spaces between worlds. Thanks
to Epicurean philosophy, man can, like Epicurus himself,
match the true gods in mental calm; cf. 3.322, 5.43-51.

80-101 Religion is more impious than its opponents

L here forestalls an objection which the previous passage
might prompt, by turning the charge of impiety back upon
religio. His thesis (the converse of that noted at 41
and 736-9) is illustrated by the example of the sacrifice
of Iphigeneia: when the Greek fleet sailed for Troy, it
was becalmed at Aulis in Boeotia on account of the anger
of the goddess Artemis, which was placated when Iphigeneia,
the daughter of the commander-in-chief Agamemnon, was summoned on the pretext of marriage to Achilles and duly sacrificed instead. L naturally overlooks the 'civilised'
version according to which the goddess spirited Iphigeneia
safely away to the Crimea. L's choice of example has been
taken as evidence of anachronism and exaggeration of the
hold of *religio* on his contemporaries (cf. Introduction
III): against this it may be argued (i) that the legendary
example sums up human sacrifice through the ages, (ii) that
human sacrifice serves as an archetypal example of the
evils of *religio,* and (iii) that instances of gruesome
punishment on religious grounds were none too remote from
the Rome of L's day; e.g. Livy records how, during the
Second Punic War (just over a century before L's birth), a
Vestal virgin and her seducer suffered the appointed penalty
for their crime by being buried alive and publicly beaten to
death respectively.

80 illud: anticipating the *ne* clause.
   in his rebus: 'in this connection'; a recurrent, somewhat
     prosaic Lucretian formula, repeated at 331, 370 and
     1052.

81 impia: the transference (see on *verna* 10 above) from
     rationis to *elementa* (which here denotes 'principles';
     contrast the technical sense at 197) circumvents the
     metrically inadmissible *īmpĭaē*. The adj. may be rendered
     'impious' both here and in 83, but more lit. denotes
     'lacking in duty', in 81 duty to the traditional gods,
     in 83 duty to the true, Epicurean gods, which overlaps
     with duty to others - in Agamemnon's case, with duty to
     his daughter.

82 indugredi: compounded with the archaic by-form of *in, indu*
     (like the classical *indoles, indigeo); īngrĕdī* would not
     fit the metre. Cf. also *indupedita* 240, *induperator* (an
     Ennian form) 4.967 and 5.1227, and *indu* itself 5.102.
   quod contra: 'but on the contrary'; *quod* is adverbial acc.,
     'as to this', as in *quod nunc* 221, *quod si* (familiar in
     prose) 180, 391 and 410 and *id* 655.
   illa: contemptuous, like *ista,* and pointing the contrast -
     'it is that (very) religion which . . .'.

83 **scelerosa atque impia**: answering *impia . . . sceleris* 81-
2, with chiasmic arrangement.

84 **quo pacto**: 'just as', 'even so' (lit. 'in the way in which'),
introducing an example of the preceding generalisation,
as at 912.
   Triviai: i.e. of Artemis, the Roman Diana, the goddess of
the crossroads (where *tres viae* meet). If *Triviai* has
its original adjectival force with *virginis*, it is one
of only four Lucretian examples of the archaic -*ai* gen.
in an adj.: he normally restricts it to nouns (cf. on
29 above). *virginis* no doubt hints that Artemis should
have protected the virgin Iphigeneia, not demanded her
sacrifice; cf. *virgineos* 87.

85 **Iphianassai**: the name is treated as a variant for *Iphigeneia*,
perhaps on account of their similar meaning ('powerful
queen', 'born powerful'): as the two are metrically
equivalent, L's preference is presumably on grounds of
euphony. He has either overlooked or confused Homer,
Iliad 9.145 and Sophocles, *Electra* 158, where Iphianassa
is a sister who survived Iphigeneia.
   turparunt: = *turpaverunt*; on L's fondness for contracted
perf. forms, see on *suemus* 60 and *irritat* 70; cf. *donarat*
(= *donaverat*) 94 below.

86 **ductores Danaum delecti**: in the context of the deed just
described, the *d* alliteration becomes mock-majestic and
contemptuous. On the gen. pl. *Danaum*, see on *divum*
1 above.
   prima virorum: 'chiefest of heroes'. L is fond of the
neut. pl. of an adj. or participle with the gen. of a
noun, a poetic idiom which spreads to Silver prose, and
often expresses a missing abstract (e.g. *sublima caeli*
340, 'the heights of heaven'). The gen. is in origin
partitive, like *virorum*, but L also extends the idiom to
cases where adj. and noun are coextensive (e.g. *strata
viarum* 315, 'paved streets'; *vera viai* 659, 'the true
path'). *prima virorum*, unusual in that the neut. is
applied to persons, ironically echoes a familiar Greek
construction (e.g. Euripides, *Medea* 916; cf. Ovid's
summa ducum in a mock-heroic context at *Amores* 1.9.37),
and implies a criticism of Greek heroic values: the
generals' ruthless conduct belies their high reputation,
and L would regard Epicurus, the philosophical warrior
of the preceding passage, as far worthier of such a
description.

87 L heightens the pathos of the description by suggesting
-99 throughout the contrast between the sacrifice and the
wedding which Iphigeneia had been promised; see on
infula 87 and on 95-9 below

87 simul: = *simulac*, as in 89 below (and often in the historians).
The main clause follows in 92.
  infula: a band of twisted wool, worn not only by priests
  and Vestal virgins, but by sacrificial victims. Iphigeneia,
  expecting simply the nuptial hairband or *vitta*, thus receives the first clue to her betrayal. Though the scene
  is Greek, some of the details, understandably enough, are
  Roman.
  cui . . . virgineos . . . comptus: 'her virgin tresses';
  the acc. is governed by the *circum* of *circumdata* (cf.
  hunc circumfusa 38-9); for the dat., see on *omnibus* 19
  above. *comptus*, based on *comere* (see on 950 below),
  appears to be a Lucretian coinage, of his favourite
  fourth decl. formation (Introduction V a): it implies
  arrangement, so suggesting the six plaits (*sex crines*)
  usual for a bride. The juxtaposition *infula virgineos*
  (see also on *virginis* 84 above) adds to the pathos.

88 pari . . . parte: 'in equal lengths'; *mālarum*, partitive
  gen., goes with *utraque*. The elaborate precision of
  the ceremonial is in sharp contrast with the primitive
  barbarity of the deed itself; for similar sneers at the
  paraphernalia of religion, cf. 739 and 5.1198ff.

89 maestum: emphatic; Agamemnon's grief is the second indication that all is not well; cf. the tears of the assembled
  troops in 91.

90 hunc propter: 'next to him'; wherever L places *propter*
  after its case, its sense is local. His postponement
  of prepositions is sometimes as bold as it is metrically
  expedient (cf. e.g. 718, 812 and 841), though it has the
  basis of the anastrophe regular e.g. in *mecum, tecum*
  and with *tenus*.
  celare: emphatic: Iphigeneia might have expected an animal
  sacrifice at her wedding but the concealing of the knife
  reveals more sinister intent.
  ministros: 'his attendants'; a general word, but often
  applied to the attendants of a priest.

92 genibus summissa: 'her knees sank beneath her and . . .'
  (lit. 'let down by her knees').
  petebat: a pictorial impf., freezing the action - there
  she was, in the act of falling.

93 in tali tempore: 'in such peril'; *in* is appropriate, for
  tempore has more than temporal sense; see on 26 above,
  where *in* is redundant, as also in 98 below.
  quibat: the verb, conjugated like *ire*, has as its subject
  the noun clause of 94.

94 I.e. the fact that she was Agamemnon's eldest child -
  princeps = *prima*. The line recalls Euripides, *Iphigeneia*
  in Aulis 1220.

95 sublata virum manibus: reminiscent of Aeschylus' λαβεῖν
    ἀέρδην (*Agamemnon* 234) but also suggestive of the mar-
    riage ceremony, in which the bride was borne aloft
    when taken from her mother's arms. This sentence re-
    presents the sacrifice as a hideous travesty of the
    wedding ceremony which Iphigeneia expected: the antithesis
    is made explicit at *non ut . . . sed . . .* 96-9. On the
    gen. pl. *virum*, see on *divum* 1 above.
  tremibunda: with fear of death, rather than with a bride's
    natural modesty.

96 deductast: again appropriate to a wedding ceremony, where
    the term is technical for the escorting of the bride
    from her own house (where the marriage normally took
    place) to the house of the groom.
  sollemni more sacrorum: 'the customary practice of the
    rites', i.e. of marriage; the *sacra*, in the event, took
    a different form. *sollemnis* denotes (i) 'annual' and
    so (ii) 'regular' and acquires the association of sol-
    emnity from its frequent application to religious ob-
    servance.

97 claro comitari Hymenaeo: 'be accompanied by the resounding
    wedding-song'; the non-deponent *comitare* is rare and
    poetic, except in the past participle passive. The name
    of the Greek god of marriage is often employed in this
    'faded' sense, a usage of the type which L justifies at
    2.655ff., where he allows *Bacchus* and *Ceres* to denote
    wine and corn. The quadrisyllabic ending, since it in-
    volves a Greek name, is of a type admitted by Virgil
    (Introduction V d), though he would have tended to
    avoid the preceding elision.

98 casta inceste: 'a pure maid impurely slain' (adapting Duff).
-9   *inceste* is separated from *concideret* for the sake of the
    antithesis.
  nubendi tempore in ipso: opposed to *hostia concideret*,
    to form a second antithesis within the clause.
  mactatu . . . parentis: L naturally follows the most
    barbarous account, in which Agamemnon acts as high priest
    and performs the deed himself; cf. Euripides, *Iphigeneia
    in Aulis* 1178. On the coined *mactatus* (found only here)
    see on *comptus* 87 above. The placing of *maesta* repre-
    sents her father's responsibility as the culmination of
    Iphigeneia's grief; the whole phrase forcefully indi-
    cates the extent to which the deed was *impius* (83).

100 The trivial purpose of the sacrifice comes as a ghastly
    anticlimax after the horror of the preceding line: the
    opposition between *hostia* and *exitus*, *maesta* and *felix
    faustusque* is pointed by their similar position in each
    line.

exitus: 'outcome'; L plays on the senses (i) result and
(ii) egress (from harbour), underlining that to
Agamemnon and his fleet a favourable outcome and egress
were identical (cf. Introduction V c).

felix faustusque: a formula from augury, used contemptuously to heighten the anticlimax; only *religio* could
describe the outcome of such an atrocity in such terms.
The religious formula prepares for the return of *religio*
(last mentioned in 83) in the famous concluding line
which follows.

101 tantum . . . malorum: 'such depths of evil'.

102-135 Fears about the hereafter must be forestalled:
the syllabus expanded

The passage is a natural sequel to the preceding one, since
both are directed against misgivings which L's hostility
to *religio*, revealed in 62-79, may inspire. L again turns
the objection inside-out, arguing that fear of death
should be an incentive to the study of his philosophy,
which alone can dispel the ignorance about the nature
of the soul from which fear of death stems: the nature
of the soul and of apparitions of the dead (subjects
covered in books 3 and 4) must accordingly be added to
the syllabus already set out in 50-61.

102 tutemet: *tu* is here given emphasis by a double suffix,
the archaic -*te* (cf. *tute* 269, 403 and 407), and -*met*
(cf. e.g. classical *egomet*). The form reappears only
at 4.915. While the emphasis points the contrast with
nobis, metrical convenience is doubtless a factor.

iam: i.e. now that you have embarked on the poem: most
conveniently translated with *quovis tempore*, 'at some
point or other hereafter'.

vatum: 'of the seers', a contemptuous term, including
poets who subscribed to religion and mythology. *vates* was
the oldest Latin term for a poet but by L's day had
fallen into contempt and been replaced by *poeta*. Virgil
was to reinstate it in the sense 'inspired bard'.

103 terriloquis: on the compound, found only here, see on
navigerum 3 above.

victus dictis: the assonance may be 'meaningful' (Introduction V c); it is the function of words to prevail
and to con-vince.

desciscere: a military metaphor, suggesting that *a nobis*
102 means 'from the Epicurean camp'; contrast the
'editorial' *nos* at 41 (see note). At 80-81 the danger

was that Memmius might not begin his study (*inire*):
it is now that, having embarked, he may abandon it.
The prolative infin. with *quaeres* replaces the *ut*
construction normal in prose: *quaerere* approximates
in sense to *conari* or *velle*, with which the infin. is
standard. The idiom illustrates the wider currency of
the infin. in poetry, where it is metrically convenient,
than in prose; cf. *valere* + infin. (108f. and 630), by
analogy with *posse*, and *suadere* and *inducere* + acc. and
infin. (140-3), where the sense approximates to that of
cogere and *iubere*.

104 quippe etenim: 'for, to be sure', a favourite Lucretian
formula.
iam: 'as things are', without Epicurean philosophy; cf.
nunc 110.
fingere: as often, implying delusion; cf. e.g. 371 and
842.

105 somnia: 'idle fancies', though the word can also denote
-6 dreams, which, as 133-5 show, can contribute to such
fancies.
vitae rationes vertere: 'overturn your principles of life',
both factual beliefs and principles of conduct. The
thought is elaborated at 3.59ff., where fear of death
is claimed to contribute to avarice, ambition, breaking
of natural ties and even suicide. The clause may contain a business metaphor, with *rationes* figuratively
suggesting accounts: *conturbare rationes* (cf. *turbare*
106) is a technical term for bankruptcy, and the pl.
fortunas is more often concrete ('wealth') than abstract
('fortunes', good or bad).
possint: consecutive subj. The repetition of the verb at
the end of successive lines seems justified by the emphasis: these things *may* happen, but must not be allowed
to.

107 merito: 'with reason' sc. may one incline to heed the seers.
finem: L regularly gives the word its older fem. gender.

109 religionibus: 'religious fears' (see on 63 above), which
to L are 'superstitions' (see on 65 above).
vatum: 'stemming from the seers'; the gen. is subjective.

110 nunc: 'as it is', for the more usual *at nunc* (169 and
340).
restandi: = *resistendi*.

111 poenas . . . timendumst: for the normal *poenae timendae
sunt*; L is fond of this construction (cf. 138 and 381-
2), in which the impersonal use of the gerundive, normal
with intransitive verbs (e.g. *legibus parendum est*) is
extended to verbs which govern a direct object. (Gram-

marians sometimes regard the form rather as a gerund
but the gerund does not elsewhere appear as subject
or have the force of obligation.) The idiom is doubtless partly influenced by Greek, where φοβητέον ἐστὶ
τιμωρίας and φοβητέαι εἰσὶ τιμωρίαι are equally normal:
its appearance in L, Varro and the jurists suggests also
an element of archaism, though Plautus has only a single
instance. The sole Ciceronian example (*de Senectute* 6 -
viam quam nobis ingrediundum sit) falls into a special
category, for the acc. may be regarded as governed by
the *in-* prefix, rather than as a genuinely direct object.

113 Of these alternatives, the soul's birth (*nata sit*) is an
aspect of its mortality, taken up in 114, its entry into
the body at birth (*nascentibus insinuetur*) entails its
previous existence and is an aspect of its immortality,
taken up in 115-6. Ancient philosophers were arguably
more consistent than modern believers in thinking that
the immortality of the soul involved not only its everlasting survival after the body's death, but also its
everlasting existence prior to the body's birth. Thus,
in seeking to prove the soul's mortality in book 3, L
argues both against its survival (3.425-669) and its
pre-existence (3.670-783). For the Epicurean the soul's
birth and death implied one another: indeed, anything
subject to birth and death must be an atomic compound,
once created and ultimately destructible, so that *nativus*
(cf. *nata* and *nascentibus* here) becomes for L a virtual
synonym of *mortalis*.
nata: the assonance with *natura* 112, which is etymologically
connected (see on 21 above), is perhaps designed to load
the question, mirroring L's conviction that by nature
the soul is indeed *nata*; cf. *officium corporis / officere*
336-7.
nascentibus: sc. *nobis*; the antithesis with *nata* has point -
'whether the soul itself has a birth (and so is mortal)
or whether only its hosts have a birth (so that only they
are mortal)'.
insinuetur: 'works its way into'; the verb can be used
of causing to enter (hence the passive and reflexive uses
here and at 116) or of entering (as at 409): the thing
entered is usually expressed by a dat. (*nascentibus*),
but at 116 and 409 by the acc. (*pecudes, latebras*), which
can be seen as governed by the *in-* prefix. The word denotes entry which is devious or difficult and can be
sinister, suggesting pernicious or disruptive infiltration.
It is a favourite Lucretian term for atomic permeation
and especially, as here and at 116, for the entry of a
ready-made soul into the body: this usage is loaded and
incredulous, for L regards such devious infiltration
by the soul as so difficult as to be impossible.

114 simul . . . nobiscum: i.e. together with the body.

morte dirempta: 'shattered by death'; in Epicurean theory, resolved into component atoms.

115 Two versions of immortality theory are here considered,
-6 survival in an underworld (115) and transmigration of souls or metempsychosis (116), the theory held most notably by Pythagoras. The mention of the latter illustrates that when L attacks fear of death, primitive fear of punishment in Tartarus, suggested by *aeternas poenas* 111, is not his only target; cf. Introduction III.

115 Orci: an Italian counterpart of the Greek Hades, which can denote the god of the underworld or the underworld itself.
vastasque lacunas: the adj. suggests desolation, as well as extent. *lacuna* (as at 5.1261) can denote any hollow, not necessarily one filled with water, and may here mean 'chasms', rather than alluding to the rivers of the underworld. The phrase recurs at 6.552 but in an entirely different context.

116 pecudes alias: 'beasts as well as man'; *alias* is used like the Greek ἄλλος, which can mean 'in addition' rather than 'other'. The Grecism is perhaps influenced by the Empedoclean ἄνθρωποί τε καὶ ἄλλων ἔθνεα θηρῶν (Diels B.26.4). *pecudes* is not here restricted to farm animals, as at 14, 163 and 257.
divinitus: a sarcastic addition; divine intervention has to be invoked to explain the suspension of natural law entailed by this fantastic theory.

117 Ennius here appears as a champion of metempsychosis. At
-26 the beginning of the *Annales* he had described how the distinguished history of his soul had been revealed to him by the ghost of Homer, its previous hosts including a peacock, Homer himself, and Pythagoras (cf. Persius 6.10). Despite his merciless mockery of this aspect of his philosophy, L would have had more sympathy with the author of the *Euhemerus* and *Epicharmus* (cf. Introduction IV) in other philosophical areas, and in his generous praise of Ennius' literary achievement (117-9) he indirectly acknowledges at the beginning of the poem his debt to Ennius as his main literary model in Latin (Introduction V a).

117 Ennius: the assonance with *perenni* (118) suggests an *omen in nomine* and that Ennius and literary immortality are inseparable, as the juxtaposition *Ennius aeternis* in 121 below seems to confirm, but it does not follow that L intends an etymology of *Ennius* (Introduction V c).

noster: indicating primarily nationality, but also a
measure of affection: it became a stock epithet of Ennius
amongst Roman writers.

118 Helicone: the hill of the Greek Muses in Boeotia and also
the site of Ennius' vision of Homer referred to in
124-6.
perenni fronde: abl. of quality with *coronam*.

119 per . . . hominum: 'throughout the Italian races of mankind'; *Italas* is appropriate to *gentis* and need not be
regarded as transferred, like *verna* 10. The phrase
gains in emphasis by being placed outside the *quae*
clause of which it is part: *Italas* answers *noster* /
Helicone, 117-8 (cf. *Graiorum* / *Latinis* 136-7). L thus
sees Ennius as a pioneer in having introduced Greek-
influenced poetry to Italy: his introduction of the
Greek hexameter into Latin was something for which L had
particular reason to be grateful.
clara clueret: 'was to win fair fame'; the subj. is consecutive. *cluere*, an archaic verb, sometimes used by L
= *esse* (e.g. 580), here has the full force of the Greek
κλύειν (cf. 449), 'be spoken of (as bright)'. The alliteration fits the re-echoing of Ennius' fame throughout Italy.

120 L here pokes fun at Ennius for believing in an underworld
-6 as well as in the transmigration of souls. Since the
body decayed at death and the soul was otherwise engaged, Ennius had to people his underworld with a third
entity, a sort of ghost (the *simulacra* of 123; cf.
speciem 125). It is this concept which is here the
central object of L's scorn.

120 Acherusia templa: 'the realms of Acheron', one of the rivers
of the underworld; the phrase is a direct quotation from
Ennian tragedy (*Scaenica* 107), which L employs also at
3.25 and 86. In L *templa*, though denoting 'temples' at
6.750 and 1274, usually has the archaic sense 'regions'
but is probably often not devoid of religious overtones
imparted both by its early augural sense (an area, esp.
of the sky, marked off for augural purposes) and by its
classical usage. So here there may be the idea that
Acheron is a totem before which Ennius and mankind, in
their ignorance, bow down. Applied, as most often, to
the heavens (cf. 1014, 1064 and 1105), *templa* may carry
both a reminder that superstition makes the heavens into
a temple by placing the gods there (cf. 5.1188) and an
expression of L's own quasi-religious awe at the contemplation of this aspect of the universe.

121 aeternis: see on *aeternum* 28 above.

edens: appropriate to authoritative pronouncements, including those of oracles and 'seers', and poking fun
at Ennius' oracular dogmatism.

122 qua . . . permaneant: the subj. is of *oratio obliqua*
after *exponit* and reports Ennius' view. I have substi-
tuted *qua* for Mss *quo*: the accepted interpretation
('which, he says, neither our souls nor our bodies,
but rather ghosts *endure to reach*') makes Ennius imply
that the soul perishes before it can reach Acheron, when
his view was that it was busy transmigrating (an objection
seen, but not met, by Munro). For local *qua* picking
up a noun, cf. 356 and 421. *unde* (124 below) likewise
refers back to *templa*.

123 quaedam: 'some sort of', expressing incredulity at the
whole vague concept of the ghosts.
modis pallentia miris: descriptively effective, as Virgil's
imitations of the phrase (e.g. *Georgics* 1.477) bear witness, but in L also satirical, whether the words echo or
merely paraphrase Ennius: the pallor of the ghosts is
all the more wondrous in that it is scientifically inex-
plicable, in the absence not only of their bodies, but
even of their souls.

124 An ironical situation: Ennius, in whom Homer's soul was
-6 supposedly reincarnated, scarcely needed Homer's ghost
(*speciem* 125) to impart information to which he might
have been expected to have more direct access.

124 semper florentis: doubly appropriate, (i) as a stock description of Homer's literary immortality, corresponding
to the Greek ἀειθαλοῦς; (ii) as a sarcastic allusion to
the more literal immortality assigned to him by Ennius,
who maintained that not only his soul but also his ghost
lived on.

125 lacrimas effundere salsas: a further humorous touch; Homer's
own ghost conforms with the normal behaviour of the
Homeric shade on rising to this world, in weeping at
its tenuous lot.

126 The crowning irony: Homer, the source of traditional
mythology and, according to Ennius, of the fantastic
theory of metempsychosis, is taken by Ennius to be an
authority on natural science. *rerum naturam*, applied
to the weird beliefs Ennius was prepared to swallow, is
heavily ironic and contrasts with the true *rerum natura*,
of which L gives the syllabus in the next sentence.
Despite L's admiration for Homer as a poet (summed up
at 3.1037-8), he rejected him as did Epicurus as a
philosophical teacher; cf. e.g. the criticism of Greek
epic values implied at 86.

127 cum: picked up by *tunc* 130, 'not only . . . but also';
-30 the greater emphasis which always falls on *tum* or *tunc*
in this idiom is here reinforced by *cum primis*, 'especially'. The two categories of subject-matter are
equally important: the first receives less emphasis
because it has already been mentioned (54ff. above).
superis de rebus: see on 54 above. *solis lunaeque
meatus* (subject of the indirect question *qua fiant
ratione*) are representative examples, which are covered in book 5.
habenda nobis est ratio: 'we must give an account'; in
129 *ratio* may be translated 'principle', 'way', in 130
'reasoning'. The repetition may be accidental, but L
may deliberately emphasise the word here to contrast
the irrationality of the rival beliefs.
quaeque gerantur: 'different processes (or 'types of
process'; see on 76 above) are carried on'. *fiant*
('take place') and *gerantur* are here synonymous.
in terris: this topic was not specifically mentioned in
the previous syllabus at 50-61. L is thinking of the
account of life and civilisation which ends book 5,
and of the terrestrial phenomena explained in 6.
sagaci: see on 368 below.

131 'We must see of what the soul and mind consists'; with
videndum, sc. *est*, as e.g. at 627 and 963. The topic
is treated in book 3. The distinction between *ānima*
and *animus*, which shared the same atomic constitution,
is between the 'non-logical' and the 'logical' parts
of the Epicurean soul (the ἄλογον μέρος and the λογικὸν
μέρος of the ψυχή). The *anima* was diffused throughout
the body and was responsible for physical sensation:
the *animus* was situated in the breast and responsible
not only for thought, dreams and will, but also for
emotion. In the absence of a third Latin term to embrace both (cf. on 136-45 below), L sometimes uses
either word less technically to denote the whole soul,
a practice explained at 3.421-4; cf. the all-inclusive
sense of *anima* at 112 and 122 above.
animi . . . natura: as its pairing with *anima* shows, a
mere periphrasis for *animus*; contrast *natura animai* 112,
where *natura* has its full force. L makes frequent use
of the device, and in later books of similar periphrases
involving *corpus, potestas* and *vis*; cf. *natura* with
animantum (194 and 1038), *aquae* (281), *inanis* (363),
ardoris (702) and perhaps *omnis* (419). Epicurus' use
of φύσις with dependent gen. may be assumed to be an
important influence.

132 quae res: as we learn at 4.33ff. (where the present pas-
-3 sage is strongly echoed), the allusion is to the atomic

films or effluences (*simulacra*; contrast the non-technical
meaning in 123) which in Epicurean theory constantly
stream from the surface of compounds and are responsible
both for visual perception and for thought and dreams of
these compounds. The *simulacra* which generate apparitions of the dead are an important, and representative,
example of the subject-matter of book 4, which deals
with perception in general.

nobis: dat. with *obvia*, like the three participles.

vigilantibus . . . somnoque sepultis: in both cases, according to Epicurean theory, stray *simulacra* from the
dead have been preserved to cause the apparition (thoughts
of the dead, mentioned at 4.733-4, were explained along
similar lines). Waking visions of them are covered
briefly at 4.33ff., dreams of them more fully at 4.757-
67, where, as in all dreams, appropriate *simulacra* enter
the mind, which sees the dream as reality because of the
suspension of the faculties in sleep. The qualification
that waking visions occur in illness (*morbo adfectis*)
is missing in book 4: clearly the patient's critical
faculty is suspended by his condition, as is the dream-
er's by sleep. Those who see evidence in this passage
that L himself suffered hallucinations and *insania* may
well have been anticipated in their inventiveness by
the originators of the story in the Jerome life (Introduction II): all that the passage, and others like it,
can prove is that L is a keen, clinical observer of a
number of abnormal conditions. The metaphor of *sepultis*
reinforces the idea of communion between the sleeping
and the dead, whose literal burial is summed up in 135.

134 **audireque**: aural perception of 'apparitions' is not discussed in book 4 but must have been explained in terms
of sound particles emitted by the deceased having been
preserved along with the *simulacra*. L has occasional
examples of -*que* appended to short *e*, which for reasons
of euphony was avoided by the Augustan poets and is rare
in good prose; cf. 494, 666 and 973.

135 recurs at 4.734 with *quorum* in first position in the clause.

136-145 Difficulty of the task

L here alludes to the problems (i) imposed by his poetic
medium (*versibus* 137 and *carmine* 143): these comprise
(a) the general difficulties of clearly expressing
such a technical subject (*obscura reperta* 136) in
poetry and (b) the difficulties of vocabulary imposed by
the hexameter, in which many words, including technical
and semi-technical terms, are awkward or inadmissible

(cf. Introduction IV). The choice of poetry thus ag-
gravates problem (ii), the deficiencies of the Latin
language (*egestatem linguae* 139). This famous complaint,
echoed at 832 and at 3.260 and 317, should be seen in
each case in its context. Though treated by Pliny,
Letters 4.18.1, as more general, it would appear to be
primarily a complaint about the absence of ready-made
technical vocabulary in Latin for the expression of Greek
philosophical ideas and thus parallel with the remark of
Cicero, *de Finibus* 3.1.3 - *nobis, quibus etiam verba par-
ienda sunt imponendaque nova rebus novis nomina*. This
view is supported by the immediate addition of *rerum
novitatem* (the novelty of the subject to the Romans) in
139; and when L repeats the complaint, it is because he
has no adequate vocabulary to describe (a) Anaxagoras'
homoeomeria, (b) the interaction of the four types of
soul atom and (c) the many different shapes of soul atom.
Nevertheless, L's various coinings of quite non-technical
words may be a clue that, at a secondary level, he found
more general limitations in the language, at least for
the purposes of hexameter verse composition.

L's success in overcoming the considerable difficulties
here suggested is remarkable. In so much technical discussion, few passages lack clarity and the absence of
scientific terminology is often turned to his own account: he is rarely reduced to transliteration or invention of an intrinsically technical and prosaic word, but
prefers to adapt existing vocabulary to his needs, often
thus incorporating the metaphor appropriate to his medium;
see the examples cited in Introduction IV.

136 animi: 'in my mind'; this usage, though generally replaced
 -7   by *animo*, is found in prose with certain expressions like
    angi and *pendēre* ('be in doubt'), where it was probably
    regarded as a locative. In origin, however, the form
    would appear to be an archaic gen. of relation, as shown
    e.g. by *mentis* and *sermonis* in Plautus; cf. *Trinummus*
    454 where *mentis* and *animi* are combined.
    obscura . . . inlustrare: the favourite Lucretian meta-
    phor of light and darkness is sustained throughout this
    passage; cf. *clara lumina* and *res occultas* 144-5. It
    acquires a further dimension from the suggestion of
    literal darkness in *noctes* 142, the background against
    which L diffuses the light of his poem. The darkness is
    appropriate both to the difficulty of the subject and to
    the imperceptibility of nature's processes at the atomic
    level.

138 multa . . . sit agendum: for *multa sint agenda*; see on
111 above. In this context, the unusual construction
appears designed as an example of the very point being
made.
novis: 'strange' or 'novel', applicable both to the use
of familiar words in unfamiliar meanings (L's most usual
solution where technical vocabulary is the problem) and
to the coining of metrically convenient words. The adj.
is answered by *novitatem* 139.

139 See introductory note above. The line exhibits a remarkable pattern: there is a degree of clash between ictus
and stress (Introduction V d) in each of the first five
feet and an unusual absence of coincidence. Such a
rhythm, which does not easily arise by accident, seems
designed to illustrate the difficulty of accommodating
the subject-matter to the medium; see A.W.H. Adkins,
Phoenix 31 (1977) 145-58.

140 me . . . efferre . . . suadet et inducit . . . vigilare:
-2 acc. and infin. replaces the noun clause with *ut* which
would be normal with the two main verbs in prose, where
suadere would also take a dat. of the person (though
me is appropriate to *inducit*); cf. Terence, *Hecyra* 481.
The construction is that normal with analogous verbs like
cogere or *iubere*; cf. the prolative infin. with *quaeres*
(see on *desciscere* 103 above).
virtus: 'excellence'; cf. the compliment paid to Memmius
in 26-7.
voluptas suavis amicitiae: 'the pleasure of your sweet
friendship'; not only was *voluptas* the Epicurean *summum
bonum*, but friendship was one of the two highest pleasures possible for the Epicurean (Introduction III). The
assonance of *suavis* with *suadet*, given prominence by the
initial placing of each word in its line, is based on an
etymological connection and appears 'meaningful' (Introduction V c), bringing out the central tenet of Epicurean
moral theory - that the prospect of something pleasant
(*suavis*) is automatically a spur to action (*suadet*).
vigilare: transitive, a poetic usage, denoting 'to spend
in wakefulness'.
serenas: figurative, not meteorological, with a hint of
oxymoron after *laborem* and *vigilare*. The allusion is to
mental calm (ἀταραξία) which is not only a prerequisite
for the philosophical study in which L is engaged, but
is in its turn fostered and deepened by the contemplation of the true nature of the universe, in which his
project involves him. Thus composition not only holds
out the prospect of Memmius' friendship, but allows him
to indulge in the other great Epicurean pleasure of
philosophical reflection; for his delight in his task,
cf. 924ff.

143 demum: emphasising *carmine* - 'indeed', 'what is more'. L
     has not only the problem of finding vocabulary to express
     himself clearly (*dictis*): he has the more difficult task
     of doing so metrically and poetically (*carmine*).

144 praepandere . . . convisere: both words, which contribute
  -5   to the sustained light image of the two lines (see on
     136-7 above), are rare compounds. L perhaps wishes to
     illustrate his predicament and one of his solutions by
     this resort to unfamiliar words. *penitus* further
     strengthens *convisere*, whose prefix is itself inten-
     sive, 'to see right deep down into'.

146-328 THE EXISTENCE OF PERMANENT, INVISIBLE CONSTITUENTS OF MATTER

This passage serves, in effect, as an introduction to matter, the first of the two components of the Lucretian universe, and contains a preliminary analysis which is not exclusively atomistic but would have been broadly acceptable to the Greek physicists in general, believing as they did that visible matter comprised permanent, invisible constituents, which they called 'beginnings' or 'seeds' and which may, metaphorically, conveniently be termed a 'substratum'. The atomic nature of matter is not yet stated or justified but is treated later at 483-920. Epicurus' much briefer analysis of matter in the *Letter to Herodotus* contains the same two stages (ch. 38-9 and 40-1): like L, he starts from common philosophical ground. At the same time, L sometimes in this passage introduces more exclusively Epicurean assumptions, most notably the existence of void (223) and the infinity of time (233).

L's approach to matter and its substratum is indirect: like Epicurus, *ad Hdt.* 38, he starts from the principles that nothing is created out of or destroyed into nothing (146-264). These principles, taken together, anticipate the modern theory of the Conservation of Matter, whose validity, now that matter and energy are regarded as convertible, has proved less far-reaching than was once thought. They were fundamental to the systems of the Atomists and the other Greek physicists alike (cf. e.g. Empedocles, Diels B.11 and 12; and Aristotle, *Metaphysics* 1062b, where the first principle is attributed to all the physicists); not only did they imply stability and regularity in nature and thus represent a recognition of natural law and a rejection of mythological ideas (as L implies in introducing the first of them at 146-58), but they also had important corollaries: if things were not created out of and destroyed into nothing, they could only be created out of and destroyed into the matter of which they were visibly composed. Creation and destruction could be seen to involve the aggregation and dissolution of component matter (just as growth and decay could be seen to involve its addition and loss). Though the details of these processes could not be observed, they must continue at a level below sense-perception, to prevent the component matter itself arising from or passing away into nothing. Further, if matter was not at some stage in its dissolution to be reduced to nothing, it must, at some stage below the level of sense-perception, be permanent.

Thus, to L, the alternative to creation out of nothing is creation out of 'seed' (159-60 and 205-7), the alternative to destruction into nothing destruction into component

bodies (215-6 and 248-9), and throughout the proofs of
the second principle, he stresses the permanence of the
'seed' (221, 236 and 245). The invisibility of the
substratum is implicit throughout his arguments for the
two principles and is expressly stated at 265ff., where
he proceeds to defend the assumption.

146-214 Things are not created out of nothing, but out
of the appropriate matter

146-158 Introduction

L here characteristically insists on the anti-theological
implications of his first principle and of the theories
which he is later to base upon it (*divinitus* 150; *opera
sine divum* 158). To L science and religion compete to
explain phenomena: the religious explanation, which he
regards as due merely to ignorance (153-4; cf. 5.1183-
7 and 6.54-5) is thus rendered superfluous by the scientific account. He does not here consider views which
would see the operation of scientific law against a background of some degree of divine guidance (e.g. the Stoic
theory of Divine Providence) but the argument at 5.110-
234, based on such considerations as the imperfection of
the world, contains an attempt to answer this sort of
view.

The transition to the passage is abrupt, since 136-45 are
not concerned with *terrorem* (146). Even if there is a
suspension of thought and *terrorem* refers to the general
idea of religious fear (the central subject of 62-135),
there is awkwardness in the new application of the metaphor of darkness, which stands for difficulty and imper-
ceptibility in 136-45 but for fear and ignorance in 146
(*tenebrasque*). The passage may originally have been
designed to follow 101 or 135, with *terrorem* picking up
religio or *terrificet* (133); even so it may contain a
stopgap element, for 146-8 recur in the introductions
to books 2, 3 and 6, always preceded by the simile of children afraid of the dark, after which the contrast between
literal and figurative light (147-8) is much more natural.

146 necessest . . . discutiant: the construction without *ut*,
 -8   familiar in prose, as also with e.g. *licet* (cf. 347
        and 870) and *velim*, may be regarded as a survival of
        parataxis, the subj. being in origin an independent
        jussive. This construction is frequent in L with
        necesse est (e.g. 269-70, 385-6, 389-90 and 339) as
        also is the acc. and infin. (e.g. 302, 506, 579 and 672).

lucida tela diei: a poetic elaboration of *radii solis*.
Not only does the sun 'rout' the darkness: the military
metaphor reminds us of the crusading role of the philosophy for which the sun is here an analogue; cf. the
combative Epicurus of 62-79.

naturae species ratioque: an approximation to Epicurus'
φυσιολογία (natural science); the phrase may be taken
as a hendiadys, 'the study (or 'explanation') of nature's
outward appearance'. It implies an antithesis between
nature's outward aspect and her inner (atomic) realities,
at the same time suggesting the two main instruments of
Epicurean scientific procedure, observation and reasoning on the basis of it (cf. Introduction III).

149 principium cuius: 'the beginning of this (study)'; the
reference, as in 157-8, is doubtless to the basic atomic
theory of books 1-2. This is itself to start (*exordia
sumet*) from the first principle of 150 (*hinc* anticipates
the acc. and infin. there). *cuius* is here monosyllabic,
the *i* being vocalised and the three vowels run together:
the licence is most unusual in hexameters (cf. Lucilius
640; *Catalepton* 9.35; and monosyllabic *eius* at Cicero,
Aratea 87), though it could have been avoided by trans-
posing the two opening words.

nobis: lit. 'for us', an 'ethic' dat.

150 The heavy rhythm, with five spondees, is appropriately
solemn for the enunciation of this basic truth; cf. e.g.
236.

gigni: a recurrent Lucretian term for the formation of all
types of compound, whether animal (where it is more
literal) or vegetable or inorganic (where it is more
figurative). A similar degree of metaphor is implicit
not only in the technical terms *materies* (= *mater*; see
on 171 below), *genitalia corpora* and *semina* (58-9),
but also in e.g. *nasci* 160 and *enascitur* 170, *genitali
concilio* 182-3 and *conceptum* 555.

divinitus: though his principle rules out spontaneous
generation by any agency, L characteristically specifies
its anti-theological implications; see introductory note
above.

151 quippe: introducing an explanation both of the choice of
starting point and of the necessity for the anti-theological emphasis of 150.

ita: deictic, 'as it does'.

omnis: the description of contemporary religious fear as
universal is something of an exaggeration (Introduction
III) but it is natural for an evangelist to overstate
the need for his message.

152 multa: i.e. *opera*: the noun is attracted inside the rel.
clause which follows.

fieri: here and at 154 'come about' (of processes; cf.
129): contrast 158-9 below.

153 nulla ratione: 'in no way', but there is also an opposi-
tion between *ratione* and the similarly placed *divino
numine* in 154, which suggests 'not . . . on any rational
basis'.

154 ac: sc. acc. *quae* from *quorum* 153; for the omission of
the second rel., see on *haec* 60 above.

156 quod sequimur: 'the object of our search', defined in the
two indirect questions which follow: L seeks (i) the real
source of the creation of things (the imperceptible 'seeds'
of 159-328, which are shown at 483-920 to be atoms); (ii)
the manner of the formation of atomic compounds (the
principles of which are set out in book 2).
iam . . . inde: reinforcing *tum*: 'then, as the next step
thereafter'.

158 quaeque: the neut. pl. is used synonymously with the sing.
res quaeque 157; the reference is strictly to each type
of thing; see on *cuique* 76 above.
fiant: here 'come to be', synonymous with *gigni* and *creari*,
as *nam . . . fierent* in 159 shows; contrast 152 and 154.
opera sine divum: though *sine* here follows its abl., the
order is natural, since *divum* approximates to an agreeing adj., *divina*.

159-214 Proofs

L's six arguments for his first principle all depend in the
first instance on an appeal to experience: each stresses an
aspect of the regularity and uniformity observable in the
processes of birth and growth, which can be seen to take
place only in a restricted number of situations and circum-
stances. This part of the argument is inductive: the proof
that nature is uniform in this respect depends on an appeal
to observed examples and absence of contradictory evidence.
The fixed patterns of birth and growth are, in L's view,
only explicable on the assumption that birth and growth are
not spontaneous but depend on 'fixed seed', i.e. on the
aggregation and addition of particles of the appropriate
material in each case. It should be remembered throughout
these arguments that for the Epicurean birth and growth
were closely analogous, both being aspects of a single,
continuous process.

In arguments (i), (iii) and (v) L puts the implications of
the rival hypothesis first, the facts second, while in (ii),
(iv) and (vi) this order is inverted: the alternate arrangement lends both variety and continuity to the sequence of

proofs. Similar patterning is exploited at 551-98, in
proofs (iii-vi) of the atomic nature of matter.

159-173 Proof (i) There is a fixed place for birth

159 The couplet exactly reproduces Epicurus' only argument for
-60 the principle in *ad Hdt.* (38 *ad fin.*).
159 **fierent**: as subject, sc. *res*.
   omnibu': like Ennius and Cicero (*Aratea*), L sometimes
   elides the *s* of a final short syllable in *-is* or *-us*
   before a consonant, though his forty or so examples
   (which frequently, as here, provide a fifth foot dactyl)
   represent a much smaller proportion than Ennius exhibits.
   This elision, regular in Plautus, had become old-fash-
   ioned when L wrote and is generally avoided by the
   Alexandrian school of poets. It indicates a weak pronunciation of the *s* in ordinary speech: according to
   Cicero (*Orator* 161) the dropping of *s* in final *-us* had
   once been considered a refined pronunciation but was now
   (45 B.C.) thought rather provincial (*subrusticum*). The
   marking of these elisions in the text has been adopted
   for purposes of convenience rather than of authenticity.

160 **nil**: most naturally taken as nom., antithetical with
   omne genus, though it could be adverbial acc. with
   egeret (cf. 5.263) leaving *omne genus* as subject of
   both verbs, which would be closer to the Epicurean
   original.
   semine: generic sing., as e.g. at 185; cf. English 'seed'.
   The term here serves to introduce the concept of source
   material, but is not yet restricted to the imperceptible
   'seeds' of matter and is here also applicable to the
   observable seed of plants and animals. The argument thus
   contains an appeal to experience: it can actually be observed that things are not created from nothing, but
   that seed is required; observable seed is the starting
   point in experience for the concept of imperceptible
   seed. Similarly, *genitalia corpora* (167) is a natural
   term for any sort of generative material, whether perceptible or not. But by the end of the passage L is
   beginning to think of the source material in terms of
   its imperceptible components, as *corpora prima* 171
   suggests, and in the following proofs *semen* refers more
   exclusively to the imperceptible 'seeds'.

161 **mare**: archaic by-form of the abl., replacing *mari*.
   primum: introducing the first illustration; the catalogue
   continues to 166 without further enumerative words. L
   opens with the most startlingly grotesque of his examples,
   whereby animals would not need parents at all (161-2),
   moving on a *fortiori* to cases where animals would produce
   the wrong species and trees the wrong fruit (163-6).

posset: potential subj., as are all the verbs to 168,
tracing the consequences of the hypothesis under
attack. The sing. is appropriate to the nearest of
the three subjects.

162 squamigerum: gen. pl. (cf. 2.343 and 1083), in the older
second decl. form (see on *divum* 1 above); the adj. is
used as a noun, as at 372. Both the periphrasis and
the compound (cf. on *navigerum* 3 above) lend an archaic
note.
et: L occasionally, like other Roman poets, uses *et* or *-que*
in a list which otherwise exhibits asyndeton, a combination unusual in Latin; cf. 315, 334, 455, 598 and 715.
erumpere: appropriate to birth from eggs, not to birth from
the sky, sarcastically pointing the absurdity of the consequences of creation from nothing.

163 pecudes: i.e. tame animals, as at 14.
genus omne ferarum: in asyndeton, and antithesis, with the
first group of subjects.

164 incerto partu: i.e. there would be no fixity of species:
wild and tame animals would give birth to one another
(cf. trees with the wrong fruit 165-6).
culta ac deserta tenerent: i.e. domestic and wild animals
would not be confined to their usual habitat, a consequence of *incerto partu*.

165 arboribus constare: 'remain constant on the trees'; *constare*
is here stronger than *esse* and *arboribus* is L's favourite dat. of possession or reference; cf. *rebus* in 168
below.

166 mutarentur: sc. *fructus*; the force of *idem* is not carried
on.
omnes: sc. *arbores*.

167 As birth would not depend on the appropriate source material
-8 (as there would not be *genitalia corpora* for each type of
thing), how could there be a fixed pattern of birth (how
could each type have a *mater certa*)?
quippe, ubi: 'for, when'. Usually in L (cf. 182, 242, 617
and 990) the words go together, 'seeing that', appending
a reason for a preceding assertion (cf. prose *quippe qui*
+ subj.). But here (as at 4.771 and 925; 6.854) the words
are to be taken separately: otherwise there would be a
harsh absence of connective, and the *quippe ubi* clause
would precede, instead of following, what it explains.
The subj. *essent* is potential (see on 161 above).
genitalia corpora: cf. 58, and see on *semine* 160 above.
cuique: implying each species, as also at 169, 171, 191,
206 and 213, since all the proofs concern classes of
compound; see on 76 above.

mater: partly metaphorical, insofar as it applies to the
general location of animal births (e.g. *mare, terra*),
vegetable 'birth', and even the origin of inorganic
compounds.
consistere: like *constare* 165, stronger than *esse*; the
verb reinforces the idea of fixity in *certa*.

169 at nunc: 'but as it is', introducing the Epicurean account.

170 enascitur: the subject, *quidque*, is attracted inside the
-1 local rel. clause; cf. 16.
inde . . . materies ubi . . .: 'from the place where its
matter and first bodies reside', an elucidation of *mater*
168: scientifically speaking, 'mother' = 'source of
matter'. The 'word-play' *mater* / *materies* is meaningful
(Introduction V c) and reinforces the point: the words
are in fact etymologically connected. Elsewhere (e.g.
2.998ff.; 5.795-6 and 821-2) L brings out the meaningful correspondence between *mater* and *terra*, regarding
the earth indeed as mother in that it contained the atoms
of all the world's compounds (see on 250-1 below). *mater,
materies* and *terra* were thus interrelated concepts, and
the verbal similarities mirrored their relationship.

172 hac re: causal abl., 'therefore'; a second and closely
related reason is appended in 173 to amplify the explanation.

173 secreta facultas: 'a unique capacity', to produce the
appropriate species. *secreta*, lit. 'separate', like
certis, is from root *cernere*; the combination suggests
the sense 'determined' and 'separately determined',
further emphasising the key word in the argument (*certa*
168, *certis* 169, *certis* 173; contrast *incerto* 164) and
further underlining the rigidity of nature's patterns.

174-183 Proof (ii) There is a fixed time for birth

174 cur: L is fond of adding life and urgency to an argument
-5 by presenting it in the form of a rhetorical question;
cf. e.g. 167-8 above, 199-204, 225-31, 358-9 and 378-
80 below.
calore: sc. *aestatis*, lending poetic variety to the list
of seasons.
fundi: 'pour forth', 'burst out' (lit. 'are poured forth',
suggesting profusion; cf. *fetus fundunt* 351). There is
an element of zeugma, since with *rosam* and *frumenta* the
allusion is to the arrival of buds or blooms and fattened
ears, with *vitis* (which themselves appear in spring) to
that of the grapes.
suadente: with all three abls.
videmus: the argument throughout proceeds from experience;

cf. 208 and *manifestum est* 188.

176 The prose order would be *si non quia, cum certa semina*
-7 *rerum suo tempore . . .*; for *si non quia*, 'if it is not
    because', cf. 203.
    certa: like *suo*, emphatically placed; the fixed time of
    birth must imply fixed seeds.
    suo . . . tempore: i.e. at the appropriate, favourable
    time; the prenatal processes (*semina confluxerunt*) have
    their proper time, as does generation itself (*patefit*).
    The *dum* clause (178-9) specifies the time for the latter,
    balancing *suo tempore*. The idea is opposed to 181 and to
    tempore iniquo 183.

178 adsunt: with the overtone of favouring, lending aid, which
-9 suggests a personification of the seasons; cf. *tempestas
    indulget* 805 and *arridet* 2.32.
    vivida: 'quickened' - full of literal life.
    teneras: denoting vulnerability as well as youth.

180 quod si: 'but if'; see on *quod contra* 82 above.
    fierent: as subject sc. *res* (i.e. vegetable produce
    in general) from 179.
    subito: i.e. without the prior agglomeration of *semina*
    described in 176-7.

181 incerto spatio: 'at irregular intervals'; for *spatium* =
    tempus, cf. 184 and 234.
    alienis: i.e. inappropriate and unfavourable, the exact
    opposite of *suo* 176.

182 quippe ubi: 'seeing that' (contrast 167, where see note).
-3 *forent* (= *essent*; L makes frequent use of this metrically
    convenient alternative form) and *possent* are potential
    subjs.
    genitali concilio: 'from a birth-giving concourse';
    concilium is a regular Lucretian term for (i), as here,
    the formation of a compound (= Epicurus' σύγκρισις);
    (ii) a compound itself (= Epicurus' ἄθροισμα). The
    technical usage implies a metaphor from an assembly of
    persons and may have been suggested by the latter Greek
    term. Like *primordia*, *concilium* does not in itself pre-
    suppose the atomic account of the assembling 'seeds';
    cf. 772, where it is used in describing Pluralistic
    theory, which took a completely different view of the
    source material.
    tempore iniquo: instrumental rather than temporal abl.

184-191 Proof (iii) There is a fixed time for growth

184 augendis rebus: 'for things to increase'; for the final dat.,
    see on 24 above. It is here a variant on the *ad* con-

struction of 185, which gives a scientific account of
what *augendis rebus* involves.

spatio . . . usus: 'need of time'; *usus* is a variant on
opus, common in Plautus and found also in Ciceronian
prose; cf. 219.

185 seminis ad coitum: 'to allow for the coition of seed'.
Growth, like birth (176-7), must in reality involve the
gradual aggregation of seed: proof (iii) is the application of proof (ii) to the second stage of the birth-
growth process.

186 iuvenes: i.e. mature men, making a stronger point than
would *adulescentes*.

187 e terraque: L occasionally postpones -*que*, where a preposition and its case form a unit and make the arrangement natural; cf. 542, 674, 725, 757 and 1059.
exorta: 'once they had arisen', i.e. after birth.
salirent: denoting accelerated growth.
arbusta: properly 'plantations', but in L a regular metrical equivalent, adopted also by Virgil, for the inadmissible ārbŏrēs, though not in the dat. and abl.
where ārbŏrĭbus can be used.

189 ut par est, semine certo: 'as is natural, since their seed
is fixed'; the effect of *semine certo*, whether the abl.
is of source (with *crescunt*) or circumstantial, is to
justify *ut par est*: growth is naturally gradual, for it
depends on the availability of appropriate seed.

190 A new point: growth is true to type (whereas the hypothesis
-1 under attack would result in fluctuation of species).
Fixity of species during growth, like its gradual nature,
indicates that it must involve the addition of fixed seed.
The new point amounts to an application of proof (i),
which concerned birth, to growth.
crescentes: sc. *res* either from the general context or from
omnia 188; the latter, though a bolder *constructio ad
sensum* than the converse (for which see on *perempta* 57
above) and without exact Lucretian parallel, is not for
these reasons impossible; cf. on the unique construction
with *totas* 352 below.
quidque: i.e. each species (cf. *genus* 190); see on *cuique*
167 above.

*192-8 Proof (iv) Birth and growth demand a fixed pattern of
nutrition*

192 huc accedit uti: a common Lucretian formula of transition
to a new argument or point; cf. 215, 565 and 753-5.

praeterea, porro, denique and *postremo*, introducing proofs
(ii), (iii), (v) and (vi) in this sequence, are no less
characteristic.
certis imbribus anni: i.e. rain at the usual, fixed, times
of year; the gen. is of a subjective type, in that the
year provides the rains.

193 laetificos: the earth's produce gladdens animal life; the
adj. thus prepares for the topic of animal nutrition in
the next two lines. The compound (see on *navigerum* 3
above) is found in Ennius.

194 cibo: abl. of separation with *secreta*.
natura animantum: periphrastic for *animantes*; see on 131
above.

195 propagare: in origin, a term from arboriculture (cf. *stirps*,
= 'scion'), just as *fetus*, used of vegetable produce in
193, can also denote animal progeny. The interchangeable
terms reinforce the parallel between vegetable and animal
life (192-3 and 194-5). For the long *o*, cf. 5.850; it
is more usually short, as at 20 and 280 and in the noun
propago 42. The quantity of the prefix fluctuated, even
though by Augustan times it was normally fixed as long
or short in any given word.
vitamque tueri: 'preserve their life', i.e. that of the
individual and of the species: the former gives an allusion to the nutrition essential for growth. The necessity of nutrition shows that both birth and growth depend
on the availability of appropriate seed, contained respectively in *imbribus* 192 and *cibo* 194. Though L places
the main emphasis on birth, the argument is equally
applicable to both processes.

196 In drawing the conclusion, that nothing can be created
-8   without seed (198), L adds the new point that different
types of compound may have many types of seed in common,
thus qualifying the picture so far suggested, of the
seed as fixed according to the type of compound (e.g.
191). The qualification is prompted by the mention of
rain, which provides 'seed' for all vegetable species,
and of the food of animals, which may be the same for
different species. The point is explained much more
fully in the course of 803-29 (cf. 897-914), where it
emerges (817ff.; cf. 907ff.) that what is unique in any
species of compound is the proportion, arrangement and
motions of the various types of component atom. The
highly compressed, not to say cryptic, summary of 196-
7 may well have been composed after the completion of
the book and never adequately expanded.
ut . . . putes: 'so that you should suppose'; the consecutive clause is also prescriptive.

verbis elementa: sc. *multis multa communia esse*. L's
favourite comparison between the *primordia* (the *corpora*
of 196) in compounds and the letters in words is developed at greater length at 823ff. and 912ff., cited above;
cf. also 2.688ff. and 1013ff. The analogy, which is
probably inherited from the Atomists, is close: words
have some letters in common just as different types of
compound have different types of atom in common; the
number of letters in the alphabet, and so of possible
words, is limited, as is the number of types of atom
and of types of atomic compound; but each letter may
be used an indefinite number of times, just as there is
an infinite stock of atoms of each given type. But, as
pointed out at 827-9, the atoms have more resources (e.g.
motion) to provide variety, whereas letters admit varieties of combination and arrangement alone. *elementa*
(cf. Greek στοιχεῖα) primarily denotes 'rudiments' (cf.
81) and can not only, as here, denote 'letters' but
is one of L's technical terms for the *primordia* (e.g.
2.393, 411 and 463). The double sense, exploited at
828 and 913, reinforces the link between letters and
'seeds' and further explains L's fondness for the analogy:
see also Introduction V c. The alliteration and assonance of 196-7 illustrate the point, drawing attention to
the common letters, most conspicuously *p*, *m*, *c*, *v* and *u*,
and to the repeated combination *mult-*; cf. on 814-6, 823-
6 and 912-4 below.
principiis: for *primōrdiĭs*: see on 55 above.

199-207 Proof (v) Growth has fixed limits

199 denique: 'again': most commonly used by L (contrast 17,
76 and 278) in enumerating arguments, not necessarily
the last, for which *postremo* (208; cf. 250) often serves:
denique again introduces the penultimate argument at 238.
homines tantos: like the giants of mythology, whose reality
is discounted.

200 The alliteration, with a single initial letter (*p*, *v* and *m*)
 -2 predominating in each of three successive lines, is remarkably unsophisticated for L, and acquires in the
context a derisive air, as if mocking the absurdity of the
fantastic feats featured.

200 qui . . . possent: consecutive rel.
per vada: 'through its shallows', as they were to the giants.

202 Not only size, but longevity is limited.
vitalia . . . saecla: i.e. generations of living men;
vitalia yields a characteristic, paradoxical, type of
word-play ('outlive the living'); cf. e.g. *casta / inceste*
(98), *latitantia cernunt* (642; cf. 889-90).

203 **rebus . . . gignundis:** with *reddita*, the dat. denotes
-4   the indirect object as much as purpose (cf. on 24 above):
     so too at 552 and 577f. *reddita*, as often, here denotes
     'duly given' and so 'assigned' rather than 'given back'
     (cf. 209).
     e qua . . . oriri: 'and it is determined what can arise
     from that matter' (*e qua* belongs inside the indirect
     question, with *oriri*), i.e. the component seed of men
     is such as to preclude the birth of supermen, like
     long-lived giants.

205 These lines form an appropriate conclusion to all six
-7   proofs, not just to (v): proof (vi), which is closer in
     thought to (iv) than to (v), may well be a later, slightly
     misplaced addition, suggested by the composition of
     5.206ff., from which two lines recur.

207 **aeris in teneras . . . auras:** a piece of poetic adornment
     to round off the conclusion; *teneras* here denotes 'soft',
     'yielding'.
     possint: a 'prospective' subj., combining consecutive and
     purposive force.
     proferrier: the archaic passive infin. in *-ier* for *-i* is
     generally used by L to provide a fifth foot dactyl. As
     with the *-ai* gen., Virgil's sparing imitations reflect
     that it could impart archaic dignity, as well as being
     metrically convenient. It recurs at 395, 647, 710,
     796, 802, 905, 1059 and 1088.

208-214 Proof (vi) Fixed conditions favour birth and growth

209 **manibus:** dat. with *reddere*: the earth duly rewards the hands
     which have tilled it.

210 **videlicet:** here in its root sense (*videre licet*), hence the
     archaic construction, found also in Plautus, with dep-
     endent acc. and infin.; cf. *scire licet* (uncontracted
     for *scilicet*) with the same construction at 679,
     860 and 894.

211 **fecundas . . . ortus:** repeated at 5.210-11, where *fetus*
-2   is supplied as object of *cimus*. Here, with *primordia*
     as object, *ad ortus* indicates either 'to rise' or more
     probably 'to the births (of the earth's produce)', but
     not 'to their own birth', for the *primordia* themselves
     are birthless and deathless. *fecundas* here indicates
     richness in *primordia* which are assimilable by the
     fetus and are released by tillage.
     subigentes, often applied to the soil, denotes lit.
     'turning up from beneath' but the military sense of
     subjugation is also metaphorically appropriate; cf.
     Virgil, *Georgics* 1.125.

      cimus: fourth conj. forms of this normally second conj.
verb appear also in other poets (on such fluctuation,
see Introduction V a): its compounds are regularly
fourth conj.

213 **quaeque:** i.e. all the different types of produce.

214 **multo fieri meliora:** i.e. improve greatly on their actual
performance when uncultivated. L took a melancholy
view of the earth's productivity even after tillage:
cf. the corresponding passage in book 5 and 2.1160ff.
The contrast between the real and the more desirable
hypothetical situation is not without its wry humour.
multo is not essential to the argument: without *primordia,*
any improvement would be purely random and vary in degree,
but L selects the case which provides the maximum contrast
with the harsh facts of reality.

      **215-264 Things are not destroyed into nothing, but into
their component matter**

Of the four arguments which support this principle, (i)
and (iii) are closely connected, as are (ii) and (iv).
The ABAB arrangement provides alternation between more
technical discussion and material with more obvious
poetic potential.

215-224 Statement and proof i

On the rival view, destruction would be (a) random, in
that it would not require the external force (*vis*), by
which, as can be inferred from experience, it is always
occasioned: there is here a broad correspondence with the
arguments about random birth (159-83). It would be (b)
instantaneous, whereas in fact it can be observed in most
cases that it requires a varying degree of time; cf. the
points about the gradual accumulation of seed before birth
(176-7) and during growth (186-9).

215 In denying that things are destroyed into nothing, L places
-6   his positive account of what happens at destruction first.
Regarding his first principle as established, he uses its
implications, the existence of imperceptible particles
(*corpora*), in stating the second.
   quidque in sua corpora: 'each thing into its own bodies';
as is usual in this collocation, *sua* refers to *quidque,*
even though *quidque* is not the subject.
   dissoluat: quadrisyllabic, the *v* being vocalised, as at
223; see on *suemus* 60 above.

217 **e cunctis partibus:** in all its parts, i.e. entirely.

mortale . . . partibus is a variant on 'capable of destruction into nothing'.

218 res quaeque: again strictly 'each class of thing' (see on 76 above); objects are more or less durable according to their category.

219 enim: the postponement to fifth position, unusual in L, helps to emphasise *vi*.
quae: introducing a consecutive rel. clause, as at 222-3.

220 discidium: L's regular term for atomic dissolution (Epicurus' διάλυσις and διάκρισις) but, like all his terminology at this stage, it fits other views of the 'seeds', not just the atomic one. The root meaning is 'rending asunder': the term is normally applied to persons and is technical for 'divorce'. As with its opposite, *concilium* (see on 183 above), its Lucretian sense thus involves metaphor and personification. *discidium parere* is an oxymoron; cf. *stragemque propagant* 280 and *leti fabricator* 3.472.
nexus: 'fastenings', a metaphor from tying (cf. 240 and 244) but, as with *discidium* = divorce, there may also be a hint of legal metaphor from the prose sense 'obligation'.

221 quod nunc: a variation on *nunc* (110) and *at nunc* (169); on *quod*, see on 82 above.
aeterno: the first statement of the permanence of the 'seeds', implied for the ancient physicists by the second principle (see introductory note to 146-328) but argued for more systematically by L at 483-634.

222 The *vis* may destroy the compound rapidly by external im-
-3 pact or more gradually by disruptive infiltration. The rapid destruction differs from the sudden disappearance which would follow from the rival view at 218: the prefix of *diverberet* shows that it involves disruption into parts (which is normally, up to a point, observable).
intus: here expressing motion into, for the usual *intro*; cf. e.g. 2.711, 3.171, Tacitus, *Histories* 1.35 and (despite his criticism of the usage at 1.5.50) Quintilian 11.3.99.
per inania: an anticipation of the existence of void, which the other physicists would not generally have accepted; see on 329ff. below.

224 videri: 'to be witnessed', not 'to seem'. Outside L, the true passive sense, with or without a dependent infinitive, is comparatively rare; see on 262 below and cf. 270, 308, 364, 532, 637, 776, 889, 891, 935, 960f. and 998.

225-237 Proof ii

L here develops the only argument for the principle advanced by Epicurus in *ad Hdt*. (39), where he claims that, were matter annihilated, all things would have perished, since that into which they had been broken up would not exist. L makes the point by asking how the rival view can account for the constant re-creation and replenishment of the visible world, regarding the obvious rejoinder 'from nothing' as precluded by 159-214: matter must at some level be permanent, to allow for its re-employment which alone can explain the world's constant replenishment. Essentially the same proof is presented, from a different angle, at 540-550 in the second stage of L's analysis of matter (see on 237 below).

225   I.e. if things were destroyed into nothing. L varies his
-6   expression of the rival view with skill and poetic
       resource; cf. 217. *aetas* is subject of *perimit* às well
       as of *amovet*; *quaecumque* . . . *aetas* is the object of
       perimit.

227   genus generatim: the characteristic assonance and the
       repetition of *generatim* in 229 emphasise (i) the size
       of the problem (the re-creation of all the different
       genera must be explained, (ii) the fixity and regular-
       ity of the processes of re-creation, a reminder that
       it cannot take place from nothing (cf. 159-73).
       in lumina vitae: cf. *in luminis oras* 22 etc.

228   redducit . . . redductum: for the archaic form of the
       prefix, see on *religione* 63 above. The idiomatic re-
       petition links the topics of animal birth and nutrition
       (the latter raising the topic of vegetable birth), and
       again underlines the scale of the problem.
       Venus: here the *Venus physica* of 2-20 (which the language
       of the whole sentence strongly echoes); cf. the person-
       ifications of *natura* (224) and *aetas* (225-6 and 233).
       Friedländer 29 suggests that *Venus* here meaningfully
       echoes *genus + vita* (cf. Introduction V c).
       daedala: cf. on 7 above.

230   mare: object of *suppeditant*.
       ingenui fontes: i.e. springs in the sea-bed, commonly
       supposed by the ancients to be one of the sea's sources.
       externaque longe: 'far beyond it', in antithesis with
       ingenui; the adverb serves as a reminder of the length
       of the great rivers, and so as an additional indication
       of the vast quantity of water whose replenishment has to
       be explained.

231   pascit: a metaphor developed at 5.523-5, where the heavenly
       bodies are pictured as animals grazing. The poetic image

is scientifically satisfactory insofar as the heavenly bodies were for Epicurus denser concentrations of the same fiery matter that comprised the upper air. The description is appropriate not only to the stars but to sun and moon, which in book 5 *sidera* can include.
For the threefold division of the world (227-31), see on 2-3 above; for the pattern of three rhetorical questions of decreasing length and increasing urgency (here with anaphora of *unde*), cf. e.g. Juvenal 1.51-2 and the similar pattern at 851-3 below.

232 **debet:** frequently used by L of logical, causal, or scientific necessity, whereas in classical prose it tends to be restricted to moral obligation. While providing variety with *necesse* or the gerundive and often affording a more convenient construction, L's usage perhaps often carries the suggestion that things have a duty to obey nature's laws. Normally *debet*, not the infin. (*consumpse* 233), would be in the past tense but the logical sense of the verb makes the tense-pattern natural.

233 **infinita aetas:** the assumption of the infinity of time (for Epicurus a necessary consequence of the indestructibility of atoms and void) recurs at 550, 557-8, 578, 991 and 1004: here it strengthens the argument by allowing a limitless span for destruction into nothing to have been completed. But its omission in Epicurus, *ad Hdt.* 39 reflects that the point is not indispensable.
consumpse: a striking contraction of *consumpsisse*; cf. *abstraxe* 3.650, *protraxe* 5.1159, and *confluxet* (= *confluxisset*) at 987; see also on *suemus* 60 above.
The slow, spondaic rhythm of the line is appropriate to the description of limitless time. The addition of the pleonastic *diesque* adds, if not to the sense, to the long-drawn-out effect. The use of the synonymous *eo spatio* and *anteacta aetate* works similarly in 234, where the synizesis in *anteacta* and the fourfold elision (resulting in five cases of a vowel merging into the next and the absence of a main caesura) mirrors the continuity described. Parallel effects recur in the similar context of 557-8.

234 I.e. if the matter from which the world has now been re-
-5 plenished existed in the past - the only conceivable hypothesis.
fuere: 'there existed'; sc. *ea* as antecedent of the rel. clause, alluding to the 'seeds'.
haec rerum . . . summa: 'this sum of things', i.e. our world, though the existence of others is not yet stressed; the plurality of worlds is introduced at 2.1023ff. *rerum summa*, by contrast, normally denotes the universe (or its contents); cf. 333, 502, 619, 756 and 1008.
refecta: i.e. in its present replenished state.

236 immortali . . . naturā praeditā: antithetical with *mortali corpore* (232) - the 'seeds' must be indestructible to have survived the test of time.

237 L here deduces his second principle from the permanence of the 'seeds', whereas in the related passage at 540-50 this pattern is inverted, and their permanence deduced from the second principle. Though this exposes his argument to the charge of circularity, the two ideas are mutually complementary, and both are based on the same crucial premiss, the continuing existence and constant replenishment of the visible world.

238-249 Proof iii

This amounts to a refinement on the appeal to experience implied in proof (i): it can be inferred inductively from observation not merely that a force is required for destruction, but also that the force differs according to the texture of the compound: on the rival hypothesis, destruction, as already argued, would not require a *vis* at all; it would certainly not require a special *vis* in each case.

238 vulgo: stronger than the root sense ('commonly') - 'universally', 'indiscriminately', as at 906.

239 teneret: 'held them together'.

240 I.e. more or less tightly fastened together. *indupedita* agrees with *materies*, and is a favourite Lucretian term for the 'entanglement' within a tightly knit atomic compound. For the archaic form, see on *indugredi* 82 above. *inter se* (whether *se* is sing. or pl.) is possible because *materies* is a collective noun for the 'seeds'; cf. 2.67. In atomic theory, the differing degrees of 'entanglement' depended on the atoms' shapes, and the distances of their trajects.

241 leti satis esset causa: 'would be a sufficient cause of death'; *leti* is figurative insofar as the allusion includes inanimate compounds. The adverb *satis* is here virtually adjectival with *causa*.

242 'Seeing that there would be no particles endowed with
-3 eternal body (i.e. no indestructible 'seeds') whose interweaving (to form a compound) an appropriate force in each case would need to unloosen'.
aeterno corpore: abl. of quality with *nulla*.
vis . . . quaeque: further elucidated by *satis acris vis . . . pro textura cuiusque reperta* 246-7, 'a force which proves keen enough in proportion to (i.e. to destroy) the texture of each class of thing'.

deberet: of causal necessity; see on 232 above.

244 The facts of the situation, presented in reverse order
-5 from 239-40.
  inter se . . . nexus: 'mutual fastenings'. L's attach-
  ment of prepositional phrases direct to nouns is sometimes bold: cf. 283 and 5.300-1. The idiom is common
  in Latin only (i) with *erga* or (ii) where the phrase
  is enclosed between a noun and agreeing adj.
  constant: = *sunt*.

247 obeat: prospective subj. - L here writes from the point
  of view of an experimenter (cf. *reperta*) waiting for the
  right *vis* to turn up; contrast *donec* + indic. in an apparently identical context at 222.
  textura: a Lucretian technical term for the degree of
  intricacy in an atomic compound, based, like *contextus*
  243, on the metaphor of weaving.

248 The two aspects of L's proposition are presented in re-
  -9 verse order from 215-6.
  discidio: see on 220 above.
  corpora materiai: a slight variant on the terminology so
  far used for the 'seeds'; cf. 552, 565f., 916f. and
  997.

250-264 Proof iv

L now gives a less theoretical demonstration of the transfer
of matter to replenish the world than in proof (ii), appealing to the cycle of vegetable and animal nutrition and generation, where it can be observed that the destruction of
one thing is regularly followed by the production or growth
of another: the inference is that matter is transferred.
The processes involved have already been considered from the
point of view of creation at 192ff. The poetic felicities
of the passage, which, like proof (ii), contains echoes of
the prayer to Venus, make it a fitting conclusion to the
demonstration of the two basic principles, but the details
of the description are not purely ornamental and consistently
reinforce the scientific argument.

250 Rain perishes, but (as a result) vegetable life
  -3 flourishes.

250 pereunt: i.e. as rains, but their 'seeds' are transferred.
  -1 ubi . . . praecipitavit: an invocation of the mythological
  picture of a mystic union (ἱερὸς γάμος) between father sky
  and mother earth, a union responsible for all life - to L,
  a simple enough allegory for the productive effect of rain-
  fall, developed more fully at 2.991-8, and used not simply
  for poetic reasons, but also to illustrate the truth which

a myth may contain. It had been exploited not only
by the poets - e.g. Aeschylus, *Danaides* (*TGF* 44);
Euripides, *Chrysippus* (*TGF* 839) - but by philosophers
like Anaxagoras, who influenced the Euripidean accounts.
L more often treats the mother-earth half of the relationship, where he sees embodied the scientific truths that
the earth contains the matter from which all the compounds
of our world are formed and, at the original birth of
living creatures, was literally mother (5.805-15); cf.
2.589ff. (where the myth of Cybele the Earth-Mother is
rationalised), 5.257-60, and on 170-1 above. Other philosophers sometimes developed the sky-father picture; cf.
5.318-23, where the Stoic theory that the sky's fiery
ether was the basic substance of creation is the probable
object of attack.

253 arboribus: possessive dat.
    ipsae: i.e. the trees as a whole.

254 The second illustration in the cycle: vegetable life
-61 perishes (consumed as food), but (as a result) animals
    (i) grow (ii) reproduce and feed their kind.

254 hinc . . . porro: 'hence in turn', whether *hinc*, emphatically
    repeated at 255, 257 and 259, refers to the original union
    of 250-1, or to the produce of 252-3 (a later stage in the
    same cycle).

255 laetas: 'fruitful', the same 'agricultural' sense as at 257,
    14 and 23.
    pueris: i.e. with a new generation: cf. *novis avibus* 256
    and *nova proles* 259.
    florere: 'blossom': as with *laetas*, the metaphor reinforces
    the parallel with the earlier stage of vegetable growth
    to which the word is literally appropriate.
    videmus: the argument once more depends on an appeal to
    experience.

256 frondiferasque: cf. on 18 above. As with *pabula laeta* 257
    and *teneras per herbas* 260, the richness of the background
    not only harmonises with that of the animal foreground, but
    exemplifies a new stage of vegetable growth in the constant-
    ly recurring cycle.

257 pecudes: farm-animals, as at 14 and 163.
    pingui: cf. Virgil, *Georgics* 3.124 for this use of the neut.
    adj. as a noun; the abl. is instrumental with *fessae*. The
    animals' excess fat, like the swollen udders of 259, results
    from the abundant reappearance of the 'seeds' of their
    food.

258 corpora deponunt: 'lie down'.

candens lacteus umor: unlike the Augustan poets, L admits
double adjs. unlinked by *et* but they are not usually
parallel. *lacteus umor* is a typical Lucretian periphrasis
for *lac* and the adj. does the work of a gen. of material;
cf. *uncus ferreus vomer* (313-4) and see on 945-7 below;
contrast 491 and 557-8.

261 lacte . . . novellas: 'their tender young hearts intoxi-
cated with neat milk'; for the construction, cf. on 13
above. *mero* suggests a comparison of the young creatures
as they gambol unsteadily (*artubus infirmis . . . lasciva
. . . ludit* 260-1) with a tipsy reveller. *novellas* explains their susceptibility (they are still unused to the
stuff). The diminutive, common in agricultural language,
is also a mark of Lucretian affection.

262 Conclusion. The cycle of life and death referred to here,
-4 to which L frequently returns, is a philosophical idea
which lends itself more obviously to poetic treatment
than many of his more technical topics and which inspires
some of his most memorable lines, e.g. 2.77-9, 3.971 and
5.258-60.

262 quaecumque videntur: 'whatsoever things are observed' (=
τὰ φαινόμενα); cf. *quaecumque videmus* 542. For the passive
sense of *videri*, see on 224 above. To supply *perire* out of
penitus pereunt ('things which seem to perish') is intolerably awkward: nor can *penitus perire* be supplied, since
L would have denied that compounds seem to leave no trace.

263 alid ex alio: the archaism for *aliud* is used by L only in
this combination, in which it is metrically convenient;
cf. 407 and 1115. Catullus (66.28) has the masc. *alis*.

264 morte adiută alienā: 'assisted by the death of something
else'.

265-328 The assumption of invisible 'seeds' of matter is
perfectly feasible

L here meets the objection that his substratum of matter is
invisible, as has been implied throughout the previous arguments. While such a criticism might have been levelled
against any of the Greek physicists, according to whom
matter was at least not always what it appeared to be, it
has an especial relevance for the Epicureans in view of their
insistence on sense-perception as the main criterion of knowledge: in this case they relied entirely on their second
criterion, reasoning on the basis of experience (Introduction
III). L meets the difficulty with an orthodox appeal to
analogy, citing a series of other bodies which must be agreed

to exist despite their invisibility. These comprise bodies
(i) of wind (271-97), (ii) perceived by senses other than
sight (298-304), (iii) involved in condensation and evaporation (305-10), (iv) gradually worn away from objects
(311-21), (v) involved in growth and decay (322-7): if
these invisible bodies exist, invisible 'seeds' can exist
as well. In these examples the 'seeds' are thought of as
further below the level of sense-perception than the invisible bodies, which themselves comprise groups of 'seeds';
cf. 276 and 298-304, where the invisible bodies can move
senses other than sight, which, according to Lucretian
atomic theory, single 'seeds' (in his analysis, atoms)
could not do.

265 nunc age: a formula perhaps influenced by Empedocles and
indicative of the urgency of L's didacticism; it is used
in moving on to a new topic; cf. 921 and 953.

267 ne qua forte ('in case by any chance') suggests that such
doubts are unlikely (cf. 391 and 466), coeptes that they
can only be temporary (cf. desciscere quaeres 103); both
reflect L's confidence in his conclusions.

269 'Let me tell you of bodies besides (praeterea: i.e. in
-70 addition to the 'seeds') which you must confess exist
in nature and (yet) cannot be seen'. For tute, see on
102 above: as there, the emphasis marks the antithesis
with the convinced Epicurean. For the construction of
necessest confiteare, see on 146-8 above. in rebus
here approximates to in rerum numero (446 and 691).
videri = cerni (268); see on 224 above.

271 The v alliteration (cf. on 72 above) and the two dactyls
after the slower venti vis well reflect the wind's
sudden gusting. principio is a variation on primum;
cf. 503 and 834.

272 ruit: the transitive sense (cf. 289 and 292) is rare before
L. The fact that the wind moves visible objects (271-5)
is the first indication of its material nature (cf. 304).

273 rapido: see on 15 above; the word is more relevant to the
argument in the root sense than = 'rapid'; cf. on 294
below.

275 silvifragis: for the archaic-type compound, here presumably
a Lucretian coinage (it is found nowhere else), see on
navigerum 3 above.

276 fremitu . . . murmure: the sound made by the wind is another
sign that it is material; cf. 301-3. For the effective
m alliteration, cf. 68: saevitque minaci murmure adds
as much to the sound as to the sense.

277 sunt . . . venti . . . corpora caeca: 'there exist unseen
bodies of wind', as at 295. The verb is triumphantly
emphatic, as at 368.
nimirum: a favourite asseveration of L, which he never
uses ironically.

278 The threefold division (cf. 2-3), implicit in 271-5, here
provides a tricolon climax with anaphora of *quae*. *denique* (cf. 76) reinforces the emphasis which falls on the
final member, 'indeed'.

279 verrunt: for this metaphor, cf. 5.266, 388 and 1227 and
6.624. Here the list of objects includes both places
swept (*mare, terras*) and things swept away (*nubila*).
By a similar zeugma *raptant* denotes (i) 'ravage' and
(ii) 'carry off' (cf. *rapido* 273; *corripiunt rapidique*
294).
subito: adjective.

280 The analogy between wind and water is not simply a pictur-
-297 esque illustration, but a careful development of the proof
that wind is corporeal, since its effects correspond
closely with those of the obviously material water. L
characteristically introduces an example from the
more fully perceptible world and argues from the more to the
less perceptible: from visible water to invisible wind
and from invisible wind to imperceptible 'seeds'. The
parallelism in the wind / water analogy is extremely detailed and reinforced by L's use of the language; see
especially on 280 and 290-1 below.

280 nec ratione . . . alia . . . et cum: i.e. in precisely the
-1 same way as when: *et* replaces the *ac* more usual with
alius, for reasons of euphony.
fluunt already marks the parallelism with water: its root
is echoed in *flumine* 282.
stragemque propagant: for the oxymoron, cf. on 220 above.
stragem (root *sternere*) recalls 274; it is answered at
288, where it denotes the river's havoc.

aquae . . . natura: = *aqua*; see on 131 above. *mollis*
(nom. rather than gen.) probably makes a contrast between water's usual 'gentleness' (cf. *mollibus undis* 2.
375) and the occasional violence L is about to describe,
rather than being a constant epithet, 'flowing', 'liquid'.
repente: the first point of correspondence with wind; cf.
subito turbine 279 and *vim subitam* (of water) 286. Water,
like air, is subject to sudden disturbance (Epicurean air
comprised the same atoms as wind, in which their motion
was more violent; cf. 6.685).

282 flumine abundanti: 'in swollen flood'; the overflow of the
clause to mid-line from 281 well matches the sense.

imbribus: i.e. rain-water which has swollen the mountain-
streams feeding the river.

283 montibus ex altis: for the prepositional phrase attached
to the noun *decursus*, see on *inter se nexus* 244 above.

284 The subject is *aquae natura*, whose violence increases as
the sentence progresses. Here it propels the same objects as the wind at 274-5: the echoes of *silvifragis* in
fragmina . . . *silvarum* and *arboribus* in *arbusta* (the metrical equivalent of *arbores*; see on 187 above) underline
the parallelism. *coniciens* has its root force, 'throwing
together'.

285 The alliteration (with *v* predominating) recalls the violence
  -7 of the wind at 271. The sentence-pattern matches 271-6,
     with *ita* . . . *amnis* echoing *ita* . . . *ventus* 275-6.
     venientis: with hostile overtones, as e.g. at 3.752.
     aquai vim: matching *venti vis* 271.
     molibus: dat. with *incurrit*; the 'piles' of the bridges.
     validis: abl. with *viribus*; the *validi pontes* are confronted
     with the river's (greater) strength.

288 dat: 'causes'.
  -9 sonitu magno: cf. the wind at 275-6.
     stragem: cf. the wind at 280, and see note there.
     ruitque et: Bailey's suggestion for the Mss *ruit qua*. *-que*
     joins *volvit* and *ruit* (cf. *trudunt ruuntque* 292), *et* joins
     their objects, *grandia saxa* (the stones supporting the
     bridges) and *quidquid fluctibus obstat*. In 289, the
     opening dactyls and the high proportion of coincidence
     (Introduction V d) fit the speed and ease with which the
     water carries all before it. *ruitque ita* - W. Richter,
     Textstudien zu Lukrez (1974) - would yield a further
     dactyl.

290 debent: of logical necessity; see on 232 above.
  -1 flamina . . . flumen: a meaningful word-play (Introduction
     V c), reinforcing the parallel between wind and wave.
     Though *veluti validum flumen* is syntactically part of the
     cum clause, the comparison of course extends to the whole
     of 291-4.

293 vertice torto: 'in a swirling eddy'; throughout the *quae*
     clause the language is as appropriate to the analogue,
     water, as it is to wind: only the concluding *turbine*
     (294) fits the wind alone.

294 rapidique: masc. pl. as if *venti qui*, not *flamina venti
     quae*, had preceded; for the *constructio ad sensum*, cf.
     on 190 above and 352 below. The adj. is used predicat-
     ively: the assonance with *corripiunt* seems an intentional
     reminder of its root force (see on 15 and 273 above;

Introduction V c), as well as contributing to the vigour
imparted to 293-4 by the marked predominance of *r*, *p*,
t and *nt*.

295 quare etiam atque etiam: 'therefore again and again', a
recurrent Lucretian formula of insistence on a conclusion;
cf. 1049.
sunt venti corpora caeca: cf. on 277 above.

296 factis et moribus: abl. of respect, while *magnis amnibus*
-7 is dat. with *aemula*. The phrase involves a characteristic personification of wind and its 'rival' water.
aperto corpore: abl. of quality with *sunt*, and antithetical
with *corpora caeca* 295.

298 Smells, heat and cold, and sounds, though all invisible,
-304 must be material, since only physical contact can trigger
off sensation. For the Epicurean all sensation was
parallel to that of touch: sight, smell and hearing were
all produced by material effluences which streamed from
objects and impinged on the sense-organs (cf. Introduction
III and also on 132-4 above): heat and cold were independent atomic compounds, constantly passing from one body to
another by permeation (cf. 494 and 534-5).

300 calidos aestus: a variation for *calores*; like *frigora*,
plural to denote various instances of heat and cold.
tuimur: third conj. for the normal second (contrast 152,
195 and 324); for similar fluctuation, see on 71 and
212 with Introduction V a.

301 usurpare: 'grasp': for the unusual application of the verb
to perception, cf. 4.975 and Plautus, *Trinummus* 846; as
at 60 (see note), it is used to provide a variation in
terminology. See on 60 above also for the contracted
suemus, here scanned as a disyllable.

302 corporeā constare . . . naturā: i.e. be material.
-3 sensus impellere: 'impel the senses'; as at 689, *sensus* is
half-way to the concrete meaning 'sense-organs' (Greek
αἰσθητήρια), for which Latin as yet had no technical term
(an example of *patrii sermonis egestas*; cf. 136-45) and
for which L uses *sensus* at 3.550 and 562. As explained
at 3.246ff, external impact produced sensation by initiating the appropriate motions of *anima* and body atoms in
the observer.

304 The principle here enunciated is equally fundamental to
the argument about wind (see on 272 above), where it
was taken for granted. It amounts to a virtual definition
of matter, which Epicurus would have justified inductively
from experience: material objects which can be observed
are without exception tangible.

305 fluctifrago: the coined compound (cf. *silvifragis* 275 and
see on *navigerum* 3 above) is not simply ornamental but
indicates the source of the moisture which condenses
on the clothes.

306 eaedem: a spondee by synizesis; cf. e͡ādem 480.
serescunt: a coined antonym (based on *serenus* = 'cloudless',
'dry') of the rare *uvescunt*. The assonance of the in-
ceptives at the beginning and end of the line and of
suspensae in litore and *dispansae in sole*, placed in
similar positions in 305 and 306, brings out the parallelism between the two converse processes; cf. the repeated
quo pacto in 307-8. The spondaic rhythm of *suspensae*
. . . *serescunt* fits the slow but remorseless operation
of natural processes.

307 quo pacto: often used by L in the context of natural pro-
-8 cesses, where the root meaning suggests a political
metaphor for scientific law, like *foedus* at e.g. 586
and 5.57.
persederit: the prefix suggests permeation, the stem set-
tling, as at 6.1126.
umor aquai: for the periphrasis, cf. *lacteus umor* 258, and
see on *natura* 131 above.
visumst: true passive (see on 224 above); the perfect denotes the point of view of an observer after the completion of each process.
aestu: abl. of cause, or of instrument insofar as *fugerit*
= *pulsus sit*.

309 parvas . . . partis: i.e. tiny compound particles, themselves made up of equally invisible 'seeds'.

311 quin etiam: another frequent Lucretian method of introducing a new argument or illustration; cf. 782 and 823
and on 192 above.
solis . . . annis: the addition of *solis* gives *annis* its
root meaning of 'circuits'; cf. 5.644, where it is applied to planetary or stellar orbits. Its juxtaposition,
in this special sense, with its diminutive *anulus* (lit.
'little circle') is unlikely to be accidental: the verbal correspondence reinforces the link between the contem-
poraneous, and equally inevitable, processes.
redeuntibus: i.e. repeating themselves; the phrase (without
solis) is echoed by Virgil, *Aeneid* 8.47.

312 in digito: could be taken with one of the verbs but more
probably = *qui in digito est*; see on *inter se nexus* 244
above.
subter: i.e. on the inside.
habendo: if the gerund is, as usual, active, the sentence
involves an awkward change of subject, the wearer (not

the ring) being the subject of *habendo*. L has several
such cases - cf. 533, 902, 4.1068 (echoed by Virgil,
Georgics 3.454) and 5.194; it is tempting to regard
them as survivals of a (hypothetical) archaic passive
use of the gerund.

313 **stilicidi casus**: the *figura etymologica*, since *stilicidium*
-4 derives from *stilla* + *cadere* (cf. *corripiunt rapidique*
294), which here fits the persistence of the phenomenon.
So too does the echo of *stiLicIDi Casus* in *LapIDem Cavat*,
which at the same time provides a verbal link between
cause and its inevitable effect.
uncus . . . ferreus: on the double adj., see on *candens
lacteus umor* 258 above.

315 **strataque . . . viarum**: = *strataeque viae*; see on *prima
virorum* 86 and cf. Virgil, *Aeneid* 1.422. Noun-equival-
ents coined in this manner (here qualified by an adj.
saxea; cf. 6.1283f.) are more usually abstract. For
-que after preceding asyndeton, see on 162.
iam: i.e. after the event; only the cumulative effect, not
the details of the process, can be observed.

316 **portas propter**: for the anastrophe, see on 90 above. Statues
of deities were placed at town-gates and kissed by those
entering (cf. Cicero, *Verrine* 4.94 and Varro, *de Lingua
Latina* 5.58). It is characteristic of L to use the example
of a religious observance in order to prove a scientific
point.

317 **manus . . . attenuari**: 'show *that* their hands are being
worn away'; cf. *minui videmus* 319. Only the fact of
wear is apparent, not the process.

318 **praeterque meantum**: though *praeter* could be regarded as
an adverb, probably a case of tmesis (for *praetermean-
tumque*). L refines on Ennius' sometimes extravagant use
of the licence but does not impose such rigid restrictions
as Virgil, who only divides words with an *in-* prefix, and
then only with the suffix *-que*. L normally divides words
compounded with prepositions, usually with *-que*, but occasionally with *enim* (3.262 and 860) and *quasi* (5.287
and 299). In many cases, including the four latter,
the word division fits the sense; e.g. *seque gregari*
(452) and *disque sipatis* (651) occur in the context of
separation.

319 **haec** picks up all five cases cited in 311-8.
cum sint detrita: causal - the effects of wear (which are
visible) are evidence that diminution is constantly
taking place.

320 in tempore quoque: cf. 327: 'on each occasion'; see on 26
-1   above.

   invida . . . natura videndi: 'the grudging nature of our
   sight': the assonance makes our sight (*videndi*) seem
   intrinsically grudging (*invida*) and perhaps involves
   a serious word-play, insofar as *invida* might suggest
   'un-seeing', thus yielding an oxymoron with *videndi*.

   praeclusit: a metaphor from closing the door on something;
   cf. 975.

   speciem governs the indirect question of 320 (cf. *sensus*
   at 460-1) - 'the appearance of what bodies depart . . :'.

322 dies naturaque: equivalent to 'nature in the course of
-4   time'; cf. the hendiadys *aevo macieque*, 'with the decay
   of age', in the description of the converse process at
   325.

   moderatim: this coining, with a favourite Lucretian adverbial termination (Introduction V a), produces with *paulatim*
   an assonance which points the emphasis on the adverbs and
   stresses the sureness and insistence of nature's gradual
   processes.

   oculorum acies contenta: 'straining of the eyesight' - an
   ab urbe condita type construction (see on 464-5 below).
   The line provides yet another Lucretian variation on
   the theme of invisibility, after 277, 299-301, 307-8,
   310 and 321.

   tueri has as its object the indefinite rel. clause of 322-
   3.

325 quaecumque . . . senescunt and saxa . . . are the twin sub-
-7   jects of *amittant* with *quid* postponed: transl. 'as for
   whatsoever things . . . and rocks which . . ., you cannot
   see what they lose . . .'. 326 may be a later Lucretian
   insertion (cf. 208-214), for the addition of a specific example rather blunts the antithesis between the indefinite
   clauses of 322-3 and 325.

   mare: archaic acc. with *impendent*, for the usual dat.

   vesco: here 'eating gradually', 'gnawing', from *ve-*
   ('small') and the root *ed-* ('eat'), which L characteristically echoes in *peresa*. The *s* alliteration in *vesco sale
   saxa peresa* seems imitative of the splashing of the sea-
   spray.

   possis: subj. of the indefinite second person.

328 corporibus caecis: applicable both to the tiny invisible
   compounds for whose existence the whole passage has argued,
   and to the 'seeds' of which they are composed: the ana-
   logues have now shown that the invisibility of the 'seeds'
   is no objection to L's arguments for them in 159-264.

   igitur: the postponement emphasises the crucial word, *caecis*.

   gerit res: terminology repeatedly employed by L, usually in
   the passive, of natural processes; it carries a hint of

political, administrative metaphor, especially here with
natura personified as subject.

329-417 THE EXISTENCE OF VOID

L now turns to the second component of his universe, and in
so doing parts company with the non-Atomist Greek physicists
who would have accepted his argument so far, for the Atomists were alone in positing the alternation of void with
matter throughout the universe. In the fifth century,
Parmenides had raised logical objections to the existence
of 'that which is not', and Empedocles and Anaxagoras had
demonstrated experimentally that air, the most obvious
starting point in experience for the concept of void, was
corporeal. From that time, other schools normally denied
the existence of void altogether, although the Stoics,
while denying its existence within the visible world, accepted infinite void outside it. But the Atomists, treat-
ing Parmenides' reasoning as fallacious and analysing air,
though corporeal, at least as containing more void than
the average compound, made void a fundamental component
of their universe, on the grounds reflected in L's arguments in 335-69.

The commentators exaggerate the seriousness of a problem
connected with the Epicurean and Lucretian terminology for
void or space: according to the context, the application
of the terms may be (i) limited, to denote pure void
(totally unoccupied space) or (ii) wider, to cover partly
occupied void (the combination of unoccupied and occupied
space): they may even, as shown by 427-8 (*haud . . . esse*),
refer exclusively to occupied space. Of L's most frequent
terms, *inane, vacuum* and *vacans* are most appropriate and
most often reserved for (i), *spatium* and *locus* for (ii),
but the distinction is not rigid. The overlapping is understandable (cf. English 'space'), especially when it is remembered that any point in space (in the wider sense) was
always liable to be occupied or vacated by the constantly
moving Epicurean atoms: in L, the context invariably reveals which concept is under discussion, and the overlapping
at no point invalidates the argument. Throughout the present section, L's aim is to prove that pure void is perman-
ently to be found in the universe, i.e. that space is not
entirely occupied.

329-369 Introduction and three positive proofs

L argues (i - 335-45) that void is essential to allow

motion to objects: this fundamental argument is not purely
theoretical but is based on the observation that the denser
a compound is (i.e. the less 'empty' it appears to be) the
more resistance it offers to motion; (ii - 346-57) that
experience shows that even the densest compounds can be
permeated and so must contain void; (iii - 358-69) that
the different weight of compound bodies of identical size
can only be explained on the assumption that they contain
different amounts of void. Proof (i) is thus concerned
with void outside objects, proofs (ii) and (iii) with
void inside them. All the arguments are traditional to
the Atomists: the first is summarised in Epicurus, *ad Hdt.*
40 (a passage followed more closely later at 426-8); the
two latter were used by Democritus (cf. Aristotle, *de Caelo*
309a). (i) is the most crucial and L meets replies to it
later at 370-97; (ii) and (iii) could be answered with the
assumption that the 'void' in compounds is always occupied
by other matter, e.g. air, which would be displaced by the
permeation processes described in (ii).

329 corporea . . . natura: = *corpore*, a variation on the peri-
-30 phrasis with *natura* and a genitive, for which see on
     131 above.
   stipata tenentur: 'are held packed together'; *stipatus*,
     regularly used by L to denote absence of void, is normally
     applied to persons thronged by others, and suggests his
     favourite metaphor from the animate world.

   in rebus: 'in things'; the terminology embraces both the idea
     that void exists 'in the category of things', 'in nature'
     (cf. 270), which proof (i) seeks to establish, and the idea
     that it exists 'in compounds', with which proofs (ii) and
     (iii) are specifically concerned: the latter automatically
     entails the former. One or other idea may predominate
     whenever L uses the term in discussing void, according to
     context: here and at 399 below, where the most general
     reference is called for, it is the former which predominates.
   inane: L's most general term for void, Epicurus' τὸ κενόν. L
     reflects the variety of Epicurean terms for the concept;
     cf. 334, 367 and 379 below.

331 quod . . . cognosse: 'to know this fact'; the infin. is used
     as a noun, and is subject of *sinet* as well as of *erit utile*.
     On the standard contraction, see on *suemus* 60 above.
   tibi: the personal appeal to Memmius, taken up in the con-
     clusion at 398-417, heralds a new and fundamental point.
   in multis . . . rebus: 'in many connections'; cf. on 80 above.
     L has no aversion to using *res* in a quite different sense
     from that of the preceding line and of 333.

333 de summa rerum: 'about the totality of things'; see on
235 above.

334 'Therefore (let me assure you that) there exists intangible
space, void, and emptiness'.
locus . . . intactus: a combination of Epicurus' τόπος and
ἀναφὴς φύσις; L here gives the adj. the unique sense of
'intangible' (by analogy with words like invictus), for
which he also coins intactilis at 437.
vacansque: neut. used as a noun (like inane), as at 444;
like vacuum (367), it provides another equivalent for
Epicurus' τὸ κενόν. For -que after previous asyndeton,
see on 162 above.

335 quod: connective rel., referring to void.

336 officium . . . officere: 'what is in the way of body, to get
-7 in the way' - on the meaningful word-play, see Introduction
V c. The four 'stumbling' elisions in 337, the third of
which impedes the natural main caesura, match the obstruct-
ive effect described; see Holland, 58-9.
in omni tempore: see on 26 above.

338 principium . . . cedendi . . . daret: 'would offer a start-
-9 ing point in giving way', i.e. would be first to give way,
so allowing motion to begin. The parallelism of procedere
and cedendi reflects that motion and giving way are mutually interdependent; cf. procedere / concedere at 378-9.

340 This line covers the three divisions of our visible world
(see on 2-3 above).
sublimaque caeli: for the construction, see on prima
virorum 86. For the archaic second decl. form of the adj.,
cf. exanimus 774, and see Introduction V a.

341 multa modis multis: a favourite Lucretian collocation (cf.
on 814-5 below and 1024). The repetition of multus in
different inflexions (polyptoton: cf. also 196-7 and
824) matches the multiplicity described.

342 cernimus ante oculos: the emphatic appeal to experience
is not fatuous, for Parmenides had denied the reality
of motion; see on 381 below.

343 non tam . . . quam: 'not so much . . . but rather': without
-4 void, the visible world would not merely be immobile but
the motion necessary for its creation could never have
taken place. Cf. 988-9 and 1017-20 for a parallel movement to the same, stronger point.
sollicito, privata and genita fuissent all suggest a personification of visible 'things'. genita fuissent = genita
essent: this type of plupf. (and perf.) passive, one stage

further back than usual, is an extension from cases where
the participle becomes adjectival and timeless or where
completion or 'pastness' is stressed. L, doubtless influenced by metrical convenience, has several examples:
cf. 972; 3.849 and 868; 4.150 and 813. Here the periphrasis possibly emphasises the remoteness of the
prospect.
omnino: 'in the first place'.

345 quiesset: a standard contraction for *quievisset*; see on
suemus 60 above.

346 quamvis solidae: 'however solid', i.e. free from void:
-7 *solidae* is antithetical to *raro cum corpore*, which denotes porosity. In L *quamvis* as a conjunction is normally
used closely with adjs. (including adjectival participles)
and with adverbs; it may be so taken at 376, 387, 398
and 620.
hinc: i.e. from what follows.
licet . . . cernas: on the paratactic construction, see on
146-8 above.

348 saxis ac speluncis: 'rocky caves': hendiadys.
-9 permanat: L applies this favourite term for atomic permeation
to his first example (water), to which it is literally
appropriate, and more metaphorically to his last (cold) in
355. *dissipat sese, diffunditur, inter* . . . *meant* and
transvolitant (350-5) are all variations on the same theme.
The predominance of spondees in 348 suits the description
of the densely packed rock: the water breaks through in
the single dactyl at *permanat aquarum* and finds copious
flow in the dactylic rhythm of 349.
liquidus: the normally short first *i* is here long, as at
3.427 and at 4.1259 where both quantities are found in
the same line in the appropriate context of *mixing*; cf.
liquor 453. Such metrically convenient fluctuation is
an archaic tendency (cf. on *prōpagare* 195 above).
flent: inanimate nature is again personified; there is an
element of oxymoron with *uberibus* and the phrase recalls
the Homeric θαλερὸν δάκρυον.

350 omne: = *totum*; food reaches the whole of animal bodies,
showing that even the densest parts, like bones, contain
void through which the food permeates. The same point is
made about trees (*totas* 352).

351 in tempore: 'in due season'.

352 totas: as if *arbores*, not its metrical equivalent *arbusta*
(see on 187 above), had preceded - a bold *constructio*
ad sensum without precise Lucretian parallel, though cf.
crescentes 190 and *rapidi* 294.

353 per ramos . . . omnis: 'through all the branches', complet-
ing the amplification of *totas* which began with *usque ab*
. . ., though the sense 'through the whole of their
branches' (cf. 350) would fit the argument equally well.

354 Sounds and cold were both material compounds (see on 298-
-5 304 above): their permeation of apparently solid objects
thus implies the existence in these objects of void
through which they pass.
saepta . . . clausa domorum: i.e. walls . . . doors of
houses. For the construction, see on *prima virorum* 86
above. The gen., which goes with both participles (cf.
saepta domorum 489), is truly partitive.
transvolitant: stronger than *inter* . . . *meant*, reflecting
that doors are more readily penetrated by sound than are
walls. The unique compound replaces the metrically inadmissible *trānsvŏlānt*.
rigidum: stiffness is here colourfully transferred to cold
itself from its victims: the resultant picture is of one
'dense' compound (*frigus*) itself penetrating another
(*ossa*).

356 'But unless there were empty spaces, through which the
-7 bodies of each type could pass, in no way would you see
these things taking place'. I have assumed the loss of
haec: a plural subject for *fieri* seems essential, as
the conclusion obviously covers all the processes of
348-55. For *quod nisi* = 'but unless', cf. 2.221; 6.
568 and 591; see also on *quod contra* 82 above.
sint . . . videres: the conditional is present remote and
impf. subj. would be usual throughout; *possent* is used
as though *essent* had in fact preceded. For a similar
mixture, cf. 592-7, where a present subj. is included
in the apodosis. The arrangement illustrates the greater flexibility of conditional constructions in poetry
and is probably facilitated by the survival in poetry of
an older pattern whereby the present subj. covered
remote contingencies in both present and future, the impf.
subj. such contingencies in the past.
qua: = *per quae*; see on *unde* 56 above.
corpora quaeque: i.e. the bodies which respectively make up
water, animal and plant food, sounds and cold.

358 alias aliis . . . res rebus: the word-pattern reinforces
-9 the contrast; cf. the chiasmic patterns in similar contexts at 816 and 876-7. *aliis rebus* is dat. with *praestare*, with which *pondere* is abl. of respect.
maiore figura: abl. of quality with *alias res*. *figura*
(lit. 'shape', 'outline') is a regular Lucretian substitute for the metrically inadmissible *māgnĭtūdo*.

360 tantundemst . . . corporis: 'there is just as much matter';
-1 the partitive gen. is attracted inside the correlative

clause.

glōmere: the *o* is normally short; cf. on *prōpagare* 195
and *līquidus* 349 above.

tantundem pendere par est: 'it is natural that it (the ball
of wool) should weigh just as much'. L may have in mind
the basic meaning of *par*, 'equal' (here, to expectation),
and intend a word-play with *tantundem* to underline his
point.

362 corporis: the emphasis on the key word in the argument (here
placed first for the second successive line with *quoniam*
postponed to third position in its clause) adds urgency
to the reasoning and sharpens the antithesis with *inanis*
363.

premere omnia deorsum: the natural motion of the atoms was downwards due to weight; see on 984-97 below. Matter 'presses
all things downwards' in that it falls naturally itself
and tends to depress whatever it encounters (e.g. a scale-
pan). *deōrsum* is here a spondee by synizesis, as in most
instances in L: insofar as the compression weighs down the
end of the line, the licence is not inappropriate to the
sense.

363 natura . . . inanis: = *inane*; the periphrasis (see on 131
above) here provides an antithesis with *corporis officium*
362.

364 magnumst aeque: 'is equally large'.

videtur: 'can be seen to be'; see on 224 above.

365 inanis . . . corporis: both partitive gen. with *plus*, as
-7   is *vacui* with *minus*.

gravius: = *quod gravius est*, sc. *aequeque magnum*, answering *quod . . . videtur* 364.

dedicat: synonymous with *declarat* 365 - an old sense of the
word. Both verbs vividly personify a material object,
which cries aloud the truth of L's thesis.

multo vacui minus: 'much less void'; the 'enclosing' word-
order mirrors void's position inside the compound, as
also at 514.

368 est: 'there exists', triumphantly emphatic, as at 277.

sagaci: a metaphor from the keen scent of hounds. The image
of tracking down the truth about void is picked up and
developed at 402-9.

369 admixtum rebus: 'mingled in things'; like *in rebus* (see on
330 above), applicable both to void in compounds and to
void in general. As L seems here to be drawing the inference from all three arguments, he probably again has the
more general idea in mind.

370-397 Refutation of rival views

This passage is supplementary to proof (i), for it seeks to
meet theories which would allow motion without void (the
view of Parmenides that motion was an illusion is passed
over as preposterous in 381).

Lines 370-90 deal with the theory that motion in a plenum
could take place by transposition: on this view all motion
was analogous to that of fish in water, the example introduced at 372ff.: fish and water change places but, as observation suggests, no void ever exists between them. Like
water, air (whose analysis had a fundamental bearing on the
question of the existence of void) comprised a flexible
continuum. The argument from analogy, starting from observation, is hard to fault on the basis of Epicurean Canonic and L's first reply (378-83) is no more than an application of his argument in proof (i) to the specific
example of the fish in water. His fundamental objection,
which he would have done better to make clear, is to the
rival theory's implication that pure matter can vary in
texture and sometimes, as in the case of water and air,
can be liquid or flexible: as becomes clear at 483ff.,
pure matter (comprising the atoms) was to L homogeneous
and uniformly hard and unyielding: liquidity in compounds
could accordingly only result from the admixture of void.
Secondly (384-90), L quotes the example of a pair of flat
bodies suddenly separated, arguing that on the transposition
theory a void must at least momentarily be formed between
them after separation, until air, rushing round their edges,
meets in the middle of the area they have just vacated.

In 391-7 L uses the same example of the flat bodies in
dismissing the view that air can condense and expand;
this 'elastic air' theory he may regard either as supplementary to the transposition theory, or as offering a
completely independent explanation of motion without void.
He flatly denies that air can condense and expand (395)
and argues that, even if it could, the assumption of void
would be a prerequisite (396-7): i.e. condensation must
entail a decrease, expansion an increase, in the void in
a compound. The argument against the condensation theory
is cryptically compressed (see notes *ad loc.*), and might
well have been clarified in revision.

The transposition theory was widely held by L's rivals,
including Platonists, Aristotelians and Stoics, against
all of whom 370-90 may be assumed to be directed. The
'elastic air' theory is less well attested, either as a
supplement to the transposition theory or as an independent
alternative to it; Bailey's interpretation of ἀλλοιοῦσθαι
in Aristotle (*Physics* 214a) as a reference to changes in
density is dubious.

The passage illustrates the unsympathetic and perfunctory
method of argument which L tends regularly to employ in
dismissing rival possibilities: the trait seems to have
been shared with Epicurus and stems from L's refusal to
see any problem except in the general context of the
Epicurean system: so here his ultimate objection turns on
the Epicurean analysis of matter, which is not established
until 483ff.

370 illud, defined by *quod quidam fingunt*, is subject of
-1   *possit*, and supplied again as the object of *praecurrere*,
    which is a metaphor for anticipation.
   in his rebus: cf. on 80 above.
   deducere vero: for the image of truth as a path, cf. 659
    and 1115-7.
   quidam: the vagueness is contemptuous and plays down the
    support which the theory enjoyed amongst ancient philo-
    sophers: see introductory note above.
   fingunt: again of false belief, as at 104.

372 The smooth motion is mirrored in the liquid *l* and *qu*
-4   sounds, the concealed effort in e.g. the alternating
    plosives of *post . . . pisces . . . possint*.
   cedere: the final *e* remains short before the *sq* of
    squamigeris; L has some dozen instances of this type
    of licence, which is normally avoided by the Augustan
    poets, except with otherwise inadmissible words like
    smărāgdus. Lengthening in this position is even rarer
    and the collocation is normally avoided altogether.
   squamigeris: dat. with *cedere*; for the periphrasis, cf.
    on 162 above.
   post: adverbial, 'behind them'.
   loca: in stating the rival theory, L here and at 376 uses
    his own technical term for 'space' (τόπος, see on 334
    above). His rivals held that these 'spaces' were always
    fully occupied.
   linquant: sub-oblique subj. (like *possint*, which is perhaps
    also prospective) used in reporting the rival view.
   quo: 'into which'; see on *unde* 56 above.

375 inter se . . . moveri et mutare locum: hendiadys, 'move by
-6   changing places with one another'; *moveri* has 'changed
    places' with *mutare locum*, which belongs with *inter se* -
    the word-pattern mirrors the process described.
   quamvis sint omnia plena: i.e. despite the absence of void in
    nature. *quamvis* probably goes closely with *plena*, 'how-
    ever full' (see on 346 above).
377 id . . . totum: 'the whole of this theory'; in effect
   totum strengthens *falsa*, 'wholly false'.

378 quo: 'in what direction'.

-80 procedere . . . concedere: for the meaningful assonance,
here underlined by the similar placing of the words,
cf. on 338-9 above.

tandem: 'pray', marking an indignant question.

spatium dederint: 'have made room for them'. *spatium*,
though not here fully technical, turns out later to be
a Lucretian term (= Epicurus' χώρα) applied (like *locus*)
to 'space', whether occupied or not. To L the waters
can only 'make room' because they contain pure void,
which his opponents would deny.

cum: 'when'; though causal subj. might have been expected,
the temporal relationship is stressed. The *cum* clause
answers *ni . . . latices*: L's rivals find themselves in
a vicious circle.

381 The first alternative had been adopted by Parmenides (see

-2 introductory note above); L treats it as too absurd to
warrant further refutation than the appeal to experience
at 340-2.

privandumst corpora: = *corpora privanda sunt*; see on 111
above. In this context *dicendumst* must also be impersonal,
governing an acc. and infin. (*esse admixtum . . . inane*),
where a personal construction with nom. and infin. would
be usual.

admixtum . . . rebus: see on 369 above; unless he is thinking in particular of the void in compounds like water and
air, L is again likely to have the more general application
of the term in mind.

383 'From which each thing may derive an original starting point
for motion'. The echo of *principium cedendi* (339) in
initum primum movendi illustrates the repetitive nature
of the argument.

initum: a metrical equivalent for *initium*.

capiat: the subj. is probably prospective, not merely sub-
oblique after *dicendumst*.

movendi: probably a rare intransitive usage, as at 6.595
(contrast *moveri* 375), rather than a 'passive' use of
the gerund (see on 312 above); cf. the intransitive sense
given to *trahere* 397 and *mutare* 787: such fluctuations
probably reflect archaic flexibility.

384 si: sixth word in its clause; the word-order throws emphasis

-6 on to the subject.

de concursu: 'from collision'.

lata: Lucretian shorthand; the sequel shows that he has in
mind flatness and smoothness as well as breadth.

cita: predicative, = 'quickly'.

aer . . . inane: 'it must be that air would occupy all the
void which would be created between the bodies'. *possidat*,
paratactic subj. with *necessest* (see on 146-8 above), also

contains the apodosis of the fut. remote conditional:
fiat is potential, continuing the hypothesis. *inane*
('void') is tendentious, anticipating the argument and
implied conclusion of 387-90: *spatium* or *locus* (cf. 389
and 390) would have been less loaded terms. The long gap
between *inane* and its adj. (*omne*) effectively matches and
reinforces the picture of the large space which has been
created between the bodies and which cannot be instant-
aneously filled by air. The pattern is repeated on a
smaller scale in *totum* . . . *spatium* 388-9.

387 is: i.e. *aer* (cf. *ille* 390), subject of *confluat*.
quamvis: closely with *celerantibus* (see on 346 above).
circum: i.e. round the edges of the bodies.

388 confluat: the prefix is important to the argument: if air
meets, there must previously have been void between the
parts of it which come together.
uno tempore: 'in a single instant'; *uno* is opposed to
totum.

389 primum quemque . . . locum: 'each successive place' - the
-90 spot which at successive intervals is 'first' or
'nearest'.
necessest occupet ille: again the paratactic construction,
continued in *omnia possideantur*.
deinde: disyllabic, with synizesis, as always in L.
omnia: sc. *loca*, 'the whole area'.

391 'But if anyone happens to think, at the moment when the
-4 bodies have leapt apart, that this (i.e. the replacement
of bodies by air) happens because air condenses (i.e.
can condense and expand), he is astray; for at that moment
a void which did not exist before (between the bodies) is
created, and likewise a void which did exist before (outside the bodies) is filled (by the bodies as they separate)'. The vague *id fieri* (392) must refer to air replacing the bodies after their separation, the general
topic of the preceding lines: the mention of air there has
perhaps reminded L of the 'elastic air' theory. *vacuum
tum . . . constitit ante* (393-4) seems best regarded as
no more than a dogmatic reassertion and amplification of
L's own view of what happens in his chosen example (cf.
the dogmatic attitude of 395): a void is created between
the bodies at separation (393) and, as an inevitable
complementary process, a void outside them is filled. He
then regards the argument of 384-90 as forcing the condensation theorists, no less than the transpositionists,
to admit the void they would deny. However, his new rivals
might have argued that, when the bodies met, the air between them was compressed and at least some of it remained
trapped after impact; on separation, this air would expand,
so that air was not left to 'rush round' and fill a void.
Bailey (who takes *tum* in 393 = 'in that case') and Munro

would both regard 393-4 as a claim that expansion and
condensation in themselves imply the creation and filling
of voids and they see here an application to the specific
example of the bodies of the point made more generally in
396-7. However, after the categorical assertion of 393-
4, the inclusion of the qualification *opinor*, however
confident, in a generalised restatement would be an in-
tolerable anticlimax.

dissiluere: = *dissiluerunt*; the indic. shows that the clause
is treated as independent of *putat*.

se condenseat: the present is generalising and, by Lucretian
shorthand, condensation implies also its opposite, as at
395-7. The subj. is sub-oblique in a reported reason,
as at 374. The rare compound is always elsewhere first
conj., though the simple verb (cf. 395) occasionally
shows fluctuation to second conj. elsewhere; cf. Introduction V a.

395 denserier: for the archaic passive infin., see on 207
above.

396 I.e. condensation would entail the reduction of void in a
-7 compound (and expansion an increase).

si iam posset: 'even if it could'; the *iam* marks a hypothesis accepted for the sake of argument: it more often appears with a present subj. (also expressing a remote
present conditional; see on 356-7 above), as at 968 and
in the restorations at 1071 and 1094-1101.

trahere: intransitive, as at 6.1190; cf. on *movendi* 383
above.

398-417 Conclusion: the arguments could be multiplied

This passage serves to provide some light relief after a
section of closely reasoned argument, and to spur on the
philosophical disciple; cf. 921-50 (where the tone is
rather more serious) and 1114-7. It perhaps contains a
tacit acknowledgment of the perfunctory nature of the latter part of the discussion of void; it also introduces an
important declaration of policy: L's aim throughout the
poem, and not only in connection with void (cf. 416 note),
is to present only the cardinal Epicurean arguments, which
the pupil must then follow up for himself. Epicurus had
provided a much shorter summary than L's in *ad Hdt.* 40 and
also envisaged his pupil engaging in his own research to
follow up the outline provided (*ad Hdt.* 68 and 83).

398 quamvis: closely with *multa* (see on 346 above), which is
an internal acc. with *moreris* (cf. 5.91) - 'however much

you delay'. The spondaic rhythm fits the sense, and contrasts with the more rapid movement of 399ff.

399 in rebus: see on 330 above.
fateare necessest: a favourite formula (once more paratactic); cf. 624 and 974, and (with *confiteare*) 269-
70 and 825-6.

400 praeterea: 'besides', as at 269.

401 fidem . . . corradere: 'scrape together evidence'; the
colloquial use of the verb introduces a note of ironic
self-depreciation which is sustained in the playfully
exaggerated threat of 412-7.

402 vestigia . . . sagaci: stock metaphors of the chase, which
prepare for the sustained simile of 404-9; the image was
foreshadowed at 368-9.

403 sunt: the verb, which is here unemphatic (contrast 277,
368 and 399), would not have been placed at the beginning (or end) of the line by an Augustan poet; cf. 24.
possis: consecutive subj.; the second person is not indefinite (contrast 327). The passage is addressed to
Memmius, who is named in 411.
tute: for the emphatic form of *tu*, here denoting 'by your-
self', cf. 269, and see on *tutemet* 102 above; cf. 407,
where *per te* and *ipse* reinforce the sense.

404 montivagae: gen. sing. with *ferai* (cf. 2.597 and 1081):
on the compound, see on *navigerum* 3 above.

405 naribus, intectas fronde and vestigia all reflect that
 -6 the quarry is not directly observed during the chase:
similarly, some vital scientific truths, as in the case
of void, cannot be directly observed, and are eventually
elicited by following up observable clues.
quietes: poetic use of abstract for concrete: 'resting-
places'.

407 alid: for the archaism, see on 263 above. The chain of
scientific reasoning, like the trail, is continuous.
tute: see on 403 above.

408 talibus in rebus: i.e. in the field of philosophical
 -9 investigation.
caecas . . . latebras . . . omnis: 'all the dark lairs',
answering *intectas fronde quietes* 405; for *caecus* in
this sense, cf. 1115. *omnis* emphasises that a proper
search for the truth about void must be exhaustive.
insinuare and protrahere both sustain the image, and are
appropriate to hounds wriggling through the undergrowth
and drawing the quarry from its lair. On the construction
of *insinuare*, see on 113 above.

410 pigraris: = *pigraveris*, fut. perf.; see on *suemus* 60
above.
ab re: i.e. from the task; the rhythm, with a 'protected'
final monosyllable (Introduction V d), slows down the
line as Memmius shirks.

411 de plano: 'on my own authority' - a legal phrase, denoting
an informal pronouncement, lit. 'from the floor of the
court' as opposed to *pro tribunali*, *de loco superiore*,
denoting an official declaration from a magisterial
platform. L is perhaps contrasting his usual practice
of invoking the higher authority of Epicurus.

412 fontibu': the springs of poetic invention (as at 927)
-3   though there the inspiration is pictured as external.
L may well also be thinking of the philosophical inspiration available to him from having imbibed Epicurus'
works.
suavis: similarly, L claims poetic *lepor* at 934 but goes
on to show that the poetic 'honey' serves a philosophical
end.
meo . . . diti de pectore: explanatory of *e fontibu' magnis*
in that the breast denotes the seat of the intellect,
where L's 'springs' rise. For the combination of adj.
and possessive adj., cf. on 38 above. The copious language of the couplet seems designed to mirror the in-
exhaustibility of the threatened arguments: each line
contains two chiasmically arranged noun-adj. combinations and, of the four adjs., *largos*, *magnis* and *diti*
all make the same point; the addition of *meo* to *diti*
and the combination of two local phrases (*e fontibu'* and
de pectore) contribute further to the effect. The copious
diversity of the imagery from 412-5 works in a similar
way, giving Memmius a foretaste of the threatened deluge.

414 tarda: fem. sing. with *senectus*, involving a degree of
personification.
prius: closely with *quam* 416, ' . . . before'.

415 nobis: L and Memmius.
vitai claustra: the impressive metaphor has a scientific
foundation, the interlocking union of soul and body
atoms on which life depended.

416 tibi: tantamount to a possessive dat. with *auris* 417;
see on *omnibus* 19 above.
quavis una re: 'any single topic you like'; L now generalises: void is not the only subject on which discussion
could be protracted.

417 argumentorum: the heavy word at the beginning of the line
playfully expresses the grimness of the prospect; cf. on
412-3 above.

418-482 EVERYTHING CAN BE EXPLAINED IN TERMS OF MATTER
AND VOID

418-448 Matter and void alone exist in their own right;
there is no third category of independent existence

L here moves on to an important new point: matter and
void, to which the reader has now been introduced, are
the only independent realities in the universe. The
existence of each is first reasserted (422-9): though L
has already demonstrated the existence of invisible constituents of matter, he now makes the more obvious point
that matter in its visible form exists by invoking for the
first time the fundamental principle of Epicurean Canonic,
the validity of sensation (Introduction III). In demon-
strating the existence of void (426ff.), he sums up the
earlier argument based on motion (335ff.) but adds the new
point that void must exist to provide the space occupied
by matter: the concept of void now under discussion is thus
wider than that of the previous section, which was concerned with the existence of empty space: occupied space is now
also included in the concept (see introductory note to 329-
417 above). There follow (433-44) two arguments rejecting the independent existence of any third category, arguments which are close to definitions of matter and void:
(i) if a thing admits of touch, it is matter, if not, it
is void (cf. 304): (ii - 440ff.) if a thing can act or be
acted upon, it is matter, if not, it is void. These definitions, L would claim, are based on experience and reasoning from it: he would ask an opponent how any third category could be experienced or conceived: how did an immaterial Platonic form, or an immaterial soul, for example,
differ from void?

Lines 419-32 are closely based on Epicurus, ad *Hdt*. 39-40
(though the letter is not the source of the arguments of
433-44) and constitute the longest passage in the poem
where L follows an extant Epicurean text in detail.

418 repetam: 'resume', after the digression of 398-417; the
    verb governs a prolative infin. (*pertexere*), as at 6.936-
    7, by analogy with other verbs of beginning: see on
    desciscere quaeres 103 above.

419 omnis . . . natura: i.e. the totality of existence, whether
    omnis agrees with *natura*, or is neut. gen. and the phrase
    a periphrasis for *omne*, = Epicurus' τὸ πᾶν (see on *natura*
    131 above).
    ut est . . . per se: 'as it is of itself', introducing the
    idea of independent existence, which is fundamental to the

passage, and which prepares for the contrasted idea of existence as either property or accident; cf. on *per se* 422 below and 440, 445, 462, 466 and 479; also *ipsum* in the same sense at 433. Only matter and void (and here the totality they comprise) exist in their own right.

igitur: 'then', resumptive after the final *ut* clause of 418; it belongs after *omnis* but is postponed from the main clause.

420 constitit in: 'stands composed of' (lit. 'has taken up position on'); for this perf. with the sense of present *constat*, cf. 3.178 and 440, and for examples in other authors see Munro's note *ad loc.*

rebus: here applied to matter and void (as at 450 and 504), for which L normally uses *natura*.

corpora: i.e. bodies at a perceptible as well as at an imperceptible level (cf. 483-4); at 422, where the generic *corpus* is used, L is thinking in terms of the former.

421 diversa: predicative, 'in different directions'.

422 per se: probably technical (as at 419) with *corpus esse*. It is less likely to go with *communis sensus dedicat*, 'our sensation by itself proclaims', despite the Epicurean original, αὐτὴ ἡ αἴσθησις ἐπὶ πάντων μαρτυρεῖ; after 419 the non-technical sense would be awkwardly misleading (contrast 438, where there is no danger of ambiguity): αὐτὴ is not indispensable and L is not giving a word-for-word translation.

communis . . . sensus (423): i.e. the sensation common to all men, a specialised philosophical sense: the phrase more usually denotes fellow feeling, and so sympathy, discretion, or tact.

dedicat: cf. on 367 above.

423 L here alludes to the fundamental Epicurean criteria of
-5 factual knowledge: (i) sensation (*sensus*, αἴσθησις); (ii) reasoning (*animi ratio*, λογισμός), based on and tested against experience. (i) is fundamental but affords no evidence for the invisible world (*res occultae*, τὰ ἄδηλα, e.g. atoms and void), where (ii) becomes necessary. L, following Epicurus, here rather illogically justifies the validity of (i) (which he regarded as self-evident) by suggesting that without it (ii) breaks down: i.e. sensation is valid because there is no alternative criterion. For a similar idea, cf. 699-700.

cui nisi . . . queamus: 'and unless our faith in this is strongly established as a foundation (*prima*, predicative), there will be no standard to which (*haud erit quo*) we can refer . . . and confirm . . .'.

cui: dat. with the noun *fides*; *fides valebit* implies *fidetur*.

fundata: a favourite Lucretian metaphor from building.

quo referentes: a political expression (cf. *ad senatum de aliqua re referre*) transferred to the field of scientific procedure.

queamus: prospective subj.; the rel. clause combines consecutive and purposive force.

426 locus . . . vocamus: emphatic, answering *corpus* 422; hence the placing outside the *si* clause of 427, in which the phrase grammatically belongs.

spatium: here for the first time fully technical to denote 'space' in the generic sense; see on 379 above.

quod: either agreeing with *spatium*, the nearer of the two nouns, like *nullum* 427, or perhaps to be regarded as idiomatically attracted to the number and gender of *inane* (cf. 3.94).

427 haud . . . meare: answering the two ideas introduced at
-8   421. The first argument (*haud . . . esse*) has not been advanced previously (see introductory note above) and concerns only occupied space, which could be agreed to exist even in a plenum.

quoquam diversa: 'in any direction on their different paths'.

429 id strictly applies only to the second point (*neque . . . meare*), covered at 335ff. and 370ff., but the two ideas are closely linked in the Epicurean original and in L's mind (cf. 421); matter always occupies parts of the space through which it constantly moves.

supera: L sometimes prefers this older, uncontracted form of *supra*: contrast e.g. 531.

430 praeterea: 'in addition' (to matter and void); cf. 269 and
-1   400 and contrast the more usual 'enumerative' sense at 440 below.

omni: with *inani* as well as *corpore*, 'separate from every instance of matter and void' = 'totally distinct from matter and void'. The pattern is again chiasmic.

seiunctum secretumque: an emphatic combination of synonyms with the same prefix; cf. *seiungi seque gregari* 452.

esse: emphatic, 'exists'.

432 I.e. such as to prove a sort of third category of existence. *quod* forms an anaphora with *quod* 430, and, unlike *reperta*, resists idiomatic attraction to the gender of the predicate, *natura*. The rel. clause is consecutive. *quasi* apologises for the strangeness of the idea of any third category, making it appear eccentric. *numero* is abl. of respect with *tertia*, an inessential but idiomatic addition.

433 erit: the futures, continued until 442, suggest the point

of view of an enquirer reviewing different candidates
for existence - 'whatever is going to exist', i.e. 'be
admitted to exist': cf. e.g. 615-22.
debebit: again, as at 441 below, of logical necessity:
see on 232 above.
ipsum: = *per se*; see on 419 above.

434 cui: possessive dat.
tactus: i.e. tangibility, as at 454 below.
quamvis: adverbial with *levis exiguusque*; contrast the usages
as a conjunction, for which see on 346 above.

435 augmine: abl. of measure with *augebit*, exemplifying the
-6 *figura etymologica* (cf. *stilicidi casus* 313); transl.
'amount'.
denique: closely with *vel parvo*, 'at least' ('in the
last resort').
dum sit: 'provided it exists (in the first place)'.
corporis . . . numerum: 'the tally of body' (cf. *rerum in
numero* 446): *corporis* belongs equally with *summam*.

437 intactile: cf. on *intactus* 334 above.
-8 nulla de parte: 'at no point' in its extent.
quod . . . queat: 'such as to be able' - another consecutive
rel. clause.
per se: 'through it'; contrast the technical sense of the
phrase elsewhere in the passage (see on 419 above).

440 praeterea: introducing a second argument.
per se: technical, and emphatically positioned outside
the *quodcumque* clause of which it is part.
faciet quid: i.e. will act upon something, as the antithesis with 441 makes clear. *quid* replaces the more
normal *aliquid*.

441 fungi: 'to be acted upon' (cf. 443); L always gives the verb
the unusual basic sense of 'to suffer, undergo'. *fungi*
. . . *ipsum* forms a chiasmically arranged contrast with
the abl. absolute *aliis . . . agentibus* ('while other
things work on it').

442 erit: sc. *tale*, 'or will be such that'.
res esse gerique: *res* is concrete with *esse* ('objects'),
abstract with *geri* ('processes').

443 facere et fungi pick up the first two possibilities (440-
-4 1), praebere locum the third (442).

445 per se . . . natura: 'independent nature' (or 'category');
-6 *per se* here takes on the colouring of 'independent of
matter and void', and thus paves the way for the argument about properties and accidents.
relinqui: i.e. by a philosopher analysing the universe;

L likes to talk vividly of philosophers arranging or con-
structing the universe they describe: at 569 and 658-
60 they 'admix', 'leave behind' or 'take away' void; cf.
also 515, 701-3 and 742-5.

447 I.e. either perceptible or conceivable; for the allusion
-8   to the twin criteria of Epicurean knowledge (*sensus,
     animi ratio*), cf. on 423-5 above.
     nec . . . nec subdivide the preceding general negative,
     nulla 446; the rel. clauses are again consecutive.
     sub . . . cadat: i.e. is susceptible to, falls within the
     range of.
     apisci: 'grasp'; the 'physical' sense is archaic (cf.
     5.808, 6.1235), and is here a metaphor from the direct
     forms of perception just mentioned, in all of which
     touch was fundamental (see on 298-304 above).

449-482 Everything else is a 'property' or 'accident' of
matter and void

According to L's definitions in 451-8, properties (*coniuncta*, Epicurus' συμβεβηκότα and ἀίδια παρακολουθοῦντα)
cannot be separated from a thing without its destruction
(i.e. a thing's properties make it what it is), whereas
accidents (*eventa*, Epicurus' συμπτώματα) can come and go
without destroying the essential nature of their 'host'.
The distinction would be clearer with more examples than
L, not yet having demonstrated the atomic nature of his
primordia, is in a position to advance: e.g. atoms have
the properties of size, shape and weight; they undergo
the accidents of movement in space, collision and combination; any compound body is an accident of atoms and void;
compound bodies in turn have properties, like those of
453, and suffer accidents, like the states listed in 455-
6. The relative nature of the terms is a further compli-
cation: the property of one thing may be the accident of
another; see on *servitium* 455 below.

The remainder of the discussion deals with two cases which
might be alleged to be exceptions: (i) time (459-63) and
(ii) past events (464-82). L argues (i) that the idea of
time derives simply from the relationship of events: time
is perceptible only with reference to states of motion and
of rest (i.e. to changing and unchanging situations). He
thus analyses time as an accident of occurrences, which are
themselves ultimately accidents of matter and void. In (ii)
he meets the rather naive argument that events of the remote
past (illustrated throughout by the specific example of the
Trojan War) cannot be the accidents of the generations concerned because these 'hosts' no longer exist, (a) with the
retort that these events may be labelled as the accidents
of the places concerned, (b) (471ff.) with the more funda-

mental point that without matter and void, the events could
never have taken place: they must therefore in the last
resort be accidents of matter and void.

The account of properties and accidents, and of time, appears to be a much simplified summary of Epicurus, *ad Hdt.*
68-73, the precise interpretation of which is disputed: the
treatment of past events, however, is not taken from the
letter or from any extant Epicurean source. The identity
of L's opponents in 459-82 is not certain, though *dicunt*
and *cogant* (465-6) suggest that he has specific opponents
in mind, at least in (ii). Even if Epicurus' treatment
of time was non-polemical, L may in (i) be thinking of the
Stoics, who (according to Sextus Empiricus, *Adversus Math-
ematicos* 10.218) assigned time an independent existence:
even if this is a misrepresentation, as argued by Furley
13-14, L could still be labouring under the same delusion
as Sextus. (ii) would appear relevant not only, as Furley
suggests, to Platonist theories, but also to the belief
apparently held by at least some Stoics (cf. Seneca,
Epistulae Morales 117.7) that events enjoyed bodily existence: L would naturally regard the 'body' assigned to
events as comprising a third category of existence, distinct
both from void and from body, or matter, proper.

449 quaecumque cluent: 'whatever things have names' (sc. *praeter
inane et corpora* , an idea carried over from 445); on the
verb, here with its full sense, see on 119 above. The
clause is used simply to identify and so contains an
agreed or objective fact: hence the indic., despite *invenies* and *videbis* (cf. e.g. 325-7, where however the
word-order alone would explain the mood of *senescunt* and
impendent).
coniuncta: constructed participially with a dat., as at 453-
4 and like *eventa* in 469 , but the latter, which has some
currency as a noun outside L, is allowed a gen. at 450,
467 and 482.

450 horum: neut. picking up *rebus*, as at 56-7, although here
there is no metrical convenience in the idiom.

451 nusquam: 'in no case' - more euphonious in the context
than *numquam*, for which it serves ; cf. *usquam* = *umquam*
796.
permitiali: found only here.

452 discidio: i.e. of the property's 'owner'; on the associations of the word, see on 220 above.
potis est: archaic for *potest*: cf. on *potesse* 665 below.
seiungi seque gregari: on the expressive tmesis, see on
318 above; for the repeated prefix, cf. 431.

453 liquor: on the long *i*, see on 349 above.
    aquai: archaic dat. of the same form as L's favourite gen.
    (see on 29 above). Though no other certain literary in-
    stance has survived, Quintilian vouches for its exis-
    tence (1.7.18); the long a can be explained by the analogy
    of the gen. form.

454 intactus: characteristically coined as an antonym of *tactus*,
    'intangibility'; cf. the novel sense of the adj. *intactus*
    334 and the coined *intactile* 437.

455 The list of noms. answers that of 453-4, and looks for-
-6 ward to a predicate of the form *eventa sunt*, but the
    thought changes and they are picked up in 458 by the
    acc. *haec* - a natural enough anacoluthon.
    servitium: listed as an accident because it is here treated
    as the state of a man: as the state of a slave, it would
    be a property.
    divitiaeque: for the single -*que* despite asyndeton else-
    where in the list, see on 162 above; here however -*que*
    serves to link two chiasmically arranged pairs of op-
    posites.

456 quorum adventu . . . abituque: 'at whose coming and going',
-7 answering *seiungi seque gregari* 452, while *manet incolumis*
    forms an antithesis with *permitiali discidio* 451-2.
    natura: 'the nature of a thing', i.e. of the accident's
    'host'.

458 soliti sumus: perf. with present sense, as often with this
    verb, the participle being virtually adjectival. The
    plural is either 'editorial', as at 41 and 429, or includes
    all Roman Epicureans.
    ut par est: a defence of the terminology *eventa* (lit. 'occur-
    rences') for 'accidents', with reference to the principle
    of Epicurean Canonic that words should be used in their
    natural and most obvious senses; cf. Epicurus' justifica-
    tion (*ad Hdt.* 70) of his own term συμπτώματα as κατὰ τὴν
    πλείστην φοράν.
    eventa: saved for the climax of the definition of 455-8,
    whereas in that of 451-4 *coniunctum* came first. The
    chiasmic pattern, in which 455-6 also answer 453-4, is a
    feature of the artful balance which L contrives between
    the two sentences.

459 rebus ab ipsis: emphatic, and antithetical with *per se* -
    'it is merely from occurrences that'.

460 consequitur sensus: 'there follows a sense of'; the three
-1 indirect questions, denoting past, present and future,
    depend on the noun *sensus* (cf. on *speciem* 320-1 above).
    tum: like *porro*, enumerative, while *deinde* is temporal.

sequatur: i.e. has yet to arrive.

462 per se . . . sentire: 'that anyone senses time (as existing)
-3 in its own right'; *per se* is further explained in 463,
    where *semotum* agrees predicatively with *tempus*, i.e.
    'independently of'.
    rerum motu placidaque quiete corresponds to κινήσεσι καὶ
    στάσεσιν (states of motion and rest; Epicurus, *ad Hdt.*
    70) with slight poetic elaboration.

464 Tyndaridem . . . esse: 'when they say that the rape of the
-5 daughter of Tyndareus and the subjugation in war of the
    races born of Troy exist'. *Tyndaridem . . . gentis* ex-
    emplifies the frequent idiom whereby a noun + past part-
    iciple passive expresses an abstract idea (cf. *ab urbe
    condita*, 'from the foundation of the city'). The empha-
    tic separation of *esse* from the two noun-participle com-
    binations, which stand outside the *cum* clause, alone dis-
    tinguishes the construction from the perf. passive: L
    seems to be highlighting an ambiguity in the Latin language,
    and suggesting that it has misled his Roman opponents, who
    read into *Tyndaris rapta est* ('Helen has been raped') the
    idea that 'the rape of Helen exists'.
    Tyndaridem: though Helen was strictly the daughter not of
      Tyndareus, but of his wife Leda and Zeus, the patronymic
      is traditional, and does not necessarily indicate a
      Lucretian rationalisation of the myth.

467 quando . . . abstulerit: 'on the grounds that . . .'; the
-8 subj. is used in reporting the rival argument, whereas
    quorum . . . fuerunt with indic. interposes an objective
    truth as L sees it, 'whose accidents these in fact were'.
    The perf. *fuerunt* perhaps acknowledges that these events
    can *no longer* be called the accidents of the vanished
    saecla.
    saecla: 'generations', as at 202; not 'races' (see on 20
      above), which would imply that the Greeks and Trojans
      had no living descendants.

469 'For (when the generations concerned have disappeared)
-70 whatever has taken place will be able to be called the
    accident in one case of the lands, in another simply of
    the areas.' *aliud . . . aliud* subdivides the generalised
    subject *quodcumque erit actum*. The point of the contrast
    between *terris* and *regionibus ipsis* is obscure but the
    former perhaps denotes the physical site of events, the
    latter the mere point in space where they occurred. *region-
    ibus ipsis* may be added because L realises that *terrae*
    will eventually be destroyed with our world, so that they
    are ultimately open to the same objection as *saecla*. The
    most plausible alternative is to read *saeclis* for *terris*
    (which could have arisen from a gloss on *regionibus*) -
    'in one case of the generations (as long as they survive),

in another simply of the areas (when the *saecla* have
vanished).' In any case, the lines contain a debating-
point and L's real answer to the rival case is contained
in 471-82: he is less interested in the academic question
of finding an 'immediate' host for past events, than in
showing that their 'ultimate' host must be the matter and
void which was involved in them.

471 materies . . . rerum: i.e. matter to make up compounds,
whereas in 472 *res* denotes events; cf. on *res esse gerique* 442 above.

473 ignis: the fire of passion is not only fanned (*conflatus*)
-4 and blazes up (*gliscens*): in 475 it lights the flames of
war and in 476-7 is responsible for the literal conflagration of Troy; the point that Paris' passion was the
direct cause of the Trojan War is conveyed with splendid
poetic imagination. The linking of passion and war under
the same image is also especially appropriate in that,
to the Epicurean, both were destructive and horrendous:
this moral attitude implies a criticism of traditional
epic values: cf. the treatment of Iphigeneia in 80-101.
L's use of the Trojan War to argue a philosophic point
probably also represents a conscious attempt to improve
on traditional epic, whose style is evoked in the course
of the passage.
Phrygio: an epic-style transference from *Alexandri* (another
name for Paris) to *pectore*; cf. on 10 above.
sub: 'deep in'.

475 clara: suggesting both 'bright' (thus sustaining the fire
metaphor) and 'renowned', 'famous'.

476 clam . . . Troianis: 'unknown to the Trojans': though *clam*
+ acc. is common in Plautus, the abl. construction appears
to have only one parallel, in Caesar: in this Greek context, it perhaps evokes λάθρη + gen.
durateus: a transliteration in a Homeric context of the
Homeric δουράτεος (= *ligneus*).
partu: the metaphor of the wooden horse giving birth to
its warrior occupants appears to derive from Ennius,
Scaenica 76.

477 'The whole example is rounded off by the thunder of four
words in one line' (West 86).
Graiugenarum: the compound affords a resounding, epic-style
conclusion; cf. *Troiugenas* 465 and the patronymic
Tyndaris 464 and 473.

478 funditus omnis: 'in every single case', a favourite
Lucretian collocation, though *funditus* does not always
intensify *omnis* as here; see e.g. on 572, 620 and 668
below.

479 constare . . . esse . . . cluere: here, synonymous: 'exist
-80   . . . have their being . . . have an existence'.
   ratione . . . eadem qua constet inane: i.e. *per se*. For
    the synizesis of *eādem*, cf. 306. The subj. is sub-oblique
    after *perspicere*: cf. *gerantur* 482.

481 sed magis: sc. *ita cluere* - 'but rather exist in such a
   way'.
   merito: cf. *ut par est* 458, though here L is justifying
   the argument rather than the terminology alone.

483-634 THE ATOMIC NATURE OF MATTER

In this crucial section, L continues the analysis of
matter begun in 146-328, and argues that its constituents
are eternal, indestructible, solid, single, indivisible and
immutable, i.e. atoms. The one point in this section for
which he has already argued is the permanence of matter
(215-64), on which non-Atomist Greek physicists would have
agreed: they would have differed on the crucial question of
indivisibility, holding that matter, whether in practice or
theory, was infinitely divisible, so that matter at no
stage existed in the form of an 'atom'.

In L's mind, the various aspects which he here attributes
to the constituents of matter are inextricably linked; this
is the key to the understanding of both the presentation
and the logic of his argument, which has sometimes bewild-
ered editors. Thus in the introduction (483-502) he finds
it necessary to mention only eternity, indestructibility
and solidity; in the course of the proofs other aspects
emerge and alternate, so that proofs (i) and (iv) concern
in the first instance solidity, (iii) and (v) indivisibility, (ii) eternity, (vi) immutability and (vii) both
solidity and indivisibility. Within this framework he
frequently associates one aspect with another or deduces
it from another: e.g. eternity from solidity (485-6, 518-
9 and 528-39 where indivisibility is also inferred), solidity from eternity (548-50). The inevitable connection
between the various aspects emerges in the course of the
proofs, especially at 528-39, where division appears as a
category of destruction and solidity (implying the total
absence of void) as the only guarantee of indestructibility:
for experience indicates that destruction, whether by crush-
ing or division, depends on the presence of void in the
object. Equally, solidity, indivisibility and indestructibility are regarded as essential preconditions of eternity:
a non-solid, divisible, destructible object could not con-
ceivably avoid division and destruction indefinitely (548-
50 and 577-83). On the concepts of 'singleness' and immut-

ability, see on 548 and 584-98 below.

L's treatment is far fuller than anything to be found in Epicurus, *ad Hdt*., though some ideas from the letter can be traced in his discussion; a polemical note is implicit in it from 551.

483-502 Introduction

As is natural after the generic treatment of matter in 418-82, 483-4 (which are modelled on Epicurus, *ad Hdt*. 40) distinguish the two categories of matter (compounds and components) which have already emerged in L's discussion (see on 418-448 above). After stating the indestructibility and solidity of the components (485-6), he raises the difficulty that there is no parallel in the world of experience for completely solid, and so indestructible, matter - a contention supported by examples similar to those used in 346-57 to demonstrate the presence of void in visible compounds: his reply (498ff.) is that the hypothesis of solid, and so indestructible, ultimate components is demanded by reason, the Epicurean criterion of knowledge in fields where perception cannot go (cf. 423-5, 448, and Introduction III). The reader is thus prepared for a section of predominantly theoretical argument.

483   corpora . . . partim . . . partim: i.e. some bodies . . . .,
-4   others.
      concilio . . . principiorum: 'those which consist of an
         assembly of first-beginnings'; *principiorum* is used for
         primōrdiōrum (see on 55 above).

486   stinguere: the indestructibility of the ultimate particles
         is introduced metaphorically.
      nam: indestructibility is here a consequence of solidity,
         i.e. absence of void.
      demum: with *ea* ('they and they alone'), pointing the con-
         trast with all other categories of matter, like the
         visible compounds of 489-96.

487   etsi: 'and yet': here connective, not a conjunction.
      videtur: 'it seems', as at 497; contrast the 'Lucretian'
         sense (see on 224 above).

488   in rebus: i.e. 'in nature', as at 497.
      solido . . . corpore: abl. of quality with *quicquam* 487.

489   saepta domorum: see on 354 above, where permeation by
         voces (490) also figures.

490 clamor . . . voces: 'as do shouting and voices'; sounds
   are again treated as material, as are heat and cold in
   the remaining examples: see on 298-304 and 354-5 above.
 ferrum candescit: heat has permeated the iron, proving it
   contains void: its change of colour, like the melting
   of gold and bronze (492-3) is a form of destruction (cf.
   on 670-1 below), a consequence of permeability. Except
   for *clamor ac voces* and the *calor* and *frigus* of 494-6,
   L chooses examples where permeation leads directly to
   destruction, so reinforcing the idea that absence of
   void guarantees indestructibility (485-6).

491 dissiliuntque: permeation by heat in this instance causes
   a more spectacular form of destruction.
 fero ferventi: a striking assonance, also echoing *ferrum*
   490: it perhaps suggests that *feritas* is a natural
   characteristic not only of *fervor* but also of *ferrum*:
   cf. *fera ferri corpora* 2.103f. On the double adj.
   (one participial), see on *candens lacteus umor* 258 above.
 vapore: used by L (except perhaps at 3.432) as a synonym
   for *calor* and for the associated idea of fire (567),
   rather than in the basic sense of 'steam'.

492 cum . . . tum: 'not only . . . but also'.
 -3 labefactatus: cf. *labare* 530 and *labascit* 537; this word,
   like *solvitur* and *devicta liquescit*, indicates .
   destruction: contrast *vincunt* of the 'unquenchable'
   primordia (485-6).
 rigor auri: a poetically effective 'periphrasis' (cf. on
   animi natura 131 above), preparing for the bolder metaphor *glacies aeris*, appropriate to both the gleam and
   the melting of the bronze. The idiom is further exploited
   with *lympharum rore* 496.

495 The concluding example is supported from the direct exper-
 -6 ience of a Roman banqueter holding a silver goblet: its
   temperature varies as a slave adds water (*lympharum rore*)
   to his wine. *superne* conveys the picture of the slave
   standing while the banqueter reclines. *rite* ('in the
   accepted fashion') perhaps suggests a criticism of formal Roman practice; 2.20ff. point out that luxuries like
   silver (2.27) are not required by nature for physical
   well-being and contrast the simpler pleasures of an informal picnic.
 sensimus: 'we have felt'; the perf. makes this an appeal
   to specific instances in the past, though a generalising
   present would be equally valid: from such cases the gnomic
   perfect (cf. the Greek gnomic aorist) becomes natural;
   for early examples, cf. Plautus, *Captivi* 255-6 and
   Catullus 62.42.

497 usque adeo: with the whole sentence, 'so true is it that',

as at 966 and 1006. The line picks up 487-8 (on *in rebus* and *videtur*, see notes there); *solidi nil* ('no solidity', with a partitive gen.) answers *quicquam solido corpore*.

498 vera . . . ratio naturaque rerum: a similar hendiadys to that of 148: 'true reasoning about the nature of things'; for *ratio* as an instrument of investigation, cf. 425 and 448.

499 ades: sc. *animo*, 'pay heed', as e.g. at Plautus, *Menaechmi* 643 and *Mercator* 568.
expediamus: prospective subj.

500 esse: emphatic, 'that there exist'.
aeterno: an aspect of the indestructibility claimed in 485-6 and, like it, a consequence of solidity.

501 docemus: the clause is dependent on the acc. and infin. after *expediamus* but the indic. states an objective fact: contrast the sub-oblique subjs. in 500 and 502. The content of L's doctrine is at issue, not the fact that he is advocating it; cf. the similar distinction at 55-61.

502 unde: = *ex quibus* (see on 56 above).
omnis rerum . . . summa: see on 235 above; in the context of *creata*, the phrase suggests the totality of compounds in the universe.
nunc: i.e. as we (in our own world within the universe) now witness it.

503-539 Proof i

Matter must, at some level of analysis, exist in a pure form which excludes void: at this stage a solid, discrete part-icle of matter will have been reached. This theoretical argument is presented under three aspects, of which (a) and (c) are especially closely related: (a - 503-10) where void is to be found, matter is not, and vice versa: pure, solid matter must thus ultimately be reached in an analysis of the universe; (b - 511-7) the matter in compounds must, at some level of analysis, be pure and solid in order to contain the void in the compound; (c - 520-7) matter and void alter-nate throughout the universe: an analysis of the universe must thus ultimately reveal pure, solid matter.

From the solidity of his particles L also deduces their eternity, indestructibility and indivisibility (518-9 and 528-39); while this procedure is not in the least surpris-ing (see on 483-634 above and cf. 485-6), it remains odd that the brief inference of 518-9 precedes the fuller argu-

ment of 528-39. The anomaly would presumably have been
removed in revision and could have arisen from the late insertion of 520-31 or of 520-39: these lines could have been
added after the composition of 1008-13, to which 520-7 are
close in thought, without being ideally adjusted to their
place (cf. 208-14).

The three arguments for solidity cannot be traced to an
extant Epicurean original, though the inseparable links
between solidity, indestructibility and indivisibility
are reflected in *ad Hdt.* 40-1.

503 I.e. since nature has been found to be twofold, comprising
-5   two completely different types of existence, matter and
     void. *natura* seems to do double duty, bearing its full
     sense with *duplex*, but forming a periphrasis with the gens.
     (cf. on 131 above): 'two quite different categories have
     been found to exist, viz. matter and void'.

505 This line is repeated from 482 (though the indic. here shows
     that the rel. clause is asserted as an objective fact,
     despite its dependence on *repertast*); cf. also 472, 955
     and the recurrence of *quod inane vocamus* at 369, 426, 439,
     507 and 1074. L's repetition of phrases, lines and short
     passages is perhaps partly designed to evoke and challenge
     comparison with the recurrent formulae of epic in what he
     regards as the more serious field of philosophical poetry;
     see also on 75-7 above.

506 esse . . . sibi per se puramque: 'exists for and by itself
     and in a pure form', i.e. unmixed with the other.
     utramque: fem. referring to *natura* 503.

507 quacumque vacat spatium: i.e. in unoccupied space; *spatium*
     itself is here coextensive with the universe and embraces
     occupied and unoccupied space.

508 ea: = *ibi*, picking up *quacumque* in each case.
-9   qua . . . cumque: L frequently utilises tmesis with the
     indefinite suffix; cf. 873 (and the supplement after 1114),
     also on *praeterque meantum* 318 above.
     tenet se: 'has taken up position'; the monosyllabic ending
     brings us up against matter with a jolt.

510 sunt . . . corpora prima: probably 'the primary bodies are
     . .', with the *primordia* taken for granted on the basis
     of 149-328, rather than 'there exist primary bodies (which
     are) . . .', with their existence as well as their nature
     deduced independently from the argument (as 526, *sunt ergo
     corpora certa*, might suggest). A similar question, which
     concerns the presentation, not the substance, of the argu-

ments, arises also at 538-9, 545, 565-6, 570, 574, 609 and 627: in most of these cases, the context tends to favour the first interpretation.

511 genitis in rebus: i.e. in compound objects, whereas the *primordia* have always existed and never been 'born'.

512 materiem circum solidam constare: 'that solid matter exists around it', indicating not that the enclosing matter (which comprised discrete particles) forms a continuous, unbroken envelope but that it is, by definition, totally distinct from the void which it encloses and so pure, unadulterated.

514 corpore inane suo: the word-order reproduces the pattern in nature, as at 367 (*multo vacui minus*).

515 'If you fail to leave what contains it to exist in solid form'. On the idiom of *relinquere*, see on 446 above; here and at 703, where the sense approximates both to 'allow to' and 'admit that', it governs an acc. and infin. by analogy with *pati* (cf. 3.40) and *fateri*. The subj. is of indefinite second person. *cohibet* has its original sense, without the idea of repression. The rel. clause serves to define (cf. *quaecumque cluent* 449) and so resists the sub-oblique subj. which might be expected insofar as *relinquas* = *fatearis*.

516 id: picked up by the consecutive rel. clause *quod . . .*
-7 *cohibere*.
   materiai concilium: 'an assembly of (pure) matter', not in the full technical sense of a material compound, in which it is natural to regard void as an ingredient, as indeed *inane . . . rerum* (denoting the void in compound objects) reflects.

518 The first inference, that matter exists in a solid form,
-9 is contained in the rel. clause of 518: the main clause adds the inference that such matter, despite the destructibility of all other bodies (i.e. of all compounds, *cetera*), can be eternal. On the relationship of the couplet with 528-39, see introductory note above.

520 inane: adjectival, as at 527; contrast the usual substantival use at 523 and 524.
   vacaret: continuing the hypothesis, like *complerent* and *tenerent* 522: but *vacaret* and *complerent* are doubtless also consecutive.

521 omne: 'the universe', as at 74.
   certa: (cf. 526) 'definite', suggesting in the context an antithesis with void and its admixture and thus approximating to *pura, solida*.

523 omne quod est spatium: 'the whole of space' (as at 969),
which is coextensive with the universe (*omne* 521, which
the phrase answers).

524 inani: abl. of separation with *distinctumst*: cf. *pleno*
527.

525 naviter: with both *plenum* and *vacuum*; the subject of
-6   *exstat* is 'the universe and all the space in it', from
521 and 523.

527 pleno: sc. *spatio*.
possint: consecutive subj.

528 These lines allude to the two methods of atomic dissolution
-9   distinguished at 222-3, external impact (*plagis extrin-*
secus icta), and a more gradual process of disruptive
infiltration (*penitus penetrata*). The alternatives are
respectively picked up and illustrated in 532-3 and 534-
5: the *corpora certa* are immune to them because they contain no void.
penitus penetrata: another meaningful assonance (Introduction
V c); the phrase also contributes to the *p* alliteration
in a sinister context; cf. e.g. *Pergama partu* 476.
retexi: for the weaving metaphor, cf. *contextum* 243 and
textura 247.

530 temptata labare: cf. 537, with the archaic inceptive
labascit, and *labefactatus* 492. L uses another lively
metaphor, this time suggesting destructibility rather
than divisibility. His alternation throughout this argument between words which focus on one or other idea
(*labare, collidi, conficiuntur, labascit* as opposed to
dissolui, retexi, frangi, findi in bina) illustrates that
destruction and division are synonymous in his mind.

531 The reference is not immediately obvious: it may be to 215-
64, where the eternity of matter was taken to be implied
in the principle that nothing is destroyed into nothing
(a passage mentioned also at 543-4); it could be to 485-
6 or 518-9, with *ostendimus* meaning 'indicated' rather
than 'proved'.

532 videtur: 'it is obvious that' - the Lucretian passive use
(see on 224 above); the argument is based on experience:
denser compounds (containing less void) can be seen to
be more resistant to the six types of destruction listed.

533 nec findi in bina secando: paraphrasing the root force of
ἄτομος, 'atom'. On the 'quasi-passive' use of the gerund,
see on 312 above.

534 manabile: coined, with active force (see on *genitabilis* 11

above), from L's favourite *manare* (cf. 348 and 494), to
provide a synonym for *penetralis* 535.

535 quibus omnia conficiuntur: i.e. moisture, cold and fire can
prove fatal to any compound which they permeate.

536 quo . . . magis . . . inane replaces *quo plus inanis* to
balance *tam magis* 537.
quaeque . . . res: 'each type of thing'; see on 76 above.

537 tam magis: a common Lucretian variant on *eo magis* (or
tanto magis).
his rebus: i.e. by these processes, covering both external
impact (532-3) and permeation (534-5).
penitus combines the senses 'deep down' (cf. 529), answering
intus 536, and 'thoroughly' (cf. 541); it is here applicable to both methods of dissolution (contrast 529):
destruction, whether by external impact or permeation,
goes deeper and is more thorough, the more void the
compound contains.
temptata labascit: see on 530 above.

539 uti docui: at 503-27.

540-550 Proof ii

Matter must at some stage be eternal, or things would have
been destroyed into nothing, leaving re-creation, in turn,
to take place from nothing. L here summarises the point
implicit throughout 215-64, where the permanence of matter
appeared as the corollary of the principle that nothing is
destroyed into nothing: the argument is especially closely
related to that of 225-37, despite a difference in presentation (see on 237 above). In 548-50 'solid simplicity'
(see on 548) is deduced from eternity as the only possible
explanation of the durability of the ultimate particles: ½
the pattern of argument in proof (i) is thus inverted (see
on 483-634 above).

For the corresponding passages in *ad Hdt.*, see on 225-37
above and on 551-64 (proof iii) below.

540 fuisset: 'had been' in the past, rather than *esset* ('were
now'), because on the rival theory matter would not exist
in the present.

541 antehac: spondee by synizesis; cf. *anteacta* 234.
penitus: 'utterly': see on 537 above.
res quaeque: like the neut. pl. *quaeque* 546, indicating 'each
type of thing' (as at 536), since types, rather than indiv-

idual things, recur in nature.

542 quaecumque videmus: cf. on *quaecumque videntur* 262 above.

543 supra: at 146-264.

544 quod genitum est: for the indic., despite *docui*, in this type of rel. clause, see on *quaecumque cluent* 449 above.

545 esse . . . primordia: see on 510 above.

546 quo: (second word in its clause, like *ut* 547) = *in quae*; see on *unde* 56 above.
    possint: prospective subj., the clause being purposive, like the *ut* clause which follows.

547 suppeditet: 'may be available' - intransitive, as at 1040.
    rebus reparandis: 'for the renewal of things' (i.e. visible compounds); for the dat. of purpose, see on 24 above.

548 simplicitate: a new aspect of the ultimate particle, always qualified by *solida* (cf. 574 and 609) or *aeterna* (at 612 only). 'Singleness' serves as a bridge between the notions of 'solidity' and 'indivisibility': like *solidus*, *simplex* suggests purity (contrast *duplex* of the nature of matter and void combined at 503), so that *solida simplicitas* may be seen in part as a metrical equivalent for the inadmissible *sóliditas*: but the idea of 'unity' in *simplex* also suggests an irreducible, indivisible particle of matter. Once more the various aspects of the atom merge into one another in L's mind.

549 queunt . . . servata . . . reparare: 'can they have been
-50 preserved . . . and have renewed . . .'.
    ex infinito iam tempore: as in the parallel argument at 225-37, the infinity of time is assumed; see on 233 above. Strictly *iam* goes closely with *reparare* but the word-order suggests 'from infinite time past until now' (cf. 991).

551-564 Proof iii

There must be a limit to the divisibility of matter: otherwise, since construction in nature can be seen always to take longer than destruction, matter would by now have been broken up so far that it could not reassemble quickly enough either (a) to form new compounds in the first place or (b) to allow their growth to maturity within the usual fixed span. The thought is parallel with that of proof (ii), where L argued that, without eternal matter, the world would have disappeared: he now claims that, without indivisible matter, it

would have disintegrated. Epicurus combines the ideas
behind proofs (ii) and (iii) in a single sentence (*ad Hdt.*
41: ταῦτα δέ ἐστιν ἄτομα . . ., εἴπερ μὴ μέλλει πάντα εἰς
τὸ μὴ ὃν φθαρήσεσθαι ἀλλ᾽ ἰσχῦόν τι ὑπομένειν ἐν ταῖς
διαλύσεσι τῶν συγκρίσεων); the same sentence also contains
a parallel for the inference about the 'seeds' made in
548-50 above (πλήρη τὴν φύσιν ὄντα, οὐκ ἔχοντα ὅπῃ ἤ ὅπως
διαλυθήσεται).

The discussion of indivisibility is continued in proof (v)
and proof (vii), which also concerns solidity: the three
passages foreshadow the objections levelled specifically
against the Pluralists and Anaxagoras on this score at
746-7 and 844.

Proofs (iii-vi) exhibit the same broad pattern of
alternation as that noted on 159-214, though the symmetry,
which is interrupted by 574-6, is not so exact: see also
on 583 below.

552 frangendis rebus: the dat. expresses as much the indirect
object of *finem parasset* ('had set a limit on the breakage of things') as purpose (see on 24 above); cf. the
constructions with *reddita* (203-4 and 577).

553 usque: = *usque eo*, 'so far'.

554 'That nothing, starting from a fixed time, would be able
-5 to be conceived of them and to attain the full increase
of its lifespan', i.e. to grow to full maturity (cf.
aevi contingere florem 564): the *corpora* would have
been divided so far that they could never reassemble
quickly enough to initiate, much less to complete, the
re-creation of any compound for the reason advanced in
the next line and a half.
a certo tempore: i.e. given a fixed starting point in
time as a reference, looking forward to the hypothetical
point of completion of the processes, which would never
come; in 559-60 the present is taken as the point of
reference.
conceptum: partly metaphorical, since the generalisation
is not confined to animal or to organic life - a development of the image implicit in the recurrent use of *gig-
nere* for the formation of all compounds: see on 150 above.

556 dissolvi . . . refici: the terms presuppose the atomic view
-7 that 're-creation' was only complete when full maturity
was reached and 'dissolution' began with the decline from
that maturity: before maturity, more atoms were assimilated than lost, whereas after it the reverse applied.
reficere (cf. 562 below) is a synonym for *reparare* 547,

550 and 560; cf. 235 and 263.
posse: 'can be' implying 'and is'.

557 longa . . . omnis: subject of the rel. clause of 559, which
-60   itself provides the subject of *posset* 560. The phrase
is a remarkable accumulation, mirroring the endless
piling of moment on moment in infinite time. *diei* (cf.
322), *aetas* and *temporis* are virtual synonyms for time:
aetas is qualified by a pair of parallel adjs. (see on
candens lacteus umor 258 above). Most unusual of all is
the double gen., with *anteacti temporis omnis* probably
best regarded as defining *diei* ('the long, infinite expanse of the age of all time past'). The spondaic
rhythm of 558 and the synizesis in *antêacti* contribute
to the effect; cf. on 233-4 above. For the assumption
of the infinity of time, see again on 233 above and cf.
550: here it is vital for the argument that the *corpora*
could never reassemble but not for the claim implied in
563-4 that successive generations would take longer to
reach maturity.
fregisset . . . posset: potential subjs., drawing the
consequences of the initial hypothesis of 551-2.
adhuc: i.e. in the infinite span of time up to the present
- antithetical with *reliquo tempore*, in the (infinite)
time still to come. *rēlicŭō* is an older, quadrisyllabic
form of *rĕlĭquō*; for the lengthened *e*, cf. on *religione*
63 above.

561 reddita: sc. *a natura*, answering *natura parasset* 551; cf.
577.

562 rem quamque: 'each kind of thing' (see on 541 above),
preparing for the more explicit allusion to species
in *generatim* 563.

563 I.e. successive generations of the same species reach
-4   maturity in a constant time, implying that, were matter
infinitely divisible, each generation, if it could be
created in the first place, would take longer than its
predecessor.
possint: sub-oblique subj. after *videmus* 562, but perhaps
combining prospective force.
aevi . . . florem: a Lucretian metaphor for maturity
(cf. 3.770 and 5.847), answering *summum aetatis auctum*
555.

565-576 Proof iv

Solid, hard units of matter can produce soft compounds by
the admixture of void, whereas a soft substratum of matter,
such as was postulated by Monists, Pluralists and in part by
Anaxagoras (cf. 635-920), could not produce the hard compounds

of experience.

The passage has no extant parallel in Epicurus and may be compared with the specific attacks on the soft substrata postulated by the Pluralists and Anaxagoras (753-8 and 847-58) on the different grounds that softness implies destructibility, and with 742-5, where L suggests that a soft substratum implies void which his opponents deny.

The polemical note implicit in proof (iii) is thus here sustained: though solidity was last mentioned at 548 and though proof (iv) separates two proofs concerning indivisibility, there is no reason to suspect that the arrangement is not deliberate; see introductory note to 483-634 above and cf. the interwoven arguments of 215-64: proofs (iii-vi) also exhibit a broad pattern of alternation between the hypothetical and the real (see on 551-64 above).

565 solidissima: emphatically positioned, like the antithetical *mollia* 567, outside their clauses: *cum* 566 is postponed to fourth position.

566 constant: (= *sunt*) indic., despite the concessive idea
-7 indicated by *tamen*; cf. 726-30 and 823-6. The construction is attested in early writers and not unknown in Cicero: the stressing of the temporal relation is often an adequate explanation (cf. *cum* + indic. in a causal context; see on 380 above; here the indic. also enables L's own view to be presented vividly as a fact.
omnia . . . mollia quae fiunt: 'all things which are formed soft', i.e. all soft compounds.
reddi: 'be accounted for' - a bold personal usage, for *ratio reddi* (which appears in full to form an antithesis at 572) + gen. Epicurus' use of ἀποδοθῆναι (e.g. *ad Hdt.* 55) is a probable influence.
vapores: see on 491 above; the allusion to the three other elements of Empedocles shows that here the term denotes fire: the pl. is poetic. Though the list of the four elements may suggest that L is thinking first and foremost of Empedocles, each of the four was also the basic substance in different Monist theories; cf. 705-10.

568 The appended indirect questions specify what features of the soft compounds can be explained: the construction is of the !I know thee who thou art' type; cf. 949-50.
fiant: 'are formed' - a different sense from that in 129, which the line strongly echoes.
quaeque gerantur: 'the different processes (involving them) are carried on'; *quaeque* cannot refer to the *mollia* themselves, since *geri* is applicable to a process, not to a physical compound.

569 I.e. once the admixture of void in nature (and in compound
bodies in particular; see on 330 above) has been accepted.
On the idiom of *admixtum est*, see on *relinqui* 446 above.
There is an implied antithesis with the position of rival
theorists who deny void: cf. 655ff., 745 and 843-4.

570 si . . . sint . . . poterit: the protasis (which answers
-2 *solidissima* . . . *constant* 565-6) is remote, the apodosis open. The rival hypothesis becomes more real in L's
mind as he examines its implications: the vivid construction is continued in *carebit* 573. For a similar shift, cf.
655-6. *sint* may refer either to future time ('if the
primordia were to be (thought) soft') or to present (=
prose *essent*; see on *sint*, 356 above).
unde . . . creari: the indirect question precedes *ratio
reddi*, creating a chiasmic pattern in the antithesis with
possint . . . *gerantur* 566-8. *validi silices ferrumque*
contrast with the *mollia* and *creari* picks up *fiant*.
queant: 'could' - potential in the indirect question,
continuing the remote construction of *sint*.

572 funditus: with *carebit* rather than *omnis* (see on 478 above).
-3 The assonance with *fundamenti* is a reminder of the root
force, 'from the bottom' or 'at the bottom' (for the
latter, rarer, sense, cf. 5.497); see also on 620, 668 and
993.
omnis . . . natura: 'the whole of nature'; cf. on 419 above.
principio fundamenti: 'the basis of a foundation'. *funda-
mento*, a building metaphor, would have made L's point by
itself: the addition of *principio* states his case still
more strongly and perhaps also suggests that the rival
principia fail in their basic function of providing a
principium; cf. the criticism of Anaxagoras' *primordia*
(847-50).

574 sunt . . . pollentia: sc. *corpora* = *primordia* from 566 and
570 either as subject or as predicate: 'they (the first-
bodies) are powerful . . .' or 'there exist bodies which
are powerful . . .'; see on 510 above.

575 quorum condenso magis . . . conciliatu: 'by whose denser
assemblage'; the noun is another fourth decl. coining:
cf. the abstract sense of *concilium* (see on 183 above).
omnia must refer to all comparatively hard compounds
(unless L means that all compounds become harder when
compressed).

576 validas: the verbal similarity with *solida* (574) may to L
mirror the causal connection he sees between solidity and
strength.

577-583 Proof v

If matter is infinitely divisible, bodies which have in
practice escaped division beyond a certain limit must have
survived from infinite time until now (to allow for re-
creation). But divisible matter could not have avoided division in face of the buffets of infinite time.

This passage seems designed to counter a reply to proof
(iii) along the lines that, in practice, the division of
matter did not go so far as to preclude re-creation: this
must have been the view of the Pluralists and Anaxagoras,
who are specifically criticised for allowing infinite division at 746-7 and 844, and are probably foremost in L's
mind here. The Aristotelian distinction between potential
and actual division could be a further target.

577 I.e. assuming infinite divisibility, we must still accept
-9   the argument of 540-7, that the substratum survives and
      is not subject to destruction (as the Pluralists and
      Anaxagoras would have agreed).
      si nullast . . .: the hypothesis of 551-2 is here presented
      more vividly in an open conditional; the vivid construct-
      ion continues in *constant* 581. *tamen* also makes *si* ap-
      proximate to *etsi*.
      ex aeterno tempore: the assumption again assists L's argu-
      ment (see on 233 above).
      quaeque . . . corpora rebus: 'different bodies to make
      things'; grammatically the dat. may be taken with *superare*,
      denoting purpose or advantage. *quaeque*, though doubtless
      indicating different types of body and, by transference,
      of the compounds they form, does not justify Bailey's
      assumption of an exclusive allusion to Anaxagorean
      homoeomeria; cf. 541, 546 and 562.
      superare: 'survive', as at 672 and 790; with *ex aeterno*
      tempore, the present also includes perf. sense (as with
      iamdudum).

580 'Which are such as to exist without yet having been assailed
      by any danger' (a consecutive rel. clause). The surviving
      corpora, being infinitely divisible, must mysteriously
      have escaped the perils which would inevitably have divi-
      ded them further. *clueant* = *sint*; cf. on 119 above.

581 fragili: a rather loaded term, suggesting 'easily broken'
      rather than 'breakable'.
      constant: = *sunt* (sc. 'on the rival theory'); the subject
      is still *corpora* 579.

582 discrepat . . . potuisse: sc. *ea* as subject-acc., 'it is
      inconsistent to suppose that they can have'. *discrepat*
      governs an acc. and infin. by analogy with *convenit*, its

antonym.

583 innumerabilibus plagis: in view of the infinity of time
the adj. is quite literal. For the external blow as an
agent of destruction, cf. 222 and 528: the description
fits both L's detailed analysis, in which the atoms were
in constant motion and collision and, at a more general
level of argument, the shocks to which matter can be
observed to be subject. The line is antithetical to
580, asserting the actual conditions confronting primary
matter and thus preserving the pattern of alternation
between the hypothetical and the real in proofs (iii-
vi), which was noted on 159-214 and 551-64 above.

584-598 Proof vi

Matter must at the ultimate level of analysis be immutable
or there would be no stability in nature: members of the
same species could not preserve their uniform characteristics nor would there be any limit to the number of species
which could arise.

Immutability (cf. Epicurus' ἀμετάβλητος) is a new aspect of
the constituents of matter, which to L precludes both destructibility (cf. 670-1, repeated at 792-3, where change
implies destruction) and divisibility (cf. 3.513-5, where
change must involve addition, rearrangement or subtraction
of parts, which are thus by definition separable).

The argument probably once more contains a polemical note:
according to at least some Monists and Pluralists, the basic
substance or elements underwent qualitative change to produce the visible objects of the world; on this hypothesis,
L would maintain, all manner of change becomes possible.

584 iam: 'as it is', antithetical with si . . . possent 592-3,
-5 though the juxtaposition with quoniam is not particularly
euphonious.
generatim: emphatic; the uniformity of species is the basis
of the whole argument.
reddita finis: the echo of 577 and 561 (cf. 551) is likely
to be deliberate; the observable limitations in nature reflect the limitations imposed on the unseen primordia,
which cannot change any more than they can be divided.
crescendi . . . vitamque tenendi: an allusion to growth
to full maturity, and to the full lifespan, the times for
which are both constant in a species. The former point
was made in arguing for a limit to division (554-5 and
563-4) and its repetition here illustrates that indivisibility and immutability are complementary ideas.
rebus: here living things, whether animal or vegetable;

though L would regard the whole argument as applicable to all types of compound, he illustrates it primarily from the animal world.

constat: 'is constant' - a vital point in the argument, as at 588 (cf. 165); contrast 581 above.

586 The prose order would be *et quandoquidem sancitum exstat*
-7 followed by the two indirect questions: the *quandoquidem* clause extends to *inesse* 590, with the main clause coming in 591-2.

quaeque: 'each kind of thing' (see on 76 above) alluding to species (see on *generatim* 584 above).

foedera naturai: the spondaic fifth foot and the sonorous, archaic *-ai* genitive (cf. 1116) add to the solemnity and impressiveness of the phrase (repeated at 2.302 and 5. 310). The political metaphor is far livelier than in 'scientific law', where it is ossified, and is continued in *sancitum . . . exstat* ('it stands ordained'), where the older form and sense of *sancitum* sustain the note of archaic solemnity (the 'rugged' elision of *quandoquidem* at the end of the fifth foot is not out of keeping). At the same time, the religious associations of *sancitum* (= *sanctum*) are also appropriate in L's mind to nature's sacred edicts; cf. on *sanctius* 738.

588 quicquam . . . omnia: sc. within the same species, as the example of 589-90 shows.

quin: 'but rather'; this corrective use is unusual inside a dependent clause.

constant: antithetical with *commutatur*; see on 585 above.

589 variae: 'various' (not 'variegated'), again introducing
-90 the key idea of species, which *in ordine* and *generalis* reinforce; cf. *variae gentes* 2.610, 2.1076 and 4.413; and *variae pecudes* 5.228.

ostendant: the argument is once more from the observable world (584-90) to the invisible world of the atoms (591-2).

corpore: poetic abl. of 'place where' without preposition.

591 'They must indubitably also possess a body made up of
-2 immutable matter' - sc. *volucres*, representing *omnia* (588), as the subject of this conclusion.

immutabili': the fortuitous similarity in pattern with *MaterIae* is perhaps exploited to reinforce the link between immutability and (ultimate) matter. On the suppressed *s*, unusual outside the fifth foot, see on 159 above.

quoque: i.e. as well as unchanging observable features (in the case of the birds their *maculas*).

corpus: the repetition of the word from 590 in the same position helps to suggest how inevitably the conclusion follows from the evidence.

592 nam . . .: this sentence forms a chiasmically arranged
-8 antithesis with the previous one: 592-3 (*si . . . re-*
victa) answer 591-2 (*immutabili' . . . nimirum*), while
594-8 answer 584-590, with the responsion of 594-6 to
586-7 especially marked.

592 si . . . possent . . . constet: for the mixture of tenses
-4 in a present remote conditional, cf. the converse arrangement at 356-7 (see *ad loc.*). With *possent* (597) L reverts
to the normal prose tense for the second part of the apodosis.
revicta: the metaphor indicates that change implies weakness and so destructibility.
incertum . . . constet: the verb = *sit* but L perhaps plays
on the sense crucial at 585 and 588 above; on the rival
theory only uncertainty would be constant.
quoque: exactly balancing the *quoque* of 591. A fluctuating
substratum would result also in irregular fluctuations
in the observable world.
iam: inferential, 'in that case', 'then'.

594 quid . . . haerens: this summary of the limitations imposed
-6 by natural law (which would here be violated) is repeated
from 75-7 (see *ad loc.*).

597 saecla: = *genera* (see on 20 above).
-8 naturam: the example of the birds' markings falls under
this head.
victum: 'mode of life', including the specialised sense
of 'diet'.
motusque: for -*que* after previous asyndeton, cf. on 162
above.

599-634 Proof vii

The complicated doctrine of the 'least parts' of the atom,
discussed by Epicurus in *ad Hdt.* 56-9 (which those who find
L's treatment obscure and prosaic would do well to compare),
is here used as a final confirmation of the solidity and
indivisibility of the *primordia*. The view that the atom
had parts, which could be arrived at in thought but not
of course in physical division, was an innovation in atomic
theory made by Epicurus himself. Its purpose cannot, as
Bailey implies, have been to allow extension to the atoms
(for the 'least parts' themselves possessed extension without having parts); rather it allowed the atoms sufficient
extension to admit the (finite number of) differences in
shape and size which were necessary to account for the
(finite) variety of the visible world (cf. 2.481-99, where
these differences in atomic type depend on the number and
arrangement of the component *minimae partes*). The concept
of these 'least parts' was arrived at by analogy from the
visible world: just as one could in thought distinguish a

minimum visible point on the surface of an object, beyond
which a smaller visible point could not be conceived, so
in the atom it was possible to imagine a 'least part', possessed of the minimum conceivable degree of extension (cf.
749-52 and Epicurus, *ad Hdt*. 57-9).

In (a) 599-614 and (b) 615-27 L first seeks to establish
the existence in matter (within the imperceptible *primordia*)
of a theoretical minimum without parts, i.e. of the *minima
pars*, arguing in (a) (599-602) from the technical concept
of the 'extreme point' (see on 599 below), in (b) (615-626)
from the paradox that without such a minimum the universe and
the smallest thing in it will each comprise infinite parts
and so be equal - a fallacy, since infinities are incom-
mensurable. In each case, he then proceeds to deduce the
solidity and indivisibility, and hence the eternity, of the
primordia from the nature of the *minimae partes*. In (c)
628-34 he argues that the *primordia* can never be resolved
into their *minimae partes* (whose existence is now treated
as established): since the 'least parts' themselves have
no parts, they do not possess the variety essential in the
substratum and would thus be unable to produce anew the
manifold compounds of the visible world (see on 633-4
below). This argument is the converse of 2.500-21, where
L deduces from the limit to the varieties in nature that
the differences in the types of atom are also limited.

Since the doctrine that the atom had parts was something
of a concession, which left its advocates with the task of
proving that these parts were never physically isolable, its
presentation in (a) and (b) as a proof of the solidity and
indivisibility of the *primordia* is bold and contrasts with
the more defensive position in (c). But L's discussion is
a natural sequel not only to proofs (iii) and (v), since he
now elaborates and defends his own view of the limit to
division, but also to proof (vi), since he now turns from
the immutability which produces *constancy* in nature's various
patterns to the *minimae partes* which, by allowing for varieties of immutable atom, allow for a *variety* of constant patterns in nature. The passage also constitutes an appropriate
conclusion to the whole series of proofs, since the *minima
pars* is the ultimate stage in the Epicurean analysis of
matter. Structurally the threefold presentation matches the
pattern of the opening proof in 503-39.

For a comprehensive discussion of the whole doctrine, see
D.J. Furley, *Two Studies in the Greek Atomists* (1967) 3-158,
where the Lucretian passages are examined in ch.2.

599   quoniam . . . nequeunt: 'since that body, which our senses
-601   can no longer discern (i.e. the atom), possesses in eacn

case an ultimate point'.

extremum cacumen: (lit. 'ultimate peak') = Epicurus'
ἄκρον. These terms, which suggest a point on the surface,
are applied (i) as at 749, to the minimum visible point
of an object, (ii) as here (cf. *extremum* 752), to a point
of minimum extension in an atom, a concept justified by
analogy with (i) (see introductory note above). As the text
stands, L here takes the existence of the *extremum cacumen*
of the atom for granted and then infers its lack of parts
and minimal nature; but his mere use of the term suggests
that he has in mind the argument from analogy, which appears later at 749-52. Munro supposed two lines lost
after 599, to allow the same analogy to be drawn explicitly
here.

quodque: transferred from *corporis* to *cacumen*, as shown by
cuiusque in 749; cf. *quaeque corpora rebus* 578f.

iam idiomatically denotes a point on a scale, as at 613
and 625.

601 id: i.e. the *extremum cacumen*; its lack of parts and minimal
-2 nature (ideas combined also at 625-6) follow from its being
extremum.

constat: = *est*; *minima natura* is abl. of quality.

602 nec fuit . . .: this demonstration of the inseparability of
-8 the 'least parts' is the most crucial part of the 'proof'
and depends primarily on their definition and on the view
of them as contiguous in the atom, which thus contains no
void (see on *agmine condenso* 606).

604 alterius: i.e. of the atom, like *corporis* 606.

ipsum: 'in itself' and so 'essentially'.

primaque et una: 'a part both primary and single'; *prima*,
picked up by *inde* 605, indicates the most basic conceivable
starting point for an atom; *una*, picked up by *aliae atque
aliae*, that it is but one of several components.

605 A continuation in asyndeton of the *quoniam* clause begun
-6 in 604.

aliae atque aliae: implying quite a number of *minimae partes*
per atom; the model comprising three or a few more, which
we are invited to visualise at 2.485f., is perhaps simplified for purposes of illustration.

agmine condenso: 'in serried ranks', conveying the important
technical idea of absence of void, the secret of the atom's
eternity. Like the phalanx, it owes its survival to its
cohesion. The personification of the 'least parts' (cf.
also 610-1) and the metaphor of *revelli* and *avelli* (608
and 613) enliven the technical discussion.

607 constare: = *esse*; just as the minimum visible point could
not be seen in isolation, so the 'least parts' could not
exist by themselves.

608 unde: 'in a union from which', sc. *ibi* as antecedent.
queant: consecutive subj.

609 Repeated from 548 (cf. also 574) and echoed below in
612, as L doggedly insists on his conclusion.

610 I.e. comprising a tightly (*artē*) packed, cohesive union of
'least parts': the abl. *minimis partibus* is probably one
of means. *stipata* again (cf. 329) suggests absence of void.
stipata and *cohaerent* are used by historians of military
formation and are not inconsistent with the metaphor introduced in 606.

611 This line contrasts the union of the 'least parts' in an
atom with the union of atoms to form a compound. *conciliata* has the root meaning of 'linked in a *concilium*'
(cf. on 183 above) and, like *conventu*, fits the probable
personification of 610.

612 magis: = *potius*, as at 481, 701 and 765. *aeternitas* is
here again inferred from *soliditas* and *simplicitas*.

613 unde: = *a quibus* (cf. 56).
-4 avelli quicquam . . . deminui: *concedit* here governs an acc.
and infin. instead of an *ut* clause, by analogy with *patior*
(cf. *suadere* and *inducere* at 140-2).
iam: 'any longer' - i.e. once reduction has proceeded as far
as the atom; cf. on 601 above. The line ends as abruptly
at the monosyllable as does division at the atom (see Introduction V d).
reservans semina rebus: hinting at the argument to follow
at 628-34.

615 minimum: technical for a theoretical minimum in matter (=
Epicurus' ἐλάχιστον); cf. *minima . . . natura* 602 and 626.
parvissima quaeque: 'all the smallest' - the form of the
superlative (cf. 3.199) is probably colloquial; its use
here and at 621 allows *minimus* to be reserved for the specialised, technical, sense.

616 On the spondaic fifth foot, perhaps suggestive of the tedium
of infinite division, see Introduction V d.

617 pars: sc. *dimidia*, not only out of *dimidiae* and *dimidiam*; in
-8 a mathematical context *pars* regularly denotes one part
out of two. The repetition ('half of a half . . . a half')
seems intentionally grotesque and calculated to pour scorn
on the rival view.
praefiniet: 'will foreordain a limit' - a legal term personifying the *res* (i.e. in L's view the *minimum*); L's absolute
use gives *finire* its root sense.

619 rerum . . . summam: 'the sum of things' (cf. on 235 above),

but the combination with *minimamque*, 'the smallest of
things' (in the Lucretian analysis, the *minima pars*),
suggests a play on *summam* as adj., 'the greatest of
things'. Either way, the universe is denoted.
escit: = *intererit*, 'what difference will there be'; the
rare, archaic inceptive of *esse* here serves as a future.

620   nil erit ut distet: = *nil distabit* with the verb impersonal
-1   and *nil* adverbial acc.   For the periphrasis, cf. e.g.
      2.496 and 5.517.
      funditus: with *quamvis* and *infinita*, rather than *omnis*,
      'however utterly infinite' (see on 346 and 478 above).
      funditus is also appropriate in the root sense 'at the
      bottom', since L is considering the view that in division
      the universe has no 'downward' limit (cf. on 572 above).
      omnis summa: i.e. the entire universe, probably 'the whole
      sum' (cf. 502), though *omnis* could be neuter gen. (cf. on
      419 and 572-3 above).

622   aeque: for the fallacy contained here, see introductory note
      above.

623   quod: connective, object of *reclamat* and *credere*.   For the
      vivid personification of *vera ratio* by its two verbs, cf.
      declarat 365 and *dedicat* 367.   The paradoxical consequences
      are dismissed as manifestly untenable.

624   fateare necessest: for the paratactic formula, cf. 399.

625   ea: i.e. the *minimae partes*.
      iam: see on 601 and 613 above.

627   illa: i.e. the *primordia*.   The sense is either 'you must also
      confess that those bodies are solid and eternal' or 'you
      must confess that those bodies also exist, solid and eter-
      nal' (see on 510 above).   In either case solidity and eter-
      nity follow from the existence of the *minimae partes* on
      the grounds set out more fully in (a) at 602-14.
      tibi: dat. of agent with the gerundive of obligation *faten-
      dum* (sc. *est*, as at 131), which provides a variation on
      fateare necessest 624.

629   consuesset: = *consuevisset*, an established contraction (see
      on *suemus* 60 above).
      rerum natura creatrix: this striking personification, which
      has prompted comparisons with the creative Venus of the
      book's introduction, should not obscure the fact that
      Nature has frequently appeared in a creative or re-creative
      role already (see on 56 above and the instances listed
      there - most recently 614).

630   eadem: 'in turn' (cf. on 57 above).

reparare: for infin. dependent on *valere*, cf. 108f. and
see on 103 above.

631 quae . . . aucta: subject of *possunt* 632, i.e. the *minimae*
partes, which are not 'enlarged' by themselves having
parts (*aucta* is stronger than *praedita* 625). There is
an implied contrast with the atoms, which comprise a
number of *minimae partes*.

632 ea: object of *habere*, which is to be supplied with *possunt*
-3 from the rel. clause: 'those attributes'.
genitalis . . . materies: i.e. the substratum, 'birth-
giving matter' (cf. *genitalia corpora* 58).

633 varios . . . motus: 'varieties in interlinkings, weights,
-4 blows, meetings (or collisions) and motions': *varios*
is emphatic and qualifies all five nouns, taking its
gender from the nearest (contrast the neut. pl. *quae*
summing up the list in 634). The argument presupposes
some of the doctrines of book 2: the atoms, even within
compounds, undergo constant motion and collision; their
interaction and behaviour differs according to their
differing types and so produces the varieties observable
in nature (for similar anticipations, cf. 685-7, 798-802,
817-22, 907-12 and 951-2). Here L suggests that the
minimae partes, unlike the *primordia*, admit no variety
of type (as they are without parts and are the absolute
minimum of extension, they must be identical in size,
shape and weight - cf. *similes* 605) or of behaviour. They
could thus never combine to produce even a single compound known to experience (for every compound included
more than one type of atom; 2.581ff.), much less the
variety observable in nature. Cf. also 2.720-9, where
differences in atomic behaviour are explicitly attributed
to differences in atomic type; there (as at 5.438-9) the
list of five nouns, with *intervalla* and *vias* added, recurs.
conexus: a coined compound of *nexus* (see on 220 above), involving the same metaphor of tying.
pondera: weight, together with size (on which it depended)
and shape were the three properties of the atom.
res quaeque: 'different types of process', again emphasising nature's variety.

635-920 REFUTATION OF RIVAL ANALYSES OF MATTER

This section is complementary to the preceding one, where
a polemical note was implicit from 551. L now reinforces
his own account of the substratum by ruling out others,
selecting for attack the three types of analysis of matter
which had preceded Atomism. The section is not a digression.

It is of fundamental importance: since the atomic theory
was based on reasoning from experience, it was vital
to show that rival hypotheses about the invisible, based
equally upon reasoning, would not work and that Atomism
alone was feasible. For this reason refutation of rival
views was traditional in Epicureanism and L may be drawing on Epicurus' *Epitome of the Books against the Physicists* or on polemical sections in his other works. Nor
is it surprising to find Anaxagoras' account of matter
included in L's attack, even though it is unlikely to
have been taken seriously in L's own day: a theory's
unpopularity was no proof of its falsity and from the
Epicurean viewpoint it must be shown scientifically why
it was untenable. Similarly it was insufficient to hold
Epicurean conclusions without acceptance or understanding
of the science which supported them, for confidence was
then likely to crack in time of stress (cf. 3.41ff.).

Throughout L naturally confines himself to the analysis
of matter advocated by the various philosophers under
consideration and disregards other fundamental points
in their system, whether he would accept them or not: he
is content to mention in passing the many other inspired
discoveries of the Pluralists (see on 736 and 705-33).

L's treatment is essentially unsympathetic (cf. on 370-
97 above). For, though he makes valid points against
Monists and Pluralists at 645-89 and 763-81, his repre-
sentation of the views of Anaxagoras is at least over-
simplified (see on 830-920 below) and much of the argument throughout turns on points already covered or
demonstrates the superiority of his own atomic hypothesis.
But despite the generally unsympathetic argumentation, L's
attitude to different philosophers varies considerably:
the animosity displayed towards Heraclitus and his disciples is in marked contrast with the reverence later
shown for Empedocles.

635-704 (A) The Monists, represented by Heraclitus and the
fire theorists

On Monism, see Introduction III. Though this section
deals exclusively with the fire theory, the conclusions
are applied to all forms of Monism at 705-11. It seems
likely, despite the arguments of Furley 15-16, that L's
concentration on the fire theory is to be explained not
merely because its originator Heraclitus was the last and
probably the greatest of the Monists, but also because it
had been adopted by the Stoics as the basis of their
physics, according to which everything in the universe
was composed of fire at a greater or lesser degree of

tension; in its purest form, this fire existed as the Divine Providence (πρόνοια), reason (λόγος) or spirit (πνεῦμα), which controlled the universe. This would help to explain the bitterness of L's hostility towards Heraclitus and his followers (see introductory note on 635-920 above) and fits the plurals with which L refers to the fire theorists throughout most of the passage. *inanis* and *stolidi* (see on 639 and 641 below) certainly seem to indicate that the Stoics are in mind in the introductory lines. L's complaint that his rivals deny the admixture of void (655-64) strictly fits the Stoics better than Heraclitus himself, in whose pre-Parmenidean day the controversy about void had not arisen; however, as Furley suggests, L may see a Heraclitean denial of void as implicit in his Monism.

635-644 Introduction: Heraclitus' obscurity recommends him to his disciples

635 quapropter: i.e. because the substratum (*materiem rerum*) has been shown to be atomic in 483-634.

636 ignem: the initial position, as well as the repetition in *ex igni*, emphasise the key word of this section.
summam: i.e. the universe and all its contents (= *rerum summam*; see on 235 above).

637 lapsi . . . videntur: 'can be seen to have fallen'; on the true passive sense of *videri*, cf. on 224 above. Its use with the participle perhaps evokes the Greek construction of φαίνομαι in this sense.

638 'Heraclitus, their leader, is first and foremost to enter the fray'; i.e. as originator of the fire theory he is the prime target for L's attack, followed by his disciples (notably the Stoics). In this context *primus* is unlikely to look forward to the later attacks on Empedocles and Anaxagoras. The military image, natural in a polemical section, recurs e.g. at 741; cf. also Epicurus as philosophical warrior 62-79.
Heraclitus of Ephesus, best remembered for his doctrine of continual flux (πάντα ῥεῖ, οὐδεν μένει), lived in the sixth and fifth centuries B.C. Of his life little is known; on his philosophy, see Guthrie Vol.I 403-92.
proelia: poetic pl.

639 'Illustrious on account of his dark language amongst the
-40 empty-headed more than amongst the serious-minded Greeks . . .' The oxymoron in *clarus ob obscuram linguam* involves a play on *clarus* ('bright, clear', 'famous'; cf. 475), which is also a translation of the second part

of Heraclitus' name (Snyder 117f.). The figure gains
in point from Heraclitus' nickname (ὁ σκοτεινός, 'the
dark one'). His almost proverbial obscurity, especially
serious from an Epicurean viewpoint (see on *inversis
verbis* 642), makes reconstruction of the details of his
philosophy from fragments and second-hand accounts all
the more hazardous.
> inanis . . . gravis: doubtless the Stoics and the
Epicureans respectively, deliberately inverting the
Stoic view of the two schools. It is possibly no
accident that *inanis* is here applied to philosophers
who (655ff.) deny the existence of *inane*, as if the
very emptiness of their minds disproved their contention.
> quamde: this archaic form of *quam* is attested in Ennius.

641 stolidi: as at 1068, the word (= *stulti*) strongly suggests
the Stoics, given (i) the context; (ii) the verbal similarity with *Stoici*; (iii) that the term inverts their
claim that the Stoic alone was *sapiens*, others *stulti*;
cf. on *inanis* above.

642 inversis . . . verbis: i.e. twisted, misapplied words.
The criticism is based firmly on Epicurean Canonic,
according to which (Introduction IV) words should be
used in their primary, most obvious senses. The term
itself bears its primary sense, and covers any undue
straining of language, though in view of his own practice L can scarcely be objecting to figurative language
in itself. Lines 639-44 seem designed consistently
to mimic the artificialities of Heraclitus' style, given
(i) the oxymoron in 639 and 642 (*latitantia cernunt*);
(ii) the 'inversions' of *inanis, gravis* and *stolidi*
(639-41); (iii) the culminating mixed metaphor of 644
(*fucata sonore*, 'dyed in sound', where *colore* would be
expected). Though all but the last of these expressions
are unexceptionable in themselves and though L uses
oxymoron and similar devices (e.g. 41-2, 220 and 280)
and 'inversion' of rival evaluations, especially those
of *religio* (e.g. 736-9), elsewhere, they all contribute
cumulatively to the parodic effect.

643 belle: the colloquialism for *iucunde* points the superficial-
-4 ity of the attitude of the *inanes*. By contrast the *lepor*
of L's poem (934ff.) is designed to make the truth more
palatable and is not a substitute for truth.
> tangere . . . auris: though in Lucretian physics the ears
are literally 'touched' (see on 298-304 above), the
phrase prepares for a more extravagant mixture, of sight
and sound, in *fucata sonore* (see on 642 above). *fucata*
further implies 'counterfeit' and is thus antithetical
with *vera*.

645-689 Fire cannot produce the variety observable in nature

This argument, which has some connection with 628-34, where L argued that the *minimae partes* did not admit enough variety to form the substratum, raises the fundamental difficulty in all Monist theories, which had been highlighted by Parmenides. L considers the two possible ways in which fire could change: (i - 647-64) it might condense and rarefy, but these processes, without qualitative change, could only produce compounds exhibiting the characteristics of fire in varying degrees; in any case (655ff.), as stated in connection with air at 396-7, condensation and rarefaction are impossible without void, which his opponents (here probably Heraclitus *and* the Stoics: see on 635-704 above) deny; indeed, without void, the very existence of fire as we know it is impossible. Nor (ii - 665-74) can fire lose its characteristics as a result of qualitative rather than of quantitative change, for it is then too perishable to serve as a substratum, which ought to be permanent; each time it changes, it ceases to exist as fire. Finally (675-89) L demonstrates the superiority of his own theory, in which a substratum of unchangeable atoms can produce change in the visible world by different combinations and arrangements. This is only possible if the substratum itself, unlike fire, possesses no secondary qualities (e.g. heat and brightness, colour, taste and smell) which would be bound to obtrude themselves in combination.

L's objections are designed to cover all possible explanations of the process of change: like modern critics, he may not have been sure, from the language of their accounts, which of his two alternatives Heraclitus and the Stoics respectively adopted. The indications are that Heraclitus, like Anaximenes with his air theory, believed in condensation and rarefaction; the surviving evidence for the Stoic position might reasonably be taken in the same way, even if, as suggested by Furley (15-16, cited above), such an interpretation is largely mistaken.

The final part of the argument, concerning the immutability of the substratum, corresponds closely with Epicurus, *ad Hdt.* 54.

645 possent . . . si sunt . . . creatae: 'would be able . . .
-6   if they have really been created' - perhaps a mixed
      conditional (cf. 570-2 and 655-6, where the shift is
      to a vivid apodosis); alternatively the true protasis
      to *possent* may be concealed in *cur* ('on what hypothesis',
      'given what conditions'). For the vivid presentation of
      the rival view (*si sunt*), cf. e.g. 577 and 615.

647 calidum . . . rarefieri: 'that hot fire should condense
-9 and rarefy'; the acc. and infin. stands as subject
of the 'impersonal' *prodesset*. *calidum* is not gratuitous, but looks forward to the crucial idea of fire's
natura and to *ardor* 650. For the archaic passive infin.
denserier, see on 207 above. *rarefieri* is a coinage
by analogy with e.g. *calefacere* and *liquefacere*.
si . . . haberent: 'if the parts of fire had the same
nature as fire as a whole possesses as well', i.e.
if there were no qualitative difference between fire
and its constituents (as there was in atomic theory).
super = *insuper*, though the local sense is figuratively
appropriate to a 'superstratum'.

650 acrior ardor: the assonance is well suited to the insis-
-1 tence and intensity of the heat.
partibus: to be supplied also with *disiectis disque*
sipatis to complete the antithesis; the phrases are
probably abl. absolute but could be possessive dat.
On the effectiveness of the tmesis of the otherwise
inadmissible *dissipatis*, see on *praeterque meantum*
318 above; cf. 452, as also for the emphatic repetition
of the prefix.
esset: potential, continuing the hypothetical construction
of 647-9.

652 hoc: abl. of comparison, summing up the changes of intensity of fiery qualities just illustrated.
fieri: prolative, belonging inside the *quod* clause, with
posse.
rearis: prospective subj., 'you may suppose'.

653 talibus in causis: i.e. where such causes, viz. condensa-
-4 tion and rarefaction, operate.
nedum rules out *a fortiori* a stronger point than one just
denied: more usually it introduces a phrase, here a
complete clause.
variantia: coined for the metrically inadmissible *varietas*.
queat: potential, 'could'.

655 id quoque: 'moreover', adding a supplementary point to
-6 this argument (lit. 'as to this also'); though the phrase
is unique in L, see on *quod* 82 for similar adverbial
accs.
si faciant . . . poterunt: cf. 570-2 for the same pattern
in a mixed conditional. *faciant* = 'they were to suppose',
hence the acc. and infin. (sc. *esse* with *admixtum*). The
pl. shows that Heraclitus' disciples have now also entered the lists.
rebus: here applied specifically in the first instance to
compounds (see on 369 above), of which fire is the case
in point. The criticism is thus applicable to the Stoics,
who, while denying void within the world, admitted

'infinite void outside it.
rarique relinqui: a variation on *rarefieri* 648.

657 multa sibi . . . contraria: 'many obstacles in their path'
to the admission of void. For the Monists, insofar as
the question arose at all, the main obstacle would be
the unity of their system; the Stoics were also faced
with the difficulties over void raised by Parmenides
(see on 329-417 above).
mussant: 'they are struck dumb', keeping quiet on the
question in fear and bewilderment; for *mussare* (primarily to mumble inaudibly) so used, cf. 6.1179 and
Virgil, *Aeneid* 11.344-5. No subsequent restoration
has improved on this ancient conjecture.

658 fugitant . . . relinquere: the prolative infin. is used
by analogy with verbs like *nolle* and *vereri*: see on *desciscere quaeres* 103 above, and cf. *fuge credere* 1052.
For the idiom of *relinquere* (contrast 656) and of the
antithetical *exempto* 660, see on 446 above.
inane . . . purum: totally empty, as opposed to occupied,
space.

659 ardua . . . vera viai: 'the steep path . . . the true
one'; for the construction, see on *prima virorum* 86
above. The neut. pl. is here in each case coextensive
with the noun.
dum: the temporal clause also contains the reason for
amittunt . . . viai. ardua . . . metuunt takes up *quia
. . . contraria* 657; *amittunt . . . viai* answers *mussant
. . . purum* 657-8.

660 A new point, involving a concluding *reductio ad absurdum*
-4 of the denial of void: without it, not only would condensation and rarefaction be impossible, but everything
would be fully condensed already, so that fire could not
throw off light and heat: the 'basic substance' could
not even exist in recognisable form.

660 nec rursum cernunt: beginning an antithesis with *multa sibi
cernunt contraria* 657 (they fail to see the far greater
problems in the *denial* of void). *exempto rebus inani*
(abl. absolute, with *rebus* dat. of disadvantage) similarly answers *inane relinquere purum* 658.

662 The heavy spondaic rhythm, reinforced by the staccato
effect of four successive monosyllables, is well suited
to the description of a world frozen into immobility
and contrasts with the lively dactyls of 663 which describe the true state of affairs. *nil ab se* is 'emitted'
from the rel. clause, just as compounds (normally) emit
parts from themselves; cf. 367, 385-6, 388-9 and 514 for

parallel examples of probable 'syntactical onomatopoeia'.
possit: consecutive subj., as well as sub-oblique after
cernunt.
raptim: any type of motion is impossible in a plenum
(335ff.); rapid emissions, like those of fire (663),
are all the more unaccountable.

664 ut videas: a final clause.
non . . . esse: i.e. contains void; sc. eum = ignem as
acc. subject.

665 alia . . . ratione: i.e. other than by condensation and
rarefaction, introducing the second horn of the dilemma.
potesse: the archaic form of posse, from pote (a weakened
form of potis 452) + esse.

666 ignis: the pl. here suggests 'fire-particles'.
in coetu: 'in assembly' to form a compound, equivalent to
in concilio (cf. 772), as also at 775. The sense is
similar at 1017, 1026 and 1048. The phrase prepares
for the contrast with the atomic account 675-89.
Bailey's 'in compression' fails to provide an alternative to condensation and rarefaction.
stingui: i.e. lose the characteristics of fire, as
mutareque corpus explains. The term, already used
as a metaphor for destruction at 486, is loaded and
anticipates the argument for the 'death' of fire in
668-71. But L is perhaps doing no more than sarcastically echoing Heraclitus' own account, according to
which (Aetius 1.3.11) fire was 'extinguished'.

667 'If at no point are they going to refrain from doing
this', i.e. if, unlike the Atomists, they allow qualitative change to take place right down to the level
of their primordia, thus denying an unchanging substratum. The second protasis further limits the first,
with a switch to the future: reparcent, a rare compound,
governs a prolative infin. by analogy with verbs like
desinere or nolle; cf. on fugitant relinquere 658 above.
The assonance parte reparcent has a derisive ring.

668 I.e. their fiery substratum will perish in every case
-9 of change: e.g. when fire changes into smoke, fire will
be annihilated, smoke created from nothing (possibilities
ruled out at 159-264).
nimirum: echoing scilicet 667; the obviousness of the
conclusion is heavily emphasised.
funditus: recurrent in this section in the context of
the destructibility of rival substrata, where the root
sense 'at the bottom' (see on 572 above) is appropriate
(cf. 673, 791, 797 and 854). Though combined with omnis
(see on 478 above), it should be taken separately,
'utterly', 'fundamentally', unless it does double duty.

ardor: here a variant for *ignis*, as at 682, 702 and 902.

670 The preceding assertion is justified with the fundamental
-1 axiom that change implies death, repeated in the argu-
    ment against the Pluralists at 792f., and again at 2.
    753f. and 3.519f. The Epicureans may well have derived
    it from the criticisms of the earlier physicists made
    by Parmenides and the Eleatic school. As L proceeds
    to point out, the hypothesis of a substratum of un-
    changing atoms avoided this problem.
    quodcumque: 'whenever a thing'; there is a slight ana-
    coluthon, as *hoc* does not pick up *quodcumque* but de-
    notes 'this process'.
    suis . . . finibus: i.e. from the bounds of its own nature;
    for the metaphor, cf. 76-7 (=595-6).
    continuo . . . est: i.e. automatically entails.

672 Antithetical with 668-9 and also transitional to the state-
-4 ment of the atomic position at 675ff. 673 recurs at 797
    (and twice in book 2) and in slightly varied form at
    791; 674 reappears at 757. On such repetitions (cf.
    670-1), see on 75-7 and 505 above.
    aliquid: like the Epicurean atoms.
    superare: 'survive' (as at 579); with *incolume*, it is opposed
    to *occidet*, *mutatum* and *mors* 668-71.
    ollis: 'for them', viz. *quaecumque creantur* 669; cf. *rebus*
    579, which likewise denotes 'for making compounds'. The
    archaic form of *ille* is occasionally adopted also by the
    Augustan poets.
    tibi: 'ethic' dat. - 'in case you find that . . . .'.
    renata vigescat: a poetic elaboration of *fient* 669.

675 nunc: 'as it is', introducing the true, atomic account.
    certissima: 'most definite', probably pointing the contrast
    with the ill-defined bits of fire that constitute the
    rival *primordia*.

677 quorum . . . ordine: 'through whose coming or going and
    changes of arrangement'. The assonance *abitu / aditu*
    underlines the link between parallel but opposed pro-
    cesses (cf. 305-6); the repetition in *mutato . . .*
    mutant, echoed in 686, highlights the correspondence
    between invisible and visible processes.

678 res . . . corpora: synonymous, denoting compounds. Though
    corpora = primordia in 675 and 679, the context prevents
    any ambiguity.

679 scire licet: the original, uncontracted form of *scilicet*,
    with acc. and infin. governed by *scire*; cf. 860, 894,
    and *videlicet* with the same construction at 210. *haec*
    corpora rerum is subject of *esse*, *ignea* the emphatic
    predicate.

680 A new presentation of the argument of 647-54, here pointing
-3 out the superiority of atomism: sc. *corpora* (= *primordia*)
    with *quaedam* and *cuncta* (680 and 682) and as subject of
    crearent (683).

680 decedere, abire: synonyms in asyndeton, answering *abitu*
-1 677, while *aditu* is taken up by *attribui*.

683 ignis: emphatically placed predicate (cf. *ignem* 690);
    quodcumque crearent is the subject. *foret* and *crearent*
    are both potential.
    omnimodis: = *omnibus modis*, apparently a Lucretian coining
    by analogy with *multimodis* (from *multis modis*). The point
    is that compounds would have all the qualities of fire
    and be totally indistinguishable from it.

684 A fuller statement of the position of 675-8, with the im-
-9 portant addition that the atoms differ from all the
    substances of experience. This idea is developed in
    book 2, where L argues that they lack all secondary
    qualities, such as colour, taste, smell, heat and cold
    and that they possess three properties alone, size, shape
    and weight.

684 verum: 'the truth' (contrast the connective *verum*).

685 For the anticipation of the doctrine of atomic motion and
    collision, cf. on 633-4 above.
    ordo: suggesting position relative to other *corpora*, while
    positura (coined to replace the inadmissible *positio*)
    denotes the position of an atom relative to itself (e.g.
    which way up).
    figurae: 'shapes' but suggesting also the associated idea
    of 'sizes', to which L oftens applies the term (see on
    359 above). Placing, position and shape of the atoms
    were advanced by Democritus as the three basic causes
    of varieties in compounds: to these Epicurus added var-
    ieties in the patterns of atomic motion.

686 mutatoque ordine mutant naturam: i.e. of the compound; the
-7 whole point is that the atoms themselves are unchanging
    (676). *ordine* is an oversimplification, serving as short-
    hand for the first four nouns in 685; addition and sub-
    traction of atoms (677), allowing for different *figurae*
    in the compound, should also strictly be included (cf.
    the fuller statements at 800-1 and 817-9). *quae* is to
    be supplied out of *quorum* 684 as subject of *mutant* (see
    on *haec* 60 above).
    simulata: = the inadmissible *similia*, from the rare root
    sense 'made like'.

688 praeterea: 'besides' (= *alii*), as at 269, 400 and 430.

corpora: 'bodies', including the material *simulacra* responsible for visual perception; see on 132 and, for the
physical nature of all perception, on 298-304 above.
possit: consecutive subj.

689 sensibus: see on 303 above.
nostros . . . tactus: 'and by bombardment touch our sense
of touch'. *adiectu* is another fourth decl. coinage; the
juxtaposition in *tangere tactus* of words of the same
root effectively mirrors the pattern of two tangible
things making contact.

690-704 Concluding objections

Lines 690-700 are aimed at Heraclitus himself, and crit-
icise his attitude to sense-perception: for his distrust
of the fundamental Epicurean criterion of knowledge (Introduction III), cf. Diels B.107. L's complaint is not that
the substratum of fire is often imperceptible (which the
Epicurean atoms invariably were) but that Heraclitus is
inconsistent in accepting the evidence of the senses in
the case of fire and rejecting it in all others: to L,
all visible substances are equally real and equally 'un-
real' inasmuch as sense-perception does not provide complete information about their composition. In 701-4 L
adds that any visible substance might as well be chosen
as fire (i.e. on the basis of sense-perception, as the
parallelism of language in 690-2 and 704 suggests). The
point also serves as a transition to 705-11, where L goes
on to list the very different basic substances postulated,
arbitrarily as he sees it, by the various Monists.

This concluding salvo with its accusations of lunacy (692,
698 and 704) and its sequence of indignant rhetorical
questions (699-703) completes the attack on Heraclitus and
his disciples with the same derisive contempt with which
it opened (635-44).

690 ignem . . . ignem: emphatically placed at the beginning
-1 and end of the acc. and infin. governed by *dicere*; in
690 *ignem* is predicate of *esse*.
constare: either = *esse* or used ironically to suggest 'is
constant', since L has just discussed the view that the
'constant' substance changes (665ff.).

692 facit: 'supposes', as at 655.
perdelirum esse videtur: 'seems to be raving lunacy'; the
intensive form of the already strong *delirus* (cf. 698)
is found nowhere else. *mihi videtur* 698 ('seems to me')

suggests that *videtur* here and at 704 is not a true
passive (see on 224 above), though the sense 'is obviously'
fits well in both places.

693 'For he himself fights on the side of the senses against
the senses'. This metaphorical paradox, perhaps again
intended to mimic Heraclitus' style (see on 642), is explained in what follows: Heraclitus, though opposing
sense-evidence in the case of all other visible substances, himself supports it in the case of fire. There
is irony in the description of him as even partially
'on the side of' the senses, given his general attitude
of distrust. *ipse* underlines his inconsistency.

694 unde . . . unde: = *ex quibus*, with rhetorical anaphora.
-5 hic . . . quem nominat ignem: either 'this thing which
he calls fire' with *hoc quod* attracted to the gender of
ignem or 'this fire which he names (as the only reality)'.

697 cetera: object of *cognoscere*, which is supplied with *sensus*
and *vere* from 696 to complete the antithesis.
nilo: abl. of measure of difference with *minus*.
sunt: indic. because the clause, though grammatically sub-
oblique after *credit*, is asserted on L's own authority
as a fact.

699 quo referemus: 'to what standard shall we refer?'. For
-700 the argument and the terminology, see on 423-5 above.
ipsis sensibus: abl. of comparison - 'than our very
senses'.
qui . . . notemus: 'by which we may mark off'. *qui* is the
old abl. of the rel. (= *quo*) and picks up *quid*; the clause
is purposive.

701 quare quisquam magis . . .tollat: 'why should anyone rather
remove', introducing a deliberative rhetorical question.
quisquam is used because a negative is implied; no one
has grounds to do so. On the idiom of *tollat*, the antithetical *linquere* 702 and *relinquat* 703, see on 446 above.

702 ardoris naturam: periphrastic for *ardorem* (= *ignem*), whereas at 682 *naturam* had its full force (cf. on 131 above).

703 ignis: either acc. pl. (i.e. instances of fire) or gen.
sing. (sc. *naturam*).
quidvis: 'anything you care to choose': this conjectural
restoration stresses the arbitrary nature of monistic
theories.
relinquat: for the construction with acc. and infin., see
on 515 above.

704 'For it seems (to be) equal madness to say either': *dicere*

is substantival, as at 690; *utrumque* is used for
alterutrum.

705-829 (B) The Pluralists, led by Empedocles

On Pluralism, see Introduction III. Just as in the previous
section L's aim was to refute all forms of the fire theory
and so of Monism in general, so here he aims to demolish
all versions of Pluralism (including Dualism: cf. on 712-
3 below), not merely that of Empedocles which was by far
the most refined, being designed to resist the type of
criticism levelled against Monism by Parmenides and the
Eleatics. Whereas in some versions of Pluralism the four
elements themselves changed, Empedocles maintained that
they were, like the Epicurean atoms, themselves changeless
but produced different compounds as a result of different
combinations. In addition he postulated the twin principles
of Love and Strife, which were apparently material entities
and governed the intermingling of the elements, joining
like to unlike and like to like respectively; the two predominated alternately in a recurring cosmic cycle. Though
these twin principles may have suggested to L the abstractions of the creative and destructive forces of nature (cf.
2.569-72) and though Empedocles' allegorical use of Ares
and Aphrodite in depicting the alternation of Love and
Strife may have influenced L's personification of those
creative and destructive forces in the Mars and Venus of
his proem, his criticisms of Pluralism include no mention
of this part of Empedocles' theory. He doubtless regarded
Love and Strife, literally interpreted, as concepts too
idiosyncratic, arbitrary and removed from experience to
warrant refutation.

705-733 Transition to the Pluralists: praise of Empedocles

After applying his refutation of the fire theory to all
forms of Monism in 705-11, L turns to the various versions
of Pluralism in 712-5. The praise which he proceeds to bestow upon Empedocles as the foremost of the Pluralists in
the remainder of the paragraph, thus affording temporary
relief from technical argument as at 398-417 and 921-50,
is of a lavishness usually reserved for Epicurus himself.
Empedocles appears as the greatest of Sicily's many
marvels, just as Epicurus is the greatest product of Athens
in the introduction to book 6: his genius, like that of
Epicurus, is 'divine' (see on 730-3 below). L's reverence
is based (i) on Empedocles' poetic treatment of scientific
material, from which he himself drew inspiration (Introduction IV), and (ii) on various specific aspects of his
philosophy (cf. the reference in 734-9 to the inspired dis-

coveries of Empedocles and other lesser philosophers),
quite apart from his general scientific spirit: e.g.
the Atomists, while maintaining that pluralistic analysis
had not gone far enough, still (like the Stoics) recognised
the four elements, which played an important part in their
cosmogony (cf. 5.235-317 and 416-508); unlike Heraclitus,
Empedocles insisted on the validity of the senses and also
postulated a physical basis for consciousness.

705 These lines are all but identical with 635-6, while 637
-6   is echoed in 711: the discussion of the fire theory
     ends as it began.

707 principium: 'as a beginning', or basic substance (= Greek
     ἀρχή); cf. *primordia* 712, 753 and 765 and *principiis* 740
     (both with *rerum*) applied to dualistic and pluralistic
     substrata.
     gignundis . . . rebus: purposive or possibly possessive
     dat. with *principium* (cf. on 24 above); in prose, a gen.
     might have been used in its place.
     aera: the basic substance postulated by Anaximenes. The
     form of the acc. is Greek: cf. *aethera* 1089.

708 constituēre: 'have appointed' - a similar idiom to that
     noted on *relinqui* 446 above.
     umorem: i.e. *aquam*, alluding to the theory originated by
     Thales. The chronological order of Thales, Anaximenes
     and Heraclitus is here reversed. L probably regarded
     Anaximander's theory of 'the boundless' as too meta-
     physical to warrant inclusion.

709 ipsum per se: 'entirely by itself', making the same point
     as *solo* 636 and *uno puroque* 646.
     terram: according to Aristotle, *Metaphysics* 989a, this was
     a popular, not a philosophical version of Monism. L
     might be expected to see it as containing more truth
     than the other theories, since he regarded the earth
     as containing atoms of all types and as, in a sense,
     literally 'mother' (see on 171 above).

710 omnia . . . omnis: the strategic placing of the words gives
     the repetition additional emphasis.
     in rerum naturas: = *in res*; in this periphrasis (see on
     131 above) *natura* is nowhere else plural.

711 derrasse: = *deerravisse*; cf. *desse* 43, and see on *suemus*
     60 above.
     videntur: true passive, as in the corresponding 637.

712 adde: *sc.* eos; *adde* and *adde quod* 847 serve as further

Lucretian formulae of transition.

conduplicant . . . rerum: i.e. postulate two basic substances. The refutation of 'Dualism', an earlier and
simpler form of Pluralism, is implied *a fortiori* in the
arguments soon to be advanced against the four-element
theory.

713 **iungentes**: probably metaphorical, from the basic sense
of 'yoking', 'harnessing' a pair of animals.
liquori: (cf. *umorem* 708) = *aquae*. The attribution of
air-fire Dualism is uncertain (Oenopides of Chios and
Parmenides are possible candidates). The earth-water
theory was held by Xenophanes of Colophon, the great
critic of Olympian religion and mythology.

714 **rebus**: i.e. elements (Empedocles' 'roots', ῥιζώματα).
L devises no specific term: the use of *res* (compounds)
reflects his own attitude that the four elements, while
important, were essentially just like other compounds.

715 **igni terra atque anima . . . et imbri**: for partial asyndeton in a list, see on *et* 162 above. *anima* ('breath')
is used also by Cicero as a philosophical term for the
element air. *imbri* is a more exclusively poetic variant for water. L's use of such variants and periphrases
throughout this section (e.g. 744, 770-1, 777 and 783-
6; cf. also 668, 708 and 713 above) is paralleled in
Empedocles, whose poetry so impressed him.

716 **quorum . . . cum primis**: 'foremost of these' (lit. 'with
the first'): cf. *dux, primus* of Heraclitus in 638.
Empedocles: born about 500 B.C. of noble family, he combined the roles of poet, philosopher, mystic, orator
and politician, championing the cause of democracy in
his native Acragas (Latin *Agrigentum*), declining the
kingship and later being forced to flee to the Peloponnese.
He was rumoured to have leapt into the crater of Etna
in an attempt to prove the divinity to which (see on 730
below) he laid claim. His two philosophical poems were
entitled 'On Nature' (Περὶ Φύσεως) and 'Purifications'
(Καθαρμοί); from them some 350 and 100 lines respectively
survive. See further Guthrie Vol.II 122-265.

717 It is probably no accident that at least three of the four
-25 elements figure prominently in this description of
Empedocles' native Sicily (earth and water in 717-21 and
fire in 722-5), as if to imply that his environment helped
to suggest his theory. Air is included under *caelum*
(which embraces both air and the upper, fiery ether) 725,
even though it does not receive the same emphasis. Cf.
J.M. Snyder, *Classical World* 65 (1972) 217-8.

717 triquetris terrarum . . . in oris: 'within the triangular
borders of its lands': Horace, *Satires* 2.6.55 similarly
uses *triquetra tellus* for the metrically inadmissible
Sicilia. *oris* has its primary sense (see on 22 above)
and is repeated with *terrarum* at 721, allowing the
element *terra* to receive emphasis.

718 quam: governed by *circum*; for the word-order, see on
-9 *hunc propter* 90 above.
   magnis anfractibus: because the coastline contains deep
   bays and inlets.
   aequor Ionium: the sea east of Sicily, separating it
   from Crete: the spray shows that *aequor* is here a
   general term for ocean (contrast and see on *aequora
   ponti* 8 above).
   virus: always in L the 'poison' of brine.

720 angusto . . . fretu: poetic local abl. with *rapidum*,
-1 'the sea, rushing in a narrow strait'. *rapidum* probably
   has overtones of its root sense (see on 15 above).
   undis: instrumental abl.; its repetition at the end of the
   second successive line seems to be the climax of a pattern giving prominence to the element water in 718-20
   (cf. *aequor*, *fretu* and *mare*).
   eius: for the demonstrative replacing a second rel. (here
   in a new case and postponed to the end of the clause),
   see on 60 above. The word-pattern in the line, with
   the juxtaposition of the Italian and Sicilian boundaries,
   mirrors their close proximity in nature.

722 vasta Charybdis: an echo of the Homeric ὀλοὴν Χάρυβδιν in
-3 *Odyssey* 12.428; *vasta* is active, 'devastating'. The
   whirlpool, situated at the entrance to the straits of
   Messina (*fretu* 720) on the Sicilian side and personified
   in legend as a monster, is mentioned, like Etna which
   forms the climax of the description, as one of the
   marvels of Sicily outshone by Empedocles. Against a
   background containing such traditional objects of super-
   stitious fear as Charybdis and Etna, Empedocles' rationa-
   lism is doubtless intended to appear the more heroic.
   flammarum: representing the element fire (cf. *ignis* and
   flammai fulgura 724-5) and going with *iras*.
   rursum se colligere: *se* refers to Etna, which is included
   in the subject (*Aetnaea murmura*). Though *minari* in
   older Latin often takes a present for fut. infin.,
   colligere is here accurate - 'threaten that it is (already) collecting'. *rursum*, taken up in *iterum* 724 and
   repeated in 725, stresses the reality of the danger: in
   L's day the most recent eruptions had been a series of
   four (140-122 B.C.), the last of which had destroyed
   Catana. Thucydides records three earlier ones which
   took place between the Greek settlement and 425 B.C. For

m alliteration (*minantur . . . rursum*) in a context of rumbling menace, cf. 68-9.

724 Etna is personified and the eruption seen as an eructation. The interruption of the assonance *VIS Vomat ignIS* by the monosyllabic *ut*, together with the 'violence' of the line ending (see on 69 above) and the onomatopoeia of *vis* (see on 72 above), convey an appropriately convulsive effect. **eruptos:** 'bursting forth', lit. 'caused to break forth'; the transitive usage is paralleled at 4.1115 and 6.583. **ut:** fifth word in its clause, expressing purpose.

725 **flammai fulgura:** for the authenticity of volcanic lightning, see West 7; cf. also Sophocles, *Philoctetes* 986. For the vigorous *f* alliteration in the line, cf. 490-1 and 900.

726 'While this region appears in many ways great and worthy
-7 of the wonder of the races of men and is noised abroad as a place to be seen'. For the indics. with *cum* in what is here a purely concessive context, see on 566 above. *magna* and *miranda* seem to stand in asyndeton, with *modis multis* belonging to each; the impressive alliteration helps to knit the words together. *gentibus humanis* is dat. of agent with the gerundive. For *visendaque fertur*, cf. *clara clueret* 119; *fertur* is probably characteristically closer to its root sense than usual when applied to reporting. The phrase does not necessarily imply that L had never visited the island.

728 **rebus . . . bonis** indicates that Sicily is fertile and **multa . . . vi** ('fortified by a great supply of men') that it is populous, but the metaphor of *munita* and the alternative sense of *vi* ('might'), coupled with the 'violence' of the line-ending (see on 13 above), simultaneously suggest military prowess (*virum vi* recurs in a military context at 2.326). The repulsion of the Athenian expedition by Syracuse and Sicily's prolonged resistance to Carthage may be especially in mind. Military achievement is contrasted with Empedocles' greater, philosophical and poetic, achievement in the following lines, reflecting L's scale of values (see on 70-1 above). The double alliteration adds to the impressiveness of this pregnant phrase.

730 **sanctum:** the theme of Empedocles' 'sanctity' and 'divinity' (*divini pectoris* 731 and *vix humana stirpe creatus* 733) forms the climax of the paragraph and is continued until 739: he is more like the true Epicurean gods than are the conventional gods of religion; for L's similar attitude to Epicurus himself, see introductory note to 62-79 above and on *caelo* 79 above. The passage is also an acknowledgment of the claim to divinity made, doubt-

less equally figuratively, by Empedocles himself (Diels
  B.112.11).
magis: with all three adjs.
videtur: probably 'seems', as also at 726 and 733, rather
  than the true passive (see on 224 above).

731 carmina: Empedocles' poetry, which L admired less reservedly
    than his philosophy, is a further vitally important just-
    ification of *divini*.
    pectoris: the seat of the intellect and so of poetic and
    philosophical inspiration, as at 413.

732 vociferantur: probably especially appropriate to prophetic
    utterance, so fitting the antithesis with orthodox
    religio which is implicit from 730-9. The verb is ap-
    plied to Epicurus' *ratio* at 3.14; *praeclara reperta* is
    comparable with *divina reperta* of Epicurus at 6.7.

734-762 Initial objections

The Pluralists, despite their many inspired discoveries,
are wrong about the substratum because:
(a - 742-5) they deny void, but accept (i) motion (ii)
soft compounds, including their own elements. Yet without void both (i) and (ii) are impossible, as L has demonstrated and implied respectively in the course of 329ff.
(cf. also 660-4).
(b - 746-52) they deny (i) a limit to physical division
and (ii) the existence of a theoretical minimum, positions
ruled out by proofs (iii), (v) and (vii) of the atomic
nature of matter.
(c - 753-8) their elements are soft and can be seen to be
destructible: such a substratum would leave the world to
be destroyed into nothing and re-created out of nothing.
(d - 759-62) their elements are mutually hostile, and
could never combine to produce compounds as the theory
requires.
(a), (b) and (c) involve fundamental points already covered:
they correspond with the first objections brought against
Anaxagoras at 843-58. All four arguments are relevant, but
not restricted, to Empedoclean Pluralism, though in (a)
L does not exploit Empedocles' apparently contradictory
position on void; while denying its existence, he admitted
that there were 'pores' (πόροι) in things, which Aristotle,
de Generatione et Corruptione 1.8, complains is tantamount
to the admission of void. (c) and (d), as applied to
Empedocles, are less unfair to him than Bailey suggests:
these two appeals to experience have some validity not
only against other forms of Pluralism, but also against
the specifically Empedoclean points (i) that the four elements comprised an unchangeable and indestructible substratum (ii) that they could combine harmoniously under

the influence of 'Love' (on which see introductory note
to 705-829 above).

734 supra: i.e. in 712-5; the allusion is to the Dualists and
-5   the Pluralists inferior to Empedocles. The Monists
    were dismissed at 711, and are not included in the
    criticisms of 742-62.
    partibus egregie multis: abl. of measure of difference
    with *inferiores*, 'by an outstandingly great degree' -
    a much stronger version of *multo*. The pattern of
    inferiores . . . minores is chiasmic.

736 These lines take up the theme of 730-3, developing the
-9   favourite Lucretian paradox that philosophy is more
    truly religious than orthodox religion.

    divinitus: taking up *divini* 731. On the many 'inspired'
    discoveries of Empedocles himself, see introductory
    note to 705-33 above; those of the lesser philosophers
    may include contributions to cosmology and physiology
    but L doubtless has in mind their breakaway from rel-
    igion and mythology and their quest for some sort of
    scientific law, which gives further point to his favour-
    able comparison of philosophy with religion in these
    lines. Despite his criticisms of the rival schools,
    he had a broad sympathy with their approach, including
    that of many of the Monists, even though the latter are
    not included in this tribute.

737 tamquam: apologising for the oracular metaphor of *ex adyto
    cordis* and *responsa dedere*. For the former, cf. *templaque
    mentis* 5.103, even though the primary sense of *templa* is
    'regions'. *cor*, like *pectus* 731, is the seat of the
    intellect. For the transference of the terms of relig-
    ious practice to philosophy, cf. on *agere hoc* 41 above.

738 These lines are repeated at 5.111-2 in describing L's own
-9   pronouncements; the comparison with the Delphic oracle
    may have been suggested by an epigram of Epicurus re-
    corded by Diogenes Laertius 10.12.
    sanctius: taking up *sanctum magis* 730.
    certa ⌣‿. . magis: replacing the metrically impossible
    certiore.
    Pythia: the priestess of Apollo at Delphi, who sat in
    the temple's inner shrine (*adytum* 737) on a tripod, sup-
    posedly set over a chasm exuding inspirational vapours.
    The scent of the laurel, sacred to Apollo, which she wore
    as a wreath or chewed or burnt (cf. 6.154-5), added to
    their effect. For similar sneers at the ritual of
    religio, cf. on 87-8 above and 5.1198ff.
    tripodi a: the anastrophe (see on *hunc propter* 90 above)

is more natural since *Phoebi* and *lauroque* are left to
follow *a*. The abl. in *-i* is unusual for this originally
Greek noun: L's fluctuations between *-i* and *-e* forms
of third decl. nouns sometimes lead to divergence from
normal classical usage, flexible as it sometimes is; cf.
e.g. *lapidi* 884, *fini* 978, *parti* 1111 and conversely
mare 161.
profatur: appropriate to oracular pronouncement.

740 principiis . . . in rerum: (taken up by *ibi* 741) i.e.
in the case of the substratum (cf. on 707 above).
fecere ruinas: i.e. they have (i) come to grief themselves (cf. 741 and *dabunt ruinas* 2.1145): (ii) created
ruin (for the visible world) (cf. *dabant ruinas* 5.1329)
by postulating the infinitely divisible and soft *primordia*
of 746-58, instead of the solid foundation (*fundamentum*
573) required - an effective, characteristic word-play.

741 magni magno cecidere . . . casu: 'mightily are the mighty
fallen' - a characteristically Lucretian version of the
Homeric κεῖτο μέγας μεγαλωστί (*Iliad* 16.776) with the
figura etymologica (*cecidere casu*) added to the repetition of *magnus*. The military image for philosophy recurs here: cf. 70ff. and 638. The line-ending (see on
69 above) is not inappropriate to the violence of the
fall.

742 exempto . . . relinquunt: antonyms - they 'take away'
-3 void, yet 'leave' soft compounds in their universe; for
the idiom, continued in *admiscent* 745, see on 446 above.
constituunt: 'they suppose', i.e. postulate.
The spondaic rhythm of 742 fits the static congestion implied by the rival theory, while in 743 the dense spondees
in *et res mollis raras* seem to belie the nature allowed
to the *res*.

744 solem: 'sunlight', representing fire, which can throw off
light and heat because it is rarefied (663-4); the list
opens with the four elements, implying the same *reductio
ad absurdum* as at 660-4: without void, the rival substratum could not even exist. *animalia* and *fruges* are
important in the argument of 803-29.

746 I.e. their *primordia*, unlike the atoms, are infinitely
-8 physically divisible and (*a fortiori*) do not contain a
theoretical minimum (the *minima pars* of 599ff.).
secandis corporibus: with *finem esse* the dat. is as much
possessive as final (cf. on 24 and 203-4 above), like
fragori with *pausam stare* (so too at 844).
faciunt: 'suppose': cf. on 655 above.
stare . . . consistere: stronger than *esse* (cf. 752) - 'and
that there is not an established halting-place . . . and

no firm (unshifting, absolute) minimum whatsoever'.
prorsum (balancing *omnino*) intensifies *quicquam*.
fragori: outside L, the word denotes the noise of breaking.

749 A fuller statement of the argument for the theoretical
-52 minimum of matter which was implied at 599-601 (see
notes there); it is based on the analogy of the 'ultimate
point' on the surface of visible objects, which is the
visible minimum.

749 'Although we see that each object possesses that ultimate
-50 point, which seems, judged by our senses, to be a minimum'. *cuiusque* is a possessive gen. and denotes each
visible object. *ad* + acc. denotes the criterion, as
at 3.214. *videtur* ('seems') makes a contrast with the
actual, absolute *minimum* 752: indic. is used, despite
videamus, because the clause states what L regards
as an established fact: so too with *quis* and *habent*,
despite *conicere*, in 751-2 (cf. e.g. 697 and 954).

751 **quae . . . rebus:** 'that the ultimate (point) which the
-2 things you cannot see possess forms a firm minimum for
things', i.e. the ultimate point in the invisible *primordia* constitutes an absolute minimum in nature. Three
inferences are here compressed: (i) the *primordia* must,
like visible objects, possess an *extremum cacumen*; (ii)
therefore they contain a minimum; (iii) this must be an
absolute minimum in nature. The restoration *rebus* takes
up *in rebus* 748, whereas Munro's *in illis* fits (ii) but
overlooks (iii), the crucial conclusion.

753 **huc accedit:** separated from *utqui* (an archaic, emphatic
-5 form of *ut*) by the *quoniam* clause.
primordia . . . constituunt: 'they appoint as the first-
beginnings of things soft objects' (cf. 707-8); *mollia*,
used as a noun, is the antecedent of *quae*, for the rival
primordia are tiny particles which individually cannot
be seen (*videmus*).
nativa: itself an indication of mortality (see on 113
above).
funditus: soft compounds can be seen to be 'utterly' mortal
as compounds (even though they comprise imperishable
atoms); the root sense of *funditus* (see on 668 above) is
not here applicable. The mortality of the four elements
is fully illustrated at 5.235-305.

756 L returns to a familiar theme, with 757 equivalent to 674.
-7 **iam:** inferential, after *quoniam* 753 (cf. 594).

758 **quid:** third word in its clause, 'how far'.
iam . . . habebis: 'you will now (i.e. after 146-264)
know'.

759 The subject is the four elements; *veneno* is predicative
    dat.

760 ipsa sibi inter se strongly emphasises the idea of rec-
    iprocity and mutual interaction.
    congressa: 'when they meet', in their supposed attempts
    to form a compound.
    peribunt: as when water puts out fire or fire evaporates
    water.

761 ut . . . videmus: an appeal to experience. In a storm
 -2 lightning, rain and wind (representing three of the four
    elements), so far from combining in compounds, can be
    observed to repel one another. *coacta*, whether forming
    an abl. absolute with *tempestate* or (less probably) neut.
    pl., 'driven together by a storm' (cf. *congressa* 760),
    seems to indicate that the hostile elements have to be
    brought forcibly together in the first place.

763-781 The crucial dilemma of Pluralism

If (a - 763-8) the elements change into visible compounds,
the visible compounds might just as well be called the substratum of the elements as vice versa: if (b - 770-81) the
elements remain unchanged, they can never produce the compounds of experience but will, in combination, obtrude a
combination of their own characteristics; a substratum
ought to be devoid of such secondary qualities.

The dilemma is essentially that posed in reverse order for
the fire theorists at 645-89. L's point at 665-74, that
if fire changes into other things it is destructible, is
here balanced by the idea that the four elements are no
more 'basic' than their supposed products, with which they
are constantly interchanging; the refutation of (b) corresponds closely with the argument of 647-54 (restated
at 680-3). As in the earlier passage, L concludes with
a demonstration of the superiority of Atomism, in which
the substratum is devoid of secondary qualities. The
two remaining anti-Pluralist arguments likewise end with
a statement of his own position.

Of the alternatives presented (a) was a popular version
of Pluralism and (b) the more sophisticated account of
Empedocles himself (see on 705-829 above). Lines 770-81
contain perhaps L's most serious critisicm of the Empedoclea
account, though the importance of 753-8 should not be under-
estimated.

763 rebus and res in 763-4 denote the elements, as do the
 -6

neut. pls. *illa* and *illorum* which pick them up in 765-
6 (cf. on 57 above), but in 765-6 *rerum* and *res* are
applied to the compounds which the elements are supposed
to form. The general idea emerges clearly enough and
the interchangeable terminology seems calculated to
reflect L's view of the four elements as no more than
res (see on 714 above) and to reinforce the point of
765-6 - 'how can they be called the first-beginnings
of things, rather than things instead the first-beginnings
of them, and the reverse assumed?'. Which *res*, he
essentially asks, are the *primordia* of which? Both
the elements and their 'products' are regarded as belonging to the wrong category for a substratum. For *qui =
how*, cf. 168 above. With *res illorum*, sc. *primordia
dici*; *putari* is most simply taken as impersonal.

767 These lines make clear that the theory attacked in 763-
-8 8 involves qualitative change and indicate the more
    fundamental objection which lies behind the *reductio
    ad absurdum*: change, as we have learnt at 670-1 and are
    soon to be reminded at 792-3, implies death. *gignuntur*
    also implies ultimate destruction (cf. *nativa* 754 and
    on 113 above).
    colorem: representative of the secondary qualities summed
    up in *totam naturam*.
    inter se: closely with *mutantque* (answering *alternis
    gignuntur*), 'one with another'.
    tempore ab omni: 'from time everlasting', so that it is
    impossible to say whether elements or 'products' came
    first; L's habitual assumption of the infinity of time
    is doubtless implied, strengthening the debating-point.
    As with *iamdudum*, the presents include also past sense.

769 The Mss here accidentally repeat 762.

770 sin . . . putas: introducing the second horn of the dilemma.
-1   The second person seems more appropriate to an imaginary
    philosophical adversary than to Memmius; contrast 751
    and 758 and cf. 799, 803, 824-6, 897, 907 and 915-8.
    coire: i.e. to form a compound; cf. *in concilio* 772 and
    in coetu 775. For the periphrases for the elements,
    see on 131 and 715 above.

772 ut: fifth word in its clause.
    eorum: partitive gen. with *nil*; with *naturam* sc. *suam*.

773 tibi: ethic dat., as at 673.
    esse creata: the perfect infin. with *poterit* suggests 'to
    be created from them and to exist'.

774 animans . . . exanimo: i.e. animate . . . inanimate; both
    words have their root sense, indicating possession or

lack of *anima*, though *exanimus* usually denotes 'dead'.
The allusion to animate life is a reminder of the complexity of the compounds which have to be accounted for.
animalia fruges 744 and *fruges arbusta animantes* 808
and 821 represent parallel pairings. *animans* is probably
a noun, as usual in L; with *exanimo cum corpore*, sc. *res*
from 773. The second decl. form of the adj. is not
confined to L.

775 quidque: i.e. each element.
in coetu variantis acervi: 'in the assembly of the diverse
heap'; after the personification implicit in *coire* 770
and *concilio* 772 and *coetu* here, *acervi* comes in rather
oddly and is perhaps designed to suggest that the elements defeat expectation by becoming a lifeless mass,
instead of producing exciting new qualities by their
combination.

776 mixtusque . . . manere: 'and air will be seen to remain,
-7 mixed at the same time with earth, and heat with dew';
mixtus and *manere* are best taken together. *manere*
continues the idea that no new qualities will result.
videbitur is passive (see on 224 above).

778 oportet: nowhere else used by L, the word properly denotes
moral obligation (like *debere*; see on 232 above) - 'it
behoves'. Here it suggests a personification of the
primordia, with those of the Pluralists failing to live
up to the standards required of them.

779 naturam . . . caecamque: 'a secret, hidden nature', not
simply in the sense that *primordia* should be invisible,
which those of the Pluralists, comprising tiny particles
of the elements, were, but in the sense that they should
have no secondary qualities (cf. on 684-9 above), which
would become perceptible in compounds.

780 emineat: i.e. obtrude in the compound (just as the word
obtrudes by its position outside its clause); the idea
is opposed to *clandestinam caecamque*.
quod . . . obstet: 'so as to conflict and prevent', another
consecutive rel. clause.

781 The subject is *quodcumque creatur*, i.e. any compound.
esse . . . proprie: 'to exist in its own right', by
having distinctive secondary qualities not shared with
its *primordia*.

*782-802 Attack on the theory that the four elements change
into one another.*

Such a theory was held both by Aristotle (*de Generatione et Corruptione* 2.4) and by the Stoics (Cicero, *de Natura Deorum* 2.84): the latter, while regarding fire as the ultimate constituent of the universe (see on 635-704 above), added a touch of Pluralism by postulating a cycle in which earth passed via water and air into fire, while fire passed via air and water back into earth. The Stoic account appears once more to owe much to Heraclitus, who himself talked of an 'upward and downward path' (ἄνω κάτω ὁδός) of change into and from fire, though his cycle included only three of the four elements of Pluralism and did not involve air. The theory criticised is not Empedoclean but belongs with those versions of Pluralism involving change in the elements which have already been attacked at 763-8. Against it L advances the same argument with which he countered the Monistic thesis that fire underwent change (665-74) and there are strong echoes between that passage and this: as at 675ff., he follows up the argument with a characteristic affirmation of the superiority of his own view.

782 caelo: i.e. the upper air or fiery ether, of which the
-4   heavenly bodies (*ignibus*) are denser concentrations. The description of his opponents as 'starting with' fire reverses the order of the 'upward and downward path' but still fits the Stoics well, since they regarded fire as more 'real' and 'basic' than the other elements.

    faciunt: 'suppose', as at 655.

    se vertere . . . gigni . . . creari: all these terms, like *mutare* 787, already to L imply destructibility (see on 767-8 above).

785 cuncta: neut. pl. ('they all'), defined by 786.
-6 primum, post: both adverbial.

787 cessare . . . mutare: 'shirk from changing'; *cessare*
-8   suggests ceasing culpably and so personifies *haec*, which refers to all four elements. *mutare* is here intransitive; for the fluctuation, cf. on *movendi* 383 above.

    meare: prolative infin. in asyndeton with *mutare* (cf. 680 and see on *ferae pecudes* 14 above), with alliteration serving to link the words. The repetition of the -*āre* ending, which occurs thrice in the line, and that of *terra* in 788 fits the description of a repeated cycle, though the repeated long *a* may be derisive, as it appears to be at e.g. 5.156ff.

    caelo . . . sidera mundi: answering the opening *caelo atque ignibus eius* 782. *mundus*, normally in L a term for a whole world (of which the universe contained an infinite number) is used in this context of the heavens.

789 The carefully constructed edifice of 782-8 is now collapsed
like a house of cards.
debent in this context seems to convey the same tone as
oportet 778: *primordia* have no right at all to behave
so improperly.

790 These lines re-apply the argument used at 670-4: 790-1
-3 are a variation on 672-3 and 792-3 identical with 670-
1 (see notes there). 789-793 are repeated in their
entirety at 2.750-4, a further indication of the
importance of the doctrines contained.

794 quae paulo diximus ante: i.e. the four elements, to which
-6 *ea* (796) also refers.
in commutatum veniunt: a variation on *mutantur*, involving
another fourth decl. coinage. L does not deny that the
four elements change in the sort of way postulated by
his opponents (cf. 5.235-305, where their 'destruction'
usually consists of their passing into one another).
Rather he argues that, since they do so, they cannot be
the real substratum; analysis must go further.
aliis: 'other bodies', in fact the atoms - antecedent of
the consecutive rel. clause.
usquam: tantamount to *umquam* (cf. 451).

797 This line = 673 (on which 791 above is a variation).

798 quin potius . . . constituas: 'why should you not rather
-9 suppose that'; *quin* is the negative of the interrogative
qui used at 168 and 765. The subj. has prescriptive
force.
tali: i.e. unchangeable.
forte: in this context = 'for example'.
crearint: = *creaverint*, sub-oblique perf. subj. after
constituas.

800 eadem: 'also', 'in turn' (cf. on 60 above).
-1 demptis . . . motu: a more complete summary of the atomic
variations responsible for varieties in compounds than
was given in the corresponding passage at 677 and 686.

802 'And that this is how all things (viz. compounds' are
(ex)changed, one for another'. L now generalises, moving
from changes of the four elements just exemplified, to
include changes of all types of compound. With *omnis* sc.
res from *rebus* to complete the acc. subject, to which
alias stands in partitive apposition. The plurals *alias*
aliis cover different types of compound, there being
many instances of each type. *mutarier* with the abl. suggests a new image, one of barter.

803-829 The argument from nutrition does not prove Pluralism

An imaginary opponent here points out that earth, air,
rain and sunshine are necessary for vegetable growth:
the implication is that vegetable life, and so in turn
animal life which feeds on it, comprises the four elements;
Pluralism is thus supported by the evidence of experience.
Throughout his reply L is prepared to admit that the four
elements play a fundamental role in the composition both
of vegetable and animal life (cf. 820-1): adding the example of human nutrition to those adduced by his opponent,
he points out that differing forms of life derive their
sustenance from different sources and, to explain this,
he adduces his own atomic theory, in which many types of
atom are common to many things but produce different compounds as a result of different combinations, arrangements
and motions (e.g. the 'food' of a plant and the food of a
man, though different, may contain many atoms in common
with one another and with the four elements); his account
is illustrated by his favourite analogy for the atoms, the
letters in words. L's aim is to show that Atomism fits the
facts adduced even better than does Pluralism; his main
contention is that pluralistic analysis does not go far
enough.

The argument is applicable to all versions of Pluralism.
It may be directed principally at Empedocles, whose theory
of nutrition appears consistent with the dramatised objection with which L begins. The pattern and content of the
argument have much in common with that advanced against
Anaxagoras at 897-914.

803 manifesta: like *palam* and *indicat*, stressing that the
-4 objector's appeal is to experience and is thus valid by
L's own Epicurean standards.
res omnis: i.e. all vegetable life, as the context reveals
(whereas in 803 res = 'fact'); contrast 813 and 816,
where animal life is also included.

805 nisi: 'but for the fact that' conveys the nuance of this
-8 mixed conditional, with open protasis (*indulget, fovet
tribuitque*) and remote apodosis (*possint*, which = prose
possent: see on 356 above).
tempestas: 'the season' (cf. 178), though the alternative
sense 'storm', as well as the context, helps pin it
down to the rainy season.
imbribus: dat. with *indulget*, 'gives the rains their way'.
tabe nimborum: 'through the wasting of the storm-clouds',
which fatten the plants by yielding up their own substance; the image is both poetically effective and

scientifically appropriate to the account of nutrition.
The *e* of the third decl. abl. sing. is here arbitrarily
lengthened; cf. 3.732, 3.734 and 6.1271.
arbusta: = *arbores* (see on 187 above).
calorem represents the remaining element, fire.
animantes: added because they in turn depend on plant-life,
which derives from the four elements, as food (cf. e.g.
254-61); their inclusion also serves as a cue for L's
own example of human nutrition at 809-13.

809 **scilicet et:** 'assuredly, and'; L accepts and develops the
-11 evidence before showing that his opponents' implied
inference does not go far enough in its analysis.
aridus: i.e. solid. *cibus . . . umor* suggests that human
sustenance is related to at least two of the elements,
earth and water, and prepares for the concession of
820-1.
adiuvet . . . exsoluatur: the conditional is remote fut.
(contrast 805-8), looking forward to a sudden interruption of our food supply.
iam: 'in that case': inferential, as at 594 and 756.
corpore: here appropriate in the specialised, idiomatic
sense of 'flesh' gained or lost.

812 The point that human food differs from that of other *res*
-3 (both animal and vegetable) and that different *res*
have their own different foods (summed up in *variae*
variis res rebus aluntur 816) implies a criticism of
the Pluralist account: why do not animate creatures
assimilate the four elements direct, as vegetable life
is supposed to do, and why does food differ from species
to species? Pluralism, it is implied, again fails to
explain the complexities of nature and L turns to his
own atomic account.
dubio procul: a favourite Lucretian asseveration, for
sine dubio.
nos: an emphatic final monosyllable, antithetical with
aliae . . . res.
ab rebus: *ab* may denote the source but is more probably
redundant and the abl. instrumental; cf. the simple abl.
in 816. *ab* in an instrumental context, though paralleled
in poetry, is a striking example of L's otiose use of
prepositions (see on 26 above); cf. 3.323, 429 and 567.
aliae atque aliae res: 'other things in succession'; the
use of *res* for both food (*rebus*) and its recipients,
which continues in 815-6, is perfectly natural: both are
atomic compounds, and the recipients are normally potenti
food themselves.

814 This atomic account anticipates some of the discussions of
-29 book 2; cf. especially 2.688-99, 760-2 and 1007-22, where
many of the lines are echoed or repeated.

814 Identical letters (most notably *m*) and groups of letters
-6 (*multa, multis, multarum; rerum, rebus, res, rebus;*
variis, variae) recur in different words, just as
common atoms and groups of atoms recur in different
compounds; the word-pattern mirrors the pattern in
nature and suggests that the analogy of the letters
in words (cf. 823-6, where similar patterns occur)
is already very much in L's mind. The complex interweaving of words in the sentence similarly reflects the
complexity of atomic interweaving.
nimirum quia . . . ideo: 'it is unquestionably because
. . . that'; all the emphasis lies on the explanation.
multa represents the first point of difference from
Empedocles, who assumed only four types of *primordia*,
which nevertheless produced all things by their combination in different proportions.
modis . . . multis: closely with *mixta sunt*.
multarum rerum: the possessive gen. belongs logically
with *communia*, 'common to many things'.

817 eadem . . . primordia: subject of the indirect questions
-9 of 818-9, which *magni refert* introduces.
quibus: sc. *aliis primordiis*.
positura: on the strict technical sense, see on 685 above,
though here it perhaps also includes *ordo* which is not
otherwise mentioned.
contineantur: with root force, 'are held together'.
dent motus accipiantque: i.e. as a result of the collisions
(the *concursus* of 634 and 685) constantly taking place
within the compound.

820 eadem . . . eadem: rhetorical anaphora. L concedes to his
-1 opponent that the four elements and living things contain the same *primordia* (even though he disagrees fundamentally about their nature and their methods of combination). *caelum* presumably at least includes air,
giving an allusion to all four elements (cf. 725),
though at 782 and 788 it represented the fiery ether.

822 They move in different combinations (*aliis commixta*,
answering *cum quibus contineantur* 818) and in different
ways (*alioque modo*, answering 819). The strange placing
of *commixta*, influenced by the mutual attraction of the
repeated *alius*, produces an interweaving again similar
to that of the atoms.

823 On this favourite analogy, cf. on 197 above. Empedocles
-6 (Diels B.23) had used the mixture of painters' colours
as an analogy for the mixture of his elements to produce manifold compounds; in this passage L may be presumed consciously to be putting forward a rival model,
which is scientifically more satisfactory. As at 814-
6 above (and on a smaller scale at 196-7), the language

underlines the point: the marked *m* and *v* alliteration
in 824 highlights the letters common to different
words, as does the repetition of groups of letters in
*versibus, verbis, versus ac verba; multa, multis;
sonitu sonanti* (the latter, dismissed by Bailey as 'an
emphatic redundance' too crude for the Augustan poets
and by Munro as 'a mere poetical assonance', is in
fact, like the other cases, scientifically illustrative).
Just as each of these three groups comprises different
words of closely related meaning (for *versus* comprise
verba), so different compounds with a preponderance of
common, identically arranged atoms would closely correspond; cf. also *ignis / lignum* at 901 and 912-4.

824 This line strongly echoes 814-5, pointing the closeness
of the analogy. *elementa* ('letters') is here an analogue
for *primordia* 815; elsewhere, L often employs it as a
synonym (see on 197 above), a usage implied in 828 below
(cf. also 913).

825 **cum tamen . . . necessest:** for the indic. in a concessive
-6 context, cf. on 566 above. *necessest* governs a familiar
paratactic subj., *confiteare* (see on 146-8 above).
inter se: closely with *distare*; both the lines and the
words differ 'one from another'. If the analogy is
pressed, *versus* would correspond to more complex,
larger-scale compounds than *verba* (e.g. men, as opposed
to flesh, blood, bone).
re: 'in meaning'.

827 **tantum . . . queunt:** sc. *efficere*.

828 **quae:** as antecedent, sc. *ea elementa*, drawing a distinction
between the *elementa* of the alphabet (827) and the
elementa of matter: the same term is applicable to both.
plura adhibere: 'bring more factors to bear', in addition
to mere change in order: e.g. varieties in the *concursus,
motus* and *positura* of 685 (cf. *quali . . . accipiantque*
818-9).

829 **unde:** = *ex quibus*, referring to *plura*; the clause is perhaps purposive, personifying the *primordia* as creative
agents, rather than merely consecutive.
variae res quaeque: 'all the various kinds of thing'; *variae*
reinforces the sense of *quaeque*. The allusion to the
variety of nature is a fitting end to the criticisms
of the Pluralists, since L's central objection, as with
the Monists, is that their substratum is too limited to
account for it: it also prepares for Anaxagoras, who
went to the opposite extreme.

830-920 (C) Anaxagoras and the theory of 'like parts'

According to L's account Anaxagoras held (a - 834ff.)
that every different substance (e.g. flesh, blood, bone,
gold) comprised particles like that substance, but sought
to account for the change of one substance into another
by adding the modification (b - 875ff.) that every
substance contained latent portions of every other substance - yet in, say, corn only the portions of corn
were manifest. The authenticity of (a) is supported by
the doxographers; as for (b) Anaxagoras certainly stated
that 'there is a portion of everything in everything
(with the exception of mind)' (Diels A.41), an idea which,
since it is so novel, would appear, together with its
explanation and elaboration, to have been the most fundamental part of his physical theory and not the desperate
expedient which L suggests (875ff.). His system must also
have been far more complicated than L's account of (b)
would imply. But it remains unclear how precisely
Anaxagoras reconciled the two positions or whether (as
suggested by Guthrie Vol.II 279-94) the widespread attribution to him of (a) is essentially misleading. The
reconstruction of his physical theory remains highly
problematical and controversial (cf. e.g. *Studies in
Presocratic Philosophy* (ed. R.E. Allen and D.J. Furley)
Vol.II (1975) chs. xii, xiii and xv.

Despite so much uncertainty, Anaxagoras' views are
historically interesting: by supposing a substratum including all the substances of the world he pushed Pluralism
to its ultimate limits (so accidentally anticipating, in
some respects, the modern chemical theory of the elements):
the Atomist hypothesis, while it was at the other extreme
in making the substratum of matter homogeneous, yet re-
sembled Anaxagoras' theory in that it allowed at least a
wide variety in the substratum because of the wide variety
of atomic shapes.

830-858 Homoeomeria *explained: initial objections*

After an exposition of part (a) of Anaxagoras' theory
(see introductory note on 830-920 above), L advances
against it the three basic objections with which he opened
his attack on the Pluralists (742-58): (i - 843) Anaxagoras
denies void; (ii - 844) he admits infinite division; (iii -
847-58) his substratum is insufficiently durable, for it
comprises all the substances of the visible world which
(like the elements of the Pluralists) can be seen to be
perishable.

830 **Anaxagorae:** Anaxagoras of Clazomenae in Asia Minor
(ca. 500-428 B.C.) was the first philosopher to take
up residence in Athens; the friend of Pericles and
Euripides, he subsequently fell victim to politically
motivated attack, was convicted of impiety and took
refuge at Lampsacus. He asserted the importance of
mind (νοῦς) as the prime cause but, as with the
other physicists, L's sole concern is Anaxagoras'
account of visible matter. For a full discussion,
see Guthrie Vol.II 266-338.

    homoeomerian: the Greek word (which is given its Greek
acc.) literally denotes 'likeness of parts', and
applies only to part (a) of the theory (see introductory
note above). L's claim (834) that the term is Anaxagorean has been called into question (see Guthrie Vol.
II 325-6): though later writers frequently use the noun
or its adj. with reference to his system, the word
appears nowhere in the extant fragments. The transliteration is a departure from L's usual practice, for
which he apologises on the grounds of *patrii sermonis
egestas* 831-2 (see introductory note to 136-45 above).

831 **quam Grai memorant:** i.e. as the Greeks call it.
-2 **nec:** = *et quam non.*

    nostra dicere lingua: i.e. to denote by a Latin term;
to have devised a metrical Latin word for this abstract
would have been virtually impossible.

    concedit nobis here governs an infin. (*dicere*) instead of
an ut clause; cf. the acc. and infin. at 613-4 (see note
there).

833 **ipsam rem:** 'the theory itself', as opposed to its name.

834 **principio . . . quam dicit:** 'first, as to what he calls
. . . .' - an indication that *homoeomeria* is not the whole
story. The second part of the theory follows at 875ff.
An original *quod*, whose antecedent would be the adverbial
acc. *id*, is attracted to the gender of the predicate of
dicit.

836 **ossibus:** apparently Lucretian shorthand for *partibus ossis,*
-42 for Anaxagoras certainly did not believe that bones
were made up of tiny, fully-fashioned bones; cf.
visceribus 837, *terris* 840, *ignibus* (already used of
fire-particles at 666) and *umoribus* 841, *ossa* and *venas*
863, *ossibus* and *nervis* 866, and contrast the clearer,
more accurate *sanguinis guttis* and *auri micis* 838-9.
The odd terminology, which avoids the cumbrous repetition
of *pars* and synonyms with a gen., may be designed partly
to illustrate the problems arising from the *patrii sermonis egestas* just mentioned, as may the high proportion
of 'licences' in the sentence (the archaisms *pauxillis* =

parvis and neut. *sanguen* for masc. *sanguinem* 835-7,
the suppressed *s* of *coeuntibu'* 838, the root sense of
concrescere 840, and the postponed *ex* 841); 3.260-5
exhibits a similar pattern (see also on 138-9 above).
But *ossibus* etc. are probably also calculated to make
homoeomeria appear eccentric and playfully to misrepresent it; cf. 915-20 and see introductory note there.
hic: subject of the sentence; the verbs are reserved until
839 and 842: in 842 *esse* or a synonym is supplied with
cetera and *consimili* ('like') is doubly applicable in
the context of 'like parts'.

843 esse ulla parte idem in: the three spondees and the three
elisions make the words seem as *stipata* as Anaxagoras'
particles. On *idem* ('at the same time'), see on 57
above.

844 concedit: 'admits (that there is)' - or alternatively 'permits
(there to be)', with a similar idiom to that noted on
446 and the same acc. and infin. construction as at
613-4.
corporibus . . . secandis: for the dat., cf. on 746-7
above.

846 illi: the fire theorists (655-64) and the Pluralists (742-
7).

847 quod: 'the fact that'; for the formula with *adde*, cf.
712.
imbecilla: weakness is a symptom of destructibility and
a consequence of softness (cf. *mollia* in the corresponding
anti-Pluralist argument at 753-8)
fingit: 'supposes' or 'fashions', parallel alternatives
to those with *concedit* 844 above: in either case *imbecilla
nimis* is predicative.

848 si . . . sunt: (as subject sc. *ea*, antecedent of *quae*)
-9 i.e. if such bodies deserve the name. Anaxagoras' 'substratum', for which he used σπέρματα (= *semina*), is only
once more dignified with the title *primordia*, in the
ironic context of 918.
simili . . . atque ipsae res sunt: 'similar to that of the
things (i.e. substances) themselves'. Anaxagoras himself appears to have had no specific word for 'substances'.
L's use of his own term for 'compounds' is a potential
source of confusion (see on 915-20 below).

850 neque: = *et quae non*, the acc. *quae* being supplied out of
the nom. *quae* 848; cf. on *haec* 60 above.
refrenat: the particles are pictured as galloping headlong to destruction.

851 For the pattern of rhetorical questions, essentially a
-3   tricolon with *quid horum* reinforcing the second member,
      cf. on 227-31 above.
    eorum: partitive gen. with *quid*.
    oppressu: coined for *oppressiōne*, denoting the grinding
      of the *leti dentibus*. Death is here pictured as
      an all-devouring animal.
    ignis . . . umor . . . aura: three of the Empedoclean
      elements. Earth, fire and water were mentioned at 840-
      1, and *aura* now completes the list. Anaxagoras was
      concerned to deny them special status and, according
      to Aristotle, *de Caelo* 302a-b, regarded them as mix-
      tures rather than as 'pure' substances.

854 funditus: 'fundamentally' (see on 668): every substance
    alike will be as perishable at the level of the sub-
    stratum as it is at the visible level.

855 manifesta videmus: like *ex oculis nostris*, stressing the
-6   appeal to experience. *ex* (for *ante* + acc.) reflects
      that *perire* implies disappearance from.
    vi victa: the assonance suggests that *vincere* is the
      function of *vis* (cf. 72).

857 'But to witness that things can neither . . . nor again
-8   . . . I call upon facts proved earlier', i.e. at 159-
      264. For *res* in different senses in the same sentence
      (the second involving a bold personification), cf. 803-
      4. For the form *reccidere*, see on *religione* 63 above.

859-874 How can the theory account for change?

L here adduces three examples (animal nutrition, vegetable
growth and combustion), in all of which experience suggests
that one substance is converted into another (e.g. food
into body-tissues). It follows that either the original
substance or the product includes 'unlike' parts: either
the product contains particles which still resemble the
original or the original already contains particles which
are like the product. The argument depends on the tacit
but correct assumption that the Anaxagorean *primordia*
were themselves unchanging (unlike the fire of 665-74
and the four elements of 763-8 and 782-802). A fragment
of Anaxagoras (Diels B.10), which alludes to animal
nutrition (L's first example), reveals that he himself
raised the very problem here posed by L and indicates
that L has not yet reached the most fundamental part of
Anaxagoras' theory in which an explanation was offered.

860 scire licet: cf. on 679 above.

nobis: possessive dat. with the list of nouns.
Lambinus' supplement is printed after 860 to complete
  the sense.
alienigenis ex partibus: (cf. 865, 869, 872 and 874)
  literally 'of alien-born parts' (the adj. is first found
  in L). The phrase serves as an antonym of ὁμοιομερής
  (the adj. of *homoeomeria*) - 'of like parts'. Since food
  nourishes the body-tissues, they must comprise parts
  like the food and unlike themselves. Alternatively (861-
  6), if they comprise 'like parts', the food itself must
  contain 'alien' matter, which is already like the tissues.
  With the second and third examples (867-74) only the
  second horn of this dilemma is stated but the converse
  implication is obvious enough.

861 commixto corpore: abl. of quality predicated of *cibos
    omnis.*
    dicent: the vague plural includes Anaxagoras' disciples:
      for the 'argumentative' fut., cf. e.g. 667.

863 ossaque et . . . venas: shorthand, perhaps playfully de-
    risive, for *corpora parva* of the same, as with *ossibus
    et nervis* 866; cf. on 836 above.
    omnino: lit. 'in all', so suggesting 'further', 'indeed'.

864 fiet uti . . . putetur: 'it will follow that all food
-6   . . . is to be thought'; the *uti* clause includes pre-
      scriptive force.
    liquor: balancing *aridus* and doing the work of an adj.
      For the distinction, cf. 809.
    ipse marks the antithesis with 860f., where it is the
      body-tissues which contain 'alien' matter.
    alienigenis: i.e. unlike the food.
    mixto: with all four nouns (which are in apposition to
      rebus) but agreeing in number and gender with the nearest.

867 quaecumque . . . crescunt: subject of the *si* clause of
    868. *corpora* may denote either complete examples of
    vegetable life (e.g. plants or trees), without implying
    that they are ever found *whole* within the earth, or
    possibly their component matter.

868 terris: the pls. appear to be mere variations for the sing.,
-9   as e.g. at 888-90. The consistent pls. *lignis, ligna*
      in the corresponding argument at 871-4 show that there
      is no need to take them as denoting 'earth-particles'.
    alienigenis: here neut. pl. used as a noun (as at 872 and
      874), denoting things unlike earth.
    exoriuntur: i.e. when the *corpora* (of vegetable life) grow.

870 transfer item: i.e. apply the same reasoning to another
    example; the imperative is a vivid, paratactic way of

expressing the protasis *si transferes*.
utare: paratactic subj. with *licebit*, like *consistant* with
necessest 872.

871   I have, with Lambinus and Giussani, excluded 873, *praeterea*
-4   *tellus quae corpora cumque alit auget*. It is most simply
explained as a Lucretian doublet for 867. 871-2 and 874
closely match 867-9, as *totidem verbis* has just promised.
flamma . . . fumusque cinisque: all 'products' of *ligna*.
latet: the variant on *sunt* 868 prepares for the account of
the second part of Anaxagoras' theory (cf. *latitare* 877).
alienigenis: i.e. things unlike the *ligna* and like the
'products'; the repetition (epanalepsis) emphasises the
crucial word in the conclusion. The jingle with *ligna*,
repeated in 874 with *lignis*, seems calculated to reinforce the conclusion: *ligna* and *alienigena* are as
closely linked as their names; cf. e.g. *corporis officium / officere* 336-7.
exoriuntur: i.e. at combustion.

*875-896 The solution cannot be that all things are hidden
in all things*

L here expounds part (b) of Anaxagoras' theory (see introductory note on 830-920 above), which contains the Anaxagorean answer to the problem just raised. L attacks this
part of the theory on the grounds that a substance's manifold contents would, despite Anaxagoras' denial, be visible in division; the point is illustrated with the same
three examples that were used in 859-74. Assuming that
L's exposition of (b) is essentially correct, his criticism is not necessarily as puerile as is sometimes supposed: if a lump of earth really contains all other substances, no small portion of it is required by Anaxagoras
to remain undetected; and if a substance's identity depends not only on which particles are in the majority, but
also on which are more conspicuous *and on the outer surface* (see on 878-9 below), one might certainly expect to
encounter alien matter on penetrating the surface, especially as substances would be required to contain high proportions of matter not only like themselves, but also like
the substances they habitually changed into. The invisibility of L's own atoms, to which he appeals in conclusion at
895-6, is not open to the same type of objection, for the
atoms possessed no secondary qualities. If the Anaxagorean
primordia contained the secondary qualities of all substances, it was mysterious that in aggregation they displayed those of only one substance at a time. L might have
raised further difficulties by enquiring into the mechanics
of change: if timber is converted into e.g. flame, smoke
and ash, how did particles of these products come to be
more numerous or prominent than the timber-particles which

predominated before? Though, assuming the Lucretian
interpretation to be essentially correct, Anaxagoras doubtless offered an explanation of these problems, it should
be remembered that L does not regard his own treatment
of any topic as exhaustive; see on 398-417 above.

875 linquitur: lit. 'is being left', i.e. by the argument
    so far.
    latitandi: in the technical sense of a criminal 'lying
    low' and escaping from justice, forming a pun with
    latitare 877, which denotes the invisibility of 'alien'
    substances. Though here humorous,
    the word-play again reflects a parallelism in the
    world: Anaxagoras tries to lie as low as his 'alien'
    substances. *quaedam* ('a sort of') seems to apologise
    for the metaphor and the word-play.
    tenvis: disyllabic, with the u consontalised: for the
    converse, cf. on *sŭēmus* 60 above.

876 id: in apposition to *copia* and defined by the *ut* clause.
 -7 res . . . rebus: i.e. substances (e.g. flesh, blood,
    bone) rather than compounds (e.g. men), though the term
    is open to misinterpretation (see on 849 above and 915-
    20 below). The word-order, with *omnibus rebus* enclosing
    omnis res immixtas, again matches the supposed pattern
    in nature.
    illud: i.e. the substance; for the neut. used with ref-
    erence to one of the *res*, cf. on 57 above.

878 cuius . . . locata: 'whose (particles) are mixed in the
 -9 greatest numbers and posted more conspicuously and in
    the front line'. Anaxagoras (Diels A.41) held that a
    substance's identity depended on the greater proportion
    and conspicuousness of the parts like it. L's military
    metaphor suggests that conspicuousness involves being
    on the outer surface, a point which considerably assists
    his argument but is not authenticated elsewhere. How-
    ever, it seems unlikely that arrangement would have
    played no part in the Anaxagorean account.

880 A characteristic formula of flat rejection, which L then
    proceeds to justify; cf. e.g. 377 and 789.

881 Food would be seen to contain the body-tissues of (a)
 -92 humans (b) animals (881-4 and 885-7), earth to contain
    vegetable-tissues (888-90) and wood to contain ash,
    smoke and fire (891-2): the three examples are those
    used at 859-74.

881 conveniebat: 'it would be proper'; like *decebat* 885, a
 -3 present potential (sc. if the rival theory were true).

In such contexts, Latin tends to use the indic., regarding the obligation or necessity as absolute and
the 'potentiality' as applying to the dependent infin.
(it is proper, whether or not it happens): when, as here,
impf. denotes present time, it is used by analogy with
the corresponding tense of the potential subj. and represents a compromise between the two constructions
(*convenit* / *conveniret*); cf. *debebat* 959.
quoque: i.e. in addition to displaying its own corn
particles.
saepe: L magnanimously concedes that body-tissues might
occasionally succeed in escaping detection.
minaci . . . franguntur: an allusion to pounding by a
stone pestle. *minaci* has especial point in view of
the supposed animate contents of the corn. In the
'periphrasis' *robore saxi* (cf. on 131 above) both words
have their full force.
aliquid . . . aluntur: i.e. one of the body-tissues (sc.
a partitive *eorum* as antecedent of *quae*). *nostro corpore*
is poetic local abl. without preposition. Unless *aliquid*
be regarded as shorthand for *signum alicuius*, there is a
slight zeugma: the corn emits (i) a sign (ii) an actual
tissue.

884 'And that when we grind it with stone on stone, gore
should exude'; grinding between millstones would reduce
the corn further than the pounding of 881-2, so that the
line reinforces the point. For the abl. form *lapidi*,
cf. on *tripodi* 739 above.

885 quoque saepe decebat: see on 881 above; the parallelism of
-7 the language reflects the parallelism of the argument
(*consimili ratione*). *decebat* governs the three acc.
and infin. constructions of 885-92.
herbas . . . et latices: the food and drink of sheep;
latices = *aquam*.
mittere: viz. when dissected or closely examined.
similique sapore . . . lanigerae quali . . . : 'which
taste similar to the rich milk of the wool-bearing
creatures'. *simili sapore* and *quali ubere* are abls. of
quality, the former linked by -*que* to *dulcis*. *simili
quali* is a conflation of *simili atque* and *tali quali*.
ubere lactis ('richness of milk') is a periphrasis for
'rich milk' and stands for *sapore uberis lactis*, a
compendious comparison. For the periphrastic compound
for sheep, cf. on *squamigeri* (= fish) 162 above.

888 saepe: as in 881 (see note there) and 885.
friatis: a technical agricultural term.

889 videri: true passive, as at 891: for the oxymoron with
-90 *latitare* (and *latere* in 892), cf. 642. The paradox here

underlines the flimsiness of Anaxagoras' contention.
dispertita: closely with *minute* and neut. pl. with reference to all three nouns.

891 videri: closely with *latere*, the whole phrase applying
-2 to both *cinerem fumumque* and *ignis minutos*. For *ignis*
= fire-particles, cf. 666 and *ignibus* 841.
praefracta forent: 'had been broken off at the end',
whether by nature or by man - an example from common experience. The subj. is potential (sc. were the rival
theory true), though the clause could have been treated
independently of the hypothesis, as in 882 and 884.

893 Another characteristic formula of rejection in the light
of the evidence of experience; cf. e.g. 188.

894 scire licet: see on 679 above and cf. also 860.

895 L characteristically ends by contrasting his own atomic
-6 theory, the 'proper' explanation (*debent*). *immixta*
latere in rebus reflects the degree of his agreement
with Anaxagoras, echoing 877 and 894: the vital difference is the substitution of *semina rerum* (the atoms)
for *res* (ready-made substances); the contrast is developed in the next argument.
The couplet strongly echoes 814-5; see notes there.

897-914 The argument from forest-fires does not support
Anaxagoras

An imaginary opponent here argues that it may be inferred
from the observable phenomenon of forest-fires that wood
contains flame, as an example of the presence of all things
in all things; he thus counters L's last point, that flame
can never be detected in wood (891-2). L replies that
his opponent's inference is wrong: if ready-made fire
were all the time present, it would obtrude its qualities,
i.e. the wood would always be on fire (cf. the arguments
against the fire theorists at 647-54 and 680-3 and against
the Pluralists at 770-7): this amounts to a restatement
of his position in the previous paragraph. He proceeds
once more to demonstrate the superiority of the Atomist
explanation of the phenomenon, according to which wood
contains many types of atom in common with fire but not
yet arranged as they are in fire: when a forest-fire breaks
out, the appropriate arrangement has been brought about by
friction. The analogy of the letters in words is once
more used as an illustration of the atoms in compounds,
as in the closely corresponding passage directed against
the Pluralists (803-29).

897 altis arboribus: possessive dat. with *cacumina*.
-8 vicina cacumina summa: 'neighbouring peaks . . . at the
    very top'; for the double adj., cf. 258: the two are
    not parallel, as *summa* intensifies *cacumina*.

900 flammai . . . flore: the image, though used as a poetic
    metaphor by Homer (according to Plutarch, *Moralia* 934B),
    by Aeschylus (*Prometheus Vinctus* 7), by Naevius (*TRF*
    48), and by L himself (4.450), and though especially
    appropriate to trees 'flowering' with flame, here
    also has a scientific application. The opponent regards
    the trees as implanted with ready-made particles of
    flame, which suddenly 'flower' on the outer surface:
    in 901-2 L re-interprets the image, claiming that the
    'flower' springs rather from appropriately arranged
    'seeds' of fire (which no more resemble fire themselves
    than a literal seed resembles blossom). For the triple
    f alliteration in the fierce context of flame, cf. 725.

901 scilicet et . . . tamen: 'assuredly, yet . . . neverthe-
    less', accepting the evidence (cf. 809) and the imagery
    but rejecting the interpretation of both.
    insitus: 'implanted in' (sc. by nature, at the trees'
    birth), according to the root sense and developing the
    image of *flore*. The usual arboricultural sense ('grafted
    on to') does not fit the account which L is here denying,
    according to which fire was inherent in *ligna*, not grafted
    on from outside.
    ignis: i.e. prefabricated fire (see on 900 above). The
    verbal correspondence with *lignis*, foreshadowed at 891-
    2, seems calculated to suggest the plausibility of the
    rival view: *lignis* contains *ignis* just as the substance
    wood is supposed to contain fire. At 912-4 L explicitly
    uses the correspondence to illustrate the true account:
    some letters are common to the two words, just as some
    atoms are common to the two compounds ('firtrees' and
    'fires' would serve to reproduce the effect).

902 semina . . . ardoris: see on 900 above; *ardoris* is again
-3 a variant for *ignis* (cf. e.g. 668).
    terendo: 'as a result of friction', closely with *con-
    fluxere* (cf. 177 for this metaphor for the seeds' com-
    bination). For the quasi-passive use of the gerund,
    cf. on 312 above.
    silvis: poetic local abl., as in 904 below.

904 facta: closely with *flamma*, 'ready-made flame', like the
    ignis of 901.
    abscondita: 'buried', 'hidden'; the former sense harmonises
    with the metaphor of *insitus* 901.

905 The apodosis comprises a tricolon, with asyndeton; each
-6 successive member expresses the consequences in starker,

more drastic terms. For *vulgo*, see on 238 above.
arbusta (acc.) again = *arbores* (see on 187 above).

907 paulo . . . ante: i.e. at 817-9, which are reported
-10   verbatim (after *vides*) in 908-10; see notes there and cf.
       the atomic doctrines introduced earlier at 675-8 and 684-9.

911 atque . . . lignum: the general point is now applied to
-12   the example under discussion.
       paulo inter se mutata: 'with slight changes one with
       another', of the sort outlined in 909-10. *paulo*, rather
       than *paulum*, is used because *mutata* contains a compar-
       ative idea: so too in 913 below.
       quo pacto: 'in the same way', introducing an illustration,
       as at 84. L's favourite analogy for the atoms (see on
       197 and on 823-6 above) is here carried further with
       the specific example of the words *ignis* and *lignum* (see
       on *ignis* 901 above). The rhythm here slows down (912-
       4 each contain five spondees), as if to allow for closer
       inspection of the two illustrative words.

913 mutatis . . . elementis: abl. of quality, 'have (as primary
       constituents) letters which show slight changes . . .'.
       The double sense of *elementa* (see on 197 and on 824
       above) is here exploited, as at 828. Despite the ar-
       resting similarity between *ignis* and *lignum / ligna*,
       the example illustrates only changes of combination but
       not of arrangement, since the common letters occur in
       the same *ordo* in each word.

914 cum . . . notemus: concessive - 'though we denote'; the
       two words, like the two compounds, possess common *ele-
       menta* but are still quite distinct.
       distincta voce: i.e. by a distinct sound or name in
       each case.

915-920 Reductio ad absurdum

L here returns to part (a) of Anaxagoras' theory (see
introductory note on 830-920 above): if the *primordia*
always resemble the objects of experience, this is the
death of them: a man's *primordia* will share his emotions
and laugh and cry when he does. This scornful point is
greatly elaborated at 2.973-90 (919-20 correspond closely
with 2.976-7), where it rounds off a series of arguments
for the insentience of the *primordia*. The picture of
men made up of anthropomorphic particles, which possess
not only emotions but also complete bodies with which to
express them, provides an effective satiric conclusion
and is obviously quite unfair to Anaxagoras; insofar as he
believed in *homoeomeria*, he held that men were made up
not of little men but of particles like the various tissues

(cf. 835-8), and he must have accounted for the sentience
of these *primordia* by the interaction of mind (νοῦς);
see on 830 above. But more serious objections to sentient *primordia* are to follow in the course of 2.865-990;
cf. esp. 2.907-30, where L enquires whether sentient
primordia have their own sensations or those of the whole
creature. To the Epicurean, emotion and consciousness
were functions of the soul-body compound, not of individual *primordia*. The playful misrepresentation is perhaps
also designed to reflect the problem of distinguishing
between substances (e.g. flesh, blood, bone) and complex
compounds (e.g. men); cf. the problem of distinguishing
between the substance bone and complete bones (see on 836
above). Such difficulties are accentuated by L's use of
res, which he regularly applies to 'compounds', to denote
'substances' (see on 849 and on 877 above).

The passage was probably added after the completion of
book 2 and is not perfectly adapted to its place: the
previous argument appears to have been originally intended
as the conclusion, in view of the close correspondence,
in form and content, with the final anti-Pluralist argument (803-29), while the return to *homoeomeria*, though
ending 830-920 on the note on which it began, is abrupt.
However, 897-914 and 915-20 have one theme in common -
that true *primordia* are unlike the objects of perception,
being devoid (i) of secondary qualities, (ii) of emotion
and consciousness.

915 iam: closely with *cernis*, 'as things are', 'actually'.
-7   quaecumque . . . apertis: i.e. everything in the visible
       world; the clause provides the acc. subject of *fieri*
       non posse. *fieri* denotes 'come into being'. For *cernis*
       (indic. despite *putas*), see on *quaecumque cluent* 449.
     quin . . . fingas: 'without imagining' or 'without fashion-
       ing'; *fingere* admits the same possibilities of inter-
       pretation as at 847.
     consimili natura praedita: 'endowed with similar nature'
       to perceptible things; L at last devises a Latin para-
       phrase, not for *homoeomeria*, but for its adj.

918 'This reasoning means the death of your first-beginnings
       of things'. *pereunt* is appropriate to convey: (i) that
       the theory is doomed (because it entails absurdities
       like those of 919-20); (ii) that the *primordia* must
       literally perish, as argued at 847-58, for a man's
       primordia will be as mortal as the man himself. The
       emotions of 919-20 are in fact symptomatic of this mort-
       ality: *tremulo* and *concussa* both indicate susceptibility
       to shock.

919 See introductory note above. In the context it is tempt-
-20   ing to suppose that the tears result from the violent
       laughter and that this is provoked by the fatuity of
       Anaxagoras' theory; cf. 2.979, where the *primordia*
       philosophise on their own composition.

921-1117 THE INFINITY OF THE UNIVERSE AND ITS TWO
CONSTITUENTS

L concludes his introduction to atoms and void by arguing for their infinity and for the infinity of the universe which they make up. After the long discussion of
the imperceptibly small (483-920), the transition to the
infinitely vast provides a dramatically effective conclusion for the book. The pattern is repeated in book 2.

921-950 Introduction: the author's mission

After the long and technical arguments about the ultimate
nature of matter, L spurs the reader on to the final topic
of the book with some reflections on his purpose, stressing the importance of his philosophical theme, and on
his use of the honey of poetry to sweeten his forbidding
subject-matter. The passage shows that L, while regarding
his poetic art not as an end in itself but as instrumental
in the execution of his didactic and philosophical purpose,
nevertheless sees Epicurean philosophy as a perfectly
legitimate, if original, field in which to aspire to genuine poetic success: otherwise, he would hardly talk of
his poetic ambitions in the lofty terms of 921-30.

926-50 are repeated with very slight changes as an introduction to book 4, where there is some reason to regard
the passage as a stop-gap which might have been replaced
in a finished version of the poem. The lines certainly
fit their context here in book 1; they may be compared
with the sectional conclusion at 398-417, even though
the tone there is less serious.

921 nunc age: the didactic formula (see on 265 above) is
        picked up at 953, at the end of the *exordium*.
     quod superest: object of *cognosce* and *audi*; contrast
        the more usual adverbial usage (see on 50 above):
        while applicable to the rest of the poem, it has part-
        icular reference to the final topic of book 1.
     clarius: i.e. (even) more attentively; for the insistence
        on Memmius' concentration, cf. 50-3 and 410. *clarius*
        is opposed to *obscura* 922 - an antithesis, echoing that

of 136-7 and 144-5 (and differently applied to
Heraclitus at 639), which is developed in 933-4.

922 Amongst a number of rather illogical imitations of this
-30 claim to poetic originality, Virgil, *Georgics* 3.289-
93 is the most conspicuous.

922 **animi:** on the case, see on 136 above.
sint: as subject, sc. 'my topics'.
The language, as well as the theme, is reminiscent of
136-7: other points of correspondence between this
exordium and 136-45 are the personal dedication to
Memmius (945-50; cf. 140-5) and the emphasis on L's
delight in his task (*suavem . . . amorem musarum* 924-
5 and *iuvat . . . iuvatque* 927-8), here primarily
poetic, whereas at 142 (*serenas*) the pleasure was
more philosophic.

923 **thyrso:** lit. the wand of Bacchus and his frenzied
votaries, which was twined with ivy and vine-shoots,
but here metaphorical, partly for the spur of fame
and partly for poetic inspiration, which it denotes
in Ovid, *Tristia* 4.1.43.
laudis spes magna: though such personal ambition was
strictly speaking un-Epicurean (cf. Introduction III),
L had good reason to regard it as innocuous in the
poetic field in the case of a poem preaching the
Epicurean gospel; contrast the political ambition
which he so often condemns (e.g. 2.7ff., 3.59ff,
5.1120ff.).
cor: the effect of the monosyllabic ending is in keeping
with the 'violence' of the sense: cf. e.g. on 13 above.

924 **incussit:** the repetition of the stem from 923 is a
reminder of the root force of the word ('has stricken
into'), so underlining the oxymoron with *suavem . . .
amorem*. The language is reminiscent of the activities
of *Venus physica* in 19, which reflects the parallelism,
traced in the opening prayer, between artistic and
reproductive creativity; pleasure (*blandum* 19; *suavem*
924) is in each case the prime motive.
mi: = *mihi*, doing the work of a possessive with *pectus*
(as does *omnibus* in 19).

925 **mente vigenti:** abl. of manner with *peragro*.
-6 **avia:** 'out of the way', 'off the beaten track' - introducing the idea of originality, which is strongly
emphasised by *nullius . . . solo, integros* and *novos*
in 926-8 and by the whole of 930. Despite the precedents for philosophical poetry mentioned in Introduction IV and L's own acknowledgment of the poetic
success of Empedocles in particular (731-3), L remains

the first poet to treat Epicureanism and the first
Roman poet to expound any full-scale philosophical
system. He perhaps also sees a comparison between
himself as a poetic pioneer (*avia . . . peragro*) and
Epicurus as a philosophic pioneer (*omne immensum peragravit* 74; cf. *primum . . . primusque* 66-7).

Pieridum: the Muses are so called from Pieria, a country
of Macedonia (cf. *Pierio* 946). Some accounts make
them daughters of a Macedonian king Pierus, who subsequently migrated to Boeotia, their traditional home
(cf. *Helicone* 118).

927 **solo:** the sole of the foot.
 -8 **iuvat . . . iuvatque:** the emphasis on L's own delight in
his poetic task (cf. *suavem amorem musarum* 924-5) is
designed in no small measure to stimulate the flagging
Memmius, which is the central purpose of the whole
passage.

integros . . . fontis: i.e. untasted, virgin springs of
poetic inspiration.

929 **inde . . . unde:** 'from places from which', i.e. from
-30 Epicurean philosophy.

coronam: this image for poetic achievement (begun in
novos decerpere flores 928) recalls the tribute to
Ennius in 117-9, whose originality was also stressed;
L is perhaps challenging comparison, seeing both himself and Ennius, in their different ways, as pioneers.

nulli: as in 924, the dat. again does the work of a
possessive with a part of the body (*tempora*, = the
temples, answering *capiti*, while *nulli* balances *meo*).

velarint: perf. subj. (= *velaverint*); the local rel.
clause is consecutive.

931 **primum quod . . . deinde quod:** the causal clauses give the
 -4 grounds for L's claim to the unique garland of 929-30.
At the same time the importance of the subject-matter
and the lucidity and poetic charm here claimed serve
to reassure both Memmius and the general reader and to
encourage perseverance. *primum* and *deinde* indicate
that for L the philosophical message comes first, the
poetry second: it does not follow that the poetry is
only secondary or *merely* utilitarian or that his com-
mitment to his poetic aims is less than total.

931 **artis religionum . . . nodis:** the metaphor suggests a
 -2 derivation of *religio* from *religare*; see on 63 above
and cf. *religione refrenatus* 5.114. *artīs* is abl. pl.
of the adj.

933 **lucida:** in the context of *obscura de re*, the adj. primarily
 -4 denotes lucidity (though this stylistic sense is not

regular before Quintilian). L admits the obscurity
of the themes (cf. 922) but claims, for the most part
with justification, to treat them lucidly. However,
the adj. also suggests the light of Epicurean philosophy
which dispels the darkness of ignorance and superstition
(cf. e.g. 146-8) and harmonises with the *lepor* of 934
(cf. the association of light with joy which is implicit
in *dia voluptas* 2.172 - 'divine' or 'bright' pleasure).

carmina: the position is emphatic; not only is L writing
lucidly, but he is doing so in the original medium of
poetry.

contingens: a compound of *tangere*, which may gain a wider
sense by association with *tingere*, 'to steep'; it is
picked up in 938 and 947.

cuncta: L, unlike the severest of his modern critics,
sees his poetry as enhancing the whole poem, not merely
sporadic 'purple patches' in it.

935 id: i.e. the poetic medium, the addition of *musaeus lepor*.
enim: apparently explaining the priority given to the
philosophical aim in 931-4; it is prior, for the poetry
also serves to further it.

non ab nulla ratione: 'not without reason'; *ab* perhaps
lit. denotes 'on the side of', as at 693.

videtur: sc. *esse*, 'can be seen to be'; see on 224 above.
This rather prosaic line provides a contrast with the
general elevation of the surrounding context and is
perhaps a reminder that the subject-matter will inevitably
produce some unevenness (see West 16 and 125-6).

936 This famous image, which L applies to his own technique
-42 in 943-50, is not original, appearing e.g. in Plato,
Laws 2.659e, but it is highly appropriate to the
Epicurean view of mankind as childlike, mentally and
spiritually ailing and in desperate need of the unpalatable medicine of Epicurean philosophy.

936 The prose order would be *sed veluti medentes cum . . .*;
-7 *medentes* is used as a noun (= *medici*).
pocula circum: serving for the unmetrical *pōcŭli* or *pōc-
ŭlōrum* and belonging closely with *oras*; cf on *inter
se nexus* 244 above. For the anastrophe, see on *hunc
propter* 90 above.

938 contingunt . . . dulci . . . liquore: echoing the sound
and sense of *contingens . . . lepore* 934, indicating
the point of comparison, which is confirmed by *dulci
contingere melle* in the apodosis at 947. The smooth
l sounds of 938 fit the sweetness of the honey, the slow
rhythm its viscosity.

939 puerorum aetas: i.e. children, at their tender, innocent
-41 age; the sense of *aetas* is important in the periphrasis
(contrast *absinthi laticem* 941).

labrorum tenus immediately restricts the strong *ludifi-cetur*, just as *non capiatur* immediately qualifies *decepta*. The gen. with *tenus*, which regularly follows its case, sometimes replaces the abl., perhaps by ana-logy with the Greek gen. with μέχρι.

deceptaque non capiatur: 'and be taken in but not take harm'; the play on *capi* is paralleled in Ennius, *Annales* 359 and Virgil, *Aeneid* 7.295. Here the verbal corres-pondence highlights not a correspondence but an opposi-tion in the world; see Introduction V c and cf. 978. *-que non* is regular for *neve* where the negative attaches to a single word.

943 haec ratio: i.e. Epicurean philosophy, as in 946 below:
-4 cf. e.g. 51.

videtur: 'seems'; contrast 935.

tristior: 'rather unpalatable' because of its difficulty, answering *taetra* 936 and *amarum* 940.

quibus: as antecedent, sc. *eis* with *tristior videtur*; *quibus* is dat. of the agent, a poetic construction not normally used by L, explained as a development from cases where the person interested is also the agent (e.g. 'known to me' = 'known by me') and doubtless influenced by the analogy of the dat. of the agent normal with the gerundive.

945 vulgus: not used with exclusive reference to the lower
-6 classes but a derogatory term for the uninitiated herd (cf. Horace, *Odes* 3.1.1), to which *tibi* stands in complimentary antithesis. Memmius is not prejudiced against the system (*retro abhorret*) like the *vulgus* but has been treated to a poetic exposition because he may, through unfamiliarity, find it *tristior*. The passage indicates that L hoped to interest a wider audience amongst the educated classes by writing in poetry than he could have attracted by a prose treatise; it also con-tains a natural enough exaggeration of the unpopularity of the Epicurean gospel in contemporary Italy. Some ten years later Cicero, who suggests that it was mainly popular with the uneducated masses who knew no better than to accept it, goes to the other extreme by claim-ing that it had taken over the whole of Italy (*Tusculan Disputations* 4.6-7).

volui: 'it was my wish', i.e. when contemplating the project.

suaviloquenti: on the compound, which appears in Ennius, *Annales* 303, see on *navigerum* 3 above. *Pierio*, a second adj. with *carmine* (see on 258 above), approx-imates to *musarum* and is not therefore parallel; cf. *musaeo dulci melle* 947.

947 quasi: apologising for the metaphor of *melle*, which has been prepared for by the simile of 938.

948 si . . . forte . . . possem: 'to see if I might be able';
-9 a verb of experiment, which regularly governs an indirect
    question introduced by *si*, is implied.
    tibi: possessive, for *tuum*, as in 924 and 930.
    tali ratione: 'in such a way', answering *tali pacto* 942;
    the use of *ratio* in 943 and 946 may however impart a
    hint of double sense, 'by such a system'.
    dum perspicis: the responsion with *interea perpotet* 940
    shows that *dum* = 'while'; the *dum* clause idiomatically
    resists the mood and tense normal in *oratio obliqua*.

950 qua constet compta figurā: 'and the form in which it
    stands arranged'; *comere* is used in its root sense,
    'to bring together', 'to construct': outside L, it is
    applied to arrangement of the hair or to adornment.
    For the idiom of the appended indirect question, cf. on
    568 above.

    951-957 The new topic

    Though L goes on to consider the infinity of (i) the
    universe (ii) space and (iii) matter, he here makes no
    separate mention of (i): its infinity is implied by that
    of either of its constituents and overlaps in L's mind
    with the infinity of space throughout the first part of
    the discussion (958-1007), where 'space' includes occupied
    space (cf. 507, 523 and introductory note on 329-417 above).
    In this sense, 'space' is coextensive with the universe.
    Of the two subjects here announced, matter is covered at
    1014ff., space, together with the universe, at 958ff. -
    the arrangement is chiasmic.

952 volitare invicta: poetic embroidery, for *moveri aeterna*.
    Though L has argued for the solidity and eternity of
    the atoms, which are obviously subject to motion, he
    has not yet demonstrated that this motion is unceasing,
    even in compounds once formed; *perpetuo volitare* thus
    anticipates a conclusion reached in 2.80ff.

953 summai: 'total' (contrast 963) - possibly an example of
    the archaic dative in *-ai* (cf. *aquai* 453), though there
    is no difficulty in assuming a double gen. (*summai eorum*)
    dependent on *finis*.
    quaedam: possibly a loaded use (lit. 'a sort of') implying
    that the concept of such a *finis* is strange.

954 evoluamus: the metaphor from unrolling a book is approp-
    riate to the final topic of book 1. The verb governs the
    preceding double indirect question (sc. *utrum* before *sum-
    mai*) by analogy with more straightforward verbs of explan-
    ation.

quod inane repertumst: 'the void which we have discovered', not only at 329-97, which concerned empty space, but also at 426-8, where occupied space was included in the concept. *quod . . . gerantur* (955) forms the subject of *constet* and *pateat* (957).

955 **seu:** introducing alternative terminology. The line echoes 472.

gerantur: sub-oblique subj. dependent on *pervideamus* 956; contrast the grammatically parallel *repertumst* 954, for which L vouches more categorically.

956 **pervideamus:** the prefix emphasises the vast range of the enquiry.

funditus omne: 'in its complete entirety'; for the collocation, cf. 478.

957 **constet:** = *sit*.

vasteque profundum: poetic embroidery of the central concept of infinity (*immensum*), focusing on space's depth.

958-1007 Infinity of the universe and of space

These two concepts overlap in L's mind, for the universe and the space here under discussion are coextensive (see introductory note on 951-7 above); his combination of the arguments for their infinity, which has puzzled editors, is thus perfectly natural. Of the four proofs adduced, (i) and (iv) contain specific allusion to the infinity of the universe, (iii), like the general conclusion (1002-7), to the infinity of the space in it, and (ii) to the infinity of both (*omne quod est spatium* 969 and *omne* 975). The only difficulty about the sequence of arguments lies in the fact that (i), (ii) and (iv) are closely related in thought both with one another and with 1008-13; it may be that proof (iii) was a late addition of the poet, not ideally adjusted to its position in the text.

958-967 Proof i

The universe has nothing outside it to bound it. The argument is expressed technically, and corresponds closely with Epicurus, *ad Hdt*. 41 (a passage on which L also draws later; see introductory note on 1008-51 below). It is repeated in a less theoretical form as proof (iv). As with (ii), its real basis is that the alternative to an infinite universe (or infinite space) is inconceivable.

958 omne quod est: i.e. the universe (Epicurean τὸ πᾶν),
picked up in 967 by *omne* (cf. 74, 975, 1001 and 1024).
nulla regione viarum: 'in no direction in which its paths
lead'; *regio* (from *regere*) here has its root sense (contrast the more usual, developed, sense 'region' at 965).

959 extremum: i.e. an extreme point or edge (Epicurus' ἄκρον);
contrast the more specialised technical sense (with or
without *cacumen*) at 599, 749 and 752.
debebat: potential (sc. 'were it finite'); see on *conveniebat* 881 above.

960 extremum . . . esse: 'in turn, it is obvious that nothing
-2   can have an extreme edge'; *videtur* (like *videatur* 961)
is a true passive (see on 224 above).
sit: the subj. is sub-oblique after *videtur* or makes a
proviso ('unless there be . . .').
quod finiat: 'something to bound it'.
ut videatur . . . sequatur: 'so that the point beyond which
(sc. *id* with *quo longius*) the nature of our sensation
cannot follow (the object) may be seen'. 962 is a description of the *extremum*, which can only be discerned
against the background of something beyond the object
and serving to bound it: e.g. the sea-edge can only
be seen against the background of the shore. Epicurus'
account is for once rather more lucid - 'the extremity
is seen against something else' (τὸ δ' ἄκρον παρ' ἕτερόν
τι θεωρεῖται).
haec sensus natura: cf. *natura videndi* 321; *haec* is deictic, as in *haec rerum summa* 235.

963 nunc: 'as it is'; cf. 110.
summam: i.e. the universe, as at 636, 706 and 1053; cf.
984.
fatendum: sc. *est*, as at 131.

964 As subject, sc. *summa* from 963.

965 L here brings out that the universe extends infinitely,
-7   from whatever point in it one starts; cf. 980-3 and
1005. At 3.1087ff. the infinity of time is described
in a parallel, equally awe-inspiring way.

966 quem quisque: 'whatever . . . anyone'; *quisque* renders the
-7   rel. clause indefinite and serves as subject of *relinquit*
as well as of *possedit*; for the attraction inside the
rel. clause, see on *capta* 15 above.
in omnis . . . infinitum: 'equally infinite in all directions'; *in omnis partis* answers *nulla regione viarum*
958.

968-983 Proof ii

Space can have no boundaries: a spear hurled from any
alleged limit of space must either fly on or be checked,
thus proving the existence of either void or matter beyond the alleged limit; in neither case will the extremity
of the universe have been reached. A similar argument is
used by Locke, *Essay on Human Understanding* 2.13.21.

968 si iam: 'even if'; see on 396 above.
constituatur: 'were supposed to be'.

969 omne quod est spatium: 'the whole of space', including
        occupied space (cf. 523); as this is coextensive with
        the universe, L can specify *omne* in drawing the con-
        clusion (975).
     procurrat: technical for the run taken to launch the
        spear; cf. Virgil, *Aeneid* 12.266, as also for *con-
        tortum* (971), denoting the hurling of the weapon, to
        which a rotating motion was imparted by a leather
        thong. L doubtless has in mind the image of the Roman
        fetialis declaring war by hurling a spear across the
        frontier; cf. Livy 1.32.12.

970 ultimus extremas: the juxtaposition of the synonyms
        reinforces the key idea of the supposed 'outermost
        edges' of space.

971 ire: sc. *eo* as antecedent of *quo*.
 -2 fuerit missum: = *sit missum* (see on *genita fuissent* 344
        above) ; sub-oblique subj. governed by *mavis*, 'do you
        prefer (to assume) that'.

975 effugium: 'escape' from a philosophical conclusion, as
        at 983; cf. *latitandi* applied to Anaxagoras (875).
     omne: subject of the acc. and infin. governed by *con-
        cedas* (976).

976 exempta . . . fine: a variation on *sine fine*; cf. 1007
        and *exempto inani* 660 and 742.

977 aliquid: i.e. matter, whose *officium* (336-7) is represented
        in *officiatque*. If the spear is prevented from leaving
        the universe, there must be matter outside to impede it;
        on the alternative of 979 (*foras fertur*), there is void
        beyond the alleged limit. The alternatives of 971-3
        are here presented in reverse order, producing a chiasmic
        arrangement.
     prŏbĕat: a metrically convenient contraction of *prŏhĭbĕat*
        (answering *prohibere* 973), perhaps formed by conscious

analogy with *debere* and *praebere*, which are also compounds of *habere;* cf. 3.864.

978 quominu' quo missum est: the assonance here highlights
an opposition (between the spear's goal and its failure
to reach it), rather than a correspondence, in the world
(cf. 901, 941, and Introduction V c).
    fini: 'at its mark', or 'target', whereas in 976, 979 and
982 *finis* denotes 'boundary'. The word-play seems
calculated to suggest an absurdity in the rival position:
the weapon's *finis* lies beyond the alleged *finis* of the
universe. L here for the only time employs the older
-*i* abl. of the word (see on *tripodi* 739 above).
    locet se: the staccato effect of the monosyllabic ending
(cf. Introduction V d) fits the description of a
spear thudding to its mark.

980 sequar: 'I will follow you'; the adversary is pictured
as journeying further and further through space in search
of its limits.
    locaris: contracted fut. perf., = *locaveris*; see on *suemus*
60 above.

981 extremas: the overflow of sense from 980 fits the idea of
space's alleged boundaries being constantly pushed
further and further back.
    quid . . . fiat: 'what will finally happen to the spear'.
telo is probably instrumental abl., the usual construction
with this idiom, though dat. and *de* + abl. are also found.

982 fiet uti: the repetition of the verb (in a rather different
sense) is emphatic - 'what will happen is that . . .'.
    consistere: 'stand firm'; each alleged boundary has to
be abandoned, as soon as the spear dilemma is applied.

983 'And the opportunity for flight will constantly postpone
your escape' (from my conclusion, as at 975).
    fugae . . . copia: the adversary's opportunity of fleeing
beyond each alleged boundary in search of a more satisfactory limit; this is afforded by the demonstration
that the universe extends beyond each boundary he posits.
The word-play *effugiumque fugae* is utilised to conclude
the argument with a resounding paradox: the opponent's
fuga never results in *effugium*. *fuga* is usually taken
of the spear's flight but L would then be disregarding
the alternative possibility of its being obstructed.
Interpretation is also complicated by the ambiguity of
prolatet, which can also mean 'prolong' (cf. H.B. Gotts-
chalk, *Classical Philology* 70 (1975) 42-4).

984-997 Proof iii

If there were any bottom to space, all matter would long
since have come to rest there. This is a new argument,
unrelated with (i), (ii) and (iv). It depends on the
Epicurean view that the predominant motion of the atoms
was downwards, due to weight (a view based on the gravity
of most visible objects). Despite this, motion in other
directions, due to atomic swerve and reverberation from
atomic collisions, also took place: these complications
are briefly alluded to, though not explained, in 995-7
(see notes *ad loc.*). The details of atomic motion are
not fully treated until the beginning of book 2 but L has
already stated the main premiss of the present argument,
the predominantly downward tendency of matter, at 362.

984 spatium summai totius omne: 'all the space in the whole
    universe' - synonymous with *omne quod est spatium* 969.
    The phrase is another indication that space is co-
    extensive with the universe and that the infinity of
    one overlaps in L's mind with that of the other. The
    subject, along with *undique*, is again placed outside
    its clause.

985 undique: i.e. at top, bottom and sides; this argument,
    unlike proofs (i), (ii) and (iv), relates only to depth
    and does not in itself show that space has no upper
    or outward limits.
    certis . . . oris: instrumental abl. with *inclusum*.
    consisteret is a synonym for *foret* 986.

986 iam: 'by now'; in a finite universe the supply of matter
    would necessarily be finite and, in the infinite time
    which L as usual presupposes in 991 (cf. on 233 above),
    would already have come to rest.

987 undique: 'on all sides'; in this finite universe matter
    would everywhere have sunk to the floor. The repetition
    of the word in the same emphatic position in both pro-
    tasis (985) and apodosis helps to suggest how automati-
    cally the latter follows from the former.
    ponderibus solidis: 'through the solid weight of its
    bodies'; both the adj. and the pl. suggest the separate
    atoms. The weight which causes their downward motion
    is unadulterated by void.
    confluxet: contracted for *confluxisset*; see on *consumpse*
    233 above and cf. *vixet* for *vixisset* in Virgil, *Aeneid*
    11.118.

988 These lines show the consequences which would follow for
-9 our, visible, world.

sub caeli tegmine: L uses the phrase, found also in
Cicero's *Aratea*, in two other places: here *tegmine*
forms a contrast with *imum* 987.
omnino: 'in the first place'; cf. 344 for parallel movement to a similar stronger point.

990 iaceret: potential subj.

991 ex infinito iam tempore: see on 986 above. Logically *iam*
goes with *iaceret* (990), *ex infinito tempore* with *subsidendo*; for the word-order, cf. on 550 above.
subsidendo: causal abl. The spondaic fifth foot, like
the three opening spondees, gives to the line a heaviness which ideally matches the sense and, in the context
of an event which L regards as impossible (as at 1077),
acquires an air of parody and mockery.

992 requies: L here begins a personification of the atoms
-3 which is sustained until 994 and which heightens the
contrast between the dead, stagnant universe of 986-
91 and the liveliness of the reality now described.
principiorum corporibus: 'to the bodies of the first-
beginnings' - not a mere periphrasis for *principiis*
but developing the image implied by *requies*: the atoms
are, as it were, physically tired.
nil . . . imum: 'no bottom'; if *imum* serves as a noun (as
in 987), *nil* is equivalent to *nullum* or adverbial.
funditus is appropriate not only to intensify *nil*, but
also in the root sense 'at the bottom' (see on 572
above).

994 confluere: 'congregate'; the verb (already applied to the
'seeds' at 177 and 903), though implying no personification in the inanimate context of 987, is used especially
of people and here continues the comparison with living
beings begun in 992 and sustained in *sedis ponere*. *quasi*
('as it were') either apologises for the image, or suggests that the whole idea of the atoms congregating at
the bottom is bizarre.
possint: the subj. is not only consecutive, but purposive,
sustaining the personification.

995 These lines elaborate the picture of ceaseless movement
-7 in the universe: the motion of matter in all directions
(996) provides an effective contrast with the stagnation
entailed by the rival theory but also reveals that L's
argument, which turned on the atoms' predominant downward movement, has been somewhat simplified.

995 res quaeque geruntur: 'different processes are carried on',
answering *nec res ulla geri posset* 988.

996 partibus e cunctis infernaque: 'from all sides and from

below'; upward movement receives separate mention
because it is especially striking in view of matter's
predominant downward tendency. It could be produced,
in Epicurean theory, by reverberation from collision.
The adj. *inferna* is used predicatively, replacing an
adverb.

suppeditantur: the verb, coupled with *ex infinito* 997,
suggests that L is thinking of the constant supply to
the world of atoms which replenish it from outside;
cf. 1035-6, 1040 and 1049.

997 ex infinito: sc. *spatio*, as at 1036; the absence of a
'floor' in the universe makes upward, and indeed all,
motion possible.

cita: perhaps primarily participial with *suppeditantur*
('are summoned and supplied'), though the sense 'swift'
also fits the picture of lively activity.

998-1001 Proof iv

This comprises a less technical presentation of proof
(i - 958-67).

998 ante oculos . . . videtur: marking an appeal to experience
(the verb is again a true passive). L now introduces
specific examples of the point made more generally and
technically at 959-62.

res rem: imitative juxtaposition, exploited in four of
the five cases of one thing bordering another in 998-
1000.

999 dissaepit: the metaphor from building a dividing wall
or barrier provides a colourful variant for *finire* 998
and *terminat* 1000. *collis* and *montes* exemplify similar
variation.

1001 omne: object of *finiat* but placed first, outside its
clause, and intensified by *quidem* for emphasis.

extra: adverbial with *nil est*; the line echoes *ultra
sit quod finiat* 961.

1002-1007 Conclusion

1002 natura loci: 'the nature of space' - in this context not
a mere periphrasis for *locus* (see on *animi natura* 131
above).

spatiumque profundi: 'the extent of the deep' - a new,
poetic expression for the totality of space; for the
focus on its depth, cf. *vasteque profundum* 957 and the
whole of proof (iii).

003 quod: 'such that', neut. in agreement with *spatium*,
the nearer of the two subjects. Grammatically the
acc. is appropriate only to *neque percurrere*; in 1005,
where the construction changes, *eius* may be supplied
out of it to go with *minus*.

004 perpetuo . . . aevi . . . tractu: 'in the everlasting
expanse of time'; the spatial metaphor explains the
construction which can be taken as poetic 'local' abl.
possint: the subj. is not only consecutive, but potential.
Thunderbolts were confined to specific worlds in the
universe and had a finite lifespan: *labentia* may thus
be seen as equivalent to *si labantur*.
The four spondees of the line fit the 'slow' passage of
infinite time, and contrast with the four dactyls of
1003 which reflect the speed of the thunderbolts:
neither advantage enables them to traverse infinity
and the deceleration in 1004 seems to match their
failure.

05 'Nor bring it about by their journeying that a whit
less (*prorsum minus*: sc. of space) remains to be
travelled'. For the idea, cf. 965-7 and 980-3.
restet is used impersonally with the infin. (lit. 'it
remains to travel less').

06 passim . . . in cunctas undique partis: an emphatic
-7 pleonasm (even if the last two expressions qualify
exemptis rather than *patet*), not inappropriate in a
description of the limitlessness of infinity and emphasising a point on which L has insisted from the
outset (*nulla regione viarum* 958; cf. also *in omnis
. . . partis* 966-7). The whole discussion thus ends
on the note on which it began.
copia rebus: 'room for things'; with *copia*, sc. *spatii*.
The allusion, in *rebus*, to the matter contained in
space again reflects that the space under discussion
is coextensive with the universe, since the universe
is the sum of that space and its material contents.
finibus exemptis: cf. 976.

1008-1051 The universe must comprise both infinite space
and infinite matter

L starts by developing the argument for the infinity of
the universe employed in proofs (i) and (iv) above: just
as there is nothing outside the universe to bound it, so
it itself contains nothing which could serve as its
ultimate boundary; of its two constituents, matter can
only be bounded by void, and void by matter (cf. 503-
27); where either comes to an end, the other must be

found beyond it. The universe must therefore comprise
either (a) an alternation of infinite matter and infinite
void (1011) or (b) finite void plus infinite matter or
(c) finite matter plus infinite void (1012-3 cover the
two latter). At this point there is a lacuna, which I
have filled with two lines suggested by Munro. L must
here have rejected (b) and begun the argument against
(c) which is continued in 1014-20: in infinite void,
finite matter would be scattered far and wide; all compounds would immediately be destroyed and indeed their
matter could never have assembled to form them in the
first place.

Lines 1008-20 are partly based on *ad Hdt.* 41-2, where
Epicurus also rejects possibilities (b) and (c) in turn:
1014-20 are an elaboration of his argument against
(c). In rejecting (b) L may have been content, as in
Munro's supplement, to appeal to the preceding arguments
or to argue, as does Epicurus in the passage cited, that
finite space would allow infinite matter nowhere to be.
But since his argument, unlike that of Epicurus, begins
with an emphasis on pure void (see on *inani* 1009 below),
he may here for the only time have argued separately
for the infinity of completely empty space, on the grounds
that without it the movement of an infinite supply of
matter would be impossibly inhibited (the converse of
1014-20).

Lines 1021-51 amplify the rejection of (c) and counter
possible criticisms. First L contemptuously dismisses
the idea that matter's present arrangement is due to
design (which would allow for the assembly and continued
union of finite matter in infinite space); worlds like
ours are rather the product of a long series of accidents, whose success, it is implied, demands an infinite
number of atoms available for 'experiment'. Again (1029
ff.) the mere continuation of our world's existence indicates the replacement from outside of the atoms which,
like all compounds, it is continually losing; the availability of sufficient atoms to sustain it, assuming infinite void, is only possible if matter too is infinite.
Lines 1042ff. defend this conclusion by rejecting an
alternative account: worlds cannot be held together simply
by the blows of unassimilable atoms on their surface,
even though these make a limited contribution to their
survival: and in any case the constant availability of
non-assimilated atoms to provide preservative blows
again implies the infinity of matter.

1008 ipsa modum . . . sibi . . . parare: 'set a limit to
     itself', including another variation on *finire* (see on

999 above) and suggesting an antithesis with the idea
of an external boundary considered earlier (961 and
1001). There is a suspension of thought over 1002-7.
rerum summa: i.e. the universe, as at 333 and 619; it
is picked up by *omnia* (1011).

1009 tenet: = *prohibet*, hence the construction with *ne*
(which is postponed to eighth position in its clause).
inani: the 'void' which is bounded by and bounds matter
is obviously 'pure' void, i.e. totally empty space (cf.
simplice natura pateat 1013); contrast the partly
occupied space discussed in the course of 958-1007.

1010 autem: 'in turn'; cf. 857.

1011 'So that she renders all things infinite by such alternation', i.e. so that the universe comprises an infinite alternation of matter and void. As subject sc.
natura, though in the second part of the consecutive
clause (1012-3) the subject is *alterutrum*. *omnia* is
tantamount to *omne*, though the pl. focuses on the
contents of the universe, like *rerum* in *rerum summa*
(1008).

1012 aut etiam: 'or else'.
alterutrum: i.e. either matter or void.
nisi terminet alterum eorum: 'supposing the other of them
failed to bound it'; the subj. reflects the remoteness,
in L's view, of this contingency. The partitive gen.
eorum is to be taken with both *alterutrum* and *alterum*.
The elision of *alterum* is unusual in L as well as in
Virgil; for Roman poets came to avoid the elision of
cretic words (-◡-) and of quasi-cretics (dactylic
words ending in -*m*).

1013 simplice natura: i.e. unmixed with the other. The abl.
of the adj. in -*e* is paralleled in L only by *pernice*
2.635.
tamen: i.e. though the other is finite.

1014 On the restoration of the preceding lost lines, see
introductory note above.
caeli lucida templa: a variant on Ennius' *caeli caerula
templa* (*Annales* 49); cf. 1064, 1090 and 1105 and on the
sense of *templa* see on 120 above. The line makes the
same triple division of the world as 2-3.

1015 divum corpora sancta: a stronger point - the Epicurean
gods, though material, were, unlike the world and its
inhabitants, eternal and indestructible. L here moves
from our world to the *intermundia* where his gods dwelt
(Introduction III).

1016 **sistere:** 'stand firm', i.e. hold together. The impressive
edifice built up in 1014-5 is suddenly toppled in this
dramatic line.

1017 **dispulsa suo de coetu:** 'driven apart from its assembly';
coetu (see on 666 above) is here the union of atoms
to form all compounds, including those of 1014-5. The
prefix of *dispulsa* is further stressed by *soluta* 1018.

1018 **magnum per inane:** in the hypothesis under attack void
is in fact infinite (and the *materiai copia* finite).

1019 **sive adeo potius:** 'or rather', a Lucretian pleonasm,
used to add a stronger point by way of correction;
sive adeo or *sive potius* is the normal idiom.   L
here adds to Epicurus' argument (*ad Hdt.* 42); cf.
344-5 and 989, where he moves to the same, stronger
point.
concreta creasset: 'would have combined to create';
the past participle of *concrescere* (as of *crescere*)
is deponent.

1020 **cogi:** 'to be brought together', the root sense (*co-agi*);
cf. 761. Like *con-creta* 1019, the word forms an
antithesis with *dis-iecta*.

1021 For the argument, see introductory note above. L here
-8 takes up the question of creation (mentioned in 1019-
20), whereas preservation after creation, the subject
of 1014-8, is taken up at 1029-41; the pattern is
chiasmic. Though 1021-8 are repeated with changes
and amplification at 5.419ff. (cf. also 5.187-94),
they are well suited to their context here, whether
or not they were first written for the later book. The
sarcastic allusion to purposive matter would fit a
wide range of teleological views of creation and the
passage may be seen as a general attack, rather than
as directed specifically against e.g. Anaxagorean mind
(νοῦς) or Stoic Divine Providence.

1021 **certe:** cf. *profecto* 1023; L offers no argument but
presents the absurdity of the rival view as self-
evident.
consilio: 'by design', the emphatic idea, picked up
and made more absurd by *sagaci mente* and *pepigere*
governing a deliberative question (1022-3).

1022 **suo:** monosyllabic with consonantalised *u*; cf. *sis* = *suis*,
in imitation of Ennius, at 3.1025. For interchange
of vocal and consonantal *u* (rare in hexameters with
suus), see on suemus 60 above.

1024 **mutata:** 'undergoing adaptations', viz. of motion, position

and combination, for the atoms are themselves unchangeable (584-98). The participle here loses its past
force and is equivalent to a present passive; this
usage, for which the standard 'timeless' sense of
deponents like *ratus* or *veritus* provides an analogy,
becomes increasingly common from the time of Livy
(see E.C. Woodcock, *A New Latin Syntax*, 1959, section
103). For the effect of the alliteration and interweaving of repeated words (*multa* . . . *multis*) in a
passage describing atomic movements and patterns, cf.
on 814-6 above.

1025 **ex infinito**: sc. *tempore*, which is included in the
corresponding line at 5.423; contrast 997 and 1036.
vexantur: 'have been harried'; the present denotes a
past action still continuing in the present.
plagis: the blows are those of atomic collision (cf.
633-4). This, weight and swerve were the three causes
of atomic motion (see on 984-97 above).

1026 **omne genus**: 'of every kind', an 'adjectival' acc.,
limiting the acc. pls. *motus* and *coetus*. This variant
for the more usual gen. of quality is an old idiom,
which survives in technical and colloquial language;
L has five examples with *omne genus* and one with *hoc
genus*.
experiundo: while denying design to the atoms, L per-
sists in personifying them; cf. *percita* 1025 (normally
used of persons) and see on 1048 below.

1027 'They fall at last into arrangements such as those by
-8 which this sum of things was created and holds together'.
The generalising present *deveniunt* and the use of *talis
qualibus* rather than *eas quibus* show that our world is
not unique (cf. 1042-3). L thus anticipates his demonstration of the plurality of worlds (2.1023ff.). For
haec rerum summa (= our world), cf. 235. *dispositura*
(cf. *positura* 685) is a Lucretian coining for the
inadmissible *dīspŏsĭtĭo*. For *consistit*, cf. *sistere*
1016; the word serves as a transition from creation
to preservation, the subject of 1029-41.

1029 **et . . . servata . . . efficit** (1031): still governed by
qualibus 1028 - 'and by which it has been preserved
. . . and brings it about'. *etiam* marks the topic of
preservation as a new stage in the argument.
magnos: 'long', a description applied to stellar or
planetary 'years' at 5.644.

1030 'Since it was first cast together into the appropriate
motions'; this reference back to the world's original,
chance formation hints at a technical reason for its
initial ability to hold together: to form any compound,

large or small, its atoms had to be able to 'ally (or 'harmonise') their motions' (*consociare motus* 2.111), i.e. fall into relatively stable patterns of motion which could be repeated within the compound.

1031 The growth and decay of worlds, the subject of these
-41 lines, is covered in more detail at 2.1105-74: a world, like any smaller-scale compound, continually lost atoms from its outer surface, and took in new atoms from the external supply which constantly bombarded it; it grew while it took in more atoms than it lost and decayed from the moment when it began to lose more than it took in. L there goes on to reveal that he regarded our world as past its zenith.

1031 This account of the world's replenishment is built
-4 (as at 227-31) around the familiar triple division into sea, earth and sky.

1031 fluminis undis: 'with the waters of their stream', approximating to *fluentibus undis*; in the context of *amnes* 1032, *flumen* bears its root sense.

1032 vapore: 'heat'; see on 491 above.

1033 fota . . . fetus: the assonance is once more a verbal
-4 link between physically inseparable processes (Introduction V c): warmth is a prerequisite of the earth's productivity.
summissa . . . floreat: for the former, cf. 8 and 193; both words represent metaphors from vegetable life, transferred to animal life, so stressing the parallelism between the two (cf. the use of *florere* at 255), but since in Epicurean theory animal life originally sprang from wombs put forth by the earth, the metaphor has some scientific basis.
vivant: pure metaphor; L denies literal life to the heavenly bodies at 5.11ff., though he loves to compare them with living creatures; see e.g. on *pascit* 231 above. *vivere* is even applied at 5.538 to the stationary earth without reference to its productivity.

1035 facerent: the subject (as also of *solent* 1037) is *amnes, terra, gens animantum* and *ignes* (1032-4).

1036 ex infinito: sc. *spatio*, as at 997.
suboriri: a rare compound, serving here and at 1049 as a synonym for *suppeditare* 1040 and *suppetere* 1050. The force of the prefix, which is not local ('from below'), is probably to denote succour or assistance, by analogy with expressions like *summittere subsidia* or *subvenire*.
copia: the supply of matter required to sustain our world during its lifetime, though vast, was finite, but

the implication (cf. 1014-20) is that in infinite void
the world can only be kept supplied if the universe
contains an infinite stock of the appropriate matter;
a finite quantity would be quickly dispersed.

1037 unde: = *ex qua* (see on 56 above).
amissa . . . quaeque: acc. pl., 'each type of loss'.
in tempore: 'at the right time', i.e. before the losses
result in the dissolution of 1040.

1038 veluti: the analogy with animal nutrition is not a mere
illustration but has a firm scientific basis: inanimate
compounds undergo growth and decay, depending on the
addition and loss of atoms, no less than animate creatures.
natura animantum: a periphrasis for *animantes*, as at 194,
to which the line closely corresponds; see on 131
above.

1039 corpus: 'substance'; while applicable to 'flesh' gained
or lost (cf. 810), the word is also appropriate in
the sense of 'matter', creating a responsion with
materies 1041.
omnia: i.e. all compound objects, including worlds.

1040 defecit suppeditare: lit. 'has failed to be available';
the infin., unusual with *deficere*, is used by analogy
with verbs like *desistere* and *desinere*.

1041 aversa viai: 'diverted from its path'. *viai* is gen. of
separation, an old Latin construction, several times
utilised by L (cf. *secreta teporis* 2.843 and *orba
pedum . . . manuum viduata* 5.840). The analogy of
Greek facilitated its retention and its revival in
the Augustan poets (e.g. Horace, *Odes* 3.27.69f.,
abstineto irarum).

1042 For the argument which begins here, see introductory note
-3 above. L seems to be countering a possible line of
argument, rather than refuting a view actually held
by any specific opponent.
plagae: again, as at 1025, of atoms and here (and at 1050)
applied to the impact of non-assimilable atoms on the
world's outer surface. The adverb *extrinsecus* is virtually adjectival (= *externae*).
summam . . . quaecumque est conciliata: 'any world which
has been assembled', indicating the plurality of worlds
which was implied at 1027-8; on the sense of the verb,
see on 611 above.
omnem: = *totam* (cf. 350), reinforcing *undique* ('on all
sides' or 'from all directions') and forming an antithesis with *partem* 1044; the sense 'every' spoils L's
argument by making him imply that some worlds can be
adequately preserved by such blows.

1044 partemque morari: i.e. repel the atoms which are flying
   outwards from the world at a certain point on its periphery. The passage is the only Epicurean source for
   the partially preservative effect on a world of
   external blows; elsewhere they appear as a destructive
   influence, hastening dissolution when a world or any
   compound is past its zenith (e.g. 2.1139ff.).

1045 aliae: sc. *plagae*, here the blows of the atoms which are
   assimilated by the world and are responsible for its
   replenishment (referred to at 1035-7); these L sees
   as the main cause of its preservation.
   dum: the subjs. are prospective (cf. 246-7), almost
   as if the atoms were aiming to preserve the world;
   see on *experiundo* 1026 above.
   suppleri summa: perhaps a deliberate word-play; the
   world is replenished, and the sum made up.
   queatur: an archaic use of the passive, influenced by
   the passive dependent infin. *suppleri* - an idiom
   preserved in classical Latin with *coepi*; cf. *expleri
   . . . potestur* 3.1010.

1046 interdum: the preservative effect is not only partial
   but temporary at that.
   resilire . . . coguntur: sc. by the atoms trying to escape
   from the world, which gain a temporary ascendancy and
   force the point of collision with the onrushing external
   atoms some way beyond the world's surface, leaving a gap
   through which others can make good their escape. In
   this sense the external blows are forced to 'leap back';
   the individual external atoms always rebound from
   collision but are replaced by the constant onrush of
   others, which would also drive many of those rebounding
   back towards the world.
   una: adverb, 'at the same time'.

1047 principiis rerum: i.e. the atoms which make up the world's
   compounds; *rerum* distinguishes them from the loose
   atoms responsible for the external blows.
   spatium: 'room'; not, as e.g. at 234, a synonym for
   tempus.

1048 largiri: personifying the *plagae* or the atoms responsible
   for them, like *cudere* and *resilire* above. Cf. the use
   of *fugai, coetu* and *libera* in connection with the world's
   atoms. There is a partial analogy with a beleaguered
   fortress, which the occupants are desperate to abandon,
   instead of waiting for the necessary supplies.

1049 multa: sc. *primordia*, which the world assimilates; the
   line reasserts that a world's replenishment and survival depend on an external supply of assimilable atoms
   (1035-7 and 1045). *multa* is not an understatement for
   innumera (see on *copia* 1036 above).

1050 Having denied that the external blows can be the prime
  -1   cause of a world's preservation, L turns the argument
       to his advantage by pointing out that they in turn
       imply an infinite supply of matter to produce them.
       tamen: 'despite this' and so 'in any case'.
       plagae quoque . . . ipsae: 'the mere blows too' (in
          addition to the intake of the assimilable atoms) and
          so 'even the blows'.
       suppetere: intransitive, like *suppeditare* 1040.
       infinita: again because, in infinite void, a finite stock
          of matter would be dispersed and so unavailable to
          batter a given world.
       vis: = *copia*. The nom. (instead of abl.) with *opus est*
          is an old construction, preserved especially in col-
          loquial language and with neut. pronouns; L has six
          or seven examples.

       1052-1113 Refutation of the theory of centripetal matter

       L here attacks the view that matter tends towards the
       centre of the universe, where it produces a single,
       spherical world, at the centre of which is a spherical
       earth, with antipodes, surrounded by spherical atmosphere
       and heavens. This theory would allow finite matter to
       form a world in infinite, or for that matter in finite,
       space, so that the argument is a natural sequel to the
       preceding discussion.

       L objects (i - 1070-1) that an infinite universe (which
       he now takes for granted on the strength of his previous
       arguments) can (logically) have no centre and (ii - 1071-
       82) that even if it had a centre, matter could not possibly
       become stationary on reaching it. A third argument (iii)
       begins at 1083, but is interrupted by a lacuna of 8 lines
       after 1093 (see on 1068ff. below). L begins by accusing
       his opponents of maintaining that, whereas earth and
       water are centripetal, air and fire are centrifugal (1083-
       93); after the lacuna, he is discussing the possibility
       of the escape of the world's fiery envelope of ether
       and the total destruction of the world resulting from it
       (1102-13). The missing lines most probably included an
       accusation of inconsistency and claimed that the theory
       of centrifugal fire must lead to the disastrous consequen-
       ces of 1102ff. The five lines printed in the text at
       this point (of which the second and third are by Munro)
       are included on this assumption. Munro himself regarded
       1102-13 as part of an elaborated restatement of the argu-
       ment for infinite matter advanced at 1014-8, without re-
       lating the lines to the centrifugal air and fire of 1087-
       93, but such a reconstruction fits the context less well.

A geocentric theory of the universe, such as is here
attacked, was set out by Parmenides and adopted by
Platonists, Aristotelians and Stoics, who all justified it in terms of centripetal matter. Furley 16-23,
following Bignone, attacks the common view that the
passage is directed principally or exclusively against
the Stoics. It is certainly characteristic of L to
lump his opponents together with an unidentified third
person plural (cf. his attacks on the opponents of
void, the Monists, and the Pluralists) and arguments
(i) and (ii) may well be regarded as unsympathetic
criticisms, presented from an exclusively Epicurean
point of view, of any centripetal theory (see on 1070-
1 below). However, what survives of (iii) seems more
exclusively applicable to the Stoics (see on 1083ff.,
1089-91 and 1092-3 below), while *stolidis* (1068) lends
support to the traditional view that the Stoics are
especially in mind throughout.

In pouring scorn on the theory of centripetal matter
(which up to a point anticipates the theory of gravity)
and on the idea of a spherical earth with antipodes,
Epicurus and Lucretius are guilty of a notorious error,
for which their rejection of their rivals' geocentric
view of the universe provides some compensation.

1052 **illud in his rebus:** for the formula, cf. on 80 above.
fuge credere: for the construction, see on *fugitant
relinquere* 658 above.
Memmi: a personal appeal as L enters the last lap of
the book, and a preparation for the concluding address
at 1114-7.

1053 **quod dicunt:** more pointed if contemptuous, with *in
medium summae* ('to what they call the centre of the
universe'), a meaningless phrase to L, since the
universe is infinite (argument (i), 1070-1); cf.
the contemptuous 1057, which looks forward to argument (ii). The parallel of 370-1 (*illud . . . quod
quidam fingunt*) does not prove that *quod dicunt* must
define *illud* ('this claim that they make, namely
that . . .'), since at 370 *illud* does not have an acc.
and infin. to define it, as it does here (from 1053-60).

1054 **mundi naturam:** periphrastic for *mundum*; see on *animi
natura* 131 above. The centripetal theories all entailed only a single world in the universe.
stare: 'is stable'; cf. *sistere* 1016 and *consistit* 1028.

1055 **ictibus externis:** the external *plagae* discussed at 1042-
51, which in Epicurean theory at least contributed to a
world's stability.

1056 summa atque ima . . . omnia: i.e. the whole of the
-7   world's upper and lower hemispheres. The division
      underlines the absurdity, in L's eyes, of the rival
      theory, according to which the world's *ima* tend up-
      wards. It prepares for the contemptuous parenthesis
      of 1057, which treats the world as something standing
      on itself (i.e. *summus mundus* stands on *imus mundus*).
      sint . . . nixa: a present would be expected (cf. *niti*
      1053); the perf. suggests *nitendo pervenerint*.

1058 L here moves from the world as a whole to the earth
-67   situated at its centre, which in Epicurean theory
      was flat, in the theory under attack spherical.

1058 quae pondera sunt sub terris: i.e. the bodies which
-9   his rivals claim are on the surface of the underside
      of the earth. L uses *pondera* rather than *corpora*
      (cf. 1077) to bring out the paradox; by the Epicurean
      laws of gravity, the bodies' weight should make them
      fall into the sky below them (cf. 1062-4). In *oratio
      obliqua*, *sint* rather than *sunt* would be expected (cf.
      sint 1056); the rival theory, with its attendant
      absurdity, is here expressed more vividly.
      sursum ('upwards'), in terra ('on the earth'), and
      retro . . . posta ('upside down') are all, like *pon-
      dera*, deliberately paradoxical, and calculated to pre-
      sent the rival idea as absurdly perverse. *sursum* and
      retro posta are applied, like *sub terris*, exclusively
      from the point of view of those *supra terras*; *in terra*
      is placed strategically between them applying from the
      opposite, antipodean point of view, and used of objects
      which have just been described as *sub terris*.

1060 quae: third word in its clause, into which the antecedent
      (*rerum simulacra*) is attracted. The comparison with
      reflections is used to illustrate only the position
      of antipodean bodies (*retro posta*), not their gravitat-
      ional properties (*sursum nitier*).
      nunc: 'as things are' (in our hemisphere) and so 'in our
      position'.

1061 animalia: L now moves on from inanimate nature on the
      earth (*pondera* 1058); the description culminates with
      human antipodeans (*illi* 1065).
      suppa: 'facing upwards' (a rare and archaic equivalent
      of *supina*), making the same point as *retro posta* in
      a deliberately grotesque way. Duff well compares a
      fly on a ceiling.

1063 inferiora: with *loca caeli* 1062 - 'the heavenly regions
      below them', again scornfully paradoxical.
      nostra: i.e. of those 'above' the earth.

1064 **caeli templa:** see on 1014 above.

1065 **illi:** i.e. the antipodeans. As book 5 reveals, L does
not reject the astronomy implied at this point, even
though he refuses to be dogmatic and advances a
variety of possibilities in accordance with the
doctrine of plurality of causes (Introduction III).
His quarrel is with the existence of antipodeans to
witness 'subterranean' day and night.

1066 **alternis . . . diebus:** 'they take their turn in sharing
-7 the seasons with us, and spend nights equal in length
to our days'; as acc. subject sc. *illos* out of *illi*
1065; with *diebus* sc. *nostris*. For the sense of
tempora caeli, cf. 5.231 and 6.362; here L is thinking primarily of the variations in the length of day
and night which accompany them. The two points made
here thus go closely together and develop *illi . . .
cernere* 1065-6.

1068 These lines are printed with Munro's restorations:
-75 their mutilation in the Mss appears to result from the
loss of the top corner of a right-hand page in the
single archetype from which all extant copies of L
derive. When, 26 lines later, the scribe turned over
and found the beginning of 8 lines missing, he failed
to preserve the remnants: hence the lacuna at 1094-
1101.

1068 **stolidis:** a probable clue that the Stoics are especially
in mind throughout the attack on the centripetalists;
see on 641 above.

1069 **rem:** 'a theory'; cf. the claim that the *stolidi* are
seduced by *inversis verbis* at 641-2.

1070 **nam . . . infinita:** argument (i); see introductory note
-1 above. The point has been demonstrated at 965-7 (cf.
980-3 and 1005). Though the Aristotelians, unlike the
Stoics, rejected the existence of infinite void outside the world, L would doubtless regard his argument
as applicable to them, this part of their theory having
been demolished by his previous arguments. Furley
(*loc. cit.*) points out that the Stoic Chrysippus anticipated L's criticism by contending that matter tended
not to the centre of infinite space but to its own
centre. But this does not mean that argument (i)
cannot be directed against the Stoics: as in the case
of Anaxagoras, L is liable to overlook the subtleties
of his rivals' position, nor would he be the only ancient
writer to overlook or misrepresent Chrysippus on the
point (cf. Plutarch, *de Stoicorum Repugnantiis* 44,
quoted by Furley).

1071 neque . . . repelli: argument (ii) begins here; assuming
-3 space had a centre, why should matter come to a stand-
still there (*ibi consistere* 1072), rather than be re-
pelled by it (*repelli* 1073)?
si iam . . . sit: see on 396 above.
quavis alia longe ratione: 'on whatever completely different principle you please'. Lucretian idiom (cf.
e.g. 2.881, 4.446, 5.460, 1030 and 1065) suggests
that *longe* qualifies *alia* rather than *repelli*, unless
the word here does double duty.

1074 The crux of argument (ii): L's rivals deny void its
-80 fundamental property, to yield to the motion of matter:
matter moving towards a hypothetical centre in void
would simply pass through it and could not be checked
or supported by void. The criticism is based on
Epicurean preconceptions and overlooks his rivals'
belief that the central point had never been empty
but was perpetually surrounded by a plenum of matter.

1075 per medium, per non medium: closely with *aeque* 1076 -
'at centre, at non-centre alike'. *per* is used
because of the implication of the motion of the
ponderibus (1076) through void. For *non medium* used
as a noun, illustrating L's sometimes innovatory approach to language, cf. *non sensibu'* and *non sensu* 2.
930-2.
debet: here (and at 1079) again of scientific obligation
but the normal sense of moral obligation fits the
'impropriety' of the rival theory; cf. 789.

1076 ponderibus: i.e. material bodies which possess weight;
as at 1058, the term seems designed to suggest the
Epicurean picture of weight causing downward movement,
in criticism of L's rivals.
motus quacumque feruntur: 'whatever the path of their
motion', amplifying *per medium, per non medium*.

1077 quisquam: adjectival, for the more usual *ullus*, as at
2.857, 3.234 and 875.
locus: 'point in space', echoing the technical usage
of the word in 1074.
cum venere: = *cum venerunt*. The slowness of the spondaic
ending mimics and mocks the picture of matter suddenly
coming to a halt; cf. on 991 above.
1078 ponderis and stare in ('stand still on', the converse
of *subsistere* in 1079) suggest that L is thinking exclusively in Epicurean terms of downward movement to
the 'centre'. If the terms also apply to motion to
it from other directions, their extension is doubtless
intended to underline the abnormality of the rival
concept of gravity (cf. *in terra* 1059).

1079 autem: 'in turn', introducing the converse idea; cf.
857 and 1010.
ulli: neut. adj. used as a pronoun, replacing *cuiquam* or
ulli rei.

1080 quin: = *ita ut non*.

1081 teneri . . . in concilium: 'be locked in union', a
-2 pregnant construction - 'enter into union and be held
there'.
medii cuppedine victae: 'overcome by craving for the
centre' - a sarcastic personification of matter (cf.
1021-3) to round off the argument. *cuppedo* (= *cupido*)
is unique to L.

1083ff. Argument (iii); see introductory note above. L here
qualifies his account of his rivals' theory: whereas
at 1053 they maintained that all matter was centripetal,
their position is now that earth and water are
centripetal, air and fire centrifugal. If (as 1089-
93 suggest) L is here attacking the Stoics, he seems
to misrepresent them: Zeno and Chrysippus (cf. Furley
loc. cit.) apparently held that air and fire were only
relatively centrifugal: all matter tended to the centre,
but air and fire, being weightless, did so less strongly
than earth and water, which possessed weight. The
strange denial of weight to air and fire may help to
explain L's not uncharacteristic misrepresentation, as
may the confused impression left with the doxographers
on the point: e.g. Stobaeus, *Eclogae* 1.19.4 implies that
Zenonian air and fire are centrifugal (ἀνώφοιτα).
Though Aristotelian air and fire were genuinely centrifugal, 1089-91 do not fit his scheme (see note *ad loc.*).

1083 fingunt: sceptical; cf. on 104 above.

1085 With Giussani's transposition, the lines amplify *terrarum*
-6 *atque liquoris* 1084 (with which sc. *corpora* from 1083);
the arrangement is chiasmic, with *liquoris* taken up in
1085, *terrarum* in 1086 - 'and things which are, so to
speak, contained in an earthy body', i.e. all the earth's
products, whether animal, vegetable or mineral. This
interpretation gains support from Seneca, *Quaestiones
Naturales* 2.1.2, where the phrase *omnia quae solo cont-
inentur* is similarly applied and is said to be a term
of jurisconsults. *magnasque e montibus undas* highlights
the downward tendency of river-water. For *e montibus*
attached to the noun *undas* (with *magnas* here acting
as an 'enclosing' adj.), see on 244 above.

1087 tenuis: 'insubstantial'; in fact, according to Zeno and
Chrysippus, weightless.

1089 Centrifugal fire here collects at the world's periphery
-91 to form the ether and sustain the heavenly bodies. This
was not the view of Aristotle, according to whom the
ether, complete with its heavenly bodies, comprised
the 'fifth nature', a revolving shell encircling the
world, which was quite distinct from the centrifugal
fire, which it held in place. Furley (*loc. cit.*) is
thus forced to the dubious assumption that L is here
criticising an earlier Aristotelian cosmology which
excluded the fifth body and was preferred by his immediate successors to his later system. It seems
far more likely that L is here attacking the Stoics.
tremere: a favourite Lucretian metaphor for the flickering
of light; cf. 4.404, 5.298, 587 and 697.
signis: the rhyming assonance with *ignis* 1088 is again
meaningful: the heavenly bodies comprise fire.
per caeli caerula: this assonance is taken over from
Ennius (see on 1014 above); for the construction, see
on 86 above.
pasci: for the metaphor, cf. on 231 and 1034 above.
calor: a variant for *ignis*; the two ideas have already
been linked in *calidos ignis* 1088.

1092 On the eight-line lacuna following this couplet at 1094-
-3 1101 and the five-line stopgap printed in the text at
this point, see introductory note above. In the context the *nisi* clause must have contained another allusion to centrifugal fire, by which L's opponents
explained the leafing of the topmost branches of
trees - *arboribus summos frondescere ramos* 1092.
The Stoic belief that internal fire nurtured plants,
and animals too, is attested e.g. by Stobaeus, *Eclogae*
1.538 and it is natural to assume that they explained
the upward (or centrifugal) growth of plants in
terms of the upward (or centrifugal) tendency of the
internal fire; *ignea vis . . . tendens* has been added
to complete the *nisi* clause accordingly. *scilicet*
. . . fingunt (Munro) is added to provide the apodosis
of the *quoniam* clause (1083ff.), *quin etiam . . . timen-*
dum to govern the *ne* clauses of 1102-10.

1102 The description of the world's destruction provides a
-13 fine imaginative climax for the book and also a sharp
contrast with Venus' creative activities with which it
opened. Epicurean theory itself entailed the eventual
sudden destruction of our world and the infinite number
of others like it (cf. 5.91-109). L's point is that
centrifugal fire would make its destruction immediate.
His description may also be intended to provide an
incidental, ironic contrast with the Stoics' own account
of the world's periodic destruction at the conflagration.

1102 **volucri ritu flammarum:** a scientific comparison, insofar

as the *moenia mundi* (cf. 73) comprised fiery ether
in the Stoic as well as the Epicurean system. *volucri*
may be seen as transferred from *flammarum* to *ritu* (cf.
on 10 above) but the metaphor of *volucri* is poetically
bolder.

1103 **diffugiant:** the prefix has point; the (spherical) 'walls of
the world' pass in different directions into the great void
as they flee the world's centre. *subito* in the context suggest the imminence as well as the rapidity
of their escape.
soluta: i.e. freed from the world and resolved into
atoms (cf. 1018): to L the latter would follow automatically from the former.

1104 **et ne** marks a stronger break than *neve* 1105; the dangers
are (a) the escape of fire (1102-3) and (b) the ensuing
disintegration and escape of the remaining elements
(*cetera* 1104), elaborated in 1105-1108.

1105 **caeli tonitralia templa:** i.e. the lower atmosphere,
comprising air, not ether; for *caeli templa*, see on
120 and 1014 above.
ruant . . . superne: 'fall from on high'. The sense
'rush upwards', which might be expected in the context
of centrifugal air, cannot be extracted from the Latin;
in L *superne* always denotes 'from above' or 'above' and
the meaning 'upwards', for which L uses *sursum*, is not
attested before the elder Pliny. Again, *ruere caelum*
is proverbial for the heavens *falling*. The skies
fall rather than rise because from this point the
account proceeds on Epicurean rather than Stoic
principles: the escape of centrifugal fire destroys
the world's equilibrium as an atomic compound, resulting in the rapid and total destruction of 1105-10.

1106 The earth's collapse is again a purely Epicurean con-
-8 sequence of the disruption. The rival theory would
allow both earth and water, being centripetal, to
survive the loss of centrifugal air and fire unharmed.
The earth (i) falls downwards (*se . . . subducat*),
on the disruption of the cushion of air which helped
to support it (5.534-63), and (ii) passes totally
away through the deep void (*omnis . . . abeat per
inane profundum*), as it is resolved into its component
atoms.
rerum caelique: the unusual pairing, with *rerum* denoting
terrestrial objects, well reflects the confused mingling
of the remnants of great and small in the general
catastrophe. The word-pattern, with *omnis* and *abeat*
(of the earth's dissolution) separated by *inter . . .
solventis* (of that of terrestrial objects and sky) also
matches the pattern of intermingling in nature.

corpora solventis: 'loosening their matter', right
down to the atomic level, as the next couplet shows.

1109 reliquiarum: on the long *e*, see on *religione* 63 above.

1110 desertum: stronger than L's permanent epithets for
void, like *vacuum* - 'deserted' by the world which
previously occupied it.
caeca: for the passive sense, 'invisible', cf. 277.
L continues to think in Epicurean terms. The awe-
inspiring picture provides an incidental reminder
of the two constituents of the universe which book
1 has sought to establish.

1111 Total destruction of the world must ensue, wherever the
-3 initial failure of its matter occurs. The lines reinforce the argument: only a small portion of fire
need escape to provide an initial breach, yet L's
rivals make the whole of the *moenia mundi* liable to
fly outwards.
parti: on the form of the abl., see on *tripodi* 739
above.
corpora desse: 'bodies fail', by deserting the *mundus*.
rebus: the constituents of the *mundus*.
ianua leti: the image, developed at 5.373-5, is imitated
by Virgil, *Aeneid* 2.661; it is especially appropriate
in the present context, where it denotes the breach
in the *moenia mundi*, through which the members of the
mundus issue to their destruction.
turba . . . omnis materiai: i.e. the whole confused
mass of the world's matter; the hint of personification
in *turba* (like *foras*) fits the gate-image.

1114-1117 Conclusion: exhortation of Memmius

No other book of L contains an epilogue. The idea may
have come from Epicurus, who uses sectional conclusions
in the letter to Herodotus (e.g. *ad Hdt.* 45); cf. L's
longer exhortation, used as a sectional conclusion, at
398-417.

1114 si: the Mss reading *sic* ('with a slight effort you will
master these principles, *as you have been doing*') is
intolerably weak and abrupt; I have adopted Munro's
emendation and supposed the next line lost. The
supplement printed takes the argument to be 'master
the principles of book 1 (*haec*), and with a small
effort you will grasp the lessons which remain (in
books 2-6)'. Lines 1115-7 then refer to the light

shed by L's early topics on his later ones and, appropriately in a conclusion, stress the continuity of the
subject-matter and of the whole system. Munro, taking
the argument as identical to that of 402-9, where
Memmius is to follow up the details of a specific
topic on his own, suggested *cetera iam poteris per
te tute ipse videre,* but at the end of the book this
carries the unfortunate implication that Memmius need
not bother to read books 2-6 at all.

1115 The book ends with L's favourite image of the light of
-7 Epicurean philosophy illuminating the darkness of
ignorance and fear (cf. 146-8). The description
is worked out in terms of a traveller by night, whose
way to his destination is constantly illumined (*nec
. . . pervideas*), and of one light kindling another
(*res . . . rebus;* cf. *alid ex alio clarescet*). The
passage may owe something to Ennius, *Scaenica* 398-
400 (see West 30).
  alid . . . clarescet: reminiscent of 407-9, though it
  does not follow that the application, to Memmius'
  personal researches, is here the same (see on 1114).
  caeca: 'dark', 'blinding'; cf. 408 and contrast 1110.
  quin: = *ita ut non,* as at 1080.
  ultima naturai: 'nature's last secrets'; for the
  construction, see on 86 above. The spondaic fifth
  foot, coupled with the archaic gen., adds solemnity
  to the phrase; cf. 586.
  pervideas: cf. *pernosces* and *perductus* 1114 and *ultima*
  1116; L insists on the completeness of the insight
  afforded by his philosophy.
  res . . . rebus: a vivid metaphor for one fact illuminating another.

VOCABULARY

The following abbreviations are used:

abl.: ablative	*indef.*: indefinite
acc.: accusative	*indic.*: indicative
act.: active	*inf.*: infinitive
adj.: adjective	*interr.*: interrogative
adv.: adverb	*m.*: masculine
advl.: adverbial	*n.*: neuter
c.: common	*nom.*: nominative
comp.: comparative	*pass.*: passive
conj.: conjunction	*pl.*: plural
correl.: correlative	*prep.*: preposition
dat.: dative	*pron.*: pronoun
f.: feminine	*ref.*: reflexive
gen.: genitive	*rel.*: relative
imp.: impersonal	*subj.*: subjunctive
ind.: indeclinable	*sup.*: superlative

The vocabulary is designed to cover only those meanings which are required for book 1 of Lucretius. Discussion of a word's usage is sometimes to be found in the Notes.

A

ā, ăb, prep. + abl.: from;
by; starting from; on the
side of.
ăbĕo, -īre, -i(v)i, -ĭtum:
depart.
ăbhorreo, -ēre, -ui: shrink
from, recoil from.
ăbĭtus, -ūs, m.: departure.
abscondo, -ĕre, -i, -ĭtum:
bury, hide away.
absinthĭum, -i, n.: worm-
wood.
ăbundans, -ntis: over-
flowing.
ac: and.
accēdo, -ĕre, -cessi, -sum:
approach (huc accedit uti:
in addition to this, there
is the fact that).
accendo, -ĕre, -i, -nsum:
ignite, kindle.
accĭpĭo, -ĕre, -cēpi,
-ceptum: receive, hear.
ācer, ācris, -e, (comp.
acrior): keen, fierce.
ăcervus, -i, m.: heap.
Ăchĕrūsĭus, -a, -um: of
Acheron.
ăcĭes, -ei, f.: sight.
Acrăgantinus, -a, -um: of
Acragas.
ăd, prep. + acc.: to; for;
judging by.
addo, -ĕre, -ĭdi, -ĭtum: add.
adeo: see usque adeo, sive
adeo.
adfĭcĭo, -ĕre, -fēci,
-fectum: affect.
ădhĭbĕo, -ēre, -ui, -ĭtum:
apply; bring to bear.
ădhūc: up to now.
adiectus, -ūs, m.: bombardment.
ădĭtus, -ūs, m.: arrival.
adiŭto, -āre, -āvi, -ātum:

assist, aid.
adiŭvo, -āre, -iūvi, -iūtum:
assist, aid.
admīror, -āri, -ātus sum:
marvel at, admire.
admisceo, -ēre, -ui, -mixtum,
+ dat. or in: admix in.
adsisto, -ĕre, -stĭti: stand
by, take up position.
adsto, -āre, -stĭti: stand by.
adsum, -esse, -fui: be present;
+ dat., attend; pay
attention.
adventus, -ūs, m.: arrival,
coming.
ădȳtum, -i, n.: inner shrine.
aemŭlus, -a, -um, + dat.:
emulous of.
Aenĕădae, -um, m. pl.: descendants, race, of Aeneas.
ăēnus, -a, -um: of bronze.
aequor, -ōris, n.: (level)
plain; sea.
aequus, -a, -um: untroubled;
equal (ex aequo and adv.
aeque: equally).
āēr, ăĕris, m.: air.
āĕrĭus, -a, -um: of the air.
aerumna, -ae, f.: tribula-
tion, trouble.
aes, aeris, n.: bronze.
aestifer, -a, -um: heat-
bearing.
aestus, -ūs, m.: heat.
aetās, -ātis, f.: time; age;
lifespan.
aeternus, -a, -um: eternal,
immortal.
aether, -ĕris, m.: (fiery)
ether; heavens; sky.
Aetnaeus, -a, -um: of Etna.
aevum, -i, n.: age; time; the
past; lifespan.
ăgĭto, -āre, -āvi, -ātum:
spend.

agmen, -ĭnĭs, *n.*: ranks.
ăgo, -ĕre, ēgi, actum:
do, perform; work on (age:
come!).
āiunt: they say.
Ălexander, -dri, *m.*:
Alexander, = Paris.
ălĭēnĭgĕnus, -a, -um: alien-
born, unlike.
ălĭēnŭs, -a, -um: not one's
own; unfavourable; of
another.
ălĭqui, -qua, -quod: some.
ălĭquis, -quid: someone,
something.
ălĭus, -a, aliud *and* alid:
other; as well (alius . .
alium *and* alius . . .
alius: one . . . another:
alius et: other than).
almus, -a, -um: nurturing,
life-giving.
ălo, -ĕre, -ui, -tum: nurture,
nourish.
alter, -a, -um: someone,
something, else; the other.
alternĭs: alternately, in
alternation.
altĕrŭter, -tra, -trum: one
or the other; one of the
two.
altus, -a, -um: tall, high
(*adv.* altē: deeply).
ămābĭlis, -e: lovely.
ămārŭs, -a, -um: bitter.
ămicĭtĭa, -ae, *f.*: friendship.
ămitto, -ĕre, āmĭsi, amissum:
lose.
amnis, -is, *m.*: river.
ămo, -āre, -āvi, -ātum:
love.
ămoenus, -a, -um: pleasant,
delectable.
ămor, -ōris, *m.*: love.
ămŏveo, -ēre, āmōvi, āmōtum:
remove, banish.
amplector, -i, -plexus sum:
embrace.
amplius: further.
ăn: or.
Ănaxăgŏras, -ae, *m.*:
Anaxagoras.

anfractus, -ūs, *m.*: bend,
curve.
angustus, -a, -um: narrow.
ănĭma, -ae, *f.*: soul; breath,
air.
ănĭmal, -ālis, *n.*: animal,
living creature.
ănĭmālis, -e: of living
creatures.
ănĭmans, -ntis, *c.*: animal,
living (*or* animate)
creature.
ănĭmus, -i, *m.*: mind;
intellect.
annus, -i, *m.*: year; re-
volution, orbit.
antĕ: (1) *prep.* + *acc.*,
before; (2) *adv.*, in front;
before, earlier.
antĕāctus, -a, -um: prev-
iously elapsed, past.
antĕhāc: before now.
ānŭlus, -i, *m.*: ring.
ăpĕrio, -īre, -ui, -tum:
open (apertus, -a, -um:
visible).
ăpiscor, -i, aptus sum:
grasp.
appāreo, -ēre, -ui, -itum:
be visible.
appello, -āre, -āvi, -ātum:
call, name.
ăqua, -ae, *f.*: water.
āra, -ae, *f.*: altar.
ărātrum, -i, *n.*: plough.
arbor, -ŏris, *f.*: tree.
arbusta, -ōrum, *n. pl.* =
arbores.
arceo, -ēre, -ui, -tum: hold
back, debar from.
ardor, -ōris, *m.*: heat,
fire.
ardŭus, -a, -um: steep,
lofty.
argentum, -i, *n.*: silver.
argŭmentum, -i, *n.*:
argument.
ārĭdus, -a, -um: dry, solid.
armenta, -orum, *n. pl.*:
cattle.
armĭpŏtens, -ntis: mighty
in arms.
arto, -āre, -āvi, -ātum:

compress, contract,
tighten.
artus, -a, -um, (adv. artē):
tight, tight-set.
artus, -ūs, m.: limb.
arva, -ōrum, n. pl.:
(ploughed) fields.
aspectus, -ūs, m.: appearance, sight.
aspergo, -ĕre, -rsi, -rsum:
sprinkle.
assĭdŭus, -a, -um: incessant.
at: but.
atque: and.
attĕnŭo, -āre, -āvi, -ātum:
attenuate, wear away.
attrĭbŭo, -ĕre, -i, -būtum:
allot, add.
aucto, -āre: increase.
auctus, -ūs, m.: increase,
growth.
audeo, -ēre, ausus sum: dare.
audio, -īre, -i(v)i, -ītum:
hear.
aufero, -ferre, abstŭli,
ablātum: take away.
augeo, -ēre, auxi, auctum:
increase, enlarge.
augmen, -ĭnis, n.: increment.
Aulis, -ĭdis, f.: Aulis.
aura, -ae, f.: breath, breeze,
air.
auris, -is, f.: ear.
aurum, -i, n.: gold.
auster, -tri, m.: south wind.
aut: or (aut . . . aut: either
. . . or).
autem: but; in turn.
āvello, -ĕre, āvulsi, -sum:
pluck away.
āverto, -ĕre, -i, -rsum:
turn away, divert.
ăvĭdus, -a, -um: greedy.
ăvis, -is, f.: bird.
āvĭus, -a, -um: out of the
way.

B

bellē: nicely.
bellum, -i, n.: war.

bĕnĕ: well.
bīni, -ae, -a: two (each),
twain.
blandus, -a, -um: alluring,
enticing.
bŏnus, -a, -um: good.

C

căchinno, -āre, -āvi, -ātum:
cackle.
căcūmĕn, -ĭnis, n.: point,
peak.
cădo, -ĕre, cĕcĭdi, cāsum:
fall.
caecus, -a, -um: unseen,
hidden; dark.
caelum, -i, n.: sky,
heavens.
caerŭlus, -a, -um: blue.
călĭdus, -a, -um: warm,
hot.
călor, -ōris, m.: warmth,
heat, fire.
campus, -i, m.: plain.
candens, -ntis: gleaming
white.
candesco, -ĕre, -dui:
glow white.
cănis, -is, c.: hound.
căno, -ĕre, cĕcĭni, cantum:
sing.
căpio, -ĕre, cēpi, captum:
capture, overcome; take,
derive; take in; harm.
căput, -ĭtis, n.: head.
căreo, -ēre, -ui, -ĭtum,
+ abl.: lack, be without.
carmen, -ĭnis, n.: poetry.
cārus, -a, -um: dear.
castus, -a, -um: chaste,
pure.
cāsus, -ūs, m.: fall.
causa, -ae, f.: cause.
causor, -āri, -ātus sum:
prevaricate.
căvo, -āre, -āvi, -ātum:
(make) hollow.
cēdo, -ĕre, cessi, cessum:
yield, give way.
cĕlĕro, -āre, -āvi, -ātum:

hasten.
cēlo, -āre, -āvi, -ātum:
conceal.
censeo, -ēre, -ui, -um: give
as one's opinion, suggest.
cerno, -ĕre, crēvi, crētum:
see, discĕrn.
certāmen, -ĭnis, n.:
struggle.
certē: certainly, to be
sure.
certus, -a, -um, (comp.
certior, sup. certissimus):
definite, fixed; sure;
certain.
cervix, -īcis, f.: neck.
cesso, -āre, -āvi, -ātum:
shirk.
cētĕra, -ōrum, n. pl.: the
rest.
Chărybdis, -is, f.: Charybdis.
cibātus, -ūs, m.: food,
nutriment.
cĭbus, -i, m.: food.
cĭnis, -ĕris, m.: ash.
cio, cīre (for cieo, -ēre),
cīvi, citum: summon.
circum, adv., and prep. +
acc.: round.
circumdo, -dăre, -dĕdi,
-dătum: set round.
circumfundor, -i, -fūsus sum:
embrace.
citus, -a, -um (comp. adv.
citius): swift.
cīvis, -is, m.: countryman.
clam, + abl.: unknown to.
clāmor, -ōris, m.:
shouting.
clandestīnus, -a, -um:
secret.
clāresco, -ĕre, -ārui:
become clear.
clārus, -a, -um: illustrious,
renowned; resounding;
bright; clear (clarius,
comp. adv.: more clearly).
classis, -is, f.: fleet.
claustra, -orum, n. pl.:
locks, bolts.
clausus, -a, -um (claudĕre):
closed.
clŭeo, -ēre: be spoken of,

have a name; exist.
cŏĕo, -īre, -i(v)i, -itum:
come together, coalesce.
coepisse, -tum: to have
begun.
coepto, -āre: begin.
coeptum, -i, n.: work
begun, enterprise.
coetus, -ūs, m.: coming together, assembly.
cognosco, -ĕre, -ōvi, -ĭtum:
get to know.
cōgo, -ĕre, cŏēgi, -actum:
compel; drive together.
cŏhaereo, -ēre, -haesi, -sum:
cohere.
cŏhĭbeo, -ēre, -ui, -itum:
contain.
cŏĭtus, -ūs, m.: coition.
collīdo, -ĕre, -īsi, -īsum:
crŭsh.
collĭgo, -ĕre, -lēgi,
-lectum: collect.
collis, -is, m.: hill.
cŏlor, -ōris, m.: colour.
cŏmĭto, -āre, -āvi, -ātum:
accompany.
commĕmŏro, -āre, -āvi,
-ātum: recount.
commisceo, -ēre, -ui,
-ixtum: mix together.
commūnis, -e: common.
commūtātus, -ūs, m.: change,
alteration.
commūto, -āre, -āvi, -ātum:
change, alter.
cōmo, -ĕre, -psi, -ptum:
bring together, construct.
compleo, -ēre, -ēvi, -ētum:
fill up.
comprĭmo, -ĕre, -pressi,
-sum: repress, restrain,
silence.
comptus, -ūs, m.: tress.
concēdo, -ĕre, -cessi, -sum:
yield; permit, allow; admit,
concede.
concĕlĕbro, -āre, -āvi, -ātum:
fill richly with life.
concido, -ĕre, -i:
collapse.
concilĭātus, -a, -um (con-
ciliāre): linked in union.

concĭlĭātus, -ūs, m.:
assemblage.
concĭlĭum, -i, n.: assembly.
concĭpĭo, -ĕre, -cēpi,
-ceptum: conceive.
concordĭa, -ae, f.: concord,
peace.
concresco, -ĕre, -crēvi,
-crētum: grow together,
coalesce (concretus, -a,
-um: having combined).
concursus, -ūs, m.: collision.
concŭtĭo, -ĕre, -cussi,
-cussum: shake violently.
condenseo, -ēre: condense.
condensus, -a, -um: dense.
condūco, -ĕre, -duxi, -ductum:
lead together, draw to-
gether, contract.
condŭplĭco, -āre, -āvi, -ātum:
multiply.
cōnexus, -ūs, m.: inter-
linking.
confĭcĭo, -ĕre, -fēci,
-fectum: destroy.
confirmo, -āre, -āvi, -ātum:
confirm.
confĭteor, -ēri, -fessus sum:
confess, admit.
conflo, -āre, -āvi, -ātum:
fan into flame.
conflŭo, -ĕre, -xi: stream
together, assemble.
congrĕdior, -i, -gressus sum:
meet, assemble.
cōnĭcĭo, -ĕre, -iēci, -iectum:
throw together; conjecture.
coniunctum, -i, n.: property.
cōnor, -āri, -ātus sum: try.
consĕquor, -i, -sĕcūtus sum:
ensue, be derived.
conservo, -āre, -āvi, -ātum:
conserve.
consĭlĭō: by design.
consĭmĭlis, -e: similar.
consisto, -ĕre, -stĭti: remain fixed, stand firm;
consist; be, exist; hold
together; come to a halt.
conspĭcĭo, -ĕre, -spexi,
-spectum: see, notice.
constĭtŭo, -ĕre, -i, -tūtum:

suppose; appoint; make up.
consto, -āre, -stĭti: consist,
consist of (+ abl. or ex +
abl.); remain constant; be,
exist; stand together; take
up position (constat, imp.:
it is fixed, determined).
consuesco, -ĕre, -suēvi,
-ētum: become accustomed.
consūmo, -ĕre, -psi, -ptum:
consume.
contemno, -ĕre, -tempsi,
-mptum: despise, spurn.
contendo, -ĕre, -i, -tentum:
strain; contend, maintain.
contextus, -ūs, m.: interweaving.
contĭneo, -ēre, -ui, -tentum:
hold prisoner; hold together;
contain.
contingo, -ĕre, -tĭgi, -tactum:
attain to, reach; touch,
smear with.
continŭo: immediately, automatically.
contorqueo, -ēre, -rsi,
-rtum: hurl, send whirling.
contrā: (1) adv., in opposi-
tion; on the contrary; on
the other hand; (2) prep. +
acc., against.
contrārĭus, -a, -um, + dat.:
opposed to.
convĕnit, imp.: it is fitting,
appropriate (convĕnĭens,
-ntis: appropriate, harmon-
ious).
conventus, -ūs, m.: as-
sembling, meeting.
converto, -ĕre, -i, -rsum:
alter.
convĭso, -ĕre: gain insight
into.
cŏŏrior, -iri, -ortus sum:
arise.
cōpĭa, -ae, f.: supply;
opportunity; room.
cor, cordis, n.: heart.
cōram, adv.: face to face.
cŏrōna, -ae, f.: crown,
garland.
corpŏrĕus, -a, -um: corporeal,

material.

corpus, -ŏris, n.: body;
matter; substance; flesh.

corrādo, -ĕre, -āsi, -āsum:
scrape together.

corrĭpio, -ĕre, -ui, -reptum:
snatch hold of.

crĕātrix, -ĭcis, f.:
creatress.

crēber, -bra, -brum (adv.
crebro): repeated.

crēdo, -ĕre, -ĭdi, -ĭtum:
believe (crēdita, -ōrum,
n. pl.: beliefs).

crĕmo, -āre, -āvi, -ātum:
burn up.

crĕo, -āre, -āvi, -ātum:
create.

cresco, -ere, crĕvi, crētum:
grow.

crŭor, -ōris, m.: blood,
gore.

cūdo, -ĕre: beat, hammer.

cultus, -a, -um: cultivated
(culta, -ōrum, n. pl.:
cultivated places).

cum: (1) prep. + acc., with;
(2) conj., when; since, because; although (cum . . .
tum and cum . . . tunc: not
only but also).

cŭmŭlo, -āre, -āvi, -ātum:
accumulate, heap up.

cunctus, -a, -um: all.

cŭpĭdē: eagerly, with
longing.

cŭpĭo, -īre (for -ĕre), -i(v)i,
-ītum: desire, yearn.

cuppēdo, -ĭnis, f. (= cŭpĭdo):
craving.

cur: why.

cūra, -ae, f.: care.

cursus, -ūs, m.: (swift)
course.

D

daedalus, -a, -um: inventive.

Dănăi, -um, m. pl.: Danaans,
Greeks.

dē, prep. + abl.: about, concerning; from, out of.

dĕa, -ae, f.: goddess.

dēbeo, -ēre, -ui, -ĭtum:
ought; need to; must.

dēcēdo, -ĕre, -cessi, -sum:
depart.

dēcerpo, -ĕre, -si, -tum:
pluck off.

dĕcet, imp.: it is fitting.

dēcĭpio, -ĕre, -cēpi,
-ceptum: deceive.

dēclāro, -āre, -āvi, -ātum:
declare.

dēcresco, -ĕre, -crēvi,
-crētum: diminish, shrink.

dēcŭrsus, -ūs, m.: downrush.

dēdĭco, -āre, -āvi, -ātum:
proclaim.

dēdūco, -ĕre, -duxi,
-ductum: escort; lead
aside.

dēfĕro, -ferre, -tŭli,
-lātum: bring down.

dēfĭcio, -ĕre, -fēci,
-fectum: fail.

dēĭndĕ: then, next.

dēlĭgo, -ĕre, -lēgi, -lectum:
choose out.

dēlīrus, -a, -um: mad.

dēmentĭa, -ae, f.: madness,
lunacy.

dēmĭnŭo, -ĕre, -i, -ūtum:
diminish, take away from.

dēmo, -ĕre, -psi, -ptum:
take away.

dēmum: indeed (is demum:
he and only he).

dēnĭque: in short; indeed;
again; finally, at least.

dens, -ntis, m.: tooth.

denseo, -ēre: condense.

densus, -a, -um: dense.

dĕorsum: downwards.

dēpōno, -ĕre, -pŏsui,
-pŏsitum: lay down, rest.

dē(e)rro, -āre, -āvi, -ātum:
stray away.

dēscisco, -ĕre, -scĭvi,
-scĭtum: desert.

dēsertus, -a, -um (dēsĕrĕre):
deserted (dēserta, -ōrum,
n. pl.: waste lands).

dēsum, dē(e)sse, dēfŭi, +
dat.: fail.

dētĕro, -ĕre, -trīvi,
-trītum: wear away.
dēvĕnio, -īre, -vēni,
-ventum: arrive.
dēvinco, -ĕre, -vīci, -victum:
vanquish.
dexter, -tra, -trum: right.
dīco, -ĕre, dixi, dictum: say;
mention; speak of; call
(dicta, -orum, n. pl.:
words).
dīes, -ēī, m.: season; day;
time.
diffĕro, -ferre, distŭli,
dīlatum: scatter; carry
away.
difficĭlis, -e: difficult.
diffīdo, -ĕre, -fisus sum,
+ dat.: distrust.
difflŭo, -ĕre: waste away,
be dissolved.
diffŭgio, -ĕre, -fūgi: flee
apart.
diffundo, -ĕre, -fūdi,
-fūsum: spread out, diffuse.
dĭgĭtŭs, -i, m.: finger.
dīmĭdĭa pars: a half.
dirimo, -ĕre, -ēmi, -emptum:
shatter, sunder.
dīs, dīte (gen. dītis): rich
(= dīves, divītis).
discĭdium, -i, n.: sundering.
discrĕpat, imp.: is is inconsistent.
discŭtio, -ĕre, -cussi, -sum:
dĭspel.
disĭcio, -ĕre, -iēci, -iectum:
scatter, throw apart.
dispando, -ĕre, -pansum:
spread out.
dispello, -ĕre, -pŭli,
-pulsum: drive apart.
dispergo, -ĕre, -rsi, -rsum:
disperse.
dispertio, -īre, -i(v)i,
-ītum: divide up.
dispōno, -ĕre, -pŏsui,
-pos(i)tum: set out.
dispŏsĭtūra, -ae, f.:
arrangement.
dissaepio, -īre, -psi,
-ptum: wall off, fence off.
dissĕro, -ĕre, -ui, -tum:
discourse.
dissĭlĭo, -īre, -ui: leap
apart.
dissĭmĭlis, -e: dissimilar.
dissĭpo, -āre, -āvi, -ātum:
disperse.
dissolvo, -ĕre, -i, -lūtum:
dissolve, break up.
distentus, -a, -um (disten-
dĕre): distended.
distinguo, -ĕre, -nxi,
-nctum: distinguish, mark
off (distinctus, -a, -um:
distinct).
disto, -āre: differ (distat,
imp.: there is a difference).
disturbo, -āre, -āvi, -ātum:
disturb, disorder.
dius, -a, -um: bright;
divine.
dīvello, -ĕre, -i, -vulsum:
tear asunder.
dīverbĕro, -āre, -ātum:
lash apart.
dīversus, -a, -um: in a
different (or an opposite)
direction.
dīvido, -ĕre, -vīsi, -vīsum:
divide, share.
dīvīnitus, adv.: by divine
power.
dīvīnus, -a, -um: divine.
dīvītiae, -ārum, f. pl.:
riches.
dīvus, -a, (gen. -i, -ae):
god, goddess.
do, dăre, dĕdi, dătum: give,
grant, offer, impart;
cause (se dare: pass, issue).
dŏceo, -ēre, -ui, -tum:
teach, show.
dŏmus, -ī and -ūs, f.: home,
house.
dōnec: until.
dōno, -āre, -āvi, -ātum:
endow with.
dōnŭm, -i, n.: gift.
dŭbĭō prŏcŭl: beyond doubt.
dŭbĭto, -āre, -āvi, -ātum:
be in doubt.
ductor, -ōris, m.: leader.
dulcis, -e: sweet.
dum: while; until; provided

that.

dŭŏ, -ae, -ŏ: two.

duplex, -ĭcis: twofold.

dūrătĕus, -a, -um: wooden.

dūro, -āre, -āvi, -ātum:
endure, survive.

dux, dŭcis, m.: leader.

E

ē, ex, prep. + abl.: from,
out of, as a result of.

ĕā, adv.: there.

ēdo, -ĕre, -ĭdi, -ĭtum:
proclaim.

effĕro, -ferre, extŭli,
ēlātum: carry out, bring
out.

effĭcio, -ĕre, -fēci,
-fectum: bring it about,
cause; make up.

effringo, -ĕre, -frēgi,
-fractum: break open.

effŭgio, -ĕre, -fūgi: escape.

effŭgĭum, -i, n.: escape.

effundo, -ĕre, -fūdi,
-fūsum: shed.

ĕgeo, -ēre, -ui, + abl.:
need.

ĕgestas, -ātis, f.: poverty.

ĕgŏ, mĕi: I.

ēgrĕgĭē: outstandingly.

ĕlĕmenta, -ōrum, n. pl.:
rudiments; letters.

ēmĭneo, -ēre, -ui: obtrude.

Empĕdŏclēs, -is, m.:
Empedocles.

ēnascor, -i, ēnātus sum:
be born from.

ĕnim: for.

Ennĭus, -i, m.: Ennius.

ĕo, īre, i(v)i, ĭtum: go,
proceed.

ĕquus, -i, m.: horse.

ergō: therefore.

ērĭpio, -ĕre, -ui, ēreptum:
snatch away.

erro, -āre, -āvi, -ātum: go
astray.

error, -ōris, m.: error,
delusion.

ērumpo, -ĕre, ērūpi,
ēruptum: burst out, hatch;
make burst out.

esco (for ĕro): begin to be.

et: and; also (et . . . et:
both . . . and).

ĕtĕnim: for indeed.

ĕtĭam: even; also; again
(etiam atque etiam: again
and again).

etsi: even though, and yet.

ēventum, -i, n.: accident.

ēvolvo, -ĕre, -i, -lūtum:
unfold.

exăequo, -āre, -āvi, -ātum,
+ acc. and dat.: make equal
to, exalt to.

exănĭmus, -a, -um: inanimate.

excello, -ĕre, -ui, -lsum:
excel.

exĕo, -īre, -i(v)i, -ĭtum:
come out, issue.

exĭgŭus, -a, -um: slight.

eximo, -ĕre, -ēmi, -emptum:
take away.

exĭtĭum, -i, n.: destruction.

exitus, -ūs, m.: egress;
result, outcome.

exordĭum, -i, n.: beginning,
starting point.

exŏrior, -īri, -tus sum:
rise up, come to birth;
arise from.

expando, -ĕre, -i, -nsum:
unfold.

expĕdio, -īre, -i(v)i, -ĭtum:
explain, unfold.

expĕrior, -īri, -tus sum:
test.

expleo, -ēre, -ēvi, -ētum:
fill out.

expōno, -ĕre, -pŏsui,
-pŏsitum: expound, explain,
recount.

exsisto, -ĕre, -stĭti: come
forth, come to be.

exsolvo, -ĕre, -i, -lūtum:
unloosen, release.

exsto, -āre, -stiti: be,
exist; stand; be left.

externus, -a, -um: external.

extrā, adv. and prep. + acc.:

outside, beyond.

extrēmus, -a, -um: extreme, ultimate (extremum, -i, n.: extreme point; extreme edge).

extrinsĕcus, adv.: from outside.

F

făcĭlis, -e: easy.

făcio, -ĕre, fēci, factum: act upon; suppose; do; make, create; bring about (facta, -ōrum, n. pl.: deeds).

făcultas, -ātis, f.: opportunity; capacity.

fallo, -ĕre, fĕfelli, falsum: escape (the notice of).

falsus, -a, -um: false.

fāma, -ae, f.: report, stories.

făteor, -ēri, fassus sum: confess, admit.

fauces, -ium, f. pl.: throat.

faustus, -a, -um: propitious.

făvōnĭus, -i, m.: the west wind.

fēcundus, -a, -um: fertile.

fēlix, -īcis: fortunate.

fĕra, -ae, f.: wild beast.

fĕro, ferre, tŭli, lātum: bear; carry; report.

ferrĕus, -a, -um: of iron.

ferrum, -i, n.: sword; iron.

fĕrus, -a, -um: fierce, wild.

fervens, -ntis (fervēre): fervent.

fessus, -a, -um: wearied.

fētus, -ūs, m.: fruit, produce.

fĭdēlis, -e: loyal, faithful.

fĭdes, -ei, f.: evidence, credence; faith.

figūra, -ae, f.: shape, outline, size; form.

findo, -ĕre, fĭdi, fissum: split.

fingo, -ĕre, -nxi, fictum: fashion, devise, imagine.

fīnio, -īre, -i(v)i, -ītum: limit, bound (fīnītus, -a,

-um: limited, finite).

fīnis, -is, f.: end, limit, bound, boundary; mark, target.

fĭo, fĭeri, factus sum: become; take place, come about; come to be, be created (fit, imp. + dat. or abl.: become of, happen to).

flābra, -ōrum, n. pl.: blasts.

flāmen, -ĭnis, n.: blast.

flamma, -ae, f.: flame.

flammo, -āre, -āvi, -ātum: flame, blaze.

flāvus, -a, -um: yellow.

fleo, -ēre, -ēvi, -ētum: weep.

flōreo, -ēre, -ui: flourish, flower, blossom.

flōs, -ōris, m.: flower.

fluctĭfrăgus, -a, -um: wave-breaking.

fluctus, -ūs, m.: wave.

fluĭto, -āre, -āvi, -ātum: flow.

flūmen, -ĭnis, n.: river; flowing.

fluo, -ĕre, -xi, -xum: flow.

flŭvĭus, -i, m.: river.

foedē: hideously.

foedus, -ĕris, n.: treaty, covenant.

fons, -ntis, m.: spring, fountain.

fŏras, adv.: outside.

forma, -ae, f.: beauty.

formīdō, -ĭnis, f.: dread.

fortĕ (abl. of fors): by chance.

fortūna, -ae, f.: fortune.

fŏveo, -ēre, fōvi, fōtum: warm.

frăgĭlis, -e: breakable, fragile.

fragmen, -ĭnis, n.: fragment.

frăgor, -ōris, m.: breakage.

frango, -ĕre, frēgi, fractum: break.

frĕmĭtus, -ūs, m.: roar.

frētus, -ūs, m.: channel,
strait.
frīgus, -ŏris, n.: cold.
frīo, -āre, -āvi, -ātum:
crumble.
frondesco, -ĕre: grow into
leaf.
frondĭfer, -a, -um: leaf-
bearing, leafy.
frons, -ndis, f.: leaf,
foliage.
frons, -ntis, f.: front.
fructus, -ūs, m.: fruit,
produce.
frūges, -um, f. pl.: produce,
crops.
frūgĭfĕrens, -ntis: fruit-
bearing, fruitful.
frūmenta, -ōrum, n. pl.: corn,
grain.
fūcātus, -a, -um: dyed,
painted, tricked out.
fŭga, -ae, f.: flight.
fŭgio, -ĕre, fūgi, fŭgĭtum:
flee, flee from.
fŭgĭto, -āre, -āvi, -ātum:
flee from.
fulgeo, -ēre, -lsi: shine.
fulgur, -ŭris, n.: lightning.
fulmen, -ĭnis, n.: thunder-
bolt.
fūmus, -i, m.: smoke.
fundāmentum, -i, n.:
foundation.
fundĭtus, adv.: absolutely;
utterly; at (from) the
bottom, fundamentally.
fundo, -āre, -āvi, -ātum:
found, establish.
fundo, -ĕre, fūdi, fūsum:
pour forth.
fungor, -i, functus sum: be
acted upon.

G

gĕnae, -ārum, f. pl.: cheeks.
gĕnĕrālis, -e: of the species.
gĕnĕrātim: according to
species, after one's kind.
gĕnĕtrix, -īcis, f.: giver of
birth, creatress.

gĕnĭtābĭlis, -e)
gĕnĭtālis, -e } : birth-giving.
gens, -ntis, f.: people,
race.
gĕnu, -ūs, n.: knee.
gĕnus, -ĕris, n.: race,
species, kind.
gĕro, -ĕre, gessi, gestum:
carry on, conduct; bear
(res gestae: events).
gigno, -ĕre, gĕnui, -ĭtum:
give birth to.
glăcĭes, -ei, f.: ice.
glaucus, -a, -um: grey-
green.
glēba, -ae, f.: clod of
earth.
glisco, -ĕre: blaze up.
glōmus, -ĕris, n.: ball,
mass.
Grāĭŭgĕnae, -ārum, m. pl.:
sons of the Greeks.
Grāius, -a, -um: Greek.
grandesco, -ĕre: grow great.
grandis, -e: great, large.
grăvĭs, -e (comp. grăvĭor,
-ius: adv. grăvĭter):
heavy; serious.
grăvo, -āre, -āvi, -ātum:
make heavy.
grĕmium, -i, n.: bosom, lap.
gŭberno, -āre, -āvi, -ātum:
steer.
gutta, -ae, f.: drop.

H

hăbeo, -ēre, -ui, -ĭtum:
have, possess; wear; know;
hold on to.
haereo, -ēre, haesi, -sum:
cling, be fixed; cleave
together.
haud: not.
haurio, -īre, hausi, -stum:
drink, drain.
haustus, -ūs, m.: draught.
Hĕlĭcon, -ōnis, m.: Helicon.
Hērāclītus, -i, m.:
Heraclitus.
herba, -ae, f.: grass.
hic, haec, hoc: this (person

_or thing).
hĭc, *adv.*: here, at this
 point.
hinc: hence, from this, as
 a result of this.
Hŏmērus, -i, *m.*: Homer.
hŏmo, -ĭnis, *m.*: man.
hŏmŏeŏmĕrĭa, -ae, *f.*:
 homoeomeria.
hōra, -ae, *f.*: hour.
horrĭbĭlis, -e: horrible,
 dreadful.
hostĭa, -ae, *f.*: sacrificial
 victim.
hūc: *see* accedit.
hūmānus, -a, -um: human.
Hȳmĕnaeus, -i, *m.*: wedding-
 song.

I

iăceo, -ēre, -ui: lie prostrate, lie.
iăcio, -ĕre, iēci, iactum:
 throw.
iam: now; by now; already; as
 it is; in that case, then
 (si iam: even if).
iānua, -ae, *f.*: gate.
ibĭ: there.
īcio, -ĕre, īci, ictum:
 strike.
ictus, -ūs, *m.*: blow, impact.
īdem, ĕădem, ĭdem: the same
 (person or thing); in turn;
 also.
ideo: for this reason.
ĭgĭtur: therefore; then.
ignĕus, -a, -um: fiery.
ignis, -is, *m.*: fire.
ignōro, -āre, -āvi, -ātum:
 not know.
ille, -a, -ud: that (person
 or thing).
imbēcillus, -a, -um: weak.
imber, -bris, *m.*: rain.
immensus, -a, -um: measure-
 less, infinite.
immisceo, -ēre, -ui, -xtum:
 mix in.
immŏdĕrātus, -a, -um: unbound-
 ed, to infinity.

immortālis, -e: immortal.
immūtābĭlis, -e: immutable.
impello, -ĕre, -pŭli, -lsum:
 impel, impinge upon.
impendeo, -ēre: overhang.
impĕtus, -ūs, *m.*: attack,
 blow.
impĭus, -a, -um: impious.
imprōvĭdus, -a, -um: taken
 unawares.
īmus, -a, -um: bottom-most,
 at the bottom (īmum, -i,
 n.: the bottom).
in, *prep.* (1) + *acc.*: into,
 towards; (2) + *abl.*: in,
 on, at.
inānis, -e: empty; vain,
 frivolous (inane, -is, *n.*:
 void, empty space).
incendĭum, -i, *n.*: fire.
incertus, -a, -um: indeter-
 minate, irregular, un-
 certain.
incestē: unchastely,
 impurely.
incĭpio, -ĕre, -cēpi,
 -ceptum: begin.
incĭtus, -a, -um: roused
 to violence.
inclūsus, -a, -um (includĕre):
 enclosed.
inclŭtus, -a, -um: illustrious.
incŏlŭmis, -e: unharmed,
 intact.
incultus, -a, -um: uncultivated.
incurro, -ĕre, -i, -cursum
 + *dat.*: attack, assail.
incŭtio, -ĕre, -cussi, -sum:
 strike into, instil into.
indĕ: next; thence.
indico, -āre, -āvi, -ātum:
 indicate.
indūco, -ĕre, -duxi, -ductum:
 lead; induce, urge.
indŭgrĕdior, -i, -gressus
 sum (= ingredi): enter,
 set foot on.
indulgeo, -ēre, -lsi, -ltum,
 + *dat.*: indulge.
indŭpĕdio, -īre, -i(v)i,
 -itum (= impedire):

entangle.
ĭnĕo, -īre, -i(v)i, -ĭtum:
enter, enter upon, enter
into.
infans, -ntis, c.: infant.
infĕrior, -ius: inferior,
lesser; below.
infernus, -a, -um: from
below.
infīnītus, -a, -um:
infinite.
infirmus, -a, -um: unsteady.
inflammo, -āre, -āvi, -ātum:
inflame, set fire to.
infŭla, -ae, f.: fillet,
hairband.
infundo, -ĕre, -fūdi, -fūsum:
pour in.
ingens, -ntis: huge.
ingĕnŭus, -a, -um: native,
inborn.
inhio, -āre, -āvi, -ātum:
gape; gaze with longing.
inĭmīcus, -a, -um: hostile.
inīquus, -a, -um: troubled;
unfavourable.
inĭtus, -ūs, m.: approach;
starting point.
inlustro, -āre, -āvi, -ātum:
illumine.
innŭmĕrābilis, -e:
innumerable.
inquam: say.
insĕro, -ĕre, -sēvi, -sĭtum:
implant.
insignis, -e: conspicuous,
outstanding.
insĭnŭo, -āre, -āvi, -ātum:
act., pass., and ref.: find
one's way into, wriggle into.
insisto, -ĕre, -stĭti: set
foot on.
instinguo, -ĕre, -nxi, -nctum:
incite.
insto, -āre, -stĭti: + dat.,
stand over, press upon; be
on hand, go on.
insŭla, -ae, f.: island.
insum, -esse, -fŭi: be
present in (or on); reside.
intactĭlis, -e }
intactus, -a, -um} : intangible.
intactus, -ūs, m.: intang-

ibility.
intĕger, -gra, -grum: un-
touched, virgin.
intĕgo, -ĕre, -texi, -tectum:
cover.
integro, -āre, -āvi, -ātum:
renew, replenish.
intellĕgo, -ĕre, -lexi,
-lectum: understand.
inter, prep. + acc.: bet-
ween, among, amidst.
interdum: sometimes, at
times.
intĕrĕā: meanwhile.
intĕrĕo, -īre, -i(v)i,
-ĭtum: perish, be destroyed.
intĕrimo, -ĕre, -ēmi,
-emptum: destroy.
intus, adv.: within, inside.
invĕnio, -īre, -vēni,
-vēntum: find.
inversus, -a, -um: inverted,
twisted.
invictus, -a, -um: unconquer-
ed, invincible.
invidus, -a, -um: grudging.
Īŏnĭus, -a, -um: Ionian.
Īphĭanassa, -ae, f.:
Iphianassa (for Iphigeneia).
ipse, -a, -um: himself, herself, itself.
ira, -ae, f.: anger.
irrĕvŏcābilis, -e: beyond
recall.
irrīto, -āre, -āvi, -ātum:
provoke, excite.
is, ĕa, id: he, she, it;
that (person or thing).
ĭtă: in this way, like this,
so; in such a way; in the
same way.
Ītălĭa, -ae, f.: Italy.
Ītălus, -a, -um: Italian.
ĭtem: in turn; likewise.
ĭter, itineris, n.: path.
ĭtĕrum, adv.: again, once
more.
iungo, -ĕre, -nxi, -nctum:
join, yoke.
iŭvĕnis, -is, m.: young man.
iŭvo, -āre, iūvi, iūtum:
help, assist, bless (iuvat,
imp.: it delights).

L

lăbasco, -ĕre: begin to totter, be undermined.

lăbĕfacto, -āre, -āvi, -ātum: make molten, dissolve, undermine.

lăbo, -āre, -āvi, -ātum: totter, be undermined.

lābor, -i, lapsus sum: glide; stumble, fall.

lăbor, -ōris, m.: toil.

lăbōro, -āre, -āvi, -ātum: suffer.

labra, -ōrum, n. pl.: lips.

lac, -ctis, n.: milk.

lacrima, -ae, f.: tear.

lactĕus, -a, -um: of milk.

lăcūna, -ae, f.: chasm; pool.

laetifĭcus, -a, -um: gladdening.

laetus, -a, -um: fertile, fruitful; glad.

lāna, -ae, f.: wool.

languidus, -a, -um (comp. languidior): weak.

lānigĕrae, -ārum, f. pl.: fleecy creatures.

lăpis, -ĭdis, m.: stone.

largior, -īri, -ītus sum: bestow.

largus, -a, -um: copious.

lascīvus, -a, -um: sportive.

lătebra, -ae, f.: lurking-place, lair.

lăteo, -ēre, -ui: lie hidden.

lătex, -ĭcis, m.: liquid; water.

Lătīnus, -a, -um: Latin.

lătĭto, -āre, -āvi, -ātum: lurk, lie hidden, lie low.

lātus, -a, -um: broad.

laurus, -i, f.: laurel.

laus, -dis, f.: praise, fame.

lĕpĭdus, -a, -um: charming, seductive.

lĕpor, -ōris, m.: charm, allure, delight.

lētum, -i, n.: death.

lĕvis, -e (comp. levior): light.

līber, -a, -um: free.

lībertas, -ātis, f.: freedom.

lĭcet, imp.: it is possible.

lignum, -i, n.: timber, wood.

lingua, -ae, f.: language, tongue.

lĭnquo, -ĕre, līqui: leave.

liquesco, -ĕre: melt, liquefy.

lĭquĭdus, -a, -um: liquid.

līquor, -ōris, m.: liquidity; liquid; water.

lītus, -ōris, n.: shore.

lŏco, -āre, -āvi, -ātum: place, station.

lŏcus, -i, m. (pl. lŏca, n.): place, region; space; room.

longus, -a, -um: long (adv. longē, comp. longius: far, further).

lŏquēla, -ae, f.: utterance.

lūcĭdus, -a, -um: shining; lucid, full of light.

lūdĭfĭco, -āre, -āvi, -ātum: mock.

lūdo, -ĕre, lūsi, -sum: frolic.

lūmen, -ĭnis, n.: light.

lūna, -ae, f.: moon.

lympha, -ae, f.: water.

M

măcĭes, -ei, f.: decay, emaciation.

mactātus, -ūs, m.: sacrificial blow.

măcŭla, -ae, f.: marking.

maestus, -a, -um: sad.

măgis: more; rather.

magnus, -a, -um (comp. māior): great, large; long.

mālae, -ārum, f. pl.: cheeks.

mālo, malle, mālui: prefer.

mălum, -i, n.: evil.

mānābĭlis, -e: permeating.

măneo, -ēre, -si, -sum: remain.

mănifestus, -a, -um: manifest, apparent, visible.

māno, -āre, -āvi, -ātum: flow.

mănus, -ūs, f.: hand.
măre, -is, n.: sea.
māter, -tris, f.: mother.
mātĕria, -ae and mātĕrĭes,
  -ei, f.: matter.
Māvors, -rtis, m.: Mars.
mĕātus, -ūs, m.: course,
  journey.
mĕdentes, -ntium (medēri), m.
  pl.: healers (= mĕdĭci).
mĕdĭum, -i, n.: the middle,
  centre.
mel, mellis, n.: honey.
mĕlior, -ius: better.
membra, -ōrum, n. pl.: limbs.
Memmĭădes, -ae, m.: son,
  scion of the Memmii.
Memmĭus, -i, m.: Memmius.
mĕmŏro, -āre, -āvi, -ātum:
  speak of.
mens, -ntis, f.: mind,
  heart.
mĕo, -āre, -āvi, -ātum:
  travel.
mĕritō: justifiably, with
  reason.
mĕrus, -a, -um: undiluted.
mĕtuo, -ĕre, -i, -ūtum: fear.
mĕtus, -ūs, m.: fear.
mĕus, -a, -um: my.
mīca, -ae, f.: grain.
mīlĭtia, -ae, f.: warfare.
minae, -ārum, f. pl.:
  threats.
mĭnax, -ācis: menacing.
minĭmus, -a, -um: minimal,
  least, smallest (minimum,
  -i, n.: a minimum).
mĭnister, -tri, m.: attendant.
minĭtor, -āri, -ātus sum:
  threaten, menace.
mĭnor, -āri, -ātus sum:
  threaten.
mĭnor, -us: smaller, less
  great (adv. minus: less).
mĭnŭo, -ĕre, -i, -nūtum:
  diminish (minūtus, -a, -um:
  minute: adv. minūtē:
  minutely).
mīror, -āri, -ātus sum:
  wonder at.
mīrus, -a, -um: wondrous.
misceo, -ēre, -ui, mixtum:
mix.
mĭser, -a, -um: wretched.
mitto, -ĕre, mīsi, missum:
  despatch, emit, send.
mŏdĕrātim: slowly, stage by
  stage.
mŏdus, -i, m.; way; limit.
moenĭa, -ĭum, n. pl.: walls,
  ramparts.
moenus, -ĕris, n. (= mūnus):
  task, work.
mōles, -is, f.: pile.
mollis, -e: gentle; flowing;
  soft.
mons, -ntis, m.: mountain.
montĭvăgus, -a, -um:
  mountain-roaming.
morbus, -i, m.: disease.
mŏror, -āri, -ātus sum:
  delay, hold back.
mors, -rtis, f.: death.
mortālis, -e: mortal, destructible (mortāles, -ium,
  m. pl.: mortals).
mōs, mōris, m.: custom,
  habit; pl., character.
mōtus, -ūs, m.: motion.
mŏveo, -ēre, mōvi, mōtum:
  move.
multĭmŏdīs: in many ways.
multus, -a, -um: much; pl.,
  many.
mundus, -i, m.: world;
  heavens.
mūnio, -īre, -i(v)i, -ītum:
  fortify.
murmur, -ŭris, n.: murmur,
  rumble.
mūsae, -ārum, f. pl.: the
  Muses.
mūsaeus, -a, -um: of the
  Muses.
musso, -āre, -āvi, -ātum:
  be struck dumb.
mūto, -āre, -āvi, -ātum:
  change; exchange.
mūtus, -a, -um: dumb.

N

nam: for.
namque: for indeed.

nāres, -ium, f. pl.: nostrils.
nascor, -i, nātus sum: be
born.
nātīvus, -a, -um: subject to
birth.
nātūra, -ae, f.: nature.
nāviger, -a, -um: ship-
bearing.
nāvis, -is, f.: ship.
nāviter: completely.
nē, + subj.: in order that
. . . not; that, in case;
that . . . not; to prevent.
-ně: interrogative suffix.
nec, něque: and not; repeated,
neither . . . nor.
něcesse, ind. adj.: necessary
(necesse est: it must be
that).
necně: or not.
nēdum: much less.
něgo, -āre, -āvi, -ātum:
deny.
nempě: assuredly.
nēquāquam: by no means, in
no way.
něqueo, -īre, -i(v)i: be
unable.
nervus, -i, m.: sinew.
něvě: and in case.
nexus, -ūs, m.: fastening,
tie, bond.
nī = nisi.
nīl, ind., and nīlum, -i, n.:
nothing.
nimbus, -i, m.: storm-cloud.
nimīrum, adv.: indubitably.
nimis, adv.: too.
nisi: if . . . not, unless;
except.
niteo, -ēre, -ui: shine,
gleam.
nitidus, -a, -um: gleaming,
resplendent.
nītor, -i, -xus sum: strive,
push.
nocturnus, -a, -um: nocturnal,
by night.
nōdus, -i, m.: knot.
nōmen, -inis, n.: name.
nōmino, -āre, -āvi, -ātum:
call, name.
nōn: not.

nondum: not yet.
nos, nostri: we.
nosco, -ěre, nōvi, nōtum:
realise, get to know.
noster, -tra, -trum: our.
něto, -āre, -āvi, -ātum:
mark off; denote.
něvellus, -a, -um: young
little.
něvitas, -ātis, f.: novelty.
něvo, -āre, -āvi, -ātum:
renew.
něvus, -a, -um: new.
nox, noctis, f.: night.
nūbila, -ōrum, n. pl.: clouds.
nūbo, -ěre, nupsi, nuptum:
marry.
nullus, -a, -um: no.
nūmen, -inis, n.: divine will,
divine power.
numěrus, -ī, m.: number;
tally.
numquam: never.
nunc: as it is; now.
nusquam: nowhere; in no case.

o

ob, prep. + acc.: on account
of.
oběo, -īre, -i(v)i, -itum:
meet, encounter.
obscūrus, -a, -um: obscure,
dark.
obsisto, -ěre, -stiti: stand
one's ground; + dat., resist.
obsto, -āre, -stiti: + dat.,
stand in the way of;
obstruct.
obtěro, -ěre, -trīvi, -trītum:
crush, trample on.
obvius, -a, -um: in one's
path.
occido, -ěre, -i, -cāsum:
pass away, perish.
occultus, -a, -um: hidden (adv.
occultē: secretly).
occupo, -āre, -āvi, -ātum:
seize.
oculus, -i, m.: eye.
odor, -ōris, m.: smell,
odour.

officĭo, -ĕre, -fēci,
-fectum: get in the way,
impede.
officĭum, -i, n.: duty,
function, characteristic.
ollę = ille.
omnĭmŏdīs: in every way.
omnīnō: at all, in the first
place, indeed.
omnis, -e: every; the whole
of; all (omne, -is, n.: the
universe).
ŏpella, -ae, f.: slight
effort.
ŏpĕra, -ae, f.: effort.
ŏpĭmus, -a, -um: rich.
ŏpīnor, -ārī, -ātus sum:
think, opine.
ŏportet, imp.: it behoves.
oppressus, -ūs, m.: grinding,
attrition.
opprimo, -ĕre, -pressi, -sum:
oppress.
ŏpus, -ĕris, n.: work (magno
opere: greatly: opus est +
abl. or nom.: there is need
of).
ōra, -ae, f.: border, edge;
region.
Orcus, -i, m.: Hell.
ordō, -ĭnis, m.: order,
arrangement.
ŏrior, -īri, ortus sum:
arise, come to be.
orno, -āre, -āvi, -ātum:
adorn.
ortus, -ūs, m.: birth.
ōs, ōris, n.: mouth; face.
ŏs, ossis, n.: bone.
ostendo, -ĕre, -i, -nsum:
show.

P

pābŭla, -ōrum, n. pl.:
pastures; food.
pactum, -i (pangĕre), n.:
agreement; abl., way.
pălam: openly.
palleo, -ēre, -ui: be pale.
pando, -ĕre, -i, -nsum: unfold, explain.

pango, -ĕre, pĕpĭgi, pactum:
construct, compose; agree,
determine.
pār, păris: equal; natural,
reasonable (părĭter, adv.:
equally).
părens, -ntis, c.: parent.
părĭlis, -e: equal.
părio, -ĕre, pĕpĕri, partum:
give birth to, create.
păro, -āre, -āvi, -ātum:
produce; prepare, set.
pars, -rtis, f.: part;
direction; degree.
partim . . . partim: partly
. . . partly.
partus, -ūs, m.: birth.
parvus, -a, -um: small (sup.
parvissimus = minimus).
pasco, -ĕre, pāvi, pastum:
feed, feast (pascor, -i,
-stus sum: feed (oneself),
graze).
passim: everywhere, on all
sides.
pătĕfăcio, -ĕre, -fēci,
-factum (pass. pătĕfīo,
-fĭĕri): lay open, reveal.
păteo, -ēre, -ui: stretch
out, extend.
păter, -tris, m.: father.
pătior, -i, passus sum:
allow.
patria, -ae, f.: native
land, country.
patrĭus, -a, -um: of a
father; native.
paucus, -a, -um: few.
paulātim: gradually.
paulō, paulum, advl.: a
little.
paupertas, -ātis, f.: poverty.
pausa, -ae, f.: stop, halting
place.
pauxillus, -a, -um: very
tiny.
pax, pācis, f.: peace.
pectus, -ŏris, n.: breast.
pĕcus, -ŭdis, f.: tame
animal; beast.
pendeo, -ēre, pĕpendi:
hang; depend (on).
pendo, -ĕre, pĕpendi, pensum:

weigh.

pĕnetrālis, -e: penetrative,
piercing.

pĕnetro, -āre, -āvi, -ātum:
penetrate.

pĕnitus, adv.: thoroughly,
utterly, deeply.

pĕpĭgi: see pango.

pĕr: prep. + acc.: through.

pĕragro, -āre, -āvi, -ātum:
traverse.

percello, -ĕre, -cŭli, -lsum:
strike, smite.

percio, -īre, -i(v)i, -ĭtum:
stimulate, excite.

percĭpio, -ĕre, -cēpi,
-ceptum: fully grasp,
understand.

percurro, -ĕre, -i, -cursum:
tear through, rush through.

percŭtio, -ĕre, -cussi,
-cussum: strike, smite.

perdēlĭrus, -a, -um:
thoroughly mad.

perdūco, -ĕre, -duxi, -ductum:
lead on.

pĕrĕdo, -ĕre, -ēdi, -ēsum:
eat through.

pĕrennis, -e: perennial,
undying.

pĕrĕo, -īre, -i(v)i, -ĭtum:
perish.

perfĭcio, -ĕre, -fēci,
-fectum: complete.

perfŭro, -ĕre: rage through.

Pergăma, -ōrum, n. pl.:
Pergamum, the citadel of
Troy.

pergo, -ĕre, perrexi,
perrectum: + inf., proceed
to, make to, aim to.

pĕrīc(ŭ)lum, -i, n.: danger.

pĕrĭmo, -ĕre, -ēmi, -emptum:
destroy.

permagnus, -a, -um: very
great.

permăneo, -ēre, -nsi, -nsum:
abide, endure.

permāno, -āre, -āvi, -ātum:
permeate, seep through.

permisceo, -ēre, -ui, -xtum:
mix thoroughly, intermingle.

permĭtĭālis, -e: destructive.

permūto, -āre, -āvi, -ātum:
alter, rearrange.

pernosco, -ĕre, -nōvi, -nōtum:
become fully acquainted
with.

perpĕtŭus, -a, -um: ever-
lasting (perpetuō, adv.:
perpetually).

perpōto, -āre, -āvi, -ātum:
drink up, drain.

persaepĕ: very often.

persīdo, -ĕre, -sēdi, -sessum:
seep through and settle.

perspĭcio, -ĕre, -spexi,
-spectum: perceive, see
revealed.

persulto, -āre, -āvi, -ātum:
leap through.

pertexo, -ĕre, -ui, -textum:
weave to completion.

pervādo, -ĕre, -vāsi, -um:
arrive, attain.

pervᵉrsus, -a, -um: perverse.

pervideo, -ēre, -vīdi, -vīsum:
examine; see as far as.

pervinco, -ĕre, -vīci,
-victum: win through, be
triumphant.

pēs, pĕdis, m.: foot.

pĕto, -ĕre, -i(v)i, -ītum:
seek.

Phoebus, -i, m.: Phoebus
(Apollo).

Phrȳgĭus, -a, -um: Phrygian,
Trojan.

Pĭerĭdes, -um, f. pl.: daughters of Pierus (the Muses).

Pĭerius, -a, -um: Pierian.

pigro, -āre, -āvi, -ātum:
shirk.

pingue, -is, n.: fat,
plumpness.

piscis, -is, m.: fish.

plăcĭdus, -a, -um: calm,
serene, peaceful.

plāco, -āre, -āvi, -ātum:
placate, calm.

plāga, -ae, f.: blow.

plānus, -a, -um: level (de
plāno: on one's own authority).

plēnus, -a, -um: full, fully
occupied.

plērumque: for the most part.
plumbum, -i, *n.*: lead.
plūrimus, -a, -um: most.
plūs, -ūris: more.
pōculum, -i, *n.*: cup, goblet.
poena, -ae, *f.*: punishment.
pollens, -ntis: powerful.
pondus, -ĕris, *n.*: weight.
pōno, -ĕre, pŏsŭi, pos(ĭ)tum:
  place, establish.
pons, -ntis, *m.*: bridge.
pontus, -i, *m.*: sea, ocean,
  the deep.
porrō: further, in turn.
porta, -ae, *f.*: door.
porto, -āre, -āvi, -ātum:
  carry (off).
pŏsitūra, -ae, *f.*: position.
possīdeo, -ēre, -sēdi,
  -sessum: hold, have possession of.
possīdo, -ĕre, -sēdi,
  -sessum: occupy, take
  possession of.
possum, posse *and* pŏtesse,
  pŏtŭi: be able.
post, *adv.*: behind; after-
  wards.
posthāc: hereafter.
postremō: finally.
pŏtestas, -ātis, *f.*: power.
pŏtĭs, *ind. adj.*: able.
pŏtius: rather.
praebeo, -ēre, -ui, -ĭtum:
  provide.
praecipito, -āre, -āvi,
  -ātum: precipitate, cast
  headlong down.
praeclārus, -a, -um (*comp.*
  praeclārior): outstanding.
praeclūdo, -ĕre, -ūsi, -ūsum:
  shut off.
praecurro, -ĕre, -i, -cursum:
  anticipate.
praeditus, -a, -um, + *abl.*:
  endowed with.
praefīnio, -īre, -i(v)i,
  -ītum: fix a limit in
  advance.
praefringo, -ĕre, -frēgi,
  -fractum: break off at the
  end.
praepando, -ĕre: spread

before.
praesertim: especially.
praesto, -āre, -stĭti + *dat.*:
  excel, surpass, exceed.
praetĕr, *prep.* + *acc.*: besides,
  in addition to, apart from.
praetĕrĕā: besides, in addition; moreover.
praetĕritus, -a, -um: past.
praetermĕo, -āre, -āvi, -ātum:
  pass by.
prĕmo, -ĕre, pressi, -sum:
  press.
prīmordia, -ōrum, *n. pl.*:
  first-beginnings.
prīmum, *adv.*: first.
prīmus, -a, -um: first;
  primary (cum primis:
  especially; foremost).
princeps, -ĭpis, *adj.*: first.
prīncipĭum, -i, *n.*: beginning,
  starting point (principio
  = primum: principiorum *and*
  principiis = primordiorum
  and primordiis).
prĭor, -ius: earlier.
prĭus, *adv.*: before, first
  (prius quam, *conj.*: before).
privo, -āre, -āvi, -atum,
  + *abl.*: deprive of.
prō, *prep.* + *abl.*: in proportion to (sua pro parte:
  for its part).
prōbeo = prŏhĭbeo.
prōbo, -āre, -āvi, -ātum:
  prove; recommend.
prōcēdo, -ĕre, -cessi, -sum:
  proceed, advance.
prōcresco, -ĕre: grow forth.
prōcumbo, -ĕre, -cŭbui, -ĭtum:
  incline (channel) one's
  force.
prōcurro, -ĕre, -i, -cursum:
  run forward.
proelium -i, *n.*: battle.
prŏfectō: assuredly.
prōfĕro, -ferre, -tŭli,
  -lātum: bear forth.
prŏficiscor, -i, -fectus sum:
  set out, start.
prŏfor, -āri, -ātus sum:
  proclaim, prophesy.
prŏfundo, -ĕre, -fūdi, -fūsum:

let flow down.
prŏfundus, -a, -um: deep
   (prŏfundum, -i, n.: the
   deep).
prŏhibeo, -ēre, -ui, -ĭtum:
   prevent, hinder.
prŏīnde: therefore.
prōlāto, -āre, -āvi, -ātum:
   put off.
prōles, -is, f.: offspring,
   progeny.
prōmitto, -ĕre, -mīsi,
   -missum: promise.
promptus, -ūs, m.: visibility
   (in promptu: conspicuous).
prŏpāgo, -āre, -āvi, -ātum:
   propagate, generate.
prŏpāgo, -inis, f.: scion,
   offspring.
propriē: in one's own right.
proptĕr, prep. + acc.: near;
   on account of.
proptĕrĕā: for this reason.
prorsum: at all, absolutely,
   utterly.
prōsum, -desse, -fŭi: + dat.,
   avail, benefit (prōdest,
   imp.: it is of avail).
prōtrăho, -ĕre, -traxi,
   -tractum: drag forth.
pŭeri, -ōrum, m. pl.:
   children.
pugno, -āre, -āvi, -ātum:
   fight, conflict.
punctum, -i, n.: moment.
pūrus, -a, -um: pure,
   unmixed.
pŭto, -āre, -āvi, -ātum:
   think.
Pȳthĭa, -ae, f.: the Pythian
   priestess of Apollo, at
   the Delphic oracle.

Q

quā, adv.: where, by which.
quācumque, adv.: wherever.
quaero, -ĕre, quaesīvi,
   -sītum: seek, search,
   enquire.
quālis, -e: what sort of
   (talis . . . qualis:

such . . . as).
quam: (1) + adj., how; (2)
   than (tam . . . quam: as
   much . . . as; as . . .as).
quamdĕ: than.
quamquam: although.
quamvis: although, however.
quando: since.
quandŏquĭdem: since indeed.
quantus, -a, -um, correl.
   with tantus(dem): as.
quāpropter: therefore.
quārē: therefore; interr.,
   why.
quăsī: as it were, so to
   speak.
quattŭŏr, ind.: four.
-quĕ: and.
queo, -īre, -i(v)i, -ĭtum:
   be able.
quī, quae, quod: (1) rel.,
   who, which (qui, old abl.
   s.: whereby: quo magis:
   the more); (2) interr.,
   which, what (qui, old abl.
   s.: how); (3) indef. (f.
   s. quă), any.
quiă: because.
quīcumque, quaecumque,
   quodcumque: whoever, whatever, whichever.
quīdam, quaedam, quiddam
   (pron.) and quoddam (adj.):
   a certain (person or thing);
   a sort of.
quĭdem: indeed, for its part.
quĭes, -ētis, f.: resting-
   place; rest.
quĭesco, -ĕre, -ēvi, -ētum:
   fall silent, become still.
quīlĭbĕt, quaelibet, quodlibet,
   adj.: any you like, any
   whatsoever.
quīn: (1) + indic., but rather;
   why not? (quin etiam: nay
   further, what is more);
   (2) + subj., so as not to,
   without.
quīnam, quaenam, quodnam,
   interr.: which, what.
quippĕ: for (quippe ubi:
   seeing that).
quis, quid: (1) interr., who,

what; (2) *indef*., someone,
something; anyone, any-
thing.

quisquam, quicquam: anyone,
anything; *adj*., = ullus,
any.

quisque, quaeque, quidque
(*pron*.) and quodque (*adj*.):
each (person or thing);
each kind (type, species)
of (person or thing).

quisquis, quidquid: whoever,
whatever.

quivis, quaevis, quidvis
(*pron*.) and quodvis (*adj*.):
any (one, thing) you like,
any (one, thing) whatsoever.

quō, *adv*.: (1) *rel*., whither,
into which; (2) *interr*.,
whither?, in what direction?,
to what?.

quod: because.

quōminus: so as to prevent.

quoniam: since, because.

quōquam, *adv*.: in any
direction.

quŏque: also.

R

radius, -i, *m*.: ray.

rādix, -icis, *f*.: root.

rāmus, -i, *m*.: branch.

răpax, -ācis: rapacious.

răpidus, -a, -um: rushing,
tearing.

răpio, -ĕre, -ui, -tum:
carry off, rape.

raptim: rapidly.

rapto, -āre, -āvi, -ātum:
ravage, carry off.

rārēfio, -fieri, -factus
sum: rarefy.

rārus, -a, -um: rarefied,
porous.

ratio, -ōnis, *f*.: philosophy,
lore, reasoning, reason;
principle; way;
explanation (rationem
habere, reddere: give an
account).

reccido, -ĕre, -i, -cāsum

(*for* rĕcidĕre): fall back,
relapse; fall off.

rĕcēdo, -ĕre, -cessi, -sum:
shrink back.

rĕcipio, -ĕre, -cēpi, -ceptum:
accept.

reclāmo, -āre, -āvi, -ātum:
cry out against.

recrĕo, -āre, -āvi, -ātum:
refresh.

rectius, *comp. adv*.: more
correctly.

rĕcŭbo, -āre, -ui, -itum:
recline.

reddo, -ĕre, -idi, -itum:
give, allot, assign;
account for; render.

reddūco, -ĕre, -duxi, -ductum
(*for* rĕdūcere): bring back.

rĕdĕo, -ire, -i(v)i, -itum:
return.

rĕdigo, -ĕre, -ēgi, -actum:
bring back, reduce.

rĕfĕro, -ferre, -ttŭli,
-lātum: bring back (as
the prize of victory);
refer; reproduce.

rēfert, *imp*.: it makes a
difference (*with* magni,
permagni, a great, very
great, difference).

rĕficio, -ĕre, -fēci, -fectum:
re-create, replenish.

refrēno, -āre, -āvi, -ātum:
rein back.

rĕgio, -ōnis, *f*.: region;
direction.

rĕgo, -ĕre, rexi, rectum:
rule.

rĕicio, -ĕre, -iēci, -iectum:
throw back.

rēlicŭus, -a, -um:
remaining.

rēligio, -onis, *f*.: religion;
religious scruple, religious
fear.

rĕlinquo, -ĕre, -liqui,
-lictum: leave.

rēliquiae, -ārum, *f. pl*.:
remains, remnants.

rĕmăneo, -ēre, -si, -sum:
remain.

rĕnascor, -i, -natus sum:

be reborn.

rĕor, rēri, rătus sum: think.

rĕparco, -ĕre: refrain from.

rĕpăro, -āre, -āvi, -ātum:
re-create, replace, make
good.

rĕpello, -ĕre, -ppŭli,
-pulsum: repel, remove.

rĕpente: suddenly.

rĕpĕrio, -īre, reppĕri,
rĕpertum: find (rĕperta,
-ōrum, n. pl.: discoveries).

rĕpĕto, -ĕre, -i(v)i, -ītum:
seek again, resume; with a
+ abl., go back to (in an
enquiry).

repleo, -ēre, -ēvi, -ētum:
fill up.

rĕpōno, -ĕre, -pŏsui,
pos(ĭ)tum: place back, rest.

rĕpugno, -āre, -āvi, -ātum:
fight.

rĕquĭes, -ētis, f.: respite.

rĕquiesco, -ĕre, -ēvi, -ētum:
come to rest.

rĕquīro, -ĕre, -īsi(v)i,
-isītum: search after;
ask, enquire.

rēs, rēi, f.: thing; situation,
affair, matter; subject-
matter, topic; task; event;
fact; meaning; theory.

rĕsĕro, -āre, -āvi, -ātum:
unlock.

rĕservo, -āre, -āvi, -ātum:
preserve.

rĕsilio, -īre, -ui: leap
back.

rĕsolvo, -ĕre, -i, -lūtum:
resolve, break up; loosen,
unlock.

responsa, -ōrum, n. pl.:
responses.

resto, -āre, -stĭti: resist;
remain.

rĕsŭpīnus, -a, -um: lying
back.

rĕtexo, -ĕre, -ui, -tum:
unweave, unravel.

rĕtĭneo, -ēre, -ui, -tentum:
hold.

retrō: in the reverse way;
back again; back.

rĕvello, -ĕre, -i, -vulsum:
pluck away.

rĕvertor, -i, -versus sum:
revert, return.

rĕvinco, -ĕre, -vīci,
-victum: overcome.

rĕvŏco, -āre, -āvi, -ātum:
summon back.

rex, rēgis, m.: king.

rīdeo, -ēre, rīsi, -sum:
smile, laugh.

rĭgĭdus, -a, -um: stiff.

rĭgor, -ōris, m.: stiffness.

rīsus, -ūs, m.: laughter.

rītĕ: duly, in established
fashion.

rītus, -ūs, m.: fashion.

rōbur, -ōris, n.: hardness,
strength.

Rōmāni, -ōrum, m. pl.:
the Romans.

rōs, rōris, m.: dew,
moisture.

rŏsa, -ae, f.: rose.

rŏtans, -ntis: whirling.

ruīna, -ae, f.: ruin (ruinas
facere: come to grief;
create ruin).

rŭo, -ĕre, -i, -tum: carry
headlong; fall.

rursum and rursus: again,
once more, in turn.

S

sacra, -ōrum, n. pl.: sacred
rites.

saec(ŭ)la, -ōrum, n. pl.:
races; generations.

saepĕ (comp. saepius): often.

saeptus, -a, -um (saepīre):
walled off.

saevio, -īre, -ii, -ītum:
rage, vent one's frenzy.

saevus, -a, -um: savage.

săgax, -ācis: keen, keen-
scented.

săl, -is, n.: salt.

sălio, -īre, -ui, -tum: leap
up.

salsus, -a, -um: salt.

salus, -ūtis, f.: safety.

salūto, -āre, -āvi, -ātum:
greet.

sancio, -īre, -i(v)i, -ītum
(for -nxi, -nctum):
ordain.

sanctus, -a, -um (comp. adv.
sanctius): sacred.

sanguen, n., and sanguis,
m., -inis: blood.

sanies, abl. -ē: matter,
the serous part of the
blood.

sapor, -ōris, m.: taste.

satis: enough, sufficiently.

saxeus, -a, -um: of stone.

saxum, -i, n.: rock, boulder.

scelerōsus, -a, -um:
criminal.

scelus, -eris, n.: crime.

scilicet: obviously,
assuredly, certainly.

scio, -īre, -īvi, -ītum:
know.

scrībo, -ere, -ipsi, -iptum:
write.

scrūtor, -āri, -ātus sum:
scrutinise.

sē and sēse, acc., sui:
himself, herself, itself.

sēcerno, -ere, -crēvi,
-crētum: separate (secrētus:
separate, distinct, unique).

seco, -āre, -ui, -tum: cut,
divide.

sed: but.

sēdes, -is, f.: resting-
place, abode.

sēgrego, -āre, -āvi, -ātum:
detach, sever.

sēiungo, -ere, -nxi, -nctum:
separate.

semel: once.

sēmen, -inis, n.: seed.

sēmoveo, -ēre, -mōvi,
-mōtum: remove.

semper: always.

senectus, -ūtis, f.: old
age.

senesco, -ere, senui: grow
old.

sensus, -ūs, m.: sensation,
sense; pl., the senses.

sentio, -īre, -nsi, -nsum:
perceive, feel.

sepelio, -īre, -i(v)i,
-pultum: bury.

sequor, -i, -cūtus sum:
follow, pursue.

serēnus, -a, -um: serene.

seresco, -ere: become dry.

sermo, -ōnis, m.: language,
tongue.

serpo, -ere, -si, -tum:
creep, steal.

servitium, -i, n.: slavery.

servo, -āre, -āvi, -ātum:
preserve.

seu: or.

si: if.

sīc: thus, in this way, so.

sidus, -eris, n.: star.

signīfico, -āre, -āvi, -ātum:
give signs of, reveal,
make known.

signum, -i, n.: sign; constel-
lation; statue.

silex, -icis, m.: flint.

silva, -ae, f.: wood, forest.

silvifragus, -a, -um:
forest-rending.

similis, -e: similar.

simplex, -icis: single,
unmixed.

simplicitas, -ātis, f.:
singleness.

simul, adv.: at the same time.

simul and simul ac, conj.:
as soon as.

simulācrum, -i, n.: image;
ghost; reflection.

simulātus, -a, -um, + dat.:
like.

sin: but if.

sine, prep. + abl.: without.

sino, -ere, sīvi, situm:
allow.

sisto, -ere, stiti: stand
firm; stand.

situs, -a, -um: situated.

sīve: or if (sive . . . sive:
whether . . . or; sive
adeo potius: or rather).

socius, -i, m., and -a, -ae,
f.: ally.

sōl, -is, m.: sun; sunshine,
sunlight.

sŏleo, -ēre, -ĭtus sum: be
wont, accustomed.
sŏlĭdus, -a, -um (sup.
-issimus): solid.
sollemnis, -e: customary,
time-hallowed.
sollĭcĭtus, -a, -um:
restless.
sŏlum, -i, n.: soil; sole of
the foot.
sōlus, -a, -um: alone.
solvo, -ĕre, -i, -lūtum:
loosen, dissolve.
somnĭa, -ōrum, n. pl.:
fancies, delusions.
somnus, -i, m.: sleep.
sŏnans, -ntis (sonāre):
resounding.
sŏnĭtus, -ūs, m.: sound.
sŏnor, -ōris, m.: sound.
sōpio, -īre, -i(v)i, -ītum:
lull.
spătĭum, -i, n.: interval,
time; space, room.
spĕcĭes, -ei, f.: appearance;
apparition.
spēlunca, -ae, f.: cave.
spēro, -āre, -āvi, -ātum:
hope for.
spēs, spei, f.: hope.
spīrĭtus, -ūs, m.: breath.
spontĕ sŭā: of one's own
accord, spontaneously.
squāmĭgĕri, -um, m. pl.:
scaly creatures.
sterno, -ĕre, strāvi,
strātum: strew; level,
pave.
stĭlĭcĭdĭum, -i, n.: falling
(dripping) water.
stinguo, -ĕre, -nxi, -nctum:
extinguish.
stīpo, -āre, -āvi, -ātum:
crowd, pack tight.
stirps, -is, f.: stock.
sto, -āre, stĕti, stătum:
be established; stand firm;
stand.
stŏlĭdus, -a, -um: foolish.
strāges, -is, f.:
devastation.
stŭdeo, -ēre, -ui: desire.
stŭdĭum, -i, n.: devotion.

suādeo, -ēre, suāsi, -sum:
prompt; urge.
suāvĭlŏquens, -ntis: sweet-
speaking.
suāvis, -e: sweet, delightful,
honeyed.
sŭb, prep.: + abl., beneath;
deep in; + acc., within
the range of.
subdūco, -ĕre, -duxi, -ductum:
take away (from beneath).
subĭcio, -ĕre, -iēci,
-iectum, + dat.: cast
beneath.
sŭbĭgo, -ĕre, -ēgi, -actum:
turn up; subdue.
sŭbĭtus, -a, -um (adv.
subito): sudden.
sublīmus, -a, -um: high,
lofty.
sŭbŏrior, -īri, -ortus sum:
be supplied.
subsīdo, -ĕre, -sēdi, -sessum:
subside, sink down.
subsisto, -ĕre, -stĭti, +
dat.: support.
subter, prep. + acc., and adv.:
beneath, underneath.
suesco, -ĕre, suēvi, suētum:
become accustomed.
sum, esse, fŭi: be, exist.
summa, -ae, f.: sum, totality,
total.
summitto, -ĕre, -mīsi,
-missum: send up (from
below); lower, let down.
summus, -a, -um: highest,
supreme; fullest; at the
top; topmost.
sūmo, -ĕre, -psi, -ptum:
take; assume.
sŭpĕr, adv.: above, from above;
as well.
sŭpĕrā and supra, adv.: above.
sŭperne, adv.: from above.
sŭpĕro, -āre, -āvi, -ātum:
survive.
sŭpĕrsum, -esse, -fŭi:
remain.
sŭpĕrus, -a, -um: above,
on high.
suppĕdito, -āre, -āvi, -ātum:
supply; be available.

suppĕto, -ĕre, -i(v)i, -ītum:
be available, be in supply.

suppleo, -ēre, -ēvi, -ētum:
replenish, make up.

suppus, -a, -um: facing
upwards.

suprēmus, -a, -um: at the
top; final.

surgo, -ĕre, -rexi, -rectum:
rise.

sursum, adv.: upwards.

suspendo, -ĕre, -i, -nsum:
hang up.

suspicio, -ĕre, -spexi,
-spectum: look up.

sŭus, -a, -um: his, her,
its (own).

T

tābes, -is, f.: wasting.

tactus, -ūs, m.: touch; sense
of touch; tangibility.

taeter, -tra, -trum:
repulsive.

tālis, -e: such.

tam: + adj., so (tam . . .
quam: as much . . . as; as
. . . as: tam magis: the
more).

tămĕn: however.

tamquam: as it were, so
to speak.

tandem: pray; at last.

tango, -ĕre, tĕtigi, tactum:
touch.

tantundem, -īdem, n.: just as
much (advl.: quite equally).

tantus, -a, -um: so great;
n. s., so much.

tardus, -ạ, -um: sluggish.

tegmen, -inis, n.: roof,
vault.

tellūs, -ūris, f.: earth.

tēlum, -i, n.: shaft;
weapon.

tempestas, -ātis, f.: season;
storm.

templa, -ōrum, n. pl.:
regions.

tempto, -āre, -āvi, -ātum:
test, assail.

tempus, -ŏris, n.: time;
crisis, peril; season; pl.,
temples.

tendo, -ĕre, tĕtendi, tensum:
tend, strive (towards).

tĕnebrae, -ārum, f. pl.:
darkness.

tĕneo, -ēre, -ui, -tum:
occupy, possess, hold, hold
together; restrain, prevent
(se tenere: have one's
position).

tĕnĕr, -a, -um: tender; soft,
yielding.

tĕnŭis, -e: slender, insubstantial.

tĕnŭo, -āre, -āvi, -ātum:
attenuate, wear thin.

tĕnŭs, + gen.: as far as.

tĕres, -ĕtis: smooth,
rounded, shapely.

termĭno, -āre, -āvi, -ātum:
border, bound.

termĭnus, -i, m.: boundary,
boundary-stone.

tĕro, -ĕre, trīvi, trītum:
grind; rub; tread.

terra, -ae, f.: earth.

terrēnus, -a, -um: earthy.

terrĭfico, -āre: terrify.

terrilŏquus, -a, -um:
terror-speaking.

terror, -ōris, m.: terror.

tertĭus, -a, -um: third.

testor, -āri, -ātus sum:
call to witness.

textūra, -ae, f.: texture.

thyrsus, -i, m.: Bacchic
wand, goad, spur.

tĭmeo, -ēre, -ui: fear.

tĭmor, -ōris, m.: fear.

tŏlĕro, -āre, -āvi, -ātum:
tolerate, withstand.

tollo, -ĕre, sustŭli,
sublātum: raise; remove.

tŏnitrālis, -e: thundery.

tortus, -a, -um (torquēre):
swirling.

tŏtĭdem, ind.: the same
number of.

tŏtĭens, adv.: so often.

tōtus, -a, -um: whole, the
whole of.

tracto, -āre, -āvi, -ātum:
  handle, try.
tractus, -ūs, m.: expanse.
trăho, -ĕre, traxi, -ctum:
  contract.
trāno, -āre, -āvi, -ātum:
  swim across.
tranquillus, -a, -um:
  tranquil.
transeo, -īre, -i(v)i,
  -ĭtum: cross, traverse;
  pass through.
transfĕro, -ferre, -tŭli,
  -lātum: re-apply.
transĭgo, -ĕre, -ēgi,
  -actum: transact.
transvŏlito, -āre, -āvi,
  -ātum: fly through.
trĕmibundus, -a, -um:
  trembling, shaking.
tremo, -ĕre, -ui: tremble,
  quiver.
trĕmŭlus, -a, -um:
  trembling.
trĭbŭo, -ĕre, -i, -ūtum:
  assign, bestow, add.
trĭpūs, -pŏdis, m.: tripod.
triquetrus, -a, -um: three-
  cornered.
tristior, -ius: rather
  forbidding.
Trivia, -ae, f.: Artemis,
  Diana, goddess of
  crossroads.
Trōiāni, -ōrum, m. pl.: the
  Trojans.
Trōiŭgena, -ae, c.: born of
  Troy.
trūdo, -ĕre, -si, -sum:
  thrust, impel.
truncus, -i, m.: trunk.
tū, tŭi: thou, you (s.).
tŭeor, -ēri (and tŭor, -i),
  -ĭtus sum: behold; watch
  over, preserve.
tum: then; again; at that
  moment.
turba, -ae, f.: crowd, mass.
turbĭdus, -a, -um: seething.
turbo, -āre, -āvi, -ātum:
  confuse, confound.
turbo, -ĭnis, m.: whirlwind,
  tornado.

turpo, -āre, -āvi, -ātum:
  pollute, defile.
tŭtĕ and tŭtĕmĕt: emphatic
  forms of tu.
tūtō, adv.: safely.
tŭus, -a, -um: thy, your (s.).
Tyndăris, -ĭdis, f.: daughter
  of Tyndareus, Helen.

U

ŭbĕr, -is, n.: udder; richness.
ūbĕr, -is, adj.: rich.
ŭbĭ: when; since; where.
ŭbicumque: wherever.
ullŭs, -a, -um: any.
ultimus, -a, -um: at the
  extremity (ultima, -orum,
  n. pl.: ultimate secrets).
ultrā, adv.: beyond.
ūmecto, -āre, -āvi, -ātum:
  moisten, bedew.
ūmŏr, -ōris, m.: moisture,
  juice, liquid.
umquam: ever.
ūnā, adv.: at the same time.
uncus, -a, -um: curved.
unda, -ae, f.: wave.
undĕ, rel. and interr.:
  whence, from which, from
  what.
undĭque: everywhere, from (on)
  all sides.
ūnus, -a, -um: one, a single,
  alone.
urbs, -is, f.: city.
usquam: anywhere; in any
  instance.
usquĕ: so far (usque ab: right
  from: usque ădĕō: to such an
  extent; so true is it that).
ūsurpo, -āre, -āvi, -ātum:
  term; grasp.
ūsus est + abl.: there is need
  of.
ut and ŭtī (also utqui): (1)
  + indic., as (ut semel: when
  once, since first); (2) +
  subj., that; so that; in
  order that.
ŭterque, utraque, utrumque:
  each (of two); either

(= alteruter).
ūtĭlis, -ĕ: advantageous.
ūtor, -i, ūsus sum: use.
utrum . . . an: whether . . .
  or; either . . . or . . . ?
ūvesco, -ĕre: grow damp.

V

văcillo, -āre, -āvi, -ātum:
  sway, reel.
văco, -āre, -āvi, -ātum: be
  empty (vacans, -ntis, n.:
  emptiness).
văcŭus, -a, -um: unpreoc-
  cupied; empty (vacuum, -i,
  n.: void).
vădum, -i, n.: a shallow.
văgor, -āri, -ātus sum:
  wander.
văleo, -ēre, -ui: be strong,
  firm; + inf., have the power,
  strength, to.
vălesco, -ĕre: grow well,
  strong.
vălĭdus, -a, -um: strong,
  powerful.
vānus, -a, -um: empty,
  idle, vain.
văpor, -ōris, m.: heat,
  fire.
vărians, -ntis (variāre):
  varying, diverse.
vărĭantĭa, -ae, f.: variety,
  diversity.
vărĭus, -a, -um: different,
  various, varied.
vastus, -a, -um: vast,
  desolate; devastating
  (vastē, adv.: vastly).
vātes, -is, m.: seer.
-vĕ: or, and.
vĕl . . . vĕl: either . . . or.
vēlo, -āre, -āvi, -ātum:
  cover, shade.
vĕlŭtī: just like; just as.
vēna, -ae, f.: vein.
vĕnēno esse: be poisonous,
  deadly.
vĕnio, -īre, vēni, ventum:
  come, approach.
ventus, -i, m.: wind.

Vĕnus, -ĕris, f.: Venus.
vēr, -is, n.: spring.
verbĕro, -āre, -āvi, -ātum:
  lash.
verbum, -i, n.: word.
vĕreor, -ēri, -ĭtus sum:
  fear.
vernus, -a, -um: vernal, of
  spring.
vērō, adv.: but.
verro, -ĕre, -i, -rsum:
  sweep.
versus, -ūs, m.: verse,
  line of poetry.
vertex, -ĭcis, m.: eddy.
verto, -ĕre, -i, -rsum:
  overturn; turn, change.
vērum, adv.: but.
vērus, -a, -um: true (adv.
  vērē: truly: vērum, -i,
  n.: the truth).
vescus, -a, -um: gnawing.
vestīgĭa, -ōrum, n. pl.:
  traces, tracks.
vestis, -is, f.: garment.
vĕtustas, -ātis, f.: old
  age.
vexo, -āre, -āvi, -ātum:
  harry.
via, -ae, f.: path, way.
vīcīnus, -a, -um: neigh-
  bouring.
vĭcissim: in turn.
victor, -ōris, m.: victor.
victōrĭa, -ae, f.: victory.
victus, -ūs, m.: way of
  life; diet.
vidēlicet: + acc. and inf.,
  it is obvious that; adv.,
  to be sure.
vĭdeo, -ēre, vīdi, vīsum:
  see; pass., seem OR be
  seen.
vĭgeo, -ēre, -ui: be vigorous,
  thrive.
vĭgesco, -ĕre, -ui: begin to
  flourish, wax strong.
vĭgĭlo, -āre, -āvi, -ātum:
  be awake; spend awake.
vinco, -ĕre, vīci, victum:
  conquer, overcome, surpass,
  prevail.
vir, -i, m.: man, hero.

vǐrens, -ntis (virēre):
̬verdant.̬
viresco, -ěre: become
veɾdạnt.
virginěus, -a, -um: of a
maiden̬
virgo, -ǐnis, f.: maiden.
virtus, -ūtis, f.: valour;
̲excellence.
vīrus, -i, n.: brine.
vīs, pl. vīres, f.: power,
might, force; supply;
pl., strength.
vǐscus, -ěris, n.: flesh.
vīso, -ěre, -i, -um: behold,
̲come to see, visit.
vīsus, -ūs, m.: eye.
vǐta, -ae, f.: life.
vītālis, -e: living.
vītǐs, -is, f.: vine.
vīvidus, -a, -um: lively,
̲vital; quickened.
vīvo, -ěre, vixi, victum:
live.
vix: scarcely.
vōcǐfěror, -āri, -ātus sum:
̬proclaim aloud.
vǒco, -āre, -āvi, -ātum:
̬call.
vǒlātilis, -e: flying.
vǒlǐto, -āre, -āvi, -ātum:
̬fly.
vǒlo, -āre, -āvi, -ātum:
̬fly.
vǒlo, velle, vǒlui: wish.
vǒlǔcer, -cris, -e: winged
(volucris, -is, f.: bird).
vǒluptas, -ātis, f.:
pleasure.
volvo, -ěre, -i, -lūtum:
̬whirl along.
vōmer, -ěris, m.: plough-
share.
vǒmo, -ěre, -ui, -ǐtum:
vomit up.
vox, vōcis, f.: voice; sound,
name.
vulgo, advl.: regularly,
indiscriminately.
vulgus, -i, n.: crowd;
common herd.
vulnus, -ěris, n.: wound.